A SINGLE TEAR

A SINGLE TEAR

W
U

A Family's Persecution, Love,

and Endurance in Communist China

N
I
N
G
K
U
N

THE ATLANTIC MONTHLY PRESS
NEW YORK

in collaboration

with Li Yikai

Library of Congress Cataloging-in-Publication Data

Wu, Ningkun.
    A single tear: a family's persecution, love, and endurance in Communist China / Wu Ningkun, in collaboration with Li Yikai.
    ISBN 0-87113-494-2
    1. Wu, Ningkun. 2. China—Biography. 3. China—Politics and government—1949–   I. Li, Yikai.   II. Title.
CT1828.W785A3   1993   951.05′092—dc20   92-23054

Design by Laura Hough

The Atlantic Monthly Press
19 Union Square West
New York, NY 10003

First printing

To My Late Mother-in-Law

Li Wang Ciyin

Who Taught Us

the Meaning of Love and Suffering

Prologue

HOW THE BOOK
CAME TO BE WRITTEN

THIS MEMOIR WOULD NEVER HAVE BEEN WRITTEN WITHOUT THE SUSTAINED AND INSPIR-
ing support of my family and so many dear friends.

Our three children, who play such an integral part in our story, are the
ones who first inspired their mother with the idea of writing down the family
history for their benefit when she visited them in Palo Alto, California, in
the fall of 1984 on her first trip to the United States. Our old friends Bill and
Ann Burton, who were hosting my wife at the time, and their good
neighbors Sam and Marilee Anderson listened to her stories hour after hour
and urged her to commit them to paper.

By the time I arrived in Palo Alto in December 1985 on my way to
England, I found Yikai had already written a narrative in Chinese that vividly
recounted a number of episodes and incidents of the tragic years we had
weathered together. Both our children and our friends insisted it was now
up to me to rewrite the whole story in English. I winced at the thought of
reliving those traumatic years, but they insisted that I owed it to the world
to tell our unique story, which is bound to throw light on this little-known
period. I was touched by the seriousness they perceived in the proposed
undertaking. I came to see that our experiences, though not particularly
horrendous, ranged over the whole duration of the Communist rule. A
memoir of those intense experiences over several decades may indeed be
unique as a testament to life in contemporary China.

It was at Cambridge University, where I was visiting in 1986 at the
invitation of Professor Derek Brewer, Chairman of the Faculty Board of
English and Master of Emmanuel College, that I began to give serious
thought to the idea of transforming our haunting memories into a memoir.
One spring evening, after dining at the high table as Professor Brewer's guest,

I found our conversation turning to my experiences in China. By the time I rose to say good night, my host had made me promise to write an autobiographical essay for the *Cambridge Review,* of which he was then the editor. The four-part essay, written in May on an ancient typewriter, took up eight pages in the June issue, under the title "From Half-Step Bridge to Cambridge." The essay's warm reception at Cambridge and elsewhere gave me further impetus to expand the family history into a book. In the essay, I summed up my story of a wasted life in a brief formula: "I came, I suffered, I survived." But have I suffered and survived in vain? That is the question. To be worthy of the suffering and survival, the least I could do was to render a truthful account of our experiences over the three tragic decades, an account that, though intensely personal, will contribute to a compassionate understanding of history and men.

In the two months that followed, I wrote an account of my wife's visits with me in prison. After our Cambridge friend Valerie Myer, a distinguished writer, had read the first draft, she immediately picked up the telephone and called her literary agent in London, who later signed an optional agreement with Hodder & Stoughton on my behalf. A month later, when my wife and I passed through Paris on our way back to Beijing, we stayed with Richard Bernstein of the *New York Times.* After reading the fragment, Richard was not only enthusiastic but peremptory in urging me to make the fragment part of a whole.

Once back in Beijing, however, I found it practically impossible to continue working on the project, for, even apart from the vicious circle of being "distracted from distraction by distraction," my mind simply declined to function in a sterile climate. By the time the student demonstrations at Tiananmen had ended in tragedy in the spring of 1989, I was resigned to shelving the project, perhaps forever. What were my personal tribulations compared with the bloody tragedies of the latest victims? Where and when would I be able to continue working on it? Some of my friends, however, felt it was now even more imperative to tell my story to the world, for it unmistakably foretold what was to come.

The following year, by happy chance, I returned to my alma mater, Manchester College in Indiana, to receive academic honors. To add to my good fortune, President William Robinson and Vice President Eldon E. Fahs readily made me an alumnus-in-residence on learning of my wish to write a memoir. So I was able to work on the project from March 1991 to March 1992 with the extraordinary moral and physical support of my college, which had nourished me with life-sustaining humane values in those formative years. Among the many other colleagues at Manchester who either took the time to read parts of the manuscript and offer critical insights or cared for me otherwise, I am particularly indebted to Dr. and Mrs. Charles Klingler; Dr. John Planer and his wife, Dr. Janina Traxler; Dr. and Mrs. Michael Rawn; and Miss Cathleen Arnoldy. Dr. John Young, former Chairman of the Board of Trustees, and his wife, Marge, two of my most large-hearted colleagues, went out of their way to support me.

Other critical readers of parts of the manuscript include Richard Bernstein, who persisted in lashing me out of my lassitude and diffidence over the years; Sandra Burton of *Time* magazine, who sent voluminous comments while working overtime at her post in Hong Kong; Edward Gargan, also of the *New York Times,* who shared Richard's enthusiasm; Professor and Mrs. William Slaughter of North Florida University, who were generous with their time and perceptions; and Mr. and Mrs. George Witwer of Kendallville, Indiana, who were the first to read several of the early chapters and comment on them with professional astuteness.

Special mention must be made of Morgan Entrekin, President of Atlantic Monthly Press, and my editor, Athena Devlin, from whose sensitive reading and judicious comments the manuscript has amply benefited.

Last but not the least, I wish to thank our children, our daughter-in-law, Robin Daughters, and our son-in-law, Mark Norman, for their sustained interest and loving support. The all-too-brief company of our little grand-children, Patrick Wu and Erik and Jasmine Wu Norman, provided a precious emotional sustenance, though they were unaware of their contribution. When old enough to read the book one day, they will see it has been written for them too, in the hope and belief that they and their offspring will live in a better world, and that what happened to their grandparents and parents will never happen again.

WU NINGKUN

Contents

CONTENTS

A SINGLE TEAR

One

THE RETURN OF A NATIVE, 1951–52

IT WAS ON A SNOWY DECEMBER MORNING IN 1943 THAT I SAW THE STATUE of Liberty for the first time, from a deck of the U.S. Army transport *George Washington*. The statue loomed large, like an embodiment of Patrick Henry's stirring war cry, "Give me liberty or give me death!," which had roused my young heart when I'd learned it in high school in my hometown of Yangzhou, on the Yangtze River, and again later, when Franklin D. Roosevelt had reiterated the cry during mankind's struggle against fascist tyranny. As an English interpreter for a group of Chinese aviators who had been sent over for training on U.S. Army air bases, I was glad to be doing my small part in the great struggle, but I had no inkling how the momentous issues involved might determine the course of my life.

Not long after their training was completed, the war ended. It had been four long years since I had left Southwestern Associated University at the end of my sophomore year to volunteer as an Air Force interpreter for the American Flying Tigers, and I could hardly wait to take up the study of English literature once again. When the 1946 fall quarter began at tiny Manchester College in Indiana, I found myself the solitary foreign student on campus. The nearly puritanical life-style was a refreshing change from life in army barracks, and the Bible and Shakespeare opened my eyes to visions of man's lofty aspirations. The simple college motto, "faith, learning, service," guided me forward in my pursuit of knowledge to serve my motherland. Two years later, I was admitted to the University of Chicago, where dozens of Chinese graduate students had preceded me. I relished the pervading atmosphere of intense intellectuality, and the Chicago school of literary criticism haunted me like a new oracle. Within three years, I was well on my way to earning a doctorate in English from a great university. By the winter of 1950, I had started working on my dissertation, "The Critical Tradition of T. S. Eliot," under my mentor, the distinguished Professor R. S. Crane. I had visions of scaling great academic heights.

But before I began to immerse myself in the vault of books in the Gothic university library, news of the renewed civil war at home kept disturbing my peace of mind. Great battles of life and death were being fought on the disaster-ridden homeland. Letters from relatives and close friends were enthusiastic and exhilarating. The tottering old regime was pronounced beyond saving, and the legendary heroes known as Communists were hailed as new saviors of the nation. Like most of my fellow Chinese students, I had grown up under the specter of national humiliation and civil war, and I yearned for the emergence of a strong and prosperous China. Now a new era seemed to have arrived with the new regime, which claimed to be not merely a new dynasty but the creator of a totally new society. Although I knew so little of the political struggles between the Nationalists and the Communists, and next to nothing of communism or Marxism, there never was any doubt in my mind that I would eventually go home and put my expertise to some good use for a new China. Meanwhile, I still had my dissertation to write, and there was no special hurry.

Unexpectedly, however, the new year of 1951 brought me a cabled request from Dr. C. W. Lu, President of Yenching University in Beijing, to replace an American professor of English who had been forced to depart due to the war in Korea. Taken by surprise, I spent the days that followed weighing the pros and cons, with friends and in my own mind. Some congratulated me on the prospect of a promising career in the great capital of a new China—I would be welcomed as a patriotic intellectual who had given up an attractive profession in the most affluent capitalist society to come home and serve the socialist motherland. Others wondered if my service with the Nationalist Air Force might not get me into trouble with the new regime. I contended that I had been a student volunteer in the national resistance against the Japanese during the coalition between the Nationalists and the Communists. To be sure, I had my doubts, but I was more homesick than I had realized. Not that I had particularly strong personal ties to return to: my parents were long since dead, I was not married or engaged, and my married younger sister was the only one of my siblings living on the mainland. Neither did I have memories of a happy childhood to go in search of. My mother had gone crazy and then killed herself before I was eight, and my father, stone-deaf and never close to me, had died when I was in my freshman year in distant Kunming. There was little to go back to, but somehow I felt an inseparable bond to the ancient homeland, which had filled my early life with poverty, grief, loneliness, humiliation, insecurity, and the ravages of war. The lure of a meaningful life in a brave new world outweighed the attraction of a doctorate and an academic future in an alien land. And perhaps I was fleeing the esoteric volumes in the university stacks in search of fresh adventures in my distant homeland.

So I cabled my acceptance, promising to return before the new school year began in September. Warm letters of welcome came not only from Yenching University but from the State Council of the People's Republic. My younger sister in Shanghai was overjoyed. And I was not deterred by dire warnings from my elder brother in Taiwan or my elder sister in Hong Kong, who portrayed the Chinese Communists as "fierce floods and savage beasts." During my two years of college in Kunming, I had come under the influence of the prevailing pro-Communist sentiments among the "progressive" faculty and leftist students. I had, in fact, become an active member of the "progressive" Evergreen Student Literary Society, through which I was initiated into Gorky's novels and handed secret Communist leaflets. Now I read avidly *The Masses and the Mainstream,* a magazine published by the Communist party of the United States, and searched bookstores for "progressive" publications. My baggage consisted mainly of trunks filled with leftist books and periodicals, including all the novels of Theodore Dreiser and Howard Fast and a three-volume standard English edition of *Das Kapital.*

On a sunny day in mid-July, I boarded the USS *President Cleveland* in San Francisco for my homebound voyage. T. D. Lee, a fellow Chinese graduate student who had taken his Ph.D. in physics the year before, together with Bill Burton, my roommate at the university, and his bride, Ann, came to see me off. When a photo had been taken and good-byes were being said, it occurred to me to ask, "Why aren't you coming home to serve the new China, T.D.?" He answered with a knowing smile, "I don't want to have my brains washed by others." As I could not figure out how brains could be washed, I did not at the time find the idea very daunting.

2

SCARCELY SIX WEEKS AFTER I RETURNED TO CHINA, THE CHINESE COMMUNIST party made the first call for thought reform among the nation's intellectuals. The call came in the form of a report given by Premier Zhou Enlai to more than three thousand teachers from universities and colleges in Beijing and Tianjin, in the Huairen (Cherishing Humanity) Hall in Zhongnanhai (the Central and South Lakes). It was my first visit to the palace and, passing armed guards in army uniform, I wondered why Mao Zedong had chosen to have his seat of power and official residence in a former imperial palace. What was the message? A symbol of the Communist triumph over feudalism or a symbol of imperial legacy in all its grandeur? Perhaps both? That's certainly what Stalin did with the Kremlin. But would it not be more consistent with the theory of the "people's power" to turn the palace into a great park for the supposed masters of the country? The Huairen Hall, where in 1915 the Qing warlord Yuan Shikai had proclaimed himself emperor for a short-lived reign of eighty-three days, was now used as an assembly hall for large top-level political meetings. I was not awed or impressed by the flashy and gaudy interior, but rather intimidated by the numerous security guards in Mao suits who patrolled the aisles, scanning the audience of academics with flashing eyes. I wondered what were the feelings among the spectators, a considerable number of whom came from leading universities in the country, including professors of national or international renown. While the security guards went back and forth on their inspection beat, the audience sat back patiently, chatting among themselves in subdued voices. The humming was abruptly stopped by an authoritative signal for silence from a large security guard on the stage.

The premier walked up the podium to thunderous applause. It had been thirteen years since I'd last seen him. In the spring of 1938, at a Nationalist army political training center in the wartime capital of Wuhan in Central China. He had lectured on the international situation to the thousands of trainees every other week for three months. It was the time of the Second Coalition between the Nationalists and the Communists. As the chief Communist representative in the National government, Zhou had served as the deputy director of the Political Department of the National Military Commission and had come to the lectures in the uniform of a Nationalist lieutenant general. Barely forty at the time, he was an energetic and tireless speaker, carrying on for four hours without a break. Never referring to domestic politics, he had dwelt on international political developments and supported his optimistic outlook with plenty of facts and analyses. Though too young to understand everything he said, I had found his optimism uplifting in the midst of crushing defeats on the battlefields.

Now a highly respected national leader in his early fifties, he looked suave and self-assertive in his well-fitting gray woolen Mao suit. The same energetic and tireless speaker, he carried on with a new confidence and authority, which reflected not only the change in his personal stature but the outcome of the civil strife of the past decades. The report lasted an unbelievable seven hours. The premier called on the nation's intellectuals, especially the "high intellectuals," to start on a course of thought reform. The intellectuals, who had come from and served the old society, were said to be imbued with the "mistaken thoughts of the bourgeois class and the petty bourgeoisie." With the proletariat as the leading class in the new society, the intellectuals must learn to criticize those mistaken thoughts and to "establish the correct stand, viewpoint, and method of the working class," in order to serve the people. The premier warned that it was going to be an arduous and even painful process, but it was imperative. He urged the university faculties of the two great cities to take the lead in carrying out thought reform among the nation's intellectuals. My mind started wandering after the first hour, and I gave up my perfunctory attempt at note-taking. Little did I know that the seven-hour report was nothing less than a declaration of war on the mind and integrity of the intelligentsia for the next forty years!

3

IT WAS NEARLY DARK WHEN WE POURED OUT OF THE FORBIDDEN GROUND. My mind went back to the day in July when T. D. Lee had deplored the prospect of brainwashing in Communist China. Now that the prospect threatened to turn into reality, my experiences of the past weeks came back to me with a new meaning.

More than two weeks after it had sailed under the Golden Gate Bridge, the ship had docked in Hong Kong, but none of the eighteen Chinese students had been allowed to go ashore, because the British considered us all either Communists or communist sympathizers. My elder sister and her husband, whom I had last seen in Chongqing shortly before my departure for America in 1943, came aboard to visit with me while arrangements were being made to transfer us to a Chinese river steamer bound for Guangzhou. The couple of hours we spent together seemed like a brief reprieve in our prolonged separation. And I would not see them again until thirty-one years later, in another country.

The first sight that caught my eye as the steamer sailed up the Pearl River into Guangzhou was a series of five-star red flags fluttering in the summer wind. My heart throbbed quickly at this symbol of an enormous new reality, which had attracted me from afar and to which I was a total stranger. This was my first visit to the southern metropolis, which was bustling with people in wooden clogs and scanty clothes. I was amazed to see no signs of the ravages of war, whereas on my tour of Tokyo during the stopover I had been depressed by the destruction in the downtown area. Here the streets were crowded with pedicabs, bicycles, and pedestrians, but there was little motor traffic. The pedicab impressed me as an improvement upon the rickshaw, which had stood for the backwardness of the old China.

At the hotel where we stayed as guests of the local government, we were assigned to clean double rooms and then politely asked to fill out detailed biographical forms and hand in our passports. In the evening we were officially welcomed at a banquet hosted by the head of the Provincial Educational Bureau. Toasts were drunk to our "victorious return to the socialist motherland to take part in socialist reconstruction!"

The next morning we were taken by a special bus to the wharf where our baggage had been unloaded for customs and police inspection. Each of us was assigned a very long table, on which all the contents of our trunks and suitcases were spread out. I knew there was no contraband in my baggage, but I was dismayed to see the methodical packing of T. D. Lee and

Bill Burton so unceremoniously undone. One police inspector pounced on my Brownie box camera (I couldn't afford a real camera), scrutinized it from all angles, and then questioned me about its function. Very simply, I opened it up for him to see it inside out. Another officer seized a thermos bottle that a friend had given me as a parting present. Made of solid steel, it was much heavier than ordinary thermoses. The baffled officer brought out a screwdriver and tried poking it here and there. Frustrated, he turned to me and asked impatiently, "How do you open this thing up?" I said apologetically, "But it's all one piece, solid steel. No way to open it up!"

In the days that followed, several other agencies hosted more banquets. We toured the few historic spots around town, as well as a couple of universities. On the last day of our stay, we were taken to a place known as the South China Revolutionary University, which turned out to be an institution for thought reform. In a bare room in a dismal building, we were shown hundreds of notebooks displayed on rows of long tables. The official who accompanied us explained that these notebooks contained the "fruits of thought reform' of the intellectuals or former Nationalist officials who had been brought here for a three- to six-month course of revolutionary education. They had been taught to review their own past from a revolutionary standpoint and to dig out the roots of evil doings and thoughts, in order to turn over a new leaf. We were advised to take a careful look at some of the writings. I went through several copies quickly and found them to be autobiographical sketches following a uniform format and using the same jargon. They were nothing but unconvincing confessions of guilt and abject self-lacerations. Bewildered, I wondered if this was what a revolutionary education was all about. After more than an hour among the depressing booklets, we were taken to hear the political commissar of the university. Dressed in a loose grass-green army uniform, the robust man in his early thirties dwelt on the superiority of Socialist China and the evils of U.S. imperialism and took to task the returned students from America before our time who had allegedly claimed that the American moon was rounder than the Chinese moon. Once he felt we had benefited from the "fruits of thought reform" on display, he dismissed us curtly, saying there was nothing else to see. There was an official farewell banquet in the evening, at which the young government workers who had been escorting us ever since we arrived sounded us out on our impressions of the revolutionary university. Most of my fellow returnees said polite things, but I was too distracted by the day's experience to engage in civilities.

After the stopover in Guangzhou, I started on the long train journey to Shanghai. This was my first visit to China's largest metropolis, which had seemed a remote mystery in my younger days, when my family could not afford to travel. Now I took in the sights and sounds with the eager curiosity of a tourist who had come a long way in time as well as space. Though disconcerted by the hustle and bustle of pedestrians, buses, bicycles, and pedicabs, I admired the skyline along the Bund, which had teased my boyish imagination in picture postcards. Gone were the foreign concessions that had wounded my budding sense of national pride, gone were the opium dens and whorehouses that had been the curse of generations. Strolling along the Huangpu River Bund, I rejoiced at the rebirth of the great city that had won notoriety throughout the world as an "adventurer's paradise."

I was happily reunited with what was left of my family—my younger sister Ninghui, who was living in the city with her husband, and my widowed stepmother, who had come from our home in Yangzhou for the reunion. Fourteen years had passed since I had said good-bye to my stepmother, as I fled the Japanese army advancing on my hometown at the age of seventeen.

When my father had remarried scarcely a year after my mother had hanged herself, the burden of bringing up six children fell on the shoulders of my stepmother. Because his deafness had prevented him from taking a paying job, Father had never been a good provider. As a sort of "gentleman farmer," he collected a little rent from the small plot of land he had inherited from his parents. With six growing children and very little income, my stepmother did the family cooking and washing and struggled to make both ends meet. Father spent most of his time smoking a long-stemmed Chinese pipe and reading a borrowed paper. He was more keen on getting me apprenticed to a pharmacist of traditional Chinese medicine than paying my way through high school. Once I nearly got kicked out of senior high because my stepmother was unable to borrow enough money to pay my tuition on time. A college education would have been out of the question, had it not been for the war, which made the universities open their doors to penniless refugee students. So I was literally a "war profiteer." Coming home again now, I was happy to find my stepmother in fair health and good spirits, although I was sad to see her gray hair and deep wrinkles. She said she was doing all right in spite of her diabetes, but coping by herself all these years, through one war after another since my father's death in 1940, must have been a bitter ordeal. She was overjoyed when I suggested that she come live with me in Beijing once the university assigned me living quarters.

It was eight years since I had said good-bye to my sister in Kunming when she was still a sophomore at our common alma mater. Now a teacher of communist politics at a suburban high school, she was full of enthusiasm for the new regime and took pride in my decision to come home and work for the New China, as she had urged me to do. My brother-in-law Zhang Yunxuan, a high school classmate of mine, was quite contented with his promising career as a senior engineer at a Shanghai steel mill. My other college friends in Shanghai were also happy to see me again and looked forward to my success as a young professor. Xiao San, who had written to warn me against the ignominy of lingering abroad as a "white Chinese," was studying Russian in preparation for translating Russian novels, while her husband, the leading novelist Ba Jin, was "observing and learning from real life" among the Chinese Volunteers in Korea. Wang Daoqian, who had recently returned from the Sorbonne, had just finished translating from the French a book of extracts and quotations from Marxist classics, to be published under the title *Marx, Engels, Lenin, and Stalin on Art and Literature*. I found the warm welcome from all of them and their own apparent happiness reassuring.

4

FROM SHANGHAI I CONTINUED MY JOURNEY TO BEIJING BY TRAIN AND AR-rived on a hot afternoon in mid-August. Meeting me at the station was Lucy Chao. Now in her late thirties, Lucy had returned to Beijing in the winter of 1948 with a Ph.D. in American literature from the University of Chicago and had since become head of the department of Western languages and literature at Yenching University. It was she who had urged me to suspend my work on my dissertation and return to meet an urgent need in her department. Slight of build, she looked even smaller in a shapeless gray cotton Mao jacket, which took me somewhat by surprise, because the new garb made her appear so different from the way she used to look in Western-style clothes at the University of Chicago. My half dozen foot lockers, suitcases, and cardboard boxes were carried out of the station on the naked backs of what Somerset Maugham had called China's "beasts of burden" and then loaded atop a horse-drawn carriage. It was my first visit to the ancient imperial city, which was now the proud capital of the People's Republic. I passed long stretches of purple walls and yellow tiles gleaming in the afternoon sun, which called up in me vague memories of stories of autocratic dynasties. There was very little auto traffic, and the pedestrians and cyclists looked relaxed and contented. But the clatter of the horse's hoofs on the pavement somehow gave me a feeling of desolation, as though I were venturing into an unknown land rather than returning home.

The carriage took us to a college commuter bus parked at the YMCA building downtown. After nearly two hours in this aging vehicle, crawling over a bumpy narrow road in disrepair, I finally arrived at the goal of my slow "pilgrim's progress." The portal of the college, flanked by giant vermilion doors and guarded by a stone lion on either side, seemed to lead into a charmed enclave of academic pursuits. The campus abounded in shady trees, and picturesque three-story buildings in classical palatial style surrounded a rock-rimmed lake. A seven-story pagoda turned out to be a water tower in disguise. Faculty housing was in separate compounds with Western-style two-story houses or Chinese bungalows.

I was put on the waiting list for a housing assignment, so I stayed as a house guest with Lucy and her husband, Chen Mengjia, who was a professor of Chinese at nearby Qinghua University and a noted archaeologist. Lean and swarthy, Chen walked with his back bent under an invisible burden, which made him appear older than his forty-odd years. Lucy's father was Dr. T. C. Chao, an Anglican bishop and dean of the Divinity School. Brought up in both China and the West, Lucy had become known as a most accomplished lady since her Yenching college days. She wrote poetry, played the piano, and had translated into Chinese T. S. Eliot's classic poem *The Waste Land* when it was still considered esoteric in England and America. Moving about gently among her elegant Ming dynasty furniture, choice objets d'art, and Steinway piano, she struck me as a heroine right out of a novel by Henry James (who was the subject of her doctoral dissertation) and thrust into a milieu as ill-fitting as her Mao jacket. I wondered what fine "moral consciousness" might be hidden under her poised presence. Unlike his naturally tactful wife, Professor Chen was gruff and outspoken. When it was announced that faculty as well as students were to take part in daily collective calisthenics, he paced the floor in circles while complaining loudly, "This is *1984* coming true, and so soon!"

When Lucy was moved to a smaller house, I went to share the three-room ground floor of a two-story house with the other bachelor professor on the English faculty, Wu Xinghua, who was tall and thin and one year my junior. I was told we were the two youngest associate professors in the history of the university. Though unable to go abroad for advanced studies because of tuberculosis, Xinghua was a master of several modern languages, including French and Italian. His essays on Chinese history, written in classical Chinese, won the admiration of professors of history and Chinese, and his poems in modern Chinese, first published at the age of sixteen, placed him among the finest poets of the late 1930s and 1940s. During the few months I shared his house, I'd often make a fire in the fireplace, sprawl on the floor in front of it, and listen to him read his poems. We'd sip a cup of coffee or a local wine with the charming name of Lotus White, which often put me to sleep. Sometimes President C. W. Lu, who had taken his Ph.D. in psychology from the University of Chicago in the 1930s, would drop in for a chat and a game of bridge. Both Professor Lu and Xinghua were brilliant conversationalists and bridge players. Life was not without its pleasures for the moment; but the moment did not last long.

There were two other professors on the English faculty: Professor Yu Da'ying, who was one of China's very few women Oxonians and was married to Professor Zeng Zhaolun, a deputy minister of higher education, and Professor Hu Jiatai, a reserved elderly man respected for his expertise in Buddhist sutras.

I took advantage of the few days left before school started to look up some of my college friends and teachers, who were either teaching at a university or working for some government agency. Most seemed contented with the new society and their positions, except for my friend Shen Congwen, the novelist. I had heard stories of his difficulties before I found my way to his home in a back alley to see for myself. Shen had been an associate professor of Chinese at the university in Kunming when I was an undergraduate in English. Though never in any of his classes, I had sent him my juvenile poems and essays for his advice and had often gravitated to his humble rooms to listen to his charming little stories. I had been spellbound by his natural, gentle voice, though his Hunan accent sometimes made him a little hard to follow. Already a celebrated writer, his classic novel *Border Town* had captured my heart. Now I found him and his wife living in three humble rooms that were not much different from the ones they had occupied in wartime Kunming, only that in the rooms of the years gone by it was like spring all the year round, whereas this abode in the imperial capital was rather bleak at the height of summer. Stripped of his post at Beijing University because of his former non-Communist convictions, he was given the job of a guide at the Palace Museum. Brushing aside my questions about his situation, he chatted and laughed as if nothing had happened, but he questioned me with a touching solicitude about my wanderings over the years. I had never forgotten his inimitable voice, but now, after ten years, looking at his face lit up with a childlike innocence and listening to his natural, smooth voice, I felt "an unspeakable feeling in the heart" (in the phrase of a classical Chinese poet) when he said, with a casual smile, "you can catch swallows on my doorstep." A writer celebrated throughout the world, a master with disciples and friends all over the earth, why should the New China have no place for such a man? As I said good-bye to him at his outer door, my mind was again troubled with vague misgivings.

Lucy asked me to teach a course in the history of English literature and another in advanced composition, both for seniors. It was my first teaching job, and I had only a couple of weeks to prepare. Worse still, there was no textbook and I was expected to put a Marxist slant on the history of England and its literature, when I knew next to nothing of Marxist theories. Among the books I had brought back from the States were *A People's History of England* by a British Marxist named Morton, a theoretical study of the history of English literature entitled *Illusion and Reality* by another British Marxist named Christopher Caudwell, and a violent attack on modern Western literature by an American Marxist, Howard Fast, under the typical

Marxist title of *Literature and Reality*. I halfheartedly tried to incorporate their ideas and terminologies into an otherwise traditional literary history. Usually I typed the lectures out on my portable Smith-Corona the day before class and only mimeographed them and handed them out to the students afterward. There were, I am sure, palpable incongruities. Some of the students who were exceptionally brilliant and well read in Western literature must have gloated over my awkward attempts to make the best of a bad job, highlighted by my shapeless gray Mao jacket, newly made on the advice of Lucy. But they ignored my Marxist dressings, raved about *Darkness at Noon* or *1984* over a glass of wine in my bare sitting room, bombarded me with questions about my experiences in the States, and borrowed American novels from my small collection. Other students who were not so brilliant but politically active also questioned me about my past and my responses to the New China. Though cautioned by Lucy and Xinghua to be careful in what I said to students, I mingled with them and spoke my mind freely, simply because I did not know how to do otherwise.

My responses to the new environment were mixed. I remembered the old China I had left behind in 1943—a land bleeding from the ravages of war and a people groaning under the yoke of a corrupt government and age-old poverty. The new government, apparently clean and committed, had the support of the people, who were able to live in peace and stability for the first time in many years. Beggars disappeared from the streets, opium-smoking was outlawed, venereal disease was being wiped out, and prostitutes were reformed into good working women, as shown in the documentary film *Our Fallen Sisters Have Stood Up*. All government workers, including college teachers and students, were entitled to free medical care. A great campaign of land reform radically changed the structure of society and freed the Chinese peasantry from the exploitation of rapacious landlords. (At the time, I was unaware of the numerous summary executions throughout the country of men and women denounced as "despotic landlords.") All this left a profound impression on me, yet I was also disturbed by the self-righteous demands for conformity and the unconditional submission of the individual to the party or the state. Communist Russia was hailed as the Big Brother and the model, at the expense of the United States, which was denounced as the arch-imperialist. At a meeting of criticism called for his benefit, a mature student in my class, Jiang the

Elder (so called because his younger cousin was in the same class), was taken to task by student activists for his pro-American and anti-Communist utterances. Unexpectedly, Huang Jizhong, my suave assistant, joined the chorus with an indignant denunciation. Later on I learned that Huang, very Americanized before the "liberation," had demonstrated his break with the old society at a public meeting on campus by violently denouncing his own mother in absentia as a landowning exploiter.

I was more than bewildered by the many-faceted new reality.

5

AS NATIONAL DAY, OCTOBER 1, DREW NEAR, THE FACULTY AS WELL AS THE student body began gathering daily on the athletic field for formation exercises, in preparation for the mass rally and parade on Tiananmen Square. An enthusiastic professor of geography shouted orders in his ex– Christian preacher's voice. As we would have the honor of being reviewed by Chairman Mao himself from the rostrum, we practiced shouting "Long live Chairman Mao!" in unison. I winced, but the example of the senior professors gave me a lesson in conformity. On the morning of the great day, we rose long before dawn and gathered on the athletic field in prearranged formations. Then, eight abreast, we marched at least a dozen miles to the heart of the imperial city to await our turn to enter the square. My legs and feet were sore, and I wondered how the senior professors were holding out. Once in the square, I was overwhelmed by the spectacle of a sea of flushed faces and the deafening shouts of "Long live Chairman Mao!" and "Long live the great, glorious, and correct Chinese Communist party!" The cries seemed to echo "Long live Generalissimo Chiang!," which had erupted from the high school freshmen in military training who were being reviewed by their "supreme leader" at the Sun Yat-sen Mausoleum in Nanjing in the summer of 1936. Was history repeating itself? Many years would pass before I took in the full impact of such a mass rally and these two oracular slogans. Luckily, this was the only time I was made to march in such a parade.

* * *

Thought reform, or brainwashing, became a new focal point of political and intellectual life among the faculty. After spending days in small groups studying Premier Zhou's report and subsequent reports by other Communist leaders, we began to apply the Communist method of "criticism and self-criticism" to the dissection of our sinful past and bourgeois mentality. Before the fall semester was half over, the country was enveloped in a new political campaign against corruption, waste, and bureaucratism, known as the Three Antis, which were blamed on corrosion by capitalist ideas. Two veteran Communists in the central government were soon executed for embezzlement of state funds. For a regime which had been in power only two years, the readiness to clean its own ranks certainly left a strong impression on me. Many innocent people, however, were suspected and accused on little evidence and then subjected to nonstop questioning and detention, setting a pattern for subsequent political campaigns. At first the university community thought such a campaign was none of their concern. They changed their minds when the party, armed with Marxist dialectics, seized upon universities as hotbeds of capitalist ideas and the Three Antis took the form of thought reform on college campuses, with professors as the main targets of attack.

At Yenching University, "U.S. imperialist cultural aggression" was singled out as the root of all evil and the Three Antis became a campaign to eliminate "Befriend U.S., Worship U.S., and Fear U.S. sentiments." A special work group of Communists was sent by the Party Committee of Beijing to conduct the campaign and take over the administration of the university. Classes were suspended and students were mobilized into small groups to look into the history of the university and the past of its leaders and faculty members. Files were removed from the president's office and scattered all over the library's main reading room to be scrutinized by student activists for evidence of cultural aggression and possible espionage. In one letter, an American professor referred to Chinese students as "guinea pigs" used in an experiment with a new teaching method. This was pounced upon as evidence of U.S. imperialists insulting and victimizing Chinese students as "pigs" and became the subject of an indignant denunciation at a big rally. I did not know what to make of what was happening around me. As head of the department, Lucy was constantly besieged by members of the work team and student activists. Xinghua was getting more and more actively involved in the campaign. I felt as if I were left drifting all alone on an uncharted sea.

The president himself, the dean of the Divinity School, and the chairman of the philosophy department, all distinguished scholars, were made to confess their sins in serving the interests of U.S. imperialism and subjected to denunciation by students and faculty members alike. Though inured to it after a while, I was nonetheless shocked by the denunciations made at a schoolwide rally against the president by Wu Xinghua, known as the President's protégé and bridge partner, and the president's only daughter, a senior at Yenching. The president's elderly maidservant, however, made news when she attempted to cut her own throat with a kitchen knife rather than denounce her master as a "cruel exploiter" under the pressure of the work group. One of the serious charges against the dean of the Divinity School, Dr. T. C. Chao, was an honorary doctorate awarded him by Princeton University in 1946 in the company of General Eisenhower, among others. "Is it not true that a man is known by the company he keeps? As we all know Eisenhower is a bloody imperialist warmonger, then what does it make the Divinity dean?" The accuser wallowed in his own rhetoric. The chairman of the philosophy department, Professor Chang Tungsun, was accused of being a suspected spy serving U.S. interests, although he had played a leading part in bringing about the "peaceful liberation" of Beijing in 1949. All three, who had publicly supported the Communists before the success of the revolution, were denounced as "U.S. imperialist elements" and summarily stripped of their posts. The president's daughter, meanwhile, was rewarded with the honor of being appointed a people's deputy to the Municipal People's Congress of Beijing.

Then all the professors were ordered to examine their past for pro-American bourgeois ideology and subjected to criticism by students at public meetings. A number of professors of Chinese and history who used to dine together, peppering their conversation with witty observations on the new order of things, were accused of forming a "reactionary clique of ten" against the New China. All were violently denounced at large public meetings and the obdurate few put in solitary confinement for repentance and confession. One professor of Chinese was so frightened that he got down on his knees and begged to be forgiven, only to be sneered at as a pitiful spineless wretch.

As a recent returnee from years of college and graduate education in America, I was ill-prepared for this sort of proceeding. I saw I was behind the times. But I was only thirty-one, I had no wish to become a pariah, I was willing to learn new things. And several female activists in my class came to my "assistance" by presenting me with "gifts," which turned out to be casual remarks I had made to some of my students. For example, I had told the girl who was working with me on an analysis of James's *The Wings of the Dove* for her B.A. thesis that I found the major Chinese newspaper the *People's Daily* quite different from American papers. For several days running before National Day, I had found on its front page no news headlines but only a few dozen political slogans for the occasion, with "Long live the Chinese Communist party!" and "Long live Chairman Mao!" leading the roll. Was that news? Now the good girls suggested, not altogether impolitely: was I not only giving vent to hostility toward socialist journalism, but perhaps trying to erode the thinking of my naive student? I shuddered, not so much because they were making a mountain out of a molehill, but rather because my casual remarks had been so carefully monitored.

By now I had moved into a two-story house in the East Compound, which I shared with Professor Zhang Fufan, who had also just returned from the United States, with an M.S. in mechanics from Stanford University. The Zhangs and their two lovely little children occupied the ground floor, and I lived upstairs with my stepmother, who had recently joined me. Zhang had been standoffish until the day he discovered we were kindred spirits, both paying for our indiscreet casual remarks. A witty man, he often bantered with his students. When his humorous remarks were brought up for criticism in the current campaign, Zhang defended himself by saying, "But Churchill also has a strong sense of humor." That did it! Now the student activists wanted him to make a special self-criticism of his admiration for the British arch-imperialist warmonger! "What can you do with such people who are utterly devoid of any sense of humor!" Zhang exclaimed to me in dismay. "I wish I could keep my mouth shut, but is freedom of silence guaranteed in the constitution?"

In our department, Lucy was the first to make a self-criticism at a plenary meeting of the faculty and students, more than a hundred people in all. She criticized herself for her absorption in literature and aloofness from politics, which was then traced to her family background and Western education. She also lamented whatever bad influences she might have had on the students who adored and emulated her. Professor Yu and Professor Wu Xinghua followed her at separate sessions. The student activists were easy on them, because they were considered to be making or aspiring to "political progress."

When it was my turn, I spoke of my tardy recognition of the great things the party had done for China, I admitted I had perhaps wasted too many years steeping myself in the study of bourgeois Western literature when the Chinese people were fighting for a new China under the leadership of the Communist party, and I expressed readiness to remold my ideology, which had been formed in Nationalist China and the United States. I thought I had gone pretty far in getting to the bottom of things. No sooner had I finished, however, than a bespectacled second-year English major jumped to his feet and called my self-criticism "superficial" and "evasive." He brandished a paperback American novel one of the seniors in my class had borrowed from me. My righteous accuser pointed to the cover, which pictured a hand with painted fingernails holding a glass of wine, and demanded with indignant eloquence, "Is this the kind of crap you've brought back from the U.S. imperialists to corrupt the young minds of the New China with?" The novel was *The Great Gatsby*. I was much more "backward" than I had realized, but I was not prepared to dump Fitzgerald's classic. Nonetheless, I had to make a more humble self-criticism a few days later before I was "passed." Xinghua was held up as an exemplary intellectual who was making rapid political progress through the current campaign and who was ready to break with the past, while I was looked upon as a "backward element." Left out of some of the various bustling faculty or student activities because of my political backwardness, I was happy to find time to finish reading Tolstoy's *War and Peace* and the Moncrieff translation of Marcel Proust's *Remembrance of Things Past* in the shaded stillness of the garden around my college house. My troubled mind regained a measure of balance by moving among sensitive souls living in distant places and times. Bridge games and poetry reading before a fire already seemed memories of a vanished past.

6

THE NEXT STEP IN THOUGHT REFORM WAS A "BE LOYAL AND HONEST CAM-paign." Every member of the faculty and the staff was required to render a detailed account of his or her past, with special emphasis on political and American connections. I had never expected I would be following so soon in the footsteps of those whose autobiographical confessions on display at the South China Revolutionary University I had confronted only a few months before. I did what was expected, however, since we had all been put in our place and nonconformity was out of the question. I had nothing on my conscience anyway, I said to myself. The fact that I had returned all the way from the United States to give myself to the New China should clear me of any suspicion.

We first met in groups of three. Each of us told his or her story to the other two, and we checked one another on inconsistencies or loopholes. Then I told my story to a larger group of faculty members. One professor of philosophy, who had openly lamented his association with idealistic European philosophy, pointed out that my past involvement with the Nationalists looked pretty suspicious and called for soul-searching on my part. Finally I wrote a painstakingly accurate and detailed autobiography from my family origin up to the day I landed in Guangzhou, concluding with a prescribed analysis of the root causes of my life—social, familial, and personal—and a pledge to step up my thought reform. But I soon learned all my compliance and honesty had gone to waste when Jian Bozan, the Marxist professor of history who had emerged as the "prince regent" of the university following the downfall of the former president, summoned me to his house.

"I have been asked by the party organization to have a word with you about your autobiography," he began in a condescending tone of voice. "You have given a broad outline of your life. Quite a complicated life, I must say, for a man of your age. It is against the party's policy to force a confession, but you still have time to add to what you have written, especially crucial omissions. It will be in your own best interest. I hope you will take advantage of this opportunity . . ." Then he lit a cigarette and started puffing smoke at me.

Taken by surprise, I bristled at the brazen insult and the implied threat from a fellow professor. "I have nothing to add," I said shortly.

"Now don't hasten yourself and don't let your feelings run away with you. We all have a past to deal with, whether we're willing to face it or not. As Marxists, we believe in facing the facts and relieving the load on one's mind by telling the party all. You must be able to recall the important things you experienced in your adult years, especially what happened recently. For instance, it was certainly a good thing that you returned to China from America, but why and how? What were the real circumstances of your return? The real motives?"

"I already gave a detailed account of them in my autobiography." Again I answered briefly.

"Indeed you did. But could you go over them, check on their accuracy and fullness, and perhaps supplement them with significant details?"

"I have nothing to add," I repeated.

"It's up to you. There is also the question of what you really did in the Nationalist Air Force, besides what you have put down."

"I have nothing to add."

"I leave it up to you. You may or may not add anything of your own free will. As I said, it's against the party's policy to force a confession, but there is still time for you—"

"I have nothing to confess. And I did not return to my own country to make a confession, Professor Jian."

I stalked out of his study, lined with thread-bound Chinese books, material evidence of an erudite Marxist historian. Professor Jian had such a large library that the university was building an addition to his house, while the common run of professors were assigned only half a house each. On the way back to my half of a house, it began to dawn on me that I was looked upon as some sort of a suspect, but of what?

When classes resumed in spring, the regular curriculum was unceremoniously dumped. I was made to give a course in progressive American fiction instead of the "useless" history of English literature. The text I used was Howard Fast's novel *The American,* which put the students to sleep. Other teachers were also forced to offer new courses and improvise politically oriented new teaching materials. But the real order of the day was group political study aimed at thought reform. The professors took turns lacerating themselves for past aberrations or slow progress on the revolutionary path. Professor Yu, the Oxonian, often broke down in speaking of her past association with her elder brother, who was even then serving as the Minister of Defense under Chiang Kai-shek in Taiwan, and avowing a thorough break with him. Xinghua said he was sorry he had to publicly criticize the former president, but it was necessary to break with him in order to make quick progress on the revolutionary path. Lucy criticized herself for not being firm like Xinghua in breaking with her own father or President Lu, her godfather. I never questioned their sincerity or integrity but only wished I could be more like them. We had gone through the same campaign together, but I was apparently lagging behind in my political progress and at a loss as to how to catch up with them.

At political discussions at Yenching and other universities, all the participants spoke as if they were unanimously converted to the materialistic philosophy of Marxism. Before long, however, we learned officially that Mao Zedong was not at all pleased with the sudden disappearance of the great scholars who had professed idealistic philosophies, Chinese and Western. He urged them and their followers to come into the open with their philosophies to confront the Marxists and seek truth from facts. No one took his words at face value, and everyone went on eulogizing Marxism and the Communist party.

Before the semester was over, the restructuring of higher education "on the Soviet Big Brother's model" was a foregone conclusion. The English faculty spent hours upon hours studying and discussing the teaching programs, teaching methods, and course contents of English departments in Soviet universities in order to reform our own. But it turned out that all the missionary colleges were to cease to exist as such and be merged into national universities. The beautiful Yenching campus was taken over by Beijing University and its faculty and staff members reassigned to universities in Beijing and other cities. Before the reassignments were announced, we were induced to pledge acceptance of whatever new jobs would be assigned us. All the faculties of the five major universities in Beijing were then sent by train to the seaside resort city of Qingdao in Shandong province for a week's summer vacation. The brief respite was apparently calculated to placate the feelings of the hundreds of university faculty who had been subjected to unprecedented political pressure over the recent months. But it was also a calculated move to get them out of the way while the university and ministry officials deliberated on their new assignments. This was my first visit to any Chinese seaside resort. Though no swimmer, I enjoyed bathing in the sea and trying to wash away, for the moment, memories of the troubling experiences of the past months.

The new assignments were announced shortly after our return to Beijing. Lucy lost her place as department chair but joined the English faculty of Beijing University as a professor of English, while Xinghua, an associate professor promoted only the year before, was appointed head of the new English faculty, made up of members from the English faculties of the five major universities, partly because of his public denunciation of the former president of Yenching. When Lucy came to my house to break the news that I was to transfer to Nankai University in the city of Tianjin, some eighty miles away, she suddenly lost her usual poise and became choked with tears. I didn't know what to say at first, but I knew how she felt. When she had urged me to cut short my doctoral work at Chicago and join her at Yenching, she had dreamed of creating a strong English faculty. Now her dream was irretrievably shattered. She had aged visibly within the recent months. Despite her unruffled appearance, it was not hard to imagine the turmoil she must have gone through, under great political pressure from the work team because of her close affiliations with her father and the president. Her husband, Chen Mengjia, who had been given a hard time at Qinghua University in the recent campaign, was transferred to the Institute of Archaeology under the Academy of Sciences. It was I who had to comfort her and reassure her it was all right, since I was not the only one to be sent away. But I knew better in my own heart, for I had returned only a year before to teach in Beijing, not Tianjin, at the special request of Yenching University. What right did they have to summarily dispose of me? But this was only my first taste of the arbitrary treatment of the individual by the all-powerful state, which would become the inflexible law of life in the decades to follow.

Two

A HIDDEN COUNTERREVOLUTIONARY, 1953–55

1

NANKAI WAS ONE OF THE THREE UNIVERSITIES THAT FORMED THE WARTIME coalition known as Southwestern Associated University, but it was a junior partner dwarfed by Beijing University and Qinghua University. When I reported to work in Tianjin in November 1952, two pedicabs took me and my stepmother from the station through dirty and crowded streets to a drab campus in the suburbs of a large commercial and industrial city. I had been promised good housing but was given two little rooms in a temporary one-story housing project with a cement floor. My stepmother occupied one room and I the other. Mother cooked our meals on a little briquet stove I had bought downtown on the afternoon of our arrival.

I was asked to teach three courses: History of English Literature, Selected Readings in American Literature, and Translation from Chinese into English. For the history course, the library happened to have a dozen copies of an introductory textbook, which were just enough for the small senior class. For the American literature course, the library had an ample supply of a Russian edition of Howard Fast's best-known novel, *Freedom Road*, which was widely read in a bad Chinese translation. For the weekly translation exercises, I selected pieces from the daily papers or current literary journals. My work load was heavier than that carried by other professors, but I had no complaint, since I was the only faculty member under the age of forty. Though frustrated in many ways, I was more than ready to assuage the students' hunger for knowledge, which reminded me so much of my early college days. In teaching the history course, I dispensed with the Marxist dressing, which I had plagiarized from Christopher Caudwell the year before, and focused instead on the humanistic tradition of

English literature from Chaucer and Shakespeare to Dickens and Thackeray, holding up Milton and Byron as Promethean fighters for freedom. I felt more than rewarded when I found my enthusiasm infectious. In lecturing on *Freedom Road,* I applied the Aristotelian method of structural analysis to the text and showed how it was constructed not as a work of art but as a work of propaganda, without passing any value judgment on the novel as a work of propaganda or a work of art. But I cited the great modern writer Lu Xun's famous dictum that "all literature is propaganda, but not all propaganda is art," in an oblique reference to the official dogma of stressing ideological correctness as the primary virtue of works of art, which was based on Mao's 1942 "Talks at the Yan'an Forum on Art and Literature." I hoped my analytical method would show my students at least one objective approach to literature. I did not know I was already intruding on grounds "where angels fear to tread."

Apart from the challenge of the invisible but pervasive repression, life was monotonous. I did not mind the difficult living conditions as much as the sterile provinciality. I was an alien in the midst of a brotherhood of middle-aged or elderly men who watched their steps and guarded their tongues. Each gave one or two courses that he had been teaching for years. Professor Gao, pallid and deaf, was always ready to sing the praises of the great party that allowed him to keep his "iron rice bowl," although he did not teach at all. They lived by the time-honored injunction, "Be worldly wise and play safe." I was not worldly wise and did not know how to play safe.

The only other member of the English faculty who had studied abroad was Miss Suhu, an unmarried professor in her fifties. Born to Cantonese parents in the United States, Miss Suhu had been inspired by a dream to serve the land of her ancestors and had come to China upon her graduation from college some thirty years ago. In spite of her decades in China, she was more at home with English than with Chinese and lived in a world of her own. An invisible wall separated her from the Chinese around her. She drank coffee, played the piano, and enjoyed eating at the only Western restaurant in town, unaware of the disapproval of her polite colleagues. On mornings when I taught two or three hours running, she would often bring me coffee. An upright piano, quite as weather-beaten as the owner herself, took up nearly half of one of the two rooms in her little college house. From time to time, at my request, she would play a familiar tune or two for me. We talked about our life experiences, literature, music, or the students who were attached to her, but never politics, for she was miraculously immune to the political happenings around her and she did not read the papers. Though we shared a common alienation, I was the more vulnerable of the two, because she no longer cared and I cared so much.

The next year, however, my Chicago roommates, Cha Liangtseng and his botanist wife Dr. Zhou Yuliang, returned to her family home in Tianjin and joined the faculty at Nankai. Also, Li Tiansheng, a former student of mine from Yenching, joined the English faculty as an assistant upon my recommendation. Their coming added a new dimension to my solitary life. As we all lived in college dormitories within walking distance, we dropped in on one another at all hours, comparing notes on literary trends and departmental or national politics. To find relief from a monotonous life, we would occasionally have a few drinks together on the weekend, or go on a bicycle ride to the picturesque older quarters of the city, which Cha had known well in his high school days.

Considered a fine poet while in college, Cha had since stopped writing poetry. But he frequently stayed up late translating *An Introduction to Literature* by a Soviet literary theorist, which quickly became a standard textbook in colleges all over China. Later on, he tackled Pushkin's poetical works one by one. Though an English scholar by profession, Cha had started learning Russian at college when it was the vogue among "progressive" students; he later focused on Russian literature at Chicago after taking his M.A. in English.

The first thing I translated was a small book I had brought back from Chicago, called *Shakespeare on the Soviet Stage,* by a Soviet Shakespearean named Morozov. I was quite impressed by the popularity of Shakespearean performances in the Soviet Union. Then, at the request of Ba Jin, I translated a biography of Dr. Norman Bethune, the Canadian surgeon who had given his life to China's war of resistance while in active service with the Communist army in 1938–39. In spite of my growing disenchantment with the realities, I could not help being deeply moved by this Western intellectual's selfless dedication to an international cause when fascism ran rampant in the world.

The thing that soured my life most was the compulsory political study sessions aimed at thought reform. Mao's writings, party newspaper editorials, and party directives on current affairs were required reading. Each faculty formed a study group, which met regularly, and one document was read aloud one or more times at each session, as if we were illiterate peasant soldiers in the Communist army. A discussion followed, and everyone was expected to lay bare his thoughts and show how the reading helped him to correct errors in his own thinking and thereby raise the level of his political consciousness. Silence was unthinkable. I soon discovered you were supposed to be always in the wrong, the party was always infallible, and raising the level of one's political consciousness was always an ongoing business. All spoke carefully with apparent earnestness, and the group leader took notes of what was said and reported to the party functionary in charge of political study after each session.

In addition, there were compulsory evening classes on Marxist rudiments for all the faculty members. One young man came from Beijing twice a week to read us the notes on Marxist philosophy that he had taken from lectures delivered by a Soviet expert at the People's University, a new institution founded under Soviet supervision. We were expected to take notes from his notes and commit them to memory for an examination at the end of the course. Most people kept themselves busy taking notes, though some others looked bored and smoked cigarettes, or simply dozed off. I never took notes, and the smoke kept me unhappily awake. Once I remarked to my elderly colleagues, "What an insult to the intelligence of the professors! It's better to doze off than to put on an act." Some of them laughed it off, others kept mum, still others called me a backward element behind my back or even to my face. I became more and more openly critical of the lack of freedom of thought and freedom of speech. Only Cha and Li shared my sentiments. Before long, I found many faculty members distancing themselves from me. I was bothered not so much by their coldness toward me as by the effect of their obsequious ways on the students. I criticized the leaders of the department and some of my colleagues, even as "baby calves are not afraid of tigers." Tigers, of course, are never afraid of baby calves!

One afternoon in the spring of 1954, I went to the regular session of political study as usual, anticipating nothing worse than the dull routine of listening to a party article read by one of the more active faculty members and everyone by turns making a little speech. I was not late, but the others had arrived early. The dingy meeting room was unusually quiet, with some twenty members of the English and Russian faculties already seated around the long table, looking serious and expectant. The ubiquitous portrait of Chairman Mao watched over the gathering. Professor Li, chairman of the department, a graying little man with cold small eyes, sat in his special wicker chair at one end of the table, looking more impassive than usual. I took the only vacant seat at the other end, so that I faced him directly. As soon as I sat down, he announced that the theme of the afternoon was "to help Comrade Wu Ningkun realize the ideological and other mistakes he has made since he came to teach in the department only one and a half years ago." Taken by surprise, I was very much a cornered calf. Had I been of a stronger character, I might have simply got up and walked out and the consequences be damned. As things were, I sat there paralyzed listening to my accusers.

Professor Yang, head of the English faculty, a gaunt and bald man in his early fifties, took the lead in "helping" me. "Mr. Wu Ningkun has been known as a patriotic intellectual, because he returned from America less than three years ago. But," he bellowed with anger, "his utterances and doings prove he has not lived up to his pretensions. All patriotic intellectuals are eager to undergo thought reform, but he called thought reform 'brainwashing,' which we all know is a reactionary term concocted by U.S. imperialism. He considered political study 'an insult to the intelligence of professors,' and derided collective reading of *People's Daily* editorials and other party documents as something fit for illiterate soldiers. The faculty night school for Marxist studies he ridiculed as a 'farce.' He boasted of never taking notes himself, and derided those who took notes as hypocrites. He said to me, 'It's better to doze off than to put on an act.' He constantly lamented what he called a 'lack of freedom of speech.' I want to know what kind of freedom of speech he wants. When Professor Gao stopped teaching because of his deafness, he expressed his heartfelt gratitude to the party for allowing him to remain on the faculty. We were all touched by the party's solicitude and his grateful feelings, but behind his back Wu called him 'a sycophant trading his soul for an iron rice bowl.' Is it not obvious that his political sentiments are not those of a patriotic intellectual who loves socialist China and supports the party? I refrain from labeling him politically. But he has surely been a bad influence, not only on the English faculty, but in the university in general."

I bristled. This man, whose scholarship I respected and who had often professed sympathy with my political sentiments, had turned on me with such sound and fury! I had been told he was furious with my careless comments on his translation, but I had never dreamed a respectable academic would stoop so low as to avenge a petty personal grudge in the name of Communist politics in which he had little faith himself!

Other colleagues spoke, one after another, citing other offhand remarks I had made. Li Jingyue, a tubercular and balding man in his forties, a former student of Professor Yang's and Professor Li's and now Li's secretary, first criticized me for my lack of respect to his worthy masters and then condemned my shocking irreverence toward Stalin. "When the great Marxist and beloved leader of the Socialist camp passed away," he recalled, "all the faculty and students of the university marched to the Soviet Consulate General with heavy hearts to mourn the great loss. Many of us cried. Only Wu Ningkun was reluctant to join the procession and showed no signs of grief." Even my success in the classroom was castigated as an attempt to show off at the expense of my colleagues. "Sheer arrogance," said one. "Individualistic heroism," said another, using the party jargon. So professional jealousy was working hand in hand with political intolerance. Only Suhu, Cha, and Li did not join the chorus. And I was not expected to defend myself. Summing up at the end of the session, the chairman pointed out that my thinking had been polluted by my American education and by my reluctance to cast off "bourgeois individualism" and accept ideological remolding. He expressed the hope that I would take in the well-meant criticism of my colleagues and "rein in at the brink of the precipice." I had no idea how well-meaning the criticism was, since those colleagues distanced themselves even further from me afterward. Even Miss Suhu stopped inviting me to coffee. I did not bother to speculate what was beyond the brink of the precipice, either. I was angry with my accusers and even more angry with myself for my naïveté in dealing with my colleagues, but I did not yet realize that the omnipresent party was behind everything, and that this encounter was to be "a minor incident implying larger probabilities." Cha and Li commiserated with me and reminded me I was not living in a free society.

2

FRUSTRATING AS MY LIFE AT NANKAI WAS, I FOUND THE CONTACT WITH MY students amply rewarding. It was not uncommon for students to visit me after class to talk over their studies or just chat freely in the privacy of a home. In the classroom, absorbed in lecturing or scribbling on the blackboard, I never saw the students as individuals, but when they sat face-to-face with me in my small room, I could take in their features and characteristics at leisure and get to know them as friends. One winter afternoon, a girl named Li Yikai came by with two of her classmates. The boys called her "Tomboy" and said she could be counted as one of the guys. All three laughed. I seemed to see Yikai for the first time: her open face shone like a full moon and she broke into a childlike laugh from time to time. Somehow this visit began to make a difference in my life. By the time the visitors said good-bye, I was resolved to get to know her better.

That Saturday night I took a bus downtown to her home address, which I had learned in the course of our conversation. It was 20 Edinburgh Lane, London Road, in the former British Concession—later changed to Happiness Lane, Chengdu Road, in the Peace District. The family lived in a Western-style three-story house. My unannounced visit created quite a stir. More flushed than usual, Yikai introduced me to her mother, her four elder brothers, and one of her three elder sisters. The family was apparently pleased with the unsolicited visit from one of her professors. We all laughed when one of her little nephews ran upstairs, yelling at the top of his voice, "Little Auntie's teacher is visiting! In a funny-looking long coat! Real funny!"

I did look funny in my long, shabby, dark blue coat, which I had picked up at a secondhand store in San Francisco, but Yikai and her folks did not seem to mind. I became a frequent visitor to their home, relishing the warmth of a traditional large family, the exact opposite of the "big socialist family." I soon learned that Yikai had lost her father at the age of four when, in the prime of his life, he'd succumbed to hypertension and heart disease. Yikai's father had worked hard running his own industries in order to strengthen China against Japanese economic aggression. When he died, he left eight young children to the care of his widow. In spite of the overwhelming odds against her, Yikai's mother quietly brought them up and gave them all a good education. Seeing her moving about the house unsteadily on her bound feet, busy with housework, I was awed by the moral strength of this frail widow who had practically no schooling at all. Motherless at an early age, I envied Yikai for the poised self-effacing love with which her mother had nurtured her and her siblings. Unsupported by philosophical or religious teachings, she knew instinctively what was good and what was evil and showed an innate compassion for the unfortunate and the wronged. For me she was the true incarnation of the traditional "virtuous wife and good mother."

The youngest of the children, Yikai grew up under the wings of a loving mother and caring siblings. The family was not rich, but well-to-do. Yikai was contented and happy. She took for granted a good life, a life free from want or fear. Active like a tomboy, she rode her bicycle fast, played on the women's volleyball team, and loved ice skating. It was she who taught me how to ride a bicycle, so we could go cycling together. I never learned to play volleyball or ice skate, but she did not seem to mind. Though eleven years my junior, she never sensed a generation gap between us. When spring came, we started dating. She had simple tastes and abhorred extravagance or vanity. We would cycle to one of the local parks, row on one of the lakes, or share a simple meal at a small restaurant or snack counter. Her innate simplicity and innocence purged my heart of the anger that was poisoning my life. When I was with her, Nankai did not feel like such a bad place after all.

Having converted to Roman Catholicism in high school at the age of fifteen, Yikai continued going to church after 1949. Though religious freedom had been written into the constitution, church attendance among college students was frowned upon by the authorities. As a former member of the Legion of Mary, Yikai had had to register with the police when it was outlawed. She had been shocked and frightened when the police raided the family home and arrested her second elder sister for her involvement with the Legion of Mary while working at the Yale-in-China Medical College in Changsha, capital of Hunan province. Her sister was sent under escort to the "scene of her crime" and then sentenced to three years in prison. Her mother wept day and night till her eyes were permanently damaged. Yikai, however, quickly recovered from the shock and prayed for her sister every day.

Yikai had entered my life at a time when I was drifting on a treacherous sea, lonely and unhappy. I was touched by the strength of this girl who never flaunted her faith, or argued with anyone about it, but quietly took it for granted. As the months went by, I seemed to have become a member of her family, which was tied together by a poignant but undemonstrative love. Her mother and siblings assumed that Yikai and I would get married when she graduated from college. And Yikai and I felt the same way. A proposal or engagement never entered our conversation, let alone a ring or a fancy wedding. We simply decided to get married on July 8, 1954, the day after school was over. I had been warned by friends of the danger of marrying a Catholic and a member of the Legion of Mary, and she, of marrying a political pariah, but we did not hesitate to throw our lot together.

As I had no church affiliation whatsoever, we were married by a Catholic priest, Father Liu of the Tianjin Cathedral, by special dispensation, but we skipped the formality of a church wedding. When the day came, we cycled to her favorite chapel in the morning, where she prayed while I sat in a pew. After a wedding banquet with my stepmother and new mother-in-law at a family restaurant in town, we left by train the same afternoon for the seaside summer resort of Qingdao for our honeymoon. We never worried about what the future might hold in store for us. We were over-brimming with happiness, so much so that we were the envy of other young people we met at the hotel or beach. One time a young man stopped us in the street. "I have watched you coming and going," he volunteered affably. "You must be from out of town, Beijing maybe. Honeymooning, perhaps?" We both laughed. "How did you know?" He was obviously pleased that he had guessed right. "Well, you look so different. So carefree, so poised, so happy!" Then we all laughed. From Qingdao we moved on, by way of Shanghai, to Suzhou and Hangzhou, the two scenic cities in East China known as "heaven on earth."

Our carefree days were brought to an abrupt halt when we returned to Nankai. The heads of the department, instead of congratulating us on our marriage as a matter of course, greeted us with the notice that Yikai would be denied a job because she had failed to ask for permission to leave the campus upon graduation while job assignments were pending. I thought it ridiculous to ask for permission to go on a honeymoon, but I was put in my place again. But so what? Yikai did not have to have a job. She could stay home and read up on Western literature. I was not to be intimidated. Yikai merrily hummed the popular song "Unity Is Strength."

We moved into an old small college house of two and a half rooms, and Mother remained with us. We lived simply on my modest pay, and Yikai seemed never to want anything. Unperturbed by the denial of a job, she went to church more often and spent most of her time reading Western classics in English or in Chinese translation. Among her favorites were *Les Misérables* by Victor Hugo and Shakespeare's *Hamlet*. At the end of my long day's work it was a joy for me to spend time talking with her about her reading. I would recite Hamlet's great soliloquies for her, especially the one that begins with "O! that this too too solid flesh would melt, . . . Or that the Everlasting had not fix'd / His canon 'gainst self-slaughter!" Or she would recite for me Ophelia's heartbreaking lament on Hamlet's derangement. Or we would take turns reading passages from an English translation of *Les Misérables*. We could not afford a radio or a good camera, so I took pictures of Yikai with my Kodak Brownie. When her married eldest sister gave us an old record player, I scoured the market of used foreign goods and bought a set of records of Beethoven's *Pastoral Symphony* and another of Bach's *Brandenburg Concertos* with the fifty yuan the City Library had given me for my English edition of *Das Kapital*. We never tired of listening to these precious records. They conjured up an idyllic island of beauty and harmony in the midst of a sea of troubles. I taught her how to play gin rummy, and she usually beat me at the game. We were contented with so little and looked forward to a happy family life.

3

IN JANUARY 1955, THE OFFICIAL *ART AND LITERARY GAZETTE* PUBLISHED AN unprecedented supplement to its monthly issue. It contained a lengthy report by Hu Feng, a veteran Communist literary theorist and critic, protesting against "the five daggers plunged into the writer's head" by the cultural bureaucrats—namely Marxism, populism, politics, thought reform, and official style. For a brief moment, the editorial note soliciting discussion led people to think this was going to be a welcome and free academic forum of theoretical and practical issues in the circles of literature and art. But soon Hu Feng came under fire as an ideological deviationist attacking the party's correct theory and practice in art and literature, and the critique spread out all over the country. In May, the *People's Daily* published Hu Feng's confession of his political and ideological errors and at the same time denounced it as insincere and treacherous. Shortly afterward, the Hu Feng affair was transformed into a counterrevolutionary conspiracy against the entire party. Several pages of the party organ were devoted to personal letters written by Hu Feng to his writer friends who shared some of his ideas, with damning running commentaries penned by Mao Zedong himself. The great leader of a great country actually stooped so low as to use private letters that must have been seized by police methods to frame an outspoken writer in his own party. Apparently there was a lot I had yet to learn about what was new in the New China!

Hu Feng's fate was sealed. At a large meeting of prominent writers and artists in Beijing he was publicly denounced as the ringleader of a secret service organization for the U.S. imperialists and the Nationalists. He was arrested on the spot and sent to jail. Then began a witch-hunt for "Hu Feng elements" throughout the country. Thousands were interrogated and at least a hundred were condemned and sent to jail. There had been many literary inquisitions throughout the long history of China, but they were supposed to be things of a dead feudal past. Now this nationwide modern literary inquisition was perpetrated in the name of the revolution and the New China, which boasted the emancipation of the Chinese people from agelong despotic oppression! And the complicity of prominent writers and artists, some of whom I knew personally, was a terrible blow to my implicit faith in writers and artists as the conscience of the nation. Nevertheless, at the political study sessions, I too joined the chorus of denunciation and despised myself for doing so. I knew the bell was not tolling for Hu Feng and other innocents alone.

Before the summer was over, the "struggle against the Hu Feng clique" escalated further into the nationwide Campaign to Uproot Hidden Counterrevolutionaries. Red banners were hung across streets all over the city, declaring, "Resolutely, thoroughly, completely, and exhaustively uproot all hidden counterrevolutionaries!" When the new school year began on September 1, 1955, the new campaign took the place of classes at the university. To be sure, I was vulnerable as a "backward element" already in political disgrace. But there was nothing hidden or counterrevolutionary about me. Surely they would not frame me just because I had a big mouth. After all, only four years ago I had returned all the way from America to serve the New China. Day after day, as I read endless denunciations of hidden counterrevolutionaries and hysterical editorials in the party organs, I could hear John Donne intoning, "Never send to know for whom the bell tolls; it tolls for thee."

Sure enough, on the very first morning of the new semester, I was hysterically denounced at a meeting of more than a hundred faculty and staff members as not only the number-one hidden counterrevolutionary at Nankai but the ringleader of a counterrevolutionary clique of four, with Cha and Li and an outspoken Russian instructor as my consorts. I was ordered to sit in the middle of the room, encircled by rings of clamorous and table-banging accusers. The fury of my accusers was so great that a frightened Russian teacher by the name of Yu Jinduo, once interpreter to the last emperor of the Qing dynasty, collapsed on the spot and had to be carried out of the room. I wondered what would have happened if this former imperial courtier had been sitting in *my* chair. After the initial bombardment, questions about my past were fired at me. I gave factual answers. Soon I saw my inquisitors were well prepared, for their questions followed chronological order and were slanted to show I had always been reactionary in my political affiliations.

"What were you doing in the city of Wuhan in the summer of 1938?" asked a young male history instructor.

"I was a war refugee looking for a rice bowl. And I also wanted to do my bit for the war of resistance. The Nationalist government was recruiting students to be trained as wartime workers for the armed forces. I signed up for a three-month training."

"What kind of training?"

"For political work in the army."

"Secret service, eh?"

"Not exactly."

"You're sly, very sly. You were in the secret service even then!"

"I was not."

"You're here to answer questions, not to talk back." Another man took over. "Who was the head of the training corps?"

"Chiang Kai-shek."

"See! You were already connected with the number-one war criminal even then. Who else?"

"Chen Cheng was the deputy commander." Chen was one of Chiang Kai-shek's top generals.

"See! Another arch-war criminal! More?"

I mentioned other Nationalist military and political leaders, all of whom had been named in the Communist blacklist of most wanted war criminals.

"Every single one a war criminal," another man interposed. "You were certainly in good company. Who else?"

"Zhou Enlai."

"You're lying!" he shot at me. "You're insulting our beloved premier. Now you're an active counterrevolutionary!"

There was an uproar

"I beg your pardon," I said calmly when the uproar subsided. "Premier Zhou was deputy director of the Political Department of the Military Commission at the time. He came every other week to lecture on the international situation. He wore the stars of a lieutenant general on the collar of his military uniform. It was during the period of wartime coalition between the Communists and the Nationalists—"

"You shut up!" The party functionary chairing the session broke in. "No one asked you for all this crap. You had better behave yourself or else! This is not your classroom You're here to confess your counterrevolutionary crimes, the sooner the better. We will expect a better attitude from you in the afternoon. Now get out."

So I got out and made my way home. It was a short distance, but it felt unbearably long. My only thought was how my pregnant wife and diabetic old mother would take this. Pushing the door open, I collapsed into a chair without a word. "What happened?" both Mother and Yikai asked anxiously at the same time. "Nothing much. I got it again," I mumbled hoarsely. "Bring him a cup of tea, Yikai." Mother's voice was shaking. But before Yikai could leave for the kitchen, the door was thrown open and several strangers barged in. Flashing a search warrant, three men and one woman announced themselves in a hostile tone as public security agents. I had never seen the men before, but I recognized the woman as an activist in the Chinese department. Two of the men ordered me to get up and proceeded to body-search me. The woman first body-searched my wife and then my mother. Then they started ransacking the little house, opening all the drawers, all the suitcases and trunks, and turning everything topsy-turvy. Finally one of the men asked me, "You got a pistol or any other weapon?" "No, nothing, just a pen," I blurted out, suddenly recalling what Napoleon had said about the pen. Another man demanded, "Where is your radio transmitter? Where have you hidden it?" No, this can't be true, I told myself, are they actually suspecting me of being a hidden spy? "I haven't even got a radio set, I can't afford it, so sorry." Visibly disappointed at not finding any material evidence of spy work, they went away with my letters, address books, notebooks, manuscripts, and sundry papers. After they had left, I looked first at the floor littered with our belongings and then up at Yikai.

"I wish they had taken away everything," I said, "so that you wouldn't have so much tidying up to do."

"Oh, I don't mind that part of it. The same thing happened to our house when Second Sister was arrested four years ago because of her Catholic affiliations."

"I'm so sorry to make you go through all this again. They could search the house as often as they liked, but I just don't see what right they had to body-search you and Mother. The whole thing is outrageous, more absurd than a bad absurdist play. I'm not going to take it lying down!"

"What right are you talking about? You are a bookworm, professor, you never understand the rules of the game. You're not living in the United States, but in Communist China." Yikai smiled at me and stretched out her hand. "I do hope nothing serious will happen to you . . ."

I knew her heart was heavy, especially because she would be giving birth to our first child in a few months' time. What assurance could I possibly give her, when I couldn't even protect her against insults from insolent agents? I wished I had not been such a fool as to put my foot in my big mouth. What had I gained but insults and injuries? I regretted my indiscretions, I was afraid. Then I suddenly remembered one of my favorite quotations from Lincoln: "To sin by silence when they should protest makes cowards out of men." Yikai interrupted my thoughts by saying I should have a bite to eat, but I had no stomach for food. It was time to go to the afternoon session of denunciation and interrogation.

On the way to the meeting room, I ran into Professor Xie of the history department. A genial fat man in his early fifties, he looked like a Happy Buddha. I smiled at him weakly, but he turned his face away and quickened his steps. When I entered the room, the encirclement was nearly complete. I took my seat in the middle and the party functionary immediately called the meeting to order.

"Wu Ningkun's behavior at the morning session was outrageous," he said sternly. "He showed no penitence, he did not confess to his counterrevolutionary crimes, past or present, he even talked back to the revolutionary comrades who were earnestly helping him come to his senses. I must warn you, Wu Ningkun, you are besieged by the revolutionary masses even as your place in this room indicates. The only way out for you lies in your surrendering to the people. The policy of the party and the government toward criminals has always been 'leniency to those who confess their crimes and severity to those who refuse to.' What course to follow—this is a question Wu Ningkun must decide for himself before it is too late. Meanwhile, I ask the revolutionary comrades to go on exposing and denouncing Wu Ningkun's counterrevolutionary crimes."

The first to speak was Professor Xie, purple with rage, looking like one of the fierce warriors guarding a Buddhist temple rather than the usual Happy Buddha. "Wu Ningkun, your behavior this morning was outrageous, absolutely intolerable. Instead of making a humble and honest confession of your crimes, you made fun of revolutionary comrades. It was flagrant resistance to the campaign and further onslaught on the party. Let me tell you, you are the number-one target of the campaign, the number-one hidden counterrevolutionary at Nankai. Your known crimes, your counterrevolutionary utterances against socialist China, are more than enough to convict you. Our great party, out of the wish to save every erring intellectual that can still be saved, is giving you this last chance to repent with the help of so many revolutionary comrades. Just now I saw you sauntering over from your home without showing the least trace of repentance. And you had the nerve, the cheek to smile." Here he started shouting.

"Have you no sense of shame left? Let me ask you, why did you smile to me on the way just now? Perhaps you were asking for my sympathy? Perhaps you wanted me to keep quiet here? No way! You drank tea with me, you discussed historical topics with me. But that was before I saw through you. Now I draw a clear line of demarcation from you, and I also ask all revolutionary comrades to do the same!"

The party functionary commended the attitude of Professor Xie, and other revolutionary comrades followed his example by shouting insults or firing questions at me one after another. The attack was focused on my bad attitude. Suddenly Shakespeare's great line "full of sound and fury, signifying nothing" sang in my ears. Before the afternoon session broke up, the party functionary announced: "Wu Ningkun will hand in a self-criticism in the morning for his reactionary attitude to the campaign and the revolutionary comrades. Wu Ningkun is forbidden to have any contact with anyone on or off campus, receive visitors, or sneak out of the campus. Any violation of these rules can only aggravate his already serious offenses. We remind you again, Wu Ningkun, it is the party's policy to mete out leniency to those who confess their crimes and severity to those who refuse to. The choice is yours, and your time is limited."

Similar denunciation sessions became a settled routine for several days running. I was exhorted daily to "confess," or to "surrender," and reminded of what the "iron fist of proletarian dictatorship" could do to my career and my family. I saw it was all psychological warfare (though psychology had been banned as a bourgeois pseudoscience), yet my mortal flesh was weak. I wished I had some crime to confess so as to escape these nerve-racking harangues and dark threats. I racked my brain trying to unearth crimes I might have committed unwittingly or crimes I had hidden even from myself. But it was fruitless, and my head ached day and night.

One morning, just as I was about to leave home for another meeting of interrogation and denunciation, I heard a commotion outside. I opened the door and saw several men in public security uniforms pushing their way through a throng of onlookers into the house of a Russian instructor across the path. Making an arrest? I wondered. It was no time for me to poke my nose into the business of others, so I went on my way. By the time I arrived on the scene of my daily ordeal, I found my inquisitors gabbing excitedly among themselves. I soon overheard that Professor Yan Yuheng, a senior member of the English faculty, was found drowned in the decorative pond in front of the library. It seemed he had been questioned in connection with the current campaign, but had refused to answer questions. He had left behind a large family. When the party functionary arrived, he announced there would be a review and discussion among the revolutionary comrades and sent me home to write confessions. When I got home, Mother looked frightened. First she said Yikai had been summoned by the campaign headquarters. Then she told me under her breath that the wife of the Russian instructor across the way had been found dead, hanging together with the man who had been rooming with them. "What for?" I asked. "I don't know and I don't ask," she whispered. "Something to do with the campaign, people say. Oh, I'm frightened to death. What about you?" What about me indeed? What comfort could I give this aging mother who had had her share of misfortune in life? I tried to put on a bold front. "They are looking into my personal history. It's to be expected. There's really nothing to worry about." "I certainly hope so," Mother said, obviously unconvinced. "But no other house has been searched." Before I could find an answer, Yikai returned.

"The campaign headquarters sent for me as soon as you had left," my young wife said calmly. "One of the women party functionaries told me you had behaved badly at the sessions, which were meant to help you. You have not confessed anything so far and their patience is limited. She said, for your sake and for my own sake, it is up to me to help you change your attitude. Then she changed her subject a little. A few individuals at the university had just taken their own lives, she said. They had resisted the campaign and come to an ignominious end. The party and the people are not to be deterred by such treachery, but unnecessary deaths should be prevented. They trust Wu Ningkun will have better sense than such scum. And they hope I will keep an eye on you. Before she had quite finished, I reassured her, 'Ningkun was so stupid as to get himself and us into this scrape, but I'm sure he will not be that stupid as to do away with his own life. He will just have to confess if he has really done anything wrong. He does not need my help, for what you have done for him is more than what he needs.' " She broke into a smile.

"Good for you, young lady! I see you are recovering from the impact of the first attack better than your man."

"I can tell they are worried by the suicides, which are not good for the image of the party as the benevolent savior. You would never stoop to that, would you?" She smiled again.

"That the Everlasting had not fix'd / His canon 'gainst self-slaughter!" I repeated the line from Hamlet's great soliloquy, which we had often recited together. She smiled again, but this time with tears in her eyes.

Following the suicides, the campaign switched to a lower key. There were no more hysterical denunciations. I was ordered to work on another autobiographical sketch at home, focusing on counterrevolutionary affiliations, utterances, thoughts, and deeds. Interrogation was carried out in the evenings instead by small groups of my "peers," mostly activists who were striving to qualify for membership in the Communist party. They no longer shouted, but were persistent and thoroughgoing. One evening, after beating about the bush with questions on my life and work at Yenching University during 1951–52, the young history instructor by the name of Lai, who had been my cordial neighbor for some months, suddenly sprang a question on me:

"What was your relationship with the counterrevolutionary clique among the students of the foreign languages department at Yenching?"

"I don't know what you're talking about."

"We're in possession of a great deal of materials relating to your activities in the clique. Some were written by your favorite reactionary students. I can tell you frankly, they have all been rounded up, including Li Tiansheng, who you brought to Nankai. We just want to give you the opportunity to save yourself by making a clean breast of your crimes. Now are you ready to talk?"

"I still don't know what you're talking about."

"All right, do you know the name ABC?"

"The ABC of what?"

"Stop pretending. You know very well it's the name of your counterrevolutionary clique."

It suddenly rang a bell. The most outspoken anti-Communist student in my class, the witty Jiang the Elder, had been accused by student activists of forming a club of reactionary students around him. "Yes, a bridge club," he had retorted laughingly, "ABC, for short. In the hands of the KGB, it could be construed into Anti-Bolshevik Club, ha-ha!" The story had gotten around, and it was laughed off.

"Now I do remember. But it was meant as a joke."

"A joke? You call anti-Bolshevik activities in socialist China a joke?"

"But there was no such club."

"Look here, it had a name, and the name was given by the ringleader of the counterrevolutionary clique, your star student Jiang. It met regularly to discuss reactionary books they had read, including *Darkness at Noon* and *1984*. You were their mentor, you took part in their discussions. Their readings furnished them with a theoretical foundation for their active opposition to communism and the New China. They engaged in spreading counterrevolutionary propaganda. Their ultimate purpose is to overthrow the party and the government. It is an active counterrevolutionary clique with a name, a leader, a mentor, a theory, and a sizable membership. Its name alone condemns itself. It has been monitored by the Public Security Ministry for a long time now. You call that a joke?"

I was flabbergasted. I saw the iron fist of proletarian dictatorship shaking before my eyes.

"I have never looked at things that way. I must think it over and recall my associations with students at Yenching and hand in a detailed report."

"I'm glad to see you're beginning to turn around. We'll wait and see."

I went home with a heavy heart, mainly because I was tormented by the thought that those bright students of mine in Beijing must have been subjected to even more brutal interrogation. When I tried to write the report, I recalled the times we spent together and parts of our conversations. But I could not for my life see anything criminal in what they said or did. They took freedom of speech for granted and resented attempts at indoctrination. That's all. My own attitude had undoubtedly given them moral support. So in my own "confession," I admitted that my unreformed Western ideology must have had a bad influence on them and said I was ready to accept my responsibility in their aberrations. But I denied the existence of such a club.

Another evening, my "peers" delved into my American years. After beating about the bush as usual, Lai the history instructor suddenly asked with a significant smirk:

"Why did you return to China in the summer of 1951, at the height of the Korean War?"

"Because this is my country." I saw no point in his question.

"You think so, eh?" he sneered. "You'd call yourself a patriot, I suppose. But patriotism has a class basis. The country you loved was feudal and capitalist China supported by U.S. imperialism, not the socialist China *we* love. Tell us now, frankly, why in the world did you come back from the United States at the time you did, when you were getting along very well as a future American Ph.D.?"

"I was invited back by Yenching University." I thought that was an incontrovertible historical fact, one a history instructor might have respected.

"Indeed," he sneered again. "We gave you a pretty good pretext, didn't we?"

"What do you mean?" I flared up. "You think I am a spy? A spy sent by the CIA, the Nationalists, and whatnot, is that it?"

"We didn't say it. You said it yourself," he retorted triumphantly.

Suddenly, however, I felt a strange relief. If this was what had been worrying them all these years, then I had nothing to worry about. My life was an open book. They might choose to misread it under the compulsion of paranoia, but the text would remain intact. From then on, I felt calm and managed to take their calculated provocation and insult with nonchalance.

4

REGULAR CLASSES BEGAN AT THE UNIVERSITY THREE WEEKS AFTER THE FIRST day of school. But the English department remained closed because three members of its small faculty were still under campus arrest and one professor had committed suicide. Interrogations gradually tapered off and I stayed home to continue writing the required autobiographical sketch. A few days after I handed it in, I was called in and told to write another one with more details. The purpose, I realized later, was obviously a ploy to detect inconsistencies between different versions. I had no fears, since I had nothing to hide. In my forced seclusion, I began translating Stendhal's classic *La Chartreuse de Parme* from a French edition sent me by Xiao San, Ba Jin's wife. The work gave my mind diversion from my present plight, and the beauty of the romantic story contrasted splendidly with the sordid politics around me. To distract me further, Yikai played gin rummy with me at night. Helpless pawns in a political game, we might as well enjoy our reprieve in the cage.

On the afternoon of January 3, 1956, while playing gin rummy with me, Yikai complained of labor pains. I threw down my cards and dashed over to the campaign headquarters, asking for leave to take her to a maternity hospital in town. The next morning, when I was again given leave to go and see her, I was overjoyed to find that our first child had been born early in the morning. It was a boy, and I named him Yiding, meaning simply "a man," in contradistinction to the god who was emerging from the current personality cult. The arrival of "a man" gave heart to the besieged parents, as the arrival of a new vital force would a besieged army.

Two weeks later, in a surprising turn of events, the publication of Premier Zhou Enlai's report on the party's policy toward intellectuals put an abrupt end to the hunt for shadow enemies. Zhou reviewed the abuse of intellectuals by party organs and officials during the five years since the Communists had come to power, which had dampened the intellectuals' initiative in playing a crucial role in the reconstruction of the New China. He attributed this abuse to the party's lack of experience in working with intellectuals and to the lack of mutual understanding. Urging party officials in responsible positions to make friends with intellectuals, he laid down new guidelines giving the intellectuals higher social status, greater freedom, and better material benefits. I was of course overjoyed and read the report carefully more than once. But my joy was premature. Before long, a young party functionary in the campaign headquarters sent for me.

"What have you been doing these days? Enjoying your life of leisure, eh?" He laughed sarcastically.

"I have been studying Premier Zhou's report." I did not think he could find fault with that, but I was once again proved naive.

"So you have an additional weapon in your hands, eh?" I was stunned and made no response. He went on, "I believe your job is still to make a confession of your counterrevolutionary offenses. A counterrevolutionary is a counterrevolutionary. The premier's report is no protection for counterrevolutionaries." Could this greenhorn radical actually be defying the great premier? I was baffled for a moment, but I quickly realized that he and his like, who had been thrown off balance by the unexpected U-turn, were desperately hoping to salvage the campaign at Nankai or to at least save face.

Soon afterward, an official from the Municipal Party Committee visiting the university sent for me. He expressed regrets that my experience in the campaign must have been very hard on me, since I had only recently returned from abroad after a prolonged absence. He reassured me that this kind of stormy political campaign "would never happen again." I took comfort from his reassurance inasmuch as I had implicit faith in the party's policy toward intellectuals newly pronounced by the respected premier. In May, I was given notice that I was to be transferred to a "party school" in Beijing and that Yikai would also get her first job there. My colleagues envied us, but Yikai did not relish the idea of living in the political center of the Communist rule and was loath to leave her family. In June, when the time came for us to leave she cried like a child with her five-month-old baby in her arms. Did her instincts tell her it was to be the beginning of an unsought-for adventure?

Three

A HUNDRED FLOWERS
AND A POISONOUS WEED,
1956–58

1

WHEN I WAS RECALLED TO BEIJING EARLY IN THE SUMMER OF 1956 AND GIVEN a new teaching job at the party school, I began to look forward to a useful academic career and a happy family life with my wife and our newborn son. Yikai was given a job as an assistant reference librarian in the faculty reading room. Though small and bleak, the campus was only a stone's throw from the fabulous Summer Palace, where we often took a stroll along the covered imperial promenade or amidst varieties of flowering trees on the lakeside, with Yiding in his wicker baby carriage. Simultaneous with my recall, to my great delight, my sister and her husband were also transferred from Shanghai to Beijing. She became vice principal of a key high school in the heart of the city and her husband a senior engineer at the prestigious Design Institute of Ferrous Metallurgy. When their son Zhang Chun, eighty days older than Yiding, came to stay with us, we would take him along on our visits to the palace. The two little cousins, sitting face-to-face in the carriage and glowing with health and happiness, seemed to personify my renewed faith in the country that I had returned to serve. My sister and brother-in-law often came to spend a weekend with us. When it was nice, we would bring the children out to the Summer Palace and have our pictures taken against the magnificent Longevity Hill or spend a leisurely afternoon boating on Kunming Lake. At the bridge table after dinner, conversation usually turned to the heartening political situation at home. The political campaign of which I had been a victim the year before was already a thing of the past. Both my sister and her husband were applying for membership in the party. Life was far from idyllic, but China seemed to be on the threshold of a period of progress and prosperity, as the party leadership eloquently and tirelessly reiterated the policy of "letting a hundred flowers bloom and a hundred schools of thought contend" advocated by Mao Zedong himself. Freedom of thought and speech, which before had been discredited as an odious bourgeois fraud, was now deemed essential to the health of a socialist state.

The party school was not a regular college, but a small training center attached to the Central Investigation Department (CID) under the Central Committee, sometimes regarded as the Chinese counterpart of the KGB or the CIA. The director of the CID was a veteran intelligence officer, General Li Kenong, who was concurrently a Deputy Foreign Minister under Zhou Enlai. The school was headed by a high CID official who remained invisible until the climax of the next political campaign. Its main function was foreign language training for handpicked students who were destined for CID assignments at home or abroad. Their professional training, which was none of our concern, was presumably given elsewhere upon graduation from the school. I would have preferred teaching at a regular university, but in a country where personal choice of jobs was condemned as a bourgeois heresy, I had to be contended with my lot. The CID cared only whether I would make a good teacher of English; they had no scruples about my political sentiments or my political past, since I would be quite "safe" in their hands.

Shortly after we reported to duty in Beijing, all the faculty members and their families, a few dozen in all, were sent to Qingdao for a few weeks' vacation. We rode first-class on the train, were accommodated at seaside villas reserved for high CID officials, and swam at a private beach guarded by armed soldiers. Uniformed soldiers who waited on us at the dinner tables insisted on addressing us as "leading cadres" in spite of our protests. "Anyone who stays here must be a leading cadre," reasoned one of them. Yikai was so amused by the earnestness of one young soldier that she whispered to me, "What would he say if he knew you were a virtual prisoner only yesterday?" It was our first taste of the caprices of the regime.

Even before the vacation was over, a wire came from Beijing assigning me to work as a senior translator for the forthcoming Eighth Communist Party Congress to be held in September in Beijing. I was expected to report to duty as soon as possible, but all the first-class sleepers had been reserved for days on end by the city's party committee to take vacationing delegates to the capital city. I suggested perhaps we could all go second-class. The business official in charge was horrified by the idea: "We would be making a serious political mistake if we did that." By the time the business official managed to put us on a first-class sleeper several days later, we found it half-empty.

In the translation department serving the congress, I found myself in the company of well-known professors of English from the great universities in Beijing, including my former housemate Wu Xinghua. We worked by shifts on the various lengthy documents of the congress and hundreds of speeches by the delegates. Sometimes we worked day and night nonstop, but no one complained. The willing cooperation of such a group of highly qualified intellectuals, mostly trained in the West or in westernized universities in the old China, was a measure of success of the regime's efforts at bringing the intellectuals into line. At the same time, these scholars in the prime of their life felt relaxed in the relatively liberal atmosphere, although most of them still observed the sagacious rule of conduct that "discretion is the better part of valor." Once, translating a speech by the great Marshal Zhu De, I threw up my hands and exclaimed, "What can you do with this ponderous style!" Professor Qian Zhongshu, the famed scholar of Chinese and Western literature and a senior fellow at the Institute of Literature under the Academy of Sciences, known for his biting wit, gave me a shocked look and put a finger on his lips while breathing a discreet "shh." Nevertheless, I was heartened by the new emphasis on economic reconstruction and the de-emphasis on class struggle in Premier Zhou Enlai's political report to the congress, which I helped translate into English. I also took comfort in the provisions in the new party constitution that were intended to forestall the emergence of a Stalinist personality cult in China. At the National Day celebrations on Tiananmen Square on October 1, following the closing of the congress, I did not march in the parade but was given a place on the grandstand facing the rostrum from which Mao Zedong watched the paraders, acknowledging their salvos of "Long live Chairman Mao!" The "long live" slogan traditionally used in hailing an emperor awakened in me memories of the nation's autocratic past, and I could not reconcile the image of the smiling messianic figure on the rostrum with the man who had unscrupulously framed and condemned the literary critic just a year before. But who was I to go against the human wave of paraders shouting themselves hoarse? I was the pride of the party school and the envy of my colleagues, although standing for hours was hardly enviable for my legs and bladder.

I did not start teaching until November, after I had done my part in finalizing the English translation of the congress documents, along with Professor Qian Zhongshu and another Oxonian, Professor Wang Zuoliang. Two reading courses and one writing course were to be my assignment, again heavier than the load carried by my colleagues. But I did not complain, for after more than a year's absence from the classroom I was itching to teach students who were eager to learn. The students were enthusiastic, and my colleagues and party bosses spoke well of me. Leading academic journals published in Beijing solicited my contributions. A new academic quarterly named *Western Languages and Literatures,* edited by Wang Zuoliang, started publication in April 1957, and the first issue carried my review of a new Chinese translation of *Hamlet* by the poet Bian Zhilin, now also a senior fellow at the Institute of Literature. In May I finished a long review of Wu Xinghua's superb translation of *Henry the Fourth.* It was to appear in the summer issue of the new journal. Also in May, a former Yenching colleague, Yang Yuemin, now managing editor of the *Literary Studies Quarterly* at the Institute of Literature, called on me to solicit a long essay on Longfellow in commemoration of the 150th anniversary of the poet's birth. *Literary Translations,* the only magazine devoted to the introduction of foreign literature, asked for a translation of *The Pearl* by John Steinbeck. I wished I had more time for reading and research, so that I could do some serious academic work. But I was not particularly discontented.

Some of my former students from Yenching University who were working in Beijing gradually turned up at my home. They recounted how they had been denounced as members of the "ABC" during the political campaign the year before and were glad it was all over. On International Labor Day, May 1, 1957, a national holiday, a dozen of them organized a sort of reunion picnic at the Summer Palace, to which Yikai and I were invited. It was an exceptionally brilliant day and the grand palace was bursting with celebrators. Bathing in the warm morning sun aboard a pleasure boat, we listened to one of my former students read a directive from the front page of the *People's Daily*. The Central Committee called on the whole party to unfold a Rectification Campaign for the laudable purpose of redressing the abuses and errors on the part of party members and party organs at all levels since the founding of the People's Republic. The Central Committee enjoined party leaders at all levels to solicit criticism from people in every walk of life, especially from intellectuals and members of "democratic" parties. The critics were urged to "air their views without reserve" for the benefit of the party and its members. They were solemnly promised: "The speaker is not to be blamed for whatever he says, while he who hears it should take warning." We all applauded the courageous decision taken by the party and naturally compared notes on what had happened to us the year before. Was the party honestly drawing a lesson from what had happened in Hungary the year before? Honestly trying to live up to its promise of bringing progress and prosperity to a new China? I was hopeful and kept my fingers crossed.

In the weeks that followed, I began reading newspapers avidly, for the first time. The *People's Daily* and other newspapers in Beijing carried numerous articles by well-known intellectuals criticizing party officials and even guidelines of the party itself. There were even calls for a multiparty system, universities governed by professors rather than party cadres, a free job market, and other liberal measures. At meetings at universities and government departments many people poured out their hearts in hopes of helping the party and its members mend their ways. My sister Ninghui, in her capacity as a nonparty vice principal of High School No. 28, aired her views on how to improve secondary education and pointed out the shortcomings in the current educational system at one of these meetings. Her speech was headlined in the official *Beijing Daily*. At Beijing University, two bus stops away from the party school, posters written in big Chinese characters covered the walls all over the campus, blooming like the proverbial hundred flowers. The party and socialist system were under fire. My former assistant Huang, now a favorite activist of the party, suddenly woke up to the new reality and joined the ranks of vociferous critics. Freedom of speech was having its day; that day was short.

Five weeks after the Rectification Campaign had been publicized with such fanfare, what has since become known as Beijing Spring was brought to a blighted end, when the "Great Leader" again personally intervened. He penned editorial after editorial for the *People's Daily,* denouncing much of the ongoing criticism as "poisonous weeds" passing themselves off as "fragrant flowers." This was not the "constructive criticism" solicited by the party, he pronounced, but vicious attacks on the party, the people, and socialism by the right wing of the bourgeoisie. Overnight, the Communist party's own Rectification Campaign turned into an all-out counteroffensive against the "bourgeois rightists." The nation, which had been granted a brief reprieve since the last political campaign, was plunged into a more ruthless antirightist struggle. The sagacious "Great Leader" let it be known at a later date that all this had been a premeditated plot to "coax a snake out of its lair," or to ensnare his critics into a trap.

2

I FELL INTO THE TRAP.

Though close to the turbulent Beijing University, the party school remained relatively unperturbed because of its special character. The party bosses of the school who had been indoctrinated in the "revolutionary cradle" of Yan'an took a wait-and-see stance. They had gone through too many political campaigns to commit themselves before they were sure which way the wind was blowing. Some of the students who were excited by the big-character posters they had read at Beijing University started putting up posters in small characters with mild criticisms of the dull political courses and the inefficient administration. I asked Vice President Feng, a Yan'an veteran, what he thought of them. "These greenhorns are too young to know what they are doing," he said enigmatically. There was some excitement and a lot of talk among the faculty members, but no one ventured to put up a poster.

One day, a party member on the English faculty asked me whether I would join them in the Rectification Campaign, meaning "to intensify my own thought reform through criticism and self-criticism."

"Hell no," I said with a laugh. "I was deep-fried in your cauldrons, and now you party members want to rectify yourselves by 'a gentle breeze and a mild rain,' as the Central Committee directive says. The party members are intoxicated with the breeze, while the masses are dampened by the rain. Wouldn't boiling water be more effective than a gentle breeze? No, thank you, none of your rectification for me. I'm already as clean as a saint, thanks to years of purgation."

By and by, faculty and staff meetings began to be called to solicit criticism to help the party carry out rectification. Trivial matters were brought up, but no one touched on anything significant. Then, one evening, Yu Wei, the senior vice president, called on me. Yu had studied in Japan in his younger days and then joined the revolutionary ranks in Yan'an. Normally a man of few words, he began by talking about his own experience in the 1942 Rectification Campaign in Yan'an, a notorious episode in the history of the party.

"Large numbers of revolutionary comrades were subjected to the severe test of trying interrogations. I was no exception. As a returned student from Japan, I was naturally a spy suspect. Some were driven to suicide, but I stood the trial and won the trust of the party."

"I admire your steadfastness under great pressure," I said. "But I don't see why the party had to resort to such police measures in testing people who had given up everything to join the revolutionary ranks."

"You must take the historical background into account. It was a time of war. The struggle with the Nationalists on the one hand and the Japanese on the other was very acute. The party could not take chances, lest enemy agents infiltrate the revolutionary ranks."

"How many such agents were caught?"

"Few, very few."

"At the cost of hurting so many good comrades?"

"Well, there's a cost for everything, and errors are inevitable. A revolutionary must look at the brighter side of things. This is why the Central Committee directive stresses that the campaign must be conducted in the manner of 'a gentle breeze and a mild rain.' Those who air their views are immune to any retaliation. That is the policy laid down by Chairman Mao. We must speak up in all sincerity to help improve the work style of the party and its members. I am dissatisfied with the way our faculty and staff meetings have been going. No one seems willing to 'air their views,' which was the purpose of the meetings. 'Chicken feathers and garlic skins' are all that has been brought up. College teachers are high intellectuals. They should say things worthy of their social function and come up with significant criticism. With your prestige at the school, I hope you will take the lead in speaking your mind at the next meeting."

"I really don't have much to say," I dodged. "I haven't been here long enough to be able to offer criticism on any significant issue."

"It doesn't have to be related to the school. You have lived in the New China long enough to have your own experiences and observations."

"My own experiences indeed! What they did to me at Nankai during the Campaign to Uproot Hidden Counterrevolutionaries was probably not much different from your own experiences in Yan'an in 1942."

"It was a mistake, but it's a thing of the past now. I reassure you, nothing will happen to you because of what you may say in the present campaign."

Some of my friends urged me to take him up on that, while others warned me against the ploy of "throwing a long line to catch a big fish." Yu Wei dropped in again on the two succeeding evenings with the same message. At the same time, Lao (Old) Liu, a former Nationalist army defector to the Communists and now secretary of the faculty party branch, also came to solicit criticism and urge me to air my views. I had no reason to question their sincerity, so I spoke up at the next faculty-staff meeting.

I began by telling how I had disrupted my doctoral work and come home to work for the New China, and what difficulties I had run into during the years since my return. I then focused on what had happened to me at Nankai during the previous political campaign in 1955.

"It was unjustifiable and preposterous. A flagrant violation of civil rights, a premeditated official lynching. Even with a phony search warrant, what right did they have to body-search my pregnant wife and aged mother? They added insult to injury, to say the least. Nankai might at least send us apologies. The campaign itself was a mistake, an attempt to stamp out freedom of thought and speech on the model of Stalinist purges, which have already been exposed and denounced by Khrushchev."

Then I lauded the party's "hundred flowers" policy and its solicitation of criticism from intellectuals as encouragement of freedom of speech. I cited the Chinese saying "Trying to stop the mouths of the people is harder than trying to stop a river from flowing," and went one step further: "Trying to stop the mouths of intellectuals is harder than trying to dam up a flood. The intelligentsia, which forms a precious small minority in a nation of hundreds of millions, should be encouraged to speak out as the conscience of China, rather than confined to the role of obsequious scholar-officials of autocratic dynasties. A people's government or a political party founded on incontrovertible truth has nothing to lose by granting freedom of speech and everything to gain from the collective wisdom of open minds. The Rectification could become a turning point in the history of the party and the People's Republic."

In foreign affairs, I suggested that the policy of "leaning to one side" might not be in the best interest of the nation. What had we gained by an unqualified confrontation with the West, when our Big Brother had at least kept on normal diplomatic relations? What had we deprived ourselves of by shutting the door against the Western world? Speaking about the teaching of English, I questioned the practice of inviting "Soviet experts" trained in their own schools to direct the teaching of English in Chinese universities staffed with professors educated in great American and British universities. Would we someday invite "Soviet experts" to direct the teaching of Chinese in Chinese universities? On the matter of theory and criticism of art and literature, I suggested that Chairman Mao's dictum of judging works of art according to ideological correctness, which was dictated by needs of wartime propaganda, might perhaps be supplemented by broader explorations in the spirit of "letting a hundred flowers bloom."

The senior vice president who was presiding over the "airing of views" expressed his appreciation of what I had proposed and asked Yikai to speak up too. She responded by saying she did not mind so much the unlawful and humiliating body search of herself when she was not even taking part in the campaign at Nankai, as much as the persecution of her innocent husband, which reminded her of the passion of Christ. Some eyebrows were raised, but Huang Hongxu, an earnest man of my age wearing thick glasses, also a professor of English and a returned student from America, showed his sympathy and approval by saying the persecution of a patriotic intellectual like me was most lamentable. "Luo Ruiqing, the minister of public security, who was responsible for victimizing innumerable innocent people in the hunt for hidden counterrevolutionaries," he suggested jocularly, "deserves to be shot." Bao Qing, a young instructor of English phonetics, vehemently aired her grievances against the party leadership at Beijing Foreign Languages Institute, where she and her husband, both English instructors, had been denounced in the same witch-hunt in 1955.

In the days that followed, our spirits were pretty high and we were often effusive, buoyed up by the "airing of views" all over the country. One day, Professor Huang asked me to join him for lunch at his home to meet a new faculty member. Cao Dun, a jovial corpulent fellow, was a college pal of Huang's and also a returned student from America. On Huang's recommendation, he had just been transferred to the school from the Foreign Languages Press, where he had worked as an English translator. We spoke quite freely, and the new man often broke into a hearty laugh. Then, one night, after a few drinks with Huang and two others in the room of Professor Xu of Beijing University, who was teaching spoken English at the party school, I brought up the four freedoms enunciated by Franklin D. Roosevelt in 1941. They had impressed me as a universal declaration of independence. "But you never realize how essential they are until you have lived in an environment that threatens to deprive you of them," I said, "just as a man would take air for granted and never realize how essential that invisible element is to his very existence. Not only are people born free but they're born free to speak. But how can one speak freely unless he is free from fear?" Finally I exclaimed in English, "Give me liberty or give me death!" Professor Huang denounced Stalin's horrendous crimes as revealed in Khrushchev's recent secret report, shouting at the end, "Long live Khrushchev!" We felt like flowers beginning to bloom.

Even when Mao launched the antirightist campaign in June, I never thought I had anything to do with it. Wasn't I only answering the call of the party to air my views without reserve? Had I not been solemnly promised immunity from reprisals? Furthermore, as I never had anything to do with capitalists, how could I be a "bourgeois rightist?" In any case, summer vacation soon began and I had to start working on the translation of Steinbeck's *The Pearl*.

3

DURING THE SUMMER VACATION, THE PARTY SCHOOL WAS RELATIVELY QUIET, but most colleges and government departments were already in the grip of the new political campaign. One day my former student Jiang the Younger came to see me and told me that both he and his elder cousin were under fire at their work units. They had both spoken up during the Rectification, challenging the one-party system and thought control. Now he wanted to lie low until it blew over. I offered him the room I used as my study. I too wished the commotion would subside, as the previous campaign had, but I had my misgivings. When he asked me what I thought would happen in the end, I felt I had to prepare him for the worst. "You have read *Darkness at Noon* and *1984*. When worse comes to worse, there will be arrests and imprisonments. History has often been dipped in the blood of martyrs. Man would have been in an even worse state today except for the sacrifices of those martyrs." After a few days, he returned to his work unit, and I never saw him again.

Before the summer vacation ended, the faculty and staff were called into frequent sessions of political study. Days were spent reading and discussing Central Committee directives on the antirightist campaign and *People's Daily* editorials, especially those known to be penned by the "Great Leader." We also reviewed the many newspaper articles targeted at well-known professors, writers, artists, and leaders of "democratic" parties who had earlier aired their views, as well as some confessions by others who had repented their mistaken views. Then the party bosses at the school made it clear that we were not to indulge in an academic study of the documents, but to relate them to ourselves and the political reality of the school.

Classes did not begin as scheduled on the first day of September. This was the third time since 1951 that university programs were shoved aside by political exigencies. Students were engaged in ferreting out and denouncing student rightists. Faculty members began to recant and confess their own errors and to inform against one another. Once again, I found myself the number-one political villain, subjected to interrogation and denunciation at dozens of small-group "study sessions" and general faculty-staff meetings. That I was a bourgeois rightist seemed a foregone conclusion before even the first meeting began. My wife was repeatedly exhorted to inform against me. Colleagues and students who had been warm and friendly a few months before started shunning me. During the meeting intermissions I would sit or stand by myself like a criminal awaiting his sentence. I felt betrayed and angry, but I knew there was nothing I could do about it. I was stupid to have taken the bait, but many seasoned eminent intellectuals and party members fared no better.

A "mass debate" followed, lasting many sessions. All that I had said, at public meetings or in private or overheard by others, was denounced as a wholesale attack on the party's domestic and foreign policies and the socialist system itself. I noticed that a neatly mimeographed handout titled "Wu Ningkun's Rightist Utterances, for Criticism and Repudiation" was distributed to "revolutionary" comrades. My only right at the "debate" was to plead guilty to whatever charge was raised against me. Any attempt at explanation or clarification of facts was shouted down as a manifestation of reactionary impenitence. Professor Yang, who had also been transferred to the school, vented his fury once again as a star witness of my sins at Nankai. A lady teacher who had done graduate work in dramatic literature at Columbia University said she had overheard me shouting "Give me liberty or give me death!" Had I or hadn't I? I pleaded guilty. "Incitation with a reactionary American slogan!" she roared, and the audience roared in agreement. A party member accused me of proposing to deep-fry party members in cauldrons of boiling oil. "Giving vent to vile class hatred!" The audience was again in an uproar. The newcomer Cao, Professor Huang's old pal, exposed the lunch in his honor at Huang's home as a rightist panel with him as an unwilling auditor suppressing his rage. His disarming hearty laugh now turned into thunderous indignation at every remark I had made and he had reconstructed.

Another day, during the noon recess, as I pushed my son in his wicker baby carriage around campus to divert my thoughts from the morning denunciation, an elderly lady colleague crossed our path. When the afternoon session began, she jumped up to accuse me of flaunting my defiance of the great campaign by parading my son all over campus. Worse still, she said, I had been heard crying, "Long live Little Dingding!," referring to my son, and making a counterrevolutionary travesty of the sacred slogan "Long live Chairman Mao!" Even my marriage was condemned as a "political union between a rightist reactionary and a reactionary Catholic." Yikai had to sit through all the general faculty-staff sessions, like "one taken to the execution ground together with the condemned" in the time-honored Chinese fashion.

Professor Huang was the only one who came to my defense. He argued that I was a patriotic intellectual who had given up an easy life and an academic career in the United States to come home and serve the New China. He admitted I might have gone too far in some of the things I had said, but allowance ought to be made for my prolonged residence abroad. In any case, he added, I had spoken freely and honestly in answer to the party's call, when others had been passive in their response. But Huang was admonished by his old pal Cao and others to mind his own class standpoint, lest he slip into the quagmire of rightists himself.

When I was interrogated by a small group of my peers in the evenings, the question of the ABC came back like a bad penny. When was it first organized? How many members in all? What books did the members read under my direction? What roles did I play? What was its political objective? Since the ABC had never actually existed, these questions were unanswerable. Why did I go to the ABC gathering at the Summer Palace on May Day? Why did I give shelter to Jiang the Younger when he fled his work unit, where he was being denounced as a counterrevolutionary? What did we talk about while he was hiding in my rooms? "He was a house guest in a private home," I answered cryptically, which brought upon my head a dire warning against evasions and implied attacks on the socialist system. Once more the question was raised: Why did I return to China in 1951 anyway? I was haunted by a recurring nightmare.

Finally, at a general faculty-staff meeting the day before the festive National Day, I was formally denounced as a "poisonous weed" of the worst kind—an "ultrarightist, a backbone element of the reactionary right wing of the bourgeoisie." My heinous crimes were characterized as antiparty, antipeople, and antisocialism, which made me a "Three-Anti" counterrevolutionary and an enemy of the people. The charges were numerous: I was born in a reactionary landlord family; I had served in the reactionary Nationalist Air Force; I had absorbed U.S. imperialist education; the motive of my return to China was unclarified; I was involved with the counterrevolutionary clique the ABC; I had taken part in their latest counterrevolutionary gathering; I maliciously attacked the great Campaign to Uproot Hidden Counterrevolutionaries as a lynching; I openly clamored for freedom of speech for rightists to overthrow the socialist China; I shouted the counterrevolutionary U.S. imperialist slogan "Give me liberty or give me death!"; I attacked the Soviet Union and Chairman Mao's policy of "leaning to one side"; I blasphemed Chairman Mao's great Marxist theory of art and literature; I was dying to deep-fry Communists in cauldrons of boiling oil; I had harbored the active counterrevolutionary Jiang the Younger in my home during the great antirightist campaign; and so on and so forth. Indignant revolutionary comrades shouted for me to "hang my head and admit my guilt." Placed in a chair by myself facing my tribunal, I burst into tears and pleaded guilty. My compulsory confession, in which I thought I had gone far in besmirching myself, was denounced as insincere and treacherous.

The meeting broke up, but Professor Huang stayed behind to shake hands with me. I had noticed an official-looking woman pacing to and fro in the back of the room and smoking continuously throughout the meeting. She also stayed behind, and now I vaguely recognized her as Mao the Frightful, another Yan'an veteran and the invisible head of the school.

"How do you feel about it?" she asked me disdainfully, puffing on her cigarette.

"I don't know what to say," I mumbled.

"It's about time that you took stock of your past and your criminal thoughts and prepared to turn over a new leaf. You ought to be grateful to us for not labeling you an active counterrevolutionary." She puffed in my face.

"Thank you," I mumbled again. In spite of it all, I was still at a loss as to how a poor scholar living from hand to mouth could have been transformed into "a backbone element" of the right wing of the propertied capitalists, with whom I never had anything to do. I had come home in good faith to serve what was lauded as a people's revolution, I had tried to put my expertise and conscience at its service, I had overlooked persecutions in previous campaigns as transient aberrations of a new regime that could still lead the nation out of the centuries of darkness. In the face of brutal reality I could no longer delude myself with wishful thinking. I paid heavily for my lesson in the omnipotence of Communist dialectics, which could transform good into evil or evil into good at will, and now I was at the mercy of the iron fist of proletarian dictatorship.

The next day, the great victory of the antirightist struggle was celebrated at Tiananmen Square and throughout the land, and I was one of the hundreds of thousands of victims on the sacrificial altar. I had been turned into an untouchable, and I wanted to be left alone to await my doom. But, no: I was told to join the faculty and staff on a holiday excursion to the Great Wall. I had not yet visited the wall, but how could I go merrymaking with people who had shouted my denunciation only the day before? I told the young party functionary who came to "invite" us that I didn't feel like going. "Oh, come on," he said. "Be a good sport. Don't take the criticism to heart, it's only meant to help you." There was command in his cheerful voice.

It was a brilliant day in early fall, the best time of the year in Beijing. The sky was blue and high, and the air was balmy. It would have been an ideal day for a family outing, had the circumstances been different. I sat with Yikai in a double seat on the chartered bus, fully intending to take a much-needed nap on the way. But shortly after the bus started, the same young party functionary came over and asked me to join Vice President Feng and two others for a card game. "But I don't know how to play the game of one hundred points," I protested. "No problem," said he, "I'll be your chief of staff." I was cornered. The game went cheerfully, as if nothing had happened at all. Since the party had not yet announced what to do with the rightists, I figured, the school authorities had decided to wait and see which way the political wind was blowing. But I felt like a mouse that the cat teases before finally devouring it.

When at last I stood face-to-face with the legendary wall I could not see what was so wonderful about this monstrous structure of huge gray bricks. My heart ached as I visualized the millions of slaves throughout the centuries, able-bodied young men torn from their parents and wives and children and driven under whips and swords to erect this monstrosity. Yikai and I climbed the wall together, apart from the group. When we reached the top, Yikai asked me, "How do you like the Seventh Wonder of the

World?" "It's a monstrosity," I said. "A monument to tyranny erected with the bones of numberless slaves by an arch-tyrant who relished burning books and burying scholars alive. And he was not alone. Emperor after emperor added to this barrier that kept the nation benighted and slavish over the centuries. Orwell should have put it in *1984,* with Dante's motto inscribed over the portal of this Mountain and Sea Pass: 'Abandon every hope, you who enter here!' "

When the two-day recess was over, the denunciation meetings resumed for the benefit of other faculty members and the students. With years of loyal service in the CID, Professor Huang might have been spared the rightist label in spite of his rightist utterances. But he had been deaf to public warnings against siding with me, and the handshake following my formal denunciation was the last straw. Meanwhile, some twenty students were labeled rightists, including a mature male student, a third-year English major, who had said the school should be administered by an academic like me rather than a party bureaucrat. One big-character poster, quibbling on his name, Xiang Qian, which means "going forward," derided him for "not going forward." He had come to China from South Korea and had worked for the CID before being sent to the school for in-service training. As a CID agent, he had looked after the well-known writer Bing Xin and her husband, Wu Wenzao, one of China's first sociologists, when they defected to the People's Republic from their Nationalist posts in Tokyo a few years ago. Wu Wenzao, a professor at the Institute of Nationalities, had already been labeled a rightist in the first wave of the campaign.

Meanwhile, we found out that Yikai was pregnant with her second child. In spite of the daily increasing stresses on us, we rejoiced over the coming of a new hope into the besieged family. A child conceived in tribulation was a simple testament to our faith in life.

Classes were scheduled to resume in November, and by request of the students I was assigned to teach all three third-year intensive reading classes, which before had been taught by three different professors. As a teacher, apparently, I could still hold my ground. Meanwhile, I was given a three-room apartment in a new two-story building that had been built as a special boon for professors, following the premier's 1956 report on the party's new policy toward intellectuals. Perhaps the campaign would be declared a mistake, just like the previous one? Perhaps right-minded party leaders were beginning to see it was doing the party and the nation nothing but harm? How could a prestigious ruling party go back on its word of honor and turn on those whose criticism it had solicited with such professed good faith? In any case, they couldn't go too far in their retaliation, could they? I kept debating with myself and hoping against hope. After all, I was a family man now and I was not prepared to be made a martyr, for my flesh was very weak.

When November came, however, I was told not to teach, but to go, together with other faculty and student rightists, to the library to catalog a mass of new and old books that had been gathering dust in the corners for months. My job was the English books. In addition, we were given menial chores. Things looked ominous.

Meanwhile, the deadline for the translation of *The Pearl* was drawing near. After each day's political session or forced labor in the library or on college grounds, I worked on it at night in my unheated study. My fingers were stiffened by the freezing cold. But I was wrapped up in the story of the young Indian pearl fisher and his wife, who fell victim to the greedy local villains because he had found the Pearl of the World. Wasn't our ordeal over the past months just like their night flight through the mountains from their ruthless trackers, the mother carrying her baby son in her arms? Kino finally came out of the mountains and foiled the designs of his treacherous enemies by throwing his precious pearl back to the sea. I was still in the dark mountains and knew not whether I could ever get out of them. Come what may, I would never throw away my pearl of the freedom of spirit, invisible but quite luminous.

4

IN EARLY MARCH, RIGHTISTS AS WELL AS REVOLUTIONARY COMRADES WERE ordered to study General Secretary Deng Xiaoping's final report on the antirightist struggle. In his capacity as director of the Anti-Rightist Headquarters under the Central Committee, he set forth the guidelines for meting out punishment to rightists. Though denounced as class enemies, rightists in general would be given administrative rather than penal punishment; severity of punishment varied with the gravity of the case. From what her colleagues said at their discussions, Yikai told me to be prepared for the worst. As the day of reckoning loomed large, my heart grew heavier and heavier. What would happen to me now? What would happen to my pregnant wife and two-year-old son and the unborn child? How had I sunk so deep into this nightmarish mire? I had been trapped and I saw no way out. Right or wrong, I was no match for the all-powerful dictatorship. I sent in one piece of self-criticism after another, pleading guilty and begging for leniency. "For in the fatness of these pursy times," I consoled myself with the bitter wisdom of Hamlet, "Virtue itself of vice must pardon beg."

On March 21, 1958, a general meeting of faculty, staff, and students was held in the student dining hall to announce officially the punishment of all those at the institute labeled rightists. I was at the top of the list: as an ultrarightist of the first order, I was to be dishonorably discharged from public employment and sent to a "state farm" for corrective education through forced labor, pending review and official approval by the State Council. This formality, which was required because of my status as a professor, was expected to take three weeks. Following the announcement, faculty members and student representatives made speeches to highlight and denounce my heinous crimes.

I sat through all the harangue less angry than resigned to the inevitable. My mind went back to those days in 1951 when I had turned a deaf ear to my relatives' and friends' dire warnings against returning to China under the new Communist rule. Now, in less than seven years, their worst fears had come true. I had been entangled in the web of class struggle. Still, I could not say it was *I* who had erred. Had I chosen not to return in 1951, more than likely I would have done so at a later date. And more than likely I would have met the same fate, given the same mesh of circumstances. I had never wished to be a martyr, and I did not feel a martyr. I could not claim noble ideals or high principles. I had no regrets, since it could not have been otherwise.

Next it was Li Tiansheng's turn. Transferred to the party school only the year before, he was also denounced as an ultrarightist and given the same punishment. A second-year English major, Zhu Qingxiu, also labeled an ultrarightist, was expelled from the school and was to be reformed through forced labor. The quiet, serious-minded youth had bought a mimeograph and stencil paper with his own money and printed leaflets to air his views in response to the call of his "Beloved Great Leader." Li and Zhu were both arrested on the spot and driven away in a public security jeep. Professor Huang, considered a marginal case, was given the label or "cap" of a rightist but spared any other punishment. All the other student rightists were expelled from the school and were to be trucked off to a village a hundred miles away to do manual labor under surveillance.

It happened to be election day, on which the formality of casting ballots for designated delegates to the Haidian District People's Congress was to be performed. After the general meeting, a junior party functionary who always reminded me of the gendarme in *Les Misérables* addressed the assembled rightists.

"You rightists are enemies of the people. But our great party is showing magnanimous leniency by treating your cases not as 'contradictions between ourselves and the enemy,' but as 'contradictions among the people.' Though your crimes are counterrevolutionary in nature, we are not treating you as enemies deserving penal punishment. It is the party's policy to turn the enemies into friends by giving you the opportunity to reform yourselves through manual labor. You are not even deprived of the right to vote. You have all criminally attacked the socialist system in one way or another. Now you see with your own eyes how socialism is infinitely superior to any other system. You should be grateful to the party from the bottom of your heart for such humane treatment. Now follow me to the polling station." Thereupon we rightists, some two dozen in all, having been led up to a large ballot box covered with bright red paper standing on a table in the middle of the dining hall, exercised our constitutional right as socialist citizens of the People's Republic of China to cast the sacred ballot for the one and only candidate.

After the polling, Yikai and I were called into the office of Mao the Frightful, the invisible woman president. The office reeked of cigarette smoke. Mao pointed with a lighted cigarette between her fingers to two chairs facing her desk.

"Well, Wu Ningkun, I don't suppose you really appreciate how lucky you are. Had you done to the Nationalists what you did to the Communists, what would they do to you?" While I fumbled for words, she answered her own question, "You would be shot, sure as hell."

"I suppose," I said weakly. "But I wouldn't know."

"Yet we have not shot you, have we? Though you fully deserve to be shot. That's the difference between the Nationalists and us," she went on. "We are not just being lenient, mind you, we try to save people like you who have committed unforgivable crimes. The punishment meted out to you may seem a little extreme in your eyes, but it will drive home the seriousness of your case and help you to turn over a new leaf. If you were an old man, we might have dealt with you differently. Oh, demotion or whatever. Since you are only thirty-eight, right? and can still serve socialism in the future, we are making sure that you reform yourself thoroughly. Do you have anything else to say for yourself?"

"No, not a thing," I said weakly again and awaited my dismissal.

"Now, Li Yikai." She turned her face to address my wife, who remained composed under the intimidating stare of Mao the Frightful. "To help you, we must ask you to give up public employment of your own free will. Tomorrow, I expect to see a big-character poster to this effect in your own handwriting. You will both get your wages next month, but they will be your last. So beginning today you must save every fen you can. No more pork in your diet!"

We were speechless. I had pleaded guilty, but they were relentless. What could we do in the face of the iron fist of proletarian dictatorship? Yikai wrote and put up the prescribed poster, to the astonishment of a colleague who still spoke to her. "You out of your mind, Li Yikai? What do you want to quit for? Aren't things bad enough in your family? What're you going to live on? You, Yiding, and the child inside you?" There was genuine concern in her voice. Yikai replied with a wry smile, "Thank you. Heaven never seals off all the exits. We'll cope."

We were evicted from our new apartment and sent back to rooms in the old building. The morning after we moved in, Pan, the chic French typist, the wife of a teacher of French and now a political activist, surprised us by barging in without even a knock on the door. She and her husband had cut us since my denunciation, although we used to be on visiting terms with one another. Ignoring my "Bonjour, Madame!" she went through our rooms and sailed out without a word. In a few minutes we suddenly realized what had happened, as the college broadcasting station announced: "The rooms of the ultrarightist Wu Ningkun were found to be in total chaos on inspection, out of keeping with the requirements of the general spring cleaning drive."

A few days later, we were summoned by the president again. "We've been reconsidering your case. I told the personnel chief, 'Look, Li Yikai has one child already and she will soon have another. You can't do this to her. Let her keep her job and earn enough to feed three mouths.' " She was all solicitude and magnanimity. "Now you understand what we mean by revolutionary humanitarianism. You have volunteered to give up your rice bowl and I'm giving it back to you. Revolutionary humanitarianism, even in dealing with the wife of an ultrarightist. Go and put up another poster and thank the party for its humane consideration."

We were again speechless. Such brazen hypocrisy was beyond our simple morals. The apparent whimsicality was nothing less than a premeditated war of nerves aimed at breaking our spirit and forcing us to put a humane veneer on their inhumanity with our own hands, in a conspiracy to dupe "the masses." I was demoralized, but that night Yikai said quietly, "In their absolute power they can do whatever they like to us. There is nothing we can do about it. But we must keep faith in life."

My sister Ninghui was also denounced as a rightist for airing her views, which had been headlined in the city party organ with approval. She was demoted and sent to a suburban farm for manual labor under surveillance. Her husband, a candidate for party membership, was denied acceptance into the party on her account. Among my former Yenching colleagues teaching at Beijing University, Huang, my former assistant, long an activist seeking party membership, had been denounced and punished as an ultrarightist for his activities this time. Xinghua, the rising young professor, was labeled a rightist because of his disapproval of following the Soviet model in English teaching. Professor Hu Jiatai did not escape the label for some careless remark or other, in spite of his discretion and Buddhist wisdom. Dr. Lucy Chao fell victim to schizophrenia when her distinguished poet and archaeologist husband got the label. Professor Yu Da'ying, the lady Oxonian, had a heart attack when her ministerial husband, a long-standing Communist fellow traveler, was denounced as an arch-rightist along with five other professors who had drafted an outline for educational reform along liberal lines. Thus, of the five professors on the former Yenching English faculty, all three men were caught, as well as the husbands of both women professors. One in each family, no misses. At Nankai, Cha Liangtseng, who had assiduously declined to attend faculty meetings called for the airing of views, was denounced as a "historical counterrevolutionary" instead, because of his wartime service with the Nationalist army. According to later government statistics, more than half a million people were labeled rightists. There were no figures for those who had been denounced but spared the label, nor of those who had been driven to insanity or suicide. The "hundred flowers" ended in a mass intellectual castration that was to plague the nation for decades to come, putting to shame the notorious emperor of the Han Dynasty who had unjustly punished only one dissident historian with physical castration. Meanwhile, activists who had performed meritorious service on the battlefield of class struggle against the rightists were rewarded with promotion and membership in the party. A generation of hypocrites and informers began to poison the moral life of the nation and paved the way for more political campaigns to come.

5

I CONTINUED CATALOGUING ENGLISH BOOKS IN THE LIBRARY PENDING FORmalization of my punishment. With the student rightists trucked off to a village for forced labor, I was pretty much left on my own under the watchful eyes of a young Beijing University graduate, who always spoke the language of party documents and *People's Daily* editorials. Ironically, among the things I was to catalog I found a heap of English translations of Russian pamphlets written by victims in Stalin's concentration camps and subsequently smuggled to the West. The stories of their physical and mental tortures affected me like nightmares, but their yearnings for freedom kept echoing in my heart. One of the pamphlets was titled *Go and Tell the West!* I could hear the writer's anguished outcry in the stillness of the deserted library, but I wondered if the West or my Western friends knew or cared what was happening to people like me in China. The vice president of the school had been right when he said "There's a cost for everything." And the cost for speaking up for freedom in socialist China was certainly high.

One day my young supervisor called me to his desk and pointed to a pile of new American books that I had ordered before the campaign started but that had just arrived from the States via the Chinese embassy in Geneva. "Do you still want these books, Wu Ningkun? Say so if you do. The payment can be deducted from your next month's paycheck, but it will be your last paycheck. If you don't, I'll put the stamp of the library on them right away." I had been waiting for these books, mostly new scholarly works by my professors at the University of Chicago; how could I not want them? But how could I afford them, now that I had only one last paycheck coming? I fingered and fondled them one by one for a few minutes, but he was getting impatient. "I have revolutionary work to attend to. And you need to go back to your labor. Be quick about it." I picked one thin volume, *The Poetry of Dylan Thomas* by Professor Elder Olson, and tore myself away from the rest. As I left his desk with the new book clutched in my hand, I heard him stamping the other books energetically, as if they were class enemies to be stamped out. That night I stayed up late to reread some of Thomas's powerful poems against Olson's brilliant analysis. In the stillness of the night I could hear again the passionate voice of the poet reciting his own poem on a visit to the University of Chicago the year before my return to China:

> *Twisting on racks when sinews give way,*
> *Strapped to a wheel, yet they shall not break;*
> *And death shall have no dominion.*

The next day, as I was winding up my day's labor at the library, I was again summoned to my young supervisor's desk. "Wu Ningkun, I am authorized by the school leadership to notify you that your punishment has met with the full approval of the higher authorities," he enunciated in his best official cadence. "You shall be picked up at two P.M., April the seventeenth, at the entrance of your dormitory and taken to a place to begin the course of your reform through forced labor. We allow you the next two days to make preparations for your new life. Therefore you need not report to me for duty in the morning as prescribed. That's all. Oh, before going home, stop at the personnel office to sign the conclusion of your case."

I found Geng Zhuang waiting for me by himself. "Come and sign the conclusion on your rightist problem." So saying, he handed me a sheet of paper with a typewritten list of six counts of my crimes and pointed to where I was to sign. As I ran over them quickly, he said impatiently, "Sign here, stop wasting my time. It's after office hours." I said nothing and signed.

* * *

I went home and gave Yikai the expected news. We were relieved that the suspense had finally ended. After briefly talking things over, we decided our two-year-old boy must be spared the trauma of seeing his daddy being picked up. So the next morning, I took him to the zoo for the last time to see the Indian elephants, which he liked so much. I bought him a big red apple from a fruit stall outside the zoo. He laughed happily when he caught sight of the elephants. "You haven't brought me to see the big elephants for such a long time now. I like them so much. You must bring me again soon! Promise, Papa?" Should I tell him the truth? Or must I lie? A farewell lie to your own two-year-old son? "As soon as I can," I choked. At the sight of an elephant rolling up bananas with its long trunk, Yiding got so excited that he started clapping, letting the apple drop near an elephant, which immediately grabbed it away with its trunk. He burst out crying, "I want my big apple back, my big red apple!" I hugged him and promised to buy him another one, and then handed him over to his nursemaid to continue his escape to my sister's home on the other side of the city. On the bus back to the school, the big apple kept hovering before my eyes like a golden image of something irretrievably lost in our life. When I told Yikai about the lost apple of gold, she smiled sadly but said nothing.

Now that there was only one day left before I was to be picked up, Yikai urged me to relax and visit the scenic Fragrant Hills, which we had never got around to visiting. I had to go by myself, since it was a weekday and she was working. I took a bus to the hills and found the park nearly deserted. I dutifully did the sights one by one and spent quite a while in the memorial hall in honor of Dr. Sun Yat-sen, the father of the first republic of China. He who had advocated uniting with the Communists and the Soviets, what would he have thought of the new republic, had he lived to this day? I could not help wondering. I ended up having a cup of tea in a deserted teahouse at the summit, from which I could get not only a bird's-eye view of the mountain scenery but a hazy distant look at the city. I ordered a small dish of fried peanuts and a couple of eggs cooked in tea leaves. When I saw the hillsides covered with lush weeds, Hamlet's familiar lines came to mind: " 'tis an unweeded garden / That grows to seed. Things rank and gross in nature / Possess it merely." After mumbling the lines a couple of times, I suddenly stopped and said to myself, "You are getting gushy, my dear! You know full well self-pity will get you nowhere. Even as President Mao the Frightful said, it's about time to take stock of my past and thoughts. Yes, but not her way. The hills are covered with a hundred flowers and the land will flourish with a hundred schools of thought. I have a garden to cultivate yet." I did not touch the peanuts or tea eggs, but had them wrapped up to take home for Yikai.

At home, Yikai had cooked two of my favorite dishes as a sort of farewell banquet for me. I had no appetite, but forced myself to eat as much as I could. She brought out a nearly empty bottle of Chinese brandy and poured what was left in it into two small glasses, although she did not drink.

"Here's to— well, what?" She smiled at me.

"To our unborn child, who will see a better world!"

"To an early return of its father!"

"I was told my absence would not be very long, but no one said just how long. It will be hard on you . . ." I felt guilty about messing up our life and leaving her to cope by herself, remembering how she had lived a sheltered life before throwing her lot in with mine.

"You mustn't worry about me, or rather us. As I said the other day, 'Heaven never seals off all the exits.' I will pray for you every day and every night. Keep faith, whatever happens, keep faith with life. How did you find the Fragrant Hills today?"

"Beautiful, absolutely gorgeous! I felt rather low at first, but then I saw the hillsides were literally covered with a hundred flowers in their glory. You and I must go and roam the hills together when I come back. The world is a beautiful garden and life is worth suffering for. Our children will certainly live in a better world. But for now you must bear the cross . . ."

"Come on, who am I not to bear the cross?" she said calmly. "I have put some changes of clothes and your toilet things in your old laundry bag. You will not know what you really need until you get there. And you don't even know where you're going, or for how long. I can always send you things you will need later on. Do you think you will have time to read books?"

71

"Probably not much. Just throw in the bag my old copy of *Hamlet* and the new edition of *Selected Poems of Du Fu* I picked up the other day, just in case. I feel as if I am going on a new adventure."

"God be with you!"

Four

THE HALF-STEP BRIDGE, 1958

1

ON APRIL 17, 1958, JUST AS THE FEW PEACH TREES ON CAMPUS WERE BURST-ing into blossoms, a drab army jeep stopped at the entrance of our old dormitory building at 2:00 P.M. sharp. Yikai silently handed me the half-empty old laundry bag before I climbed onto the backseat. I looked into her eyes, but could not bring myself to say good-bye. The dreary compound was deserted at that hour, and the event, a turning point in my life, was not even watched by the traditional crowd of spectators at an arrest or an execution.

A young driver in a grass-green army uniform drove off right away, another young soldier sitting next to him. The two smoked and jabbered all the way, kidding each other and laughing boisterously. After an hour's drive, the driver said to his companion: "We're getting there. After our job is done, I'll take you to see my girlfriend on our way back, if you behave. You were real naughty with the little bitch last night." The other soldier replied with a roguish giggle: "No question my behaving. I just wait to see how you behave with her, you plaster saint!" The driver shot back: "You talk like a rotten rightist, you stinking hooligan. If you carry on like this, I'll just dump you off right there along with my freight." Then they both had a good laugh as the jeep approached the destination.

I had thought I was being taken to a farm for physical labor. But when the jeep stopped I found myself outside an iron gate in a high wall topped by barbed wire. The gate was guarded by two uniformed soldiers holding rifles fixed with bayonets. I saw the street name Half-Step Bridge on the wall; large black characters on a big wooden plaque by the gate read BEIJING MUNICIPAL DETENTION CENTER FOR CORRECTIVE EDUCATION THROUGH

LABOR. I learned later that the center was part of the Beijing Municipal Prison. I was taken inside and handed over to a sallow-faced middle-aged officer, who stamped a receipt for "the freight." After looking at the warrant for my corrective education, he turned to me and said listlessly:

"Okay, you're from the Central Investigation Department, which is a top-secret organization. You must keep your affiliation a secret here. Which other unit do you know best in Beijing?"

"Beijing University, I suppose."

"Okay, you're from Beijing University then. Remember you're not from CID, but from Beijing University. If you aren't careful, you'll be in more trouble. Now dump your things on the table."

I did. He pushed aside my old injector razor and blades, mementos of my American years.

"Take off your watch and belt!"

I did and laid them next to the razor and blades on his table. The Gruen wristwatch was also an old memento from America.

"These items will be returned to you when you leave here. We don't want anything foolish to happen in this place, see?"

That seemed rather thoughtful, but I had trouble holding up my pants. After the initiation, I was led into a cell where some twenty men were sitting on shabby straw mats, which covered the cement floor. The men, mostly in their thirties and forties, were pale and unkempt. A strong stench of urine came from a bucket in one corner. My arrival caused a stir; they were all incredulous at having a Beijing University professor for a fellow inmate. I soon learned that only a few of them were rightists and the rest were either "historical counterrevolutionaries"—people affiliated with the previous regime in one way or another—or "bad elements"—street hooligans, pickpockets, adulterers, tramps, and the like. The inmate put in charge of the gang was a man wrinkled with age, a former Nationalist police chief named Zheng Fangwen, who was apparently in his element again. His deputy, a former Communist army platoon leader named Wang Cheng, had lost a finger in the civil war. Wang, a handsome fellow with a talent for performing Beijing opera, had served a three-year sentence for seducing a fellow officer's wife in the early fifties. Then, working at a brick kiln after serving the prison term, he got it again for stealing meal tickets from the laborers' mess. It suddenly dawned on me what a metamorphosis the "half step" had achieved for me: once I had crossed the "half step," I ceased to be a professor, an intellectual, or even a man. I was now just an "element for corrective education through labor," a common criminal, not a whit better than the pickpocket or the hooligan who slept on either side of me. No, I was worse, because thought offenses were deemed much more dangerous than petty crimes. I had been put in my place.

Squeezed in between two strange bedfellows on the cement floor during the sleepless night, I could not help reflecting on the portentous street name. I recalled two lines from a familiar Chinese verse: "One false step brings everlasting grief / One backward look shows the course of life already run!" But little did I foresee how far Half-Step Bridge was to lead me on the road to calvary!

We were fed the same meal twice a day: one piece of steamed bread made from musty corn flour, one bowl of musty corn-flour gruel, and one slice of very salty pickled turnip. No oil, no meat, no vegetables, no sugar, no cholesterol worries. The first two days, I could not stomach the food and passed it to my neighbors. "You will not have enough before long," they predicted. And they were right. Cooped up in the cell permeated with the smell of our own urine, we confessed our sins once again and denounced each other in the same way our accusers had denounced us. Except for the daily routine of emptying the full urine bucket, only occasionally were we let out of the cells to clear up the compound. On those rare occasions the fresh air and the golden sun seemed like precious gifts I had always taken for granted.

2

ONE DAY IN MAY, WE FOUND OURSELVES OUT IN THE WARM SUN EACH banging on his own aluminum or enamel washbasin to frighten sparrows. We had been ordered to take part in the concerted action of the populace known as the Campaign Against the Four Evils—namely, rats, flies, mosquitoes, and sparrows—again under the personal command of the "Great Leader." The theory was that sparrows consumed millions of tons of food grain a year, just like rats, and must therefore be exterminated like rats. As mass campaigns were deemed the effective way to deal with national problems of any kind, the populace was ordered to wage war on sparrows throughout the land during the same hours on the same day. Pursued relentlessly by the ubiquitous dinning from varieties of percussion instruments, the panic-stricken sparrows kept flying around till they dropped dead on the ground. The evil little birds proved no match for the iron fist of proletarian dictatorship. For the next few days, the local papers reported with relish, the market was flooded with fried sparrows. I did not get a taste of fried sparrows, but only a big hole in the bottom of my washbasin. I had to ask for permission to send a postcard to Yikai and ask for a replacement from home.

A few days later, on a Sunday afternoon, I was summoned to the office where I had been initiated the first day. The same sallow-faced officer pointed to a washbasin and a few other things on his table, saying, "Your wife brought these for you." I asked anxiously, "But where is she?" "You should know better," he sneered. "You're not allowed the luxury of receiving visitors in this place." It was a hot sunny day, and I shuddered at the thought of Yikai, in her advanced stage of pregnancy, trudging for hours in the hope of seeing me for a few moments and then being turned away.

It was reported much later that the extermination of sparrows had contributed to the crop failure in the next two years, as insects injurious to crops, freed from the threat of their natural enemies, ate their fill at the free Communist mess.

Toward the end of the first week of June, I had a letter from Yikai posted from the maternity ward of the Haidian District Hospital, the school being located in the administrative district of Haidian. She sent the glad tidings that she had given birth to a beautiful baby girl on the third of June and asked me to give the child a name. As I had just reread Du Fu's famous line comparing the legendary wise man Kong Ming of the Age of the Three Kingdoms to "a feather (standing for a phoenix) sailing the heavens for ever and ever," I gave her the name Yimao, or One Feather. It was the only blessing I could offer my newborn child from my dungeon. If only my child born in sorrow could one day sail the heavens!

3

THE DAY AFTER I MAILED YIKAI MY BLESSINGS AND A NAME FOR OUR DAUGHTER, we were gathered on the grounds of the center. I was surprised to see there were hundreds of us. ("I had not thought death had undone so many," I silently recited T. S. Eliot's line to myself.) We were to hear a report by a leading security official from a new state farm on Lake Xingkai in the northeastern province of Heilongjiang, bordering on Siberia. He said the new farm had recently been developed by the Public Security Bureau of Beijing to accommodate the thousands of convicts and elements under corrective education. The purpose of the establishment, he claimed, was "to reform the offenders, through forced labor, from members of the exploiting classes into new men supporting themselves by their own honest labor." The place was ominously called the Great Northern Wilderness. It was largely uninhabited and sometimes quite cold in winter, but it had rich virgin soil. Our job was to turn the great wilderness into a great socialist granary. "You will have a lot to eat. Corn, millet, rice, wheat, everything. Plenty of fish in the lake and the streams!" he reassured us with enthusiasm. After two months of incarceration on a starvation diet, we all jumped at the prospect of working in the sun on a full stomach, knowing full well we would only be doing slave labor a thousand miles away from our families. Once again I could not help admiring the dialectical finesse of the Communist party in turning a dreaded exile into a coveted boon.

In the dead of night on June 11, we were led out of the prison compound to a line of waiting city buses. The convoy moved slowly through the deserted streets, guarded by armed soldiers on either side. I said a silent farewell to the sleepy ancient seat of autocratic power, which I had returned to with such anticipation less than seven years before. Arriving at the deserted railway station, we were put on a special train patrolled by armed guards. For three days and three nights it carried us, eight hundred men in all, to the small town of Mishan. A curfew was enforced while we passed through the town to board large wooden boats, which transported us to our destination—the swampy labor reform camp on the shores of Lake Xingkai.

Five

A CHILD BORN IN
SORROW, 1958

Narrated by Li Yikai

1

WHEN NINGKUN WAS WHISKED AWAY IN AN ARMY JEEP ON THE AFTERNOON of April 17, 1958, I followed the vehicle with my eyes until it disappeared in the distance. Suddenly it was dark all around and my legs felt like jelly. A woman colleague who happened to be passing by gave me a gentle push and urged me, "Go in and lie down at once, Li Yikai. You look terrible." Back in my room, I collapsed on the bed and lost consciousness for I don't know how long, until I was roused by the little life stirring in my belly. For a moment I was alarmed. Would I have a premature delivery? But the pain soon went away. All of a sudden I burst out crying, for the first time since it all had started. And for the first time I felt so utterly alone. My sobs were interrupted by a knock on the door and a woman neighbor's loud voice calling, "Li Yikai, the Typing Room telephoned for you to go to work at once. Urgent business, they say." I got up with an effort and dragged myself to the Typing Room, where I had been reassigned since Ningkun's denunciation. The Teachers' Reading Room, where I had worked before, boasted a number of periodicals published in the United States, such as *Time, Life,* and *Reader's Digest,* which had been banned from other universities since 1949 as seditious publications. At the elite party school, teachers of English were allowed access to "periodicals from capitalist countries," so that they might be brought up-to-date on developments in the enemy camp and in the enemy language. Once Ningkun was denounced, I quickly lost the right to handle such dangerous materials and was ordered to learn on my own how to work on an old standard English typewriter. Typing, however, often gave place to political study.

As soon as I entered the Typing Room, the head typist, a woman a few years my senior known as Zuo the Leftist, greeted me in her usual deadpan tone of voice:

"Why are you so late, Li Yikai?"

"I had to wait till Wu Ningkun was gone. Then I wasn't feeling too well."

"He left at two, didn't he? And now it's past three o'clock! And swollen red eyes! What are you crying for? Still feeling sorry for him? Your tears prove you have never drawn a clear line of demarcation from the rightist. How obstinate! Come to the meeting at once. We've put this off till now. As you can see, comrades from other sections are joining us. You have sunk very deep into the quagmire of erroneous and reactionary ideas, along with your husband. We are here to help you through solemn criticism and repudiation. Will you make a self-examination first?"

"I'm sorry, I'm unprepared for this," I replied quietly.

"What? You've made so many serious mistakes and you are not even prepared to make a self-examination? Is her attitude acceptable, comrades?"

"No, of course not," the chic French typist Pan responded. "Li Yikai, we're all here to help save you from following your husband down the path to perdition. The first thing you must do is to draw a clear line of demarcation from him, you see?"

"I see, but I don't know how."

"Yes, you do," chimed in Yu Wei's wife from the personnel office in her authoritative voice. "You just don't want to because you are persisting in your reactionary class stand. You never exposed any of Wu Ningkun's rightist utterances or deeds during the entire campaign. It's all a question of your class stand. You came from a capitalist family, right?"

"My father was a patriotic national capitalist. He died from a heart disease when I was four."

"I know all that," declared the authoritative voice. "The point is, you haven't changed your class stand. On top of that, now you stick to the reactionary class stand of Wu Ningkun. That is very dangerous. Has the idea of a divorce ever occurred to you, Li Yikai? No, none of us is forcing you to divorce him. I'm just asking whether even the idea ever occurred to you?"

"No, it never occurred to me," I answered.

"See what I mean, comrades? But why not?"

"The party's policy is to 'cure the sickness and save the patient,' as we all know. Wu Ningkun is sick and the party is trying to save him—what right have I to abandon the patient? Also, I am a Catholic and the church bans divorce."

"Listen to her! Citing the party's policy and what her church says to defy us! I'll have you know, the party does not ban divorce, especially divorce from a rightist. Ding Cong's wife, for example, is getting a divorce from her rightist husband. The party and the comrades approve of her firm proletarian stand. Your religious faith is none of our business. But you forget you are a citizen of the People's Republic of China. As such, you are entitled to a divorce. As I said, no one is suggesting that you get a divorce. What do we get out of it? We're here to help you sort out your erroneous and reactionary ideas."

The others took turns in expressing agreement with the woman from personnel, exhorting me to draw a line of demarcation. Finally, in winding up the meeting, Zuo the Leftist called on me to think things over and face reality and promised more sessions of criticism for my benefit. "We won't waste more time with you today. You go home and carry on your mental struggles. We expect you to make clear at the next session how you're going to draw a line of demarcation from your rightist husband. If you persist in your stubborn ways, your problem may no longer remain a contradiction among the people. And where will you be? Go and see your God with a granitelike skull in the company of Wu Ningkun? Don't you have any feeling for your son and the child that's coming?"

I did not get back to my rooms until six o'clock, utterly exhausted. When Ningkun and Yiding were home, I used to feel cramped in the noisy tiny rooms. Now the place was as quiet as a deserted graveyard. I stepped out again to escape the sudden desolation and wandered outdoors. Colleagues and neighbors were returning from the dining hall after supper. I was on the point of greeting them when I saw they were all avoiding me. Some pretended they had not seen me, others turned their heads. So that was what they meant by complete isolation! Back in my rooms again, I saw the two tea eggs and peanuts that Ningkun had brought back from the Fragrant Hills. I remembered I had not eaten since morning and felt a pang of hunger. So I peeled an egg and was just about to bite into it when my mind went back to Ningkun. "Where is he now? Will he be given supper?

Will they beat him up? How much more insult and injury can he take? Will he kill himself when he no longer can? . . ." I choked down the hard-boiled egg with a glass of hot water, reminding myself that the little life inside me had to be fed. In the morning, I decided, I would go to Ninghui's and bring Yiding home, so I left the other egg and peanuts for him. I reminded myself I must buy him a big red apple, which was the last thing Ningkun had said before he was taken away. I stayed awake till late into the night. A thousand memories of the recent years welled up in my mind. I wished I could cry, but somehow I could not. In the end I told myself I must be brave in facing the world by myself, come what may.

In the days that followed, more sessions to "help me sort out my reactionary ideas" were held.

"At the faculty-staff meeting last May, you compared the denunciation of Wu Ningkun as a hidden counterrevolutionary at Nankai with the crucifixion of Jesus, did you not?"

"I did."

"It was outrageous! It was reactionary! How could you equate the just and well-deserved denunciation of a criminal reactionary in socialist China with the crucifixion of Jesus? Is your reactionary class stand not all too clear?"

"It was a mistake, I admit. Wu Ningkun was unworthy of the comparison. What I meant was he was equally innocent."

"What did you say? He is innocent?"

"That's what I thought at the time."

"Well, what do you think now?"

"It doesn't matter what I think now."

"You're as slippery as an eel, as stubborn as a stone, as reactionary as a rightist. We thought because you were young, recently out of college, perhaps we could still save you. But obviously your mind has been too badly poisoned by Wu Ningkun. You're more stubborn than a stone."

On another occasion, the interrogation turned on the May first picnic at the Summer Palace the year before.

"You attended the May first meeting of the ABC at the Summer Palace last year, didn't you?"

"We were invited to a picnic by Ningkun's former students."

"Slippery like an eel again! We have enough evidence to prove it was a premeditated counterrevolutionary gathering. You took part in it. What would you say is the nature of your activity?"

"We went to a picnic. I don't recall any law-breaking activity."

"We have a record of your speech at the meeting. You attacked the Campaign to Uproot Hidden Counterrevolutionaries at Nankai, very violently too, did you not?"

"We did compare notes of our experiences. At the time everybody thought the campaign had been a mistake."

"Do you still think so?"

"Does it matter what I think?"

"You are sly, very sly!" shouted Zuo the Leftist. "We'll not let you get away cheap."

Most colleagues stopped speaking to me. Cold, contemptuous, even hostile looks were shot at me, like the slings and arrows of outrageous fortune. The few women who occasionally stopped me on the way would urge me to get a divorce. "You are in your twenties, too young to be a grass widow," they would prod me with good common sense. "You are a nice girl, you got a college degree, why waste your youth waiting for him. How do you know when he will come back? Life will be hard for you as a rightist's wife, I tell you." One officious colleague even offered to match me up with a friend of hers whose wife had been labeled a rightist. Ningkun's boon companions, who used to frequent our rooms and laugh heartily with him over a few drinks, now turned their heads away when our paths happened to cross. I had always found it hard to imagine the life of a pariah, a leper, or an untouchable and never expected that I would live it myself. "But what have I done to deserve all this?" I cried out in my lonely heart.

On May 1, 1958, a year after the now infamous picnic, I was told to join an organized group tour of the model prison at Half-Step Bridge. One woman colleague even volunteered to tell me, "That's where Wu Ningkun is detained. Maybe you'll get to see him?" The visitors from the party school were first ushered into the reception room and each served a cup of tea. Then the warden gave a talk, first on the incomparable socialist policy of turning criminals into new men through forced labor, then on the history of the prison, which was a legacy from previous regimes, and finally on its size and facilities for forced labor and the kinds of convicts serving terms there. He concluded by saying, "From what you will see with your own eyes, you can tell how humanitarian our policies of reform through forced labor are. You will be able to repudiate with ironclad evidence rightist attacks on the socialist judiciary system and institutions of labor reform." After the briefing, we were taken into a workshop producing nylon socks. Male convicts wore tidy white aprons on which were printed in red: NEW LIFE NYLON SOCKS WORKSHOP, FIRST MODEL PRISON, BEIJING. They busily tended the machines. The guide told us proudly, "Our Grapes Brand products are of first-rate quality. Maybe some of you have them on right now. The best products are for export, earning foreign exchange for the state. A good example of how the dregs of society are reformed into a productive force." Then we were shown the mess hall with its rows of long tables and benches, the recreation room, where some convicts were playing cards, the reading room, where some convicts were reading the *People's Daily* and the *China Pictorial*, and finally the ward, which was divided into small cells with bunk beds. One of the women colleagues suddenly exclaimed: "Look over there! Even showers for them! We haven't got showers in our dorms. I almost feel it's too good for these enemies of the people. But it goes to prove how benevolent our party is in carrying out the policy of reforming class enemies into new men!" While I was wondering whether Ningkun was also enjoying the benevolence of the party, she turned to me and said, "We haven't seen Wu Ningkun. Well, he is not exactly a convict. He must be in an even better part. Aren't you grateful to the party?"

A few days later, I had a postcard from Ningkun asking for a washbasin to replace the one he had wrecked in frightening the sparrows to death. The address was indeed Half-Step Bridge detention center. I took a basin from home along with a mosquito net, a straw bed mat, and a straw broad-brimmed hat that he might need while laboring in the sun. I had to go to Ninghui's first because she wanted to join me. She was afraid it might not be safe for me to go by myself in my condition and she also hoped to see her brother again. It was a hot afternoon, and the bus ride, which required two transfers, took more than two hours. When the two of us got off with the sundry articles in our arms, I started asking for directions to Half-Step

Bridge. Nobody seemed to know, and one man snubbed us with a contemptuous look. After a while we approached a grizzly old man cooling himself in a doorway.

"Grandpa," I greeted him civilly. "Can you tell me how to get to Half-Step Bridge, please?"

"This is Half-Step Bridge, sister. What number you looking for?"

"I don't know the number."

"You mean the prison then?" At my nod he went on. "What are you going there for, sister?"

"My man is cooped up in the detention center."

"That's too bad. How did he end up in there? You look like nice people."

"A rightist."

"Oh! Too bad, just too bad . . . Follow the road to the end and you will run into a great wall. And that's it. Just too bad . . ."

We thanked him and walked on. The detention center was not the model place I had visited but a dingy compound in the same huge prison complex. I was told to leave my things at the desk. When I asked if I might see my husband, a sour-looking officer replied, "This is not a place for family reunions. This is an institution of proletarian dictatorship." I knew there was no arguing with him, but I wished to learn how Ningkun was being treated there. So I ventured again, "Officer, I visited the model prison on an organized tour with my colleagues from the party school just the other day. It's rather nice. Is the detention center like that?" He looked amused. "Sometimes I don't know what to make of you intellectuals," he said. "If all prisons were like that, then why should it be called the model, eh? Foreign guests often come to visit and take lots of pictures." He laughed.

I took the long bus ride home with a sinking heart and a heavy weight in my belly. Sister Ninghui was in tears.

2

I DID NOT HAVE TO CARRY THE WEIGHT INSIDE ME VERY LONG. BEFORE THE month of May was over, I had my first labor pains. By myself, I squeezed into a crowded bus bound for the district hospital a few miles away. The first question the head nurse in the maternity ward asked was, "Where is your husband?" I said, "Oh he can't come, busy taking part in manual labor." She did not seem to find it strange, saying only, "He must be a great activist then. But he will come when the child comes, certainly." My labor pains subsided, but my heartaches returned. To calm myself I prayed constantly. I did not think it proper to ask God for Ningkun's release, so I only asked that he be given the strength to endure his lot.

During visiting hours in the afternoon, families would come to see the new or expectant mothers, bringing stewed chicken, fresh fruit, or other delicacies. I never had a single visitor. To avoid nosy questions, I would retire to the lounge and read *The Imitation of Christ* or the Chinese translation of *The Pearl,* which Ningkun had completed under the most trying circumstances of his denunciation. But my fellow patients soon looked at me suspiciously. I was worried lest the identity of my husband be made known.

He did not visit when the child came into the world in the early morning of June 3. "What a lovely girl!" exclaimed the obstetrician before she cut the umbilical cord. "But where is the father? Still busy doing manual labor?" I was feeling weak, but I was surprised to hear myself blurt out unequivocally, "Yes, he has been sent away for manual labor. He was labeled a rightist." The doctor cut the cord and left without saying another word. The head nurse never spoke to me again, nor did the other nurses, except for an occasional curt necessary remark.

Two hours after giving birth to my daughter, I warily sat up in my bed and took out the postcard I had brought with me. I wrote:

Ningkun,
I gave birth to a daughter weighing 3,800 grams a little more than two hours ago at 2 A.M., June 3rd. A lovely girl! Congratulations! I'm all right. Please give her a name.

Yikai.

Stealthily removing the hospital pajamas and changing into my own clothes, I sneaked out of the hospital, keeping one hand against the wall for support, and dropped the postcard into a mailbox at the street corner. When I returned to my bed, I found a stern-looking young nurse waiting for me.

"Where did you go, Li Yikai?"

"I felt so stifled. I needed a breath of fresh air . . ."

"Don't you know you can't leave the ward without our permission?" She was angry. "It's not even three hours since you gave birth to a child. It's too hazardous. You're responsible for your own rashness, if anything happens. Do you understand?" I mumbled my apologies and she muttered something about rightists. By the time Ningkun's reply reached me several days later, he was already on his long journey of exile to the Great Northern Wilderness.

Two days later, the two grandmothers came to the hospital to take me and the new grandchild home. They brought with them Yiding and his cousin Zhang Chun, who was in his grandma's care, since both Ninghui and her husband had recently been sent away to do manual labor. I went to the discharge office to check out. The clerk looked me and my folks up and down and then remarked with amusement, "What a party to welcome you home! Two old ones and two little ones, no one to really help. Where's your husband?" I merely said, "Taking part in manual labor out of town." She shook her head and said nothing else.

My mother had come from our home in Tianjin to look after me during my confinement. None of my colleagues came to see me and the new baby, but I was contented to have Mother and Yiding with me. I tried to keep Ningkun's exile to the labor camp from Mother, but she kept asking where he was. When his first letter from the northern camp arrived, I could no longer keep it a secret. In the middle of the night she started crying, which aggravated her glaucoma. Though both Mother and I felt strongly the conspicuous absence of Ningkun, we rarely referred to him. Only Yiding would ask me from time to time, "Where is Papa? When is he coming home and taking me to see the elephants?" And I would tell him, "Papa is away doing labor like a lot of other people. He will be home before long."

Meanwhile, I took advantage of the respite at home to have heavy winter clothes made for Ningkun and sent to the northern camp. In the stillness of the night, I could almost hear Ningkun singing a local ballad of his hometown about a wife making winter clothes for her husband, who has been sent with the army of slaves to build the Great Wall during the reign of the First Emperor of the Qin Dynasty. Was history repeating itself? I shuddered to recall how the woman in the song had walked all the way from her southern home to the Great Wall to deliver the winter clothes, only to learn on her arrival that her man was long dead. In any case, I only had to take the parcel to the post office. By lucky chance I might even be able to smuggle two cans of pork stew in between the thick cotton-padded jacket and trousers, although I knew food items were forbidden in parcels sent to labor camps.

After one look at the address, the woman clerk asked me sternly, "Any eatables in the parcel?"

"Oh, no, no." I hurriedly stammered, forcing a smile.

She felt the parcel carefully. "Then what are these hard cans, eh?" she shot at me.

"Just two small cans," I stammered again, feeling like a thief caught red-handed.

"Take them out. Be quick," she ordered.

"Oh, please," I pleaded.

"You know very well you are not allowed to send foodstuffs to convicts." She raised her voice. "You deliberately violate government regulations and undermine the government's work to reform enemies of the people. You work at the university, yet you stoop so low as to lie to get your way."

I complied with her order without another word.

LABOR REFORM IN THE
WILDERNESS, 1958–60

1

THE LAKE XINGKAI STATE FARM, A FORCED LABOR CAMP, WAS SUBDIVIDED
into nine branch farms. Six of them were for penal convicts, two were for
offenders under corrective education, and No. 9 was for women. The new
arrivals were sent to the temporary site of No. 8 Branch Farm, where a
kitchen and a tool shack had already been built by an advance squad of
inmates. The first thing we did upon arrival was to put up huge tents on
the lakeside, where we would live until we could be moved to the permanent site. After settling in and a quick supper, we were gathered on a
clearing outside the tents to hear a report from the boss of the branch farm,
an officer from the public security bureau of Beijing. The gist of his report
was a stern warning against any attempt to escape, which would not only
bring on the offender severe penal punishment but end in his drowning in
the surrounding swamps or being devoured by wolves from the hills. I
couldn't imagine anyone making such a vain attempt, for the regime constantly boasted of the all-extensive meshes of socialist justice, from which
no criminal could ever hope to escape.

We started on our reform through forced labor the next morning. Our
first job was to build an earth diversion dike against inundation from the
lake so that we could then reclaim the low-lying virgin soil. Our tools were
spades, shovels, picks, rammers, and shoulder poles. We rose before dawn
and, after a quick breakfast, shouldered our tools and marched a mile to the
building site. The work gang was divided into squads of some twenty men
each, and each squad subdivided into several groups of diggers and carriers.
The diggers were usually able-bodied young men who knew how to use
the pick or the spade well. As a former professor, my hands were more agile

with the pen than with the pick or the spade, so I was assigned with another inmate, a former high school teacher, to the unskilled labor of carrying earth in a gunnysack or a huge wicker basket on a shoulder pole. As I was slow in finding the right spot for the pole, my shoulder was soon reduced to a mess of blisters and bruises. I put on a bold front and went on toughening my shoulder day in and day out, hoping like everybody else that my exertion at physical labor would put me in the good graces of the officers and bring closer the day of release.

There were no working hours: we just labored from sunrise to sunset. As the days grew longer, we labored more hours. Meanwhile, the "Wise Leader" had impetuously launched the Great Leap Forward, and the nation was to spare no efforts in "going all out, aiming high and achieving greater, quicker, better, and more economical results in building socialism." Every day, the officers asked us "When the revolutionary people are working so hard in response to the Great Leader's wise call, how much harder must you the guilty work to atone for your crimes?" So our working hours got even longer. The loads we carried got heavier and heavier, and we were urged to run faster and faster. Labor contests became the order of the day. The groups of diggers and carriers competed with each other to move the greatest volume of earth for the socialist dike under construction. Other groups charged with pounding the earth into compact layers with a wooden ram pierced the air with improvised plaintive work songs, which stirred the hearts of the laborers with familiar tunes and words of double meaning. Future historians might find a place in their chronicles for these minstrels of the labor camp. One inmate went from one building site to another like a hawker, giving sales talks through a megaphone. A former propaganda worker, he handled the job with alacrity. "Look at Wu Ningkun!" I could hardly believe my ears when I heard my name mentioned, because I had often been criticized for not carrying enough or running fast enough. "He was an intellectual who did not have enough strength to tie up a chicken. He carried very little when he first came. But look at him now, carrying as much as he can and running faster and faster! A good example of thought reform! Try harder, aim higher, and achieve greater results!" I saw the point of his holding me up as an example for the others, but I felt I was going to collapse at any moment.

Each evening, when the long-awaited blast sounded from the duty officer's whistle, we would hurriedly clean our tools in the lake and start back like homing pigeons or, rather, a routed company of soldiers. In the tent, we would lay out our huge enamel rice bowls on the dirt floor at the foot of our respective sleeping spaces for our ration of corn-flour gruel. As the gruel was always steaming hot, we would first go and wash off the day's dirt and sweat in the lake. The gruel always tasted good when we were so hungry and tired. One evening, however, I returned from the lakeside to find the golden corn gruel had turned black in the gloaming. Not trusting my shortsighted eyes, I asked my neighbor, a jolly young pickpocket, what had happened.

"Mosquitoes," he said simply.

"My goodness, what am I to do with it now?" I asked in dismay.

"Eat it. We all ate it. Animal protein, you know, professor. You didn't get that kind of good stuff at Beijing University, did you? Well, you were praised for making your Great Leap Forward today. Maybe you will be praised for eating mosquito gruel tomorrow." He laughed impishly.

I scraped off the black topping from the gruel with the big soup spoon Yikai had sent me and gobbled up the rest with relish. Mosquitoes, which were one of the things not mentioned in the pep talk by the security official in Beijing, quickly became a scourge even in daytime. There were literally billions of them, for the farm lay in the midst of swamps and grasslands. The harassment was such that we could no longer do as much work as was expected of us. In the end we were provided with an ingenious mosquito net worn around the head, at our own cost, of course. Other exposed parts of our body, however, remained susceptible to constant attacks by the bloodsuckers, which turned into beasts of prey in my nightmares under a close mosquito net.

By the summer solstice, day broke at three and the sun did not set until eight. We labored fourteen, fifteen, or sixteen hours a day. With the escalation of the Great Leap Forward, around-the-clock labor was by no means unusual, and the prescribed "biweekly Sunday" became a triweekly or monthly reprieve. The current euphemism for extra-long hours of labor was to "launch a satellite." The date set for launching the first satellite at the camp was the eve of the traditional Moon Festival late in September, which happened to be my thirty-eighth birthday. I celebrated it by harvesting rice on a neighboring branch farm all night, under a bright moon. On the night of the festival itself, when family union was traditionally celebrated throughout the land, we were exhorted to "launch another satellite to outshine the full moon" by harvesting more rice all night. Though ready to drop dead, I took comfort in lines from the famous ci-poem by the great Song dynasty poet Su Shi, celebrating the Moon Festival in exile: "Only if my love would endure / And share with me the beauteous Moon / Though a thousand miles apart!"

The winter was severe and long. The first snow fell as soon as we had finished the diversion dike and moved into permanent rows of barracks with built-in heatable brick beds called *kang*. It was the first of October, so we had the day off to celebrate National Day. The officers raved about the legendary achievements of the Great Leap Forward and bade us to double our efforts at reforming ourselves through forced labor. "The sky is the limit!" they yelled at the top of their voices. More snow fell, burying the ground under a boundless pall of oblivion. I envied the hibernating animals, who were spared the severities of winter and who would not wake up till spring brought them the joys of life. It was the season of peace and rest for local peasants, too. What could they possibly do with several feet of snow piled up through the winter months? But for those masters of Marxist dialectics, it was precisely the season to tackle what was impossible to attempt in other seasons.

The inaccessible site of the camp was a calculated choice, for it made escape virtually impossible. It was not connected with the outside world by any road or railway. The only means of transportation was the kind of primitive wooden boat that had transported us to the farm. Previous convicts had dug a narrow water channel from the lakeside to the interior, where the headquarters was located. But it was getting to be too narrow for the increasing traffic. Now that the lake and the water channel were frozen solid, it was the perfect time for turning the channel into a canal!

First, using a special ice pick, we cut the solid ice in the water channel into regular blocks. Then we piled the blocks up on either side of the channel, making two great walls of ice. One day the temperature dropped to minus 38.5 degrees Celsius and the leadership decided it was the perfect time to launch a satellite and defy the heavens. When it was time to leave the cell for the ice work, half of the inmates of the squad, including the sturdy squad leader himself, were still in bed, pleading illness. One young man simply said, "I'd rather die in bed than go out in this damned cold." The officer of the day happened to be Captain Li, who was known among us as a soldier with a soft heart. Taking in the situation at a glance, he turned to me. "Wu Ningkun, you're the squad leader for the day. Bring those who are up out to the ice work." I was taken aback and pleaded, "Me, Captain Li? Please! You know I don't even handle an ice pick!" He simply replied, "Never mind, those two or three over there can cut ice blocks for you and the others to carry. Go now, it's a satellite day." I had the funny feeling of reliving the dilemma of the Roman senator who had to accept the imperial purple or be put to death by the Praetorian Guards. At the head of a dozen men wrapped up in their heavy winter clothes, I trudged off in the deep snow to defy the heavens.

On the building site I noticed there were also fewer men working in the other squads. We worked very fast, because it was too cold to stay idle. When I saw the lunch cart coming, I hollered "Time to eat, you guys!" The kitchen inmate announced, "Corn-flour dumplings stuffed with vegetables, good stuff! No rationing today, eat as many as you like!" He fished out one from underneath the heavy cotton-padded covering and handed it to me. It was steaming, but it turned icy cold before I finished it. No one seemed to have much of an appetite. "You need your calories, you guys!" I hollered again. "Eat as many as you can! It doesn't happen every day." No one attempted a second one, and neither did I. Suddenly I discovered that two of my young carriers were missing. My God, could they have escaped? I rushed into one of the lanes between two rows of ice blocks and found the two young men huddled up with cold, as if they had been turned into ice themselves. "You want to freeze to death here, stupid?" I shouted at them. "There're better ways to die. Come on, quick, get your lunch! Don't you ever do it again, boys! What would your folks back home—" I choked up and could not finish. We failed to launch a satellite after all, for our day was cut short unexpectedly by a strong blizzard set loose by the heavens we were out to defy.

When the channel was cleared of the ice, we started widening and deepening it by removing the rock-solid frozen earth bit by bit with pickaxes. It was hard work, but it was done by free slave labor. Then spring came and the ice blocks melted. Soon there was a canal ready-made! Another example of the "industry and intelligence of the Chinese people," much vaunted by our historians and politicians, that had gone into the building of the Seventh Wonder of the World, the Great Wall of China! I recalled my forced visit to the Wall the year before, which seemed to have presaged what was in store for me. Only my ephemeral ice wall lacked the lasting tragic grandeur of the Great Wall.

The next year our winter job was to reap the reeds on the frozen lake and carry them to the site of a projected paper mill. As was the case all over the land, at the labor camp all kinds of ambitious projects were hatched out of the fever of the Great Leap Forward. The Great Northern Wilderness was to be transformed into a modern city with farms, industries, schools, cinemas, hospitals, and even a university and we would be its first builders and first inhabitants. Following the party documents and editorials in party organs, the officers raved about the "splendid prospects of communism," which were within reach and which were nothing less than heaven on earth. Among the industries was to be a giant paper mill with an annual output of hundreds of thousands of tons of paper of various kinds to serve the needs of Communist propaganda. Each of us was equipped with a crude sled with a long blade fixed at the rear end, and runners were attached to our heavy winter shoes. We pulled the sleds along with a rope across the shoulder. As the hundreds of sleds moved toward the center of the frozen lake where, miles away, the tall reeds stood, we might have been taken for a team of vacationers pursuing the pleasures of winter sports. At the push of the blade, the reeds readily fell off onto the sled in neat piles. Then we were ready to turn back and take them to the future paper mill. As a form of forced labor, it was almost fun on a nice day. The rub, however, was in the hazards. Since the weather forecasts were often unreliable, we might be caught in a blizzard and get lost on the lake, miles away from land. Then, once lost, one might freeze to death or fall into one of the unfrozen warm pockets in the lake.

One fine morning, our convoy of sleds made for the center of the frozen lake as usual. But, just as we were beginning to cut the reeds, a strong blizzard suddenly rose from nowhere and swept across the lake. Captain Li immediately blew hard on his whistle and hollered, "Going home! Going home!" Always slow on my feet, I brought up the rear. The blizzard blew harder and harder, and moving against the storm became a desperate struggle. I ducked my head, and my glasses were blown off my nose. Heavens!

I chased after them, bent down, and fumbled in the snow. The glasses were nowhere to be found, and when I lifted my head there was no one in sight. Panic-stricken, I started running and yelling "Where are you? Where are you, Captain Li? Wu Ningkun is lost!" But I stopped short at the blurry sight of a shimmering pocket of water in the midst of snow. My God, another false step would have sent me down to the abyss of the lake! I kept yelling at the top of my voice: "Captain Li, help! Wu Ningkun is lost! Help!" Before long, I heard his voice calling from a distance: "Wu Ningkun! We are here waiting for you! Follow the direction of my voice! Don't panic!" Within minutes I was with them again, to the great relief of Captain Li. Back at the camp, he told me, "Too bad you lost your glasses, but it's better than losing your life. I would have had a hard time accounting for it to the government. Did you kill yourself or did you escape to some other world? What could I say? Don't you do it again!" I promised him I wouldn't. If I had drowned in the lake, I would have given my life in vain, for the great paper mill remained on paper after all.

A variety of other jobs provided a sort of relief to backbreaking hard labor. We grew soybeans, a traditional crop of the northeastern provinces. The sight and smell of the rich black humus brought to mind the song "On the Sungari River," which lamented the loss of the dear ones following the Japanese military occupation in 1931 and told of a homeland "rich with soybean and sorghum all over the hills and plains." It had since achieved the status of a national anthem, sung by a generation of youths fleeing the flames of one war after another. Never had I dreamed that some twenty years after I fled the Japanese advancing on my hometown and after the defeat of the foreign aggressors I would be humming the same nostalgic and heartbreaking tune while doing slave labor in the land of the soybean, a thousand miles away from my own home and my loved ones.

On a summer day when there was little else to do we would be sent to the woods to cut down saplings, which we then carried to the camp in a huge bundle on our backs for use in making fences or walls. With the unruffled lake at a distance, the warm sun, the limpid air, and the lush greeneries, the marches back and forth were not at all unpleasant. Under happier circumstances, it occurred to me, this wilderness of unspoiled natural beauty might some day more profitably be developed as a summer resort. We marched to the woods in formation but returned to the camp separately, each at his own pace. The solitary walk back gave me a rare moment of privacy, in which I could indulge in conversations with myself ("Les Conversations avec Moi-même" would make a good title, I fancied) or with Yikai and Yiding in absentia, while munching the hazelnuts I had picked on the way or the wild asparagus I had found in the woods. Then, in spite of the oppressive weight on my back, I would wish the distance even greater. I was also amused to think that, bent under the great bundle of "leafy screen," I must have looked like part of the moving grove from Birnam wood advancing upon Macbeth besieged in his "Forbidden City" of Dunsinane. "Here I come, thou bloody tyrant!" I exclaimed, laughing a little at my own bravado.

2

DURING THE YEARS SINCE MY RETURN TO CHINA, I HAD BEEN TAUGHT A hundred times that the sacred mission of the proletariat was not merely to emancipate itself, but to emancipate mankind as a whole. Even enemies of one category or another, so long as they were not beyond redemption, would be emancipated from their own reactionary class stand and ideas through forced labor. Forced labor was only the means, not the end. The avowed end was thought reform of the sinners into new men. A world rid of exploitation of man by man, a brave new world of new men! To be emancipated from myself! What magnificent ideas! What splendid prospects of the future! I was fascinated.

Even while tormented on the rack of interrogation and denunciation, I never felt altogether certain that it was not I who had sinned against the new ultimate truth of Marxism, who had failed the test of an unprecedented revolution. Perhaps it was my mean understanding and vain pride that had blinded me to the incomparable superiority of the socialist system. Why was I the only one among the recent returnees from American and British universities who had sunk into the company of petty thieves and adulterers? Some of them, intelligent and scholarly, had even been accepted into the party. And were they not all honorable men, enjoying the trust of the party as well as the amenities of life? And I? The heroes on the Long March had suffered greatly climbing snow-capped mountains and crossing primeval wildernesses, but they had done it for a high ideal that they believed in. What were my sufferings for? And my poor wife and children had to suffer the consequences of my stupid indiscretions! Had I perished here, I would have been buried like any other ignominious convict. There had to be something wrong with me. I was dying to know what went on in the tormented souls of the wretches who had been condemned to die by fire during the medieval inquisition. I secretly yearned for some magic that would open my eyes to the great truth. In disgrace and ignominy, I was by no means impervious to forced reform, which the party said was aimed at "curing the sickness to save the patient." I was, at moments, almost impatient for thought reform, even though it was to be done under conditions of forced labor.

Once we were in the camp, however, forced labor left little room for thought reform. The unlimited working hours, the backbreaking labor, the hard and soft tactics were all aimed at squeezing the last ounce of strength out of the inmates day after day. Food was much improved over that at the detention center in Beijing. The standard staple was still corn flour, but of edible quality. On a day of rest or a satellite-launching day, we would be fed rice or steamed bread made of wheat flour, along with vegetables that we had grown and fish we had caught. Later on, we raised pigs, and there was even a little pork. As we were better fed, we were of course expected to work even harder. Thought reform seemed to be something remote, either of the past or of the future. For the moment, forced labor, hard labor, was everything. Jargons such as Marxist stand, viewpoint, and method; class struggle and class analysis; historical materialism and dialectical materialism; and so on and so forth, which were always on the lips of college people, went out of circulation here. In any case, most of the offenders under corrective education were either totally or practically illiterate.

There were, indeed, perfunctory reminders of thought reform. At the nightly roll call, one of the officers would occasionally remind us that we were to do forced labor for the purpose of reforming ourselves, although no one ever bothered to explain how forced labor would result in thought reform. There was no reading room, and even the *Selected Works of Mao Zedong,* ubiquitous in Beijing, was hard to find here. On some evenings, articles from a crumpled copy of the *People's Daily,* two or three weeks old, would be read aloud by a literate inmate in the flickering light of an improvised oil lamp made of an old ink bottle. Every three months there was a two-day political campaign supposedly designed to speed up the reform of the inmates. We would be enjoined to inform against each other and confess old crimes we had concealed or new crimes we'd recently committed. One petty thief who had been caught picking pockets again was vehemently denounced by his "peers." One ex-schoolteacher confessed stealing two pieces of steamed corn bread from the kitchen. The ex–police chief from the old regime denounced me for writing a reactionary poem which he had "accidentally" discovered in my absence. It was a small poem of four lines of five Chinese characters each, which I had scribbled on a back page of my volume of *Selected Poems by Du Fu* on the train to the camp, dated June 12, 1958:

> *Acquaintances I had the world over*
> *Bosom friends I now have none*
> *Only a thousand poems here*
> *To keep me company in exile*

The discovery brought no immediate repercussions, but no doubt it added a new entry in my dossier. Another rightist was accused of uttering blasphemies against the Great Leap Forward in his sleep. (Monitoring of talking in our sleep was automatic since we slept a dozen to a kang, packed like sardines.) Otherwise we spent most of the time sitting on the ground and eyeing each other in silence. Occasionally, when he could no longer bear the suspense, a guilty one would come forward with a confession.

A circuit court held an open trial from time to time, so that we would all take warning from the "negative example" of those who were given additional sentences for resisting forced reform. A young rightist, formerly a college teaching assistant in textile engineering, was given a five-year sentence after he repeatedly denied his guilt. One day, on our way back from the building site on the diversion dike, I was shocked to see a happy-go-lucky young hooligan tied to a tree with a sign in large Chinese characters behind him: THE UNREPENTANT CRIMINAL WHO ESCAPED. At an open trial he too was given a five-year sentence, which was later lengthened to fifteen years when he made a second attempt.

The one question that haunted all the inmates was how long our forced reform was to last. At first it did not worry us much, for we naively assumed it could not be too long, since we had not even been tried or sentenced. We were not criminals in the legal sense, and our offenses fell within the category of "contradictions among the people." Hadn't the party bosses at my school told me it was to be for a short time? Hadn't I exercised the right to vote even after I had been dishonorably discharged? When a special pardon was proclaimed for the last emperor and a number of former Nationalist generals on the occasion of the tenth anniversary of the founding of the People's Republic, I began to entertain illusions of release in the not too distant future. After all, those guys were war criminals, and what had I done? On the day of the anniversary, I was called into the camp commander's office for a talk.

"You've been here over a year now, Wu Ningkun. What are some of your feelings about your experience of reform?"

"I've learned to do manual labor."

"That's what you're here for. You've taken a good step forward."

Just one step forward? How many more steps must I take before I am reformed? I decided to sound him out.

"How much longer are we to undergo corrective education through forced labor, Commander?"

"It all depends. You will be released when you have thoroughly reformed yourself. The fact that you're still here means, well, Wu Ningkun, you were a professor, you can figure out what that means."

"That we are not yet thoroughly reformed. But how do we know whether or when we are thoroughly reformed?"

"When you are released!" He went on, "Anyway, what have you learned to do here?"

"Plant soybeans."

"Can you subsist on soybeans alone? You see what I mean."

There were indeed one or two inmates "released" at the end of the first year. One was a hooligan who had often gotten into brawls with other inmates. At the evening roll call one day Captain Ge warned him, in front of all the inmates, against further offenses. The next evening, Captain Ge announced that the same hooligan was released on account of "good behavior," and exhorted us to seek an early release by speeding up our thought reform. The hooligan moved into the quarters for ex-convicts who had been released, but stayed on as an "agricultural worker" on the same state farm. Another hooligan, a returned overseas Chinese from Thailand, was blown to pieces while working with dynamite. The dead man was posthumously released at a rally the next day. I was at a loss what we were supposed to learn from these examples. In any case, I could never fathom the caprice of the regime that was as mysterious as the accident of death.

One day I went to the camp clinic to ask for some pills for a bad cold. Dr. Bai, who was serving a five-year sentence for raping his patients, said to me condescendingly: "You guys think you're better off than us convicts because you have not been tried or sentenced. What you actually got is an indefinite term, indefinite, you hear? You will be kept in intolerable suspense year after year! When you do eventually get released, you will not be allowed to go home, but stay right here for the rest of your days. That's the new policy I just learned from an officer. But me, my term will be up in two months' time. When the time comes, pronto, I go home! Am I glad I'm not in your shoes!"

He was certainly right about the intolerable suspense, which the regime wielded against their victims as a ruthless weapon in their war of nerves. But he was mistaken about his own fate, for he was given five more years for some new offense before his term was up.

I was slow in coming to realize that the much-flaunted thought reform was nothing but a euphemism. In the camps, where the thin veil of euphemism was cast aside, thought reform became synonymous with brutal forced labor and naked coercion and intimidation. Unquestioning obedience was the first article of faith for offenders under corrective education as well as for convicts, whether serving their terms or kept on as "freed men."

The handsome young statistician at the branch camp who had been "released" after serving a five-year sentence for some counterrevolutionary offense or other was a perfect model of thoroughgoing thought reform. As an ex-convict, he was always respectful to the officers, always followed instructions to the last letter, always kept his statistical tables accurate and neat, and never raised his voice or said anything uncalled-for. Apparently unmarried, he never alluded to his personal life. I was dying to know what had happened to him in those five years that had turned him into such a specimen of reform through forced labor. He could not have been reformed, because no reform had ever been intended; he had somehow just learned his lesson. If the powers that be ever believed in reforming the sinners into "new men," why wouldn't they let the "new men" return to their jobs and families when they had served their terms instead of continuing to detain them at the camps against their will? Once a sinner, always a sinner!

At the height of the Great Leap Forward, we were taken to the farm headquarters to see an exhibition of a long-range plan of the Lake Xingkai State Farm for our edification. In addition to numerous charts and posters, there was a huge model of the dream city. A girl guide from the No. 9 Branch Farm for women pointed to a group of minuscule buildings in one corner, reciting her lines glibly: "That's where the future Lake Xingkai University will be located. It will teach farming, fishing, papermaking, sugar refining, and other practical skills useful to socialist reconstruction." After a pause, she added, "You've got a professor at Number Eight Branch Farm, right? There's an ideal place for him!" I shuddered at the idea. Luckily, the university never went beyond the model stage.

There were reports of inmates who had gone berserk under the intolerable suspense of an indefinite term and the prospect of perpetual confinement. Would I too succumb to the stress and strain? No, no, I promised myself, I would never do what my mother did to herself with her own hands, I must keep my sanity inviolate, keep my faith in life, come what may.

3

IN THE ABSENCE OF THOUGHT REFORM, I FOUND MUCH FOOD FOR THOUGHT, on a day of rest or when cooped up in the cell by a torrential rain or blinding blizzard, in the two small volumes of poetry I had brought with me.

Hamlet was my favorite Shakespearean play. Read in a Chinese labor camp, however, the tragedy of the Danish prince took on unexpected dimensions. All the academic analyses and critiques that had engrossed me over the years now seemed remote and irrelevant. The outcry "Denmark is a prison." echoed with a poignant immediacy and Elsinore loomed like a haunting metaphor of a treacherous repressive state. The Ghost thundered with a terrible chorus of a million victims of proletarian dictatorship. Rosencrantz and Guildenstern would have felt like fish in water, had they found their way into a modern nation of hypocrites and informers. Hamlet's losses were indeed great: a father, a mother, an angelic sweetheart, a kingdom, and his own precious life, all because of the treachery of an arch-villain and usurper. But the powerful and suspenseful action only provided a stage on which was enacted the tormenting drama in his soul. Hamlet suffered as an archetypal modern intellectual. Touched off by practical issues in the kingdom of Denmark, his anguish, emotional, moral, and metaphysical, took on cosmic dimensions and permeated the great soliloquies with an ever-haunting rhythm. When I recited them to myself on the lakeshore, I felt this anguish was the substance of the tragedy. And his great capacity for inner suffering gave the noble Dane his unique stature as a tragic hero preeminently worthy of his suffering. Ruminating on his life and death, I would say to myself "I am not Prince Hamlet," echoing Eliot's Prufrock. Rather, I often felt like one of those fellows "crawling between earth and heaven," scorned by Hamlet himself. The real question, I came to see, was neither to be or not to be, nor whether in the mind to suffer the slings and arrows of outrageous fortune, but how to be worthy of one's suffering.

Du Fu was not my favorite classical Chinese poet, in spite of his monumental stature as the "poet saint." But now, read in the labor camp, his great poems rang with the voice of the conscience of the Middle Kingdom at a time of endless and universal sufferings. Always lamenting but never despairing, he kept faith with life and transformed his poignant anguish into immortal poetry, which continued to give heart to the insulted and the injured. It was to him that I owed the inspiration, in my dungeon, of naming my child born in sorrow One Feather. I recalled how the "poet saint," constantly driven from place to place by the winds of war, had in his fifties died a pauper's death of bacillary dysentery from eating spoiled beef. Who was I to complain of a sheltered life in a socialist camp? I wanted thought reform indeed.

* * *

Gradually resigned to the prospect of an indefinite term, I took comfort in the company of my fellow inmates, as well as in the great poets of the past. One day when I was still carrying earth on the diversion dike, my right knee was accidentally cut by the sharpened edge of a spade with which a digger was filling my wicker basket. I went to the young inmate doctor who was sitting under a tree with a first-aid kit at his feet. While dressing my cut, he asked me what I had done to be where I was. I told him I was labeled an ultrarightist. When he asked me where I had worked, I hesitated for a moment and then said, "I taught at Yenching University."

"What, Yenching! Why, I was in pre-med at Yenching before entering PUMC, the Peiping Union Medical College. What did you teach?"

"I taught the English seniors when I had just returned from the States, in 1951."

"Professor, my respects. You might not have been so accessible at the university. Wasn't Li Tiansheng in your class? A good friend of mine, you know."

"Yes, indeed, and he was later my assistant at Nankai and the party school in Beijing. He was also labeled an ultrarightist and taken to the Qinghe State Farm not far from Beijing."

"Lucky dog. We had to be brought to this wilderness because Qinghe was packed to bursting. Well, you'd better get back to your labor now. Come see me at the clinic in the evening before the roll call, professor. My name is Benjamin Lee, but just Lee here, for a Christian name will land you in more trouble."

Friends in adversity, we poured out our hearts to each other. Dr. Lee had the distinction of being labeled a "rightist hooligan" because he had called his accusers names at a denunciation meeting at the hospital where he was a resident. When he was dishonorably discharged and sent to forced labor, his wife divorced him. Living all by himself in the small room that housed the clinic, he would have been driven out of his mind except for his continued absorption in medical research. Trained as a physician at the finest medical school in the country, he now delved into various concentration-camp diseases and found some exciting cures. He sent case reports with slides to his former teachers at the medical college but never got any response from them. During the famine that followed the fiasco of the Great Leap Forward, he was able to save the lives of many inmates in the camp.

Deng Muhang, another rightist inmate, was a Chinese major in college. It turned out that he had studied with Shen Congwen at the Normal University in Beijing. I was beside myself with joy when he told me he had in his shabby prisoner's bag a few of the master's works. From then on, during the hours of backbreaking labor on the diversion dike or in building the great walls of ice in freezing cold, Deng and I would chat about Shen's masterpieces, *The Border Town*, *The Long River*, his *Autobiography*, and others, diffusely, endlessly, so that sometimes we forgot our fatigue, forgot even where we were.

On a biweekly or triweekly Sunday, when some of the inmates tried to make up for lost sleep and others played cards, Deng and I would often take his few treasured books, dogeared and blackened, and sit in a quiet corner on the bank of Lake Xingkai to read aloud the parts of the works we loved the best. As Deng spoke pure Mandarin, it was always he who read what I selected. Both of us were partial to the passages having to do with water:

> Guisheng sharpened his sickle on the bank of the brook, until the cutting edge was bright and shining. He first felt the edge with his fingers, and then thrashed the water with his sickle a few times. With the coming of autumn, the water in the brook was crystal-clear, flowing very lively. Many small shrimps, with their legs clinging to a weed, swam around in the shallows, or sometimes bounced to a distance with their backs arched, as if they were very happy. Seeing this, Guisheng also felt very happy.

The water in Lake Xingkai was also crystal clear in the fall; it did not lose any luster because it had been turned into part of a labor camp. Sharpening our sickles on rocks on the lake bank, we also felt almost as happy as Guisheng did.

The one passage Deng and I never tired of reciting over and over again reads:

> Looking at the gently flowing water, I felt as if there suddenly came to my mind a little understanding of life. . . . A patch of soft afternoon sun on the hilltop touched me, pebbles as round as chess pieces at the

bottom of the river also touched me. My heart seemed to be free of dregs, transparent and candlelit, and I felt such a love, such a very warm love for everything under the sun, for the boatmen and the small boats alike!

Now, at last, I came to understand why the master's simple voice had always been so touching. There and then, his "transparent and candlelit" voice, its tender rhythm and music, made us, two young prisoners, far away from home, so happy that we forgot our sorrows and could "dream fond dreams of sailing the seas" and occasionally "look at each other in silence with tears running down our cheeks," as Su Shi put it in his heartrending ci-poem. We took sustenance from the "trickling" voice of Shen, "soft yet tenacious," which no mighty host could ever have smothered.

Most of the inmates, however, never had anything to do with Hamlet, Du Fu, or Shen Congwen. Once I found an illiterate old inmate seated on the ground in the setting sun holding a small photo in his hand. I went up to him and took a look at the photo. "What a cute little boy! Your grandson?" I said casually. "Yes, my youngest grandchild, used to be at my knees all the time," he said with a smile, his eyes shining. "But will I ever see him again? You tell me." I could hear tears in his voice. I wished I could tell him. I also wished I knew if I would see my own son again. I took out of my pocket a recent photo of Yiding and Yimao with their mother and showed it to him. "What a nice family!" he said with warm admiration. "You must miss them. You a rightist? Ai . . ." Much later, I learned the old man was among the early deaths from starvation.

Another illiterate inmate was an ex-convict in his early thirties who had served five years in a labor reform camp in the northern province of Ningxia for stabbing a man who had seduced his wife. Forced to remain on the farm after his release, Chen asked for leave to go home and visit his folks in the south. On the way back from his southern home, he had to change trains in Beijing. He discovered too late that he did not have enough money left for his train fare to Ningxia. So he decided to spend the night on a bench in the train station and try to earn some money by carrying heavy baggage for passengers boarding the train in the morning. But before morning came, he was picked up by a patrolling policeman and turned in to the detention center as an escapee from a labor camp. And he was transported here instead!

Chen could never understand how he could be caught as an escapee when he was on his way back to his farm at the end of his authorized leave. He would come to me, repeat his story over and over again in his Chinese badly distorted by a heavy Cantonese accent, and agitated and stammering a little, he would ask for an explanation. "You're a professor. You must be able to explain it to me. I beg you." It sounded like a reproach and made me feel ashamed. Perhaps it was his queer Cantonese accent that got the security officers confused. Perhaps he was too simpleminded to appreciate how the meshes of the socialist law worked! He would also ask me to write an occasional letter to his wife for him, berating her for his misfortunes. For my services, he would thrust into my pocket a handful of crackers made of bean dregs, which were part of the feed for the pigs in his care. I crunched them with a relish that was the envy of the other inmates.

It was not difficult to love "a soft patch of afternoon sun on the hills," or the boat and the ex-convict boatman, or the snow-covered wilderness, or the lake frozen solid, or even the pig crackers, but it was not so easy to love "everything under the sun." What about those officers who certainly had no love for us? Well, Captain Li at least was different. There were four officers in charge of our company of two hundred men, and Li was the most junior of the four. A demobilized local soldier, dark-complexioned and slight of stature, he spoke the earthy tongue of the peasant without a single Marxist jargon at his command. He had lost one of his eyes in the war, but we never knew which war it was, for he never bragged about his sacrifices to the nation. He had little schooling, yet he never tried to cover it up. When he saw some characters on a wall poster that he did not know, he would ask me to explain them to him with the eagerness of a schoolchild. On the other hand, when he saw how clumsy I was with the spade, he would grab it and teach me how to dig and throw up earth the easy and quick way. "I done it all my life, nothing to speak of." He sounded almost apologetic. "You never done it before, reading and writing all the time. That's real hard!"

When Captain Li was with the inmates, he never acted the officer, but instead chatted and laughed as if he were among comrades. One day when we were snowed in, he visited our cell on an inspection tour.

"Some snow, Captain Li! Does it often snow so heavily here?" I asked.

"You think this snow is heavy, Wu Ningkun? You should have seen the snow two years back when my woman had her first child. The snow on my roof was three feet deep and the door was blocked by a snow drift. Minus eighteen degrees in the room! And she had to do it there and then! I had a hard time trying to bring a pot of water to a boil for her with the little dry straw we had in the room. I had managed to have six eggs on hand for her confinement, not one more. My, oh my, I would call that some snow!"

"But this snow is heavy enough to give my feet frostbite, Captain Li," I said.

Captain Li had a ready answer. "Nonsense! Put some wula sedge in your shoes to keep your feet warm. It is one of the three treasures of the lake district: ginseng, marten fur, and wula sedge, haven't you heard?"

So saying, he pulled off one of his heavy padded shoes and put it on the kang. Then he grabbed my hand and thrust it into the shoe, urging me to feel it. I found it surprisingly warm. Looking triumphant, he put his bare foot on the kang. "Feel my foot. See how warm the wula sedge keeps it!" he said cheerfully.

"Very warm indeed," I agreed, my hand on his foot. "But I don't know how to make wula sedge shoe cushions."

Quickly he pulled a cushion out of his shoe and handed it to me. "See how nice and soft it is. All you have to do is to pound and pound on the sedge with something hard, say a brick, till it's soft like silk. It'll keep your feet warm all winter, and no socks. I can't afford socks anyway." He laughed. I followed his instructions and kept frostbite away.

Captain Li could not afford many other things either. His young wife, an illiterate peasant woman from the same village, had to do washing for inmates to add to his meager pay, which could hardly keep the couple and their two-year-old baby boy fed and clothed. There were no odd jobs to be had at the camp, because all menial labor was performed by inmates. We washed our own clothes on a day of rest, but our cotton-padded quilts had to be taken apart and washed periodically. That's where Captain Li's wife came in. I was a bit hesitant the first time I availed myself of her service. One winter morning, just as we were getting ready to march to work, I stepped up to Captain Li and stammered, "My quilt needs to be washed, Captain Li, would . . ." Before I finished, he nodded and waved me away. When I came back to the cell in the evening, I found my quilt clean-smelling and neatly folded. The compensation was eighty fen. It wasn't much, but what I earned for a day's labor was thirty fen at first, and eighty fen by the end. On a good day she could do two or three quilts, but often she had no business at all.

Nevertheless, Captain Li was always cheerful and naturally dignified. We all liked him, but word got around that the other officers did not think he assumed the proper attitude with the inmates. He seemed blissfully unaware of the fellow officers' disapproval. One early spring day, when the thaw was just beginning, we were sent into a wood in the hills to carry some logs back to the barracks. It would have been difficult to carry them downhill by a tortuous narrow trail, so we were instructed to guide them down a stream. The water was icy cold, and by the time we'd made our way out with the logs our skin was red and we were all shivering. Taking one look at our sorry plight, Captain Li at once ordered us to jump into bed and warm ourselves up. Then he went to the kitchen to order a hot drink of ginger and brown sugar for us. Before he came back we were visited by the senior officer, Captain Ge, six feet tall and with an imposing military bearing.

"What's going on here? Aren't you all supposed to be carrying logs?"

"We did, Captain Ge," replied the squad leader.

"How many trips have you made?"

"One," the squad leader said timidly.

"One trip and you're in bed warming yourselves up! Whose big idea is this?"

"Captain Li gave orders."

"He did, eh? Good, here he is. Did you give orders for these men to go to bed in broad daylight, Captain Li?"

"Yes I did," he replied calmly in his local peasant's accent, looking straight into the angry eyes of Captain Ge. "These men came out of the icy stream red and shivering all over. You don't want them to catch their death of cold, do you? That's not the way soldiers were treated in the army."

"I'm afraid you're forgetting yourself, Captain Li. These men are elements for corrective education through forced labor, not soldiers on vacation. Our duty is to be strict with them, not to spoil and pamper them. All right, we will discuss this at the officers' meeting tonight." Then, turning to us, Captain Ge shouted, "Now you all get up and carry back all the logs today!"

I could see both captains were loyal servants of the law. Only each acted according to his own understanding of what was required of him to fulfill his duty. The next day Captain Li did not show up, and I never saw him again.

We were isolated, not only from the outside world, but from the rest of the country. We were allowed to write home twice a month. At first, our mail, coming and going, was censored. What could the correspondents have said in censored mail? I told my wife I was getting along fine and there was nothing for her to worry about. She reassured me she and the two children were getting along fine and there was nothing for me to worry about. Well, we were not getting along fine and there was plenty to worry about, but the brief notes carried the comforting message that none of the family had succumbed to the tribulations. A few months later, we were told the censorship had been done away with, because we were not convicts deprived of civil rights, but fell under internal contradictions among the people. We ventured to give a few more details in our letters, but soon were told that censorship had been reinstated. No one bothered to explain why it was brought back, nor whether we still remained under internal contradictions. We still read the *People's Daily,* two or three weeks late, and tried to dig out small pieces of news buried under pages of euphoria about the splendid achievements of the Great Leap Forward and the People's Commune. We were given a vision of the land turned into a sea of fluttering red flags. Otherwise we knew little of what was really going on in the country and the world.

The farm reaped a bumper harvest of corn, rice, wheat, and soybeans in 1960, thanks to the good weather, the humus, and the slave labor. We began looking forward to larger food rations. Early in October, however, our rations were suddenly and drastically cut. The explanation was that the food we produced ourselves had to be shipped out to feed the city populace. What happened to the bumper harvests all over the land, news of which had filled the pages of the *People's Daily*? The officers never bothered to explain, and we kept the question to ourselves. Before the month was over, all the rightists on the farm, hundreds of us, were ordered to transfer to Qinghe State Farm, situated between Tianjin and the industrial city of Tangshan. Qinghe Farm was a major prison under the jurisdiction of Beijing Municipal Bureau of Public Security. No explanation was given for the sudden relocation either, but we had no doubt it would be a change for the better—better food, better treatment, better hopes of release.

Seven

GUILT BY ASSOCIATION, 1958–60

Narrated by Li Yikai

1

JULY 22, 1958, WAS THE LAST DAY OF MY EIGHT-WEEK MATERNITY LEAVE. Hardly had I finished feeding the baby after breakfast when Zuo the Leftist turned up in my shabby rooms. I was surprised by her unexpected visit and wondered if it were possible that she had actually come to congratulate me in common civility. I greeted her and offered her a seat. Brushing aside my greetings, she asked me sharply:

"Why did you not come to work today, Li Yikai?"

"I am coming to work tomorrow morning," I answered truthfully.

"You are allowed eight weeks' maternity leave, like everybody else. Fifty-six days, that is. In spite of your political mistakes, we have not deprived you of your maternity leave. Instead of showing your gratitude to the party, you overstay your leave!"

"My leave began on May the twenty-eighth—"

"No, on the twenty-seventh."

"But I didn't leave the office until almost five in the afternoon."

"The working day wasn't over, so your leave began on that day. That's all there's to it. Listen, I have revolutionary work to attend to. No more nonsense. There's urgent work awaiting you at the office." So saying, she turned back and strode out the door. I left the baby with Mother and followed her to the office. Instead of handing me my urgent assignment at once, however, she first called a meeting to criticize my failure to abide by government regulations and my neglect of my duty. I was enjoined to intensify my thought reform and warned against future violations. I thanked Zuo and the other colleagues for their help and promised not to repeat the same mistake, since it was unlikely that I should enjoy another maternity leave in the foreseeable future.

My return to work coincided with the launching of the Great Leap Forward initiated by the "Great Leader," who vowed to bring to backward China a Communist heaven on earth through a mass campaign of intensive physical labor. "Deep-plowing" was the magic for unlimited increase in agricultural production; backyard steel-smelting would enable China to outstrip England in steel output in fifteen years. For me it meant longer hours pounding on the big English typewriter, which I had only recently learned to use. I kept making mistakes, more on stencil paper than on typing paper. Zuo the Leftist gave me more stencil paper jobs to do, so that I might "learn from my own mistakes." After counting my mistakes each time, she would give me even more stencil paper jobs, so that I could "make up for my mistakes." With the escalation of the Great Leap Forward, we were required to put in extra hours. Once, I pounded away on the antiquated typewriter so late into the night that my milk oozed through my blouse. One woman colleague suggested to Zuo I might be excused from night duties, only to earn a reprimand from the leadership for wavering in her class stand and showing sympathy for rightists.

On the eve of National Day, Zuo told me to work all night to "launch a satellite," while she fulfilled the political task of attending a celebratory dance.

I made a bold appeal to her maternal instincts. "I am nursing my daughter, as you know. How can I stay up all night typing away while my baby is crying for her mama and her milk? I think I have been working hard enough, and I have typed up so many things, which nobody seems to be using."

Her face changed color and she raised her voice. "Li Yikai, you are forgetting your place. You are here to take orders from me and do what you are told to do. Stop putting on airs of a professor's wife and behave like the spouse of an ultrarightist. All revolutionary comrades are doing their utmost for the Great Leap Forward. And you, the wife of an ultrarightist, refuse to give a few hours of sleep to revolutionary work? All right, do as you please and we shall see."

I didn't wish to defy her. I had learned how to make myself very small in the last agonizing months, but I simply had to sleep with my baby and feed her during the night. Also, if I stayed up all night typing, my milk would soon dry up and my baby would starve. "No, I couldn't risk that, come what may!" I said to myself. On National Day, Zuo was honored as a model worker. Shortly after that, she was accepted into the party. She left me alone for a while. Perhaps she was too intoxicated with her new honors to bother with an ultrarightist's wife who did not know her place. Or perhaps she was waiting to "see," as she had darkly threatened.

Shortly after National Day, the college organized a three-day trip to Xushui County, some hundred miles southwest of Beijing. The purpose was to visit an experimental plot of cotton that was said to be bearing cotton bolls as large as peaches and to learn from the peasants who were so inspired by the spirit of the Great Leap Forward that they created the miracle. The "Great Leader" himself had honored the plot with a personal visit, so now it was necessary for the faithful to flock to the shrine and witness the miracle. I thought I might be excused, since I had a baby to feed. When Zuo made it clear I was wrong again, I asked whether I could bring my baby along.

"Of course not," she shot back. "What do you think this is anyway? A picnic? I'll have you know this is a political task of the first importance. Remember that Chairman Mao visited the place in person! You ought to be grateful that you are not excluded in spite of your political status. What is the feeding of a baby compared with such a significant political task, eh?"

"But what am I to do with my baby?" I was getting desperate.

"That's your problem, Li Yikai."

Left with "my problem," I scoured the neighborhood grocery stores and found two cans of condensed milk to feed the baby during my forced absence. Though the shrine was not so far away, the visit had to be stretched out over three days to lend it enough political importance. We traveled for six hours on a bumpy road. My milk began to ooze through my blouse and Mao jacket even before our two college buses arrived at the plot. Hundreds of visitors milled around the shrine to admire the cotton bolls, which were indeed bigger than usual but far from being peach-sized. We were surrounded by the strong stench of manure; one peasant told us proudly that in addition to tons of manure large quantities of fertilizer had also been applied. When night came, we were again led to the plot to witness the spectacle of a battery of spotlights turned on the little cotton plot. "As good as the fireworks at Tiananmen on the night of National Day," someone remarked admiringly. Back at the peasant's little house, where I shared a kang with half a dozen other women, I felt a growing pain in my swelling breasts. While my bedfellows slept, I applied the breast pump from time to time to relieve the pressure. The next day we were led to the cotton plot again to admire the miraculous cotton bolls and hear presentations by the production team and brigade leaders on how they were inspired by their ardent love for the Great Leader and the spirit of the Great Leap Forward. Meanwhile, the pain spread from my breasts to my arms. One young woman colleague who had also mothered two children whispered indiscreetly, "I don't understand why they made you come along, pumping away the good milk and leaving the baby home hungry and crying. If this goes on much longer, your milk will be poisoned and the baby will starve. Beyond me, totally!" It was not until the next afternoon that the pilgrims finally returned to the campus. My baby started sucking away greedily the minute I collapsed into a chair in my room.

2

DURING THIS TIME, WORD GOT AROUND THAT THE MAYOR OF BEIJING HAD launched a campaign to clean the city of political impurities, that is, class enemies of all categories, and turn the imperial capital into a "crystal city." Local police substations were busy writing off residence permits of impurities to be expelled from the city. Two days after the New Year recess, just as I was winding up the day's work, I was called into the president's office.

"Li Yikai, the country is in the midst of the Great Leap Forward," began Vice President Feng in his Shenxi dialect, while puffing on his cigarette. "New universities and colleges are springing up all over the country. One of them is Anhui University, right in the capital of the province. A new university is, of course, short of teachers, and we in Beijing are duty-bound to lend them support. The party organization has decided to assign you the honorable task of supporting Anhui University. You can teach English there and put your expertise to work. There will be no deduction in your wages. Do you have any difficulties?"

"I have two small children and I hardly know how to cope in a strange place among strange people . . ."

"The party organization took that into consideration. This is why you are being sent to Anhui instead of an outlying border region, such as Xinjiang or Qinghai. You're lucky, Li Yikai, considering . . ." He left it unfinished but I knew what he meant. "Wu Ningkun will join you there when he has completed his corrective education."

"How long will that take?" I asked eagerly.

"A year perhaps. Depends on how quickly he reforms himself. You depart on the eighth. You can get your train tickets from the business office. Good-bye, good-bye."

So casually I was disposed of! I had never wanted to come to Beijing, but I was brought here anyway. Now I had no wish to leave Beijing, but was being ordered out as an undesirable impurity. They had exiled my man hundreds of miles north, and now they were sending me into exile hundreds of miles south. So that's what Zuo was dying to "see"! Misfortune indeed never comes singly. Who was I to expect exemption from a truth universally acknowledged!

By the time I reached home I had composed myself. While feeding the baby I told my mother and mother-in-law what was happening, trying to sound as calm as I could. "I am not the only one. The Great Leap Forward is going on, and thousands of people are being sent from the capital to support the provinces. And I will get the same pay!" The two aged mothers were dismayed but restrained their feelings. My mother-in-law offered to go with me to help take care of the children.

The next morning I went to work as usual. Zuo didn't even look at me, but at the end of the day, she stopped at my desk and told me there would be a sort of farewell meeting for me in the evening. A farewell party? I couldn't believe my ears. When I went back to the office after a quick supper, there were a dozen staff members sitting around. Zuo called the meeting to order.

"This is a farewell meeting for Li Yikai. She has been transferred to Anhui University. On the basis of the many criticism meetings called for her benefit, we are to make an appraisal of her work and her political behavior over the past year. I know the comrades will be ready to give her some help before she leaves the school."

All the comrades responded to the call and took turns in making a speech. Some were mild, but several were hard-line. To conclude, Zuo asked the woman from personnel to make a summing-up.

"We are pretty familiar with Li Yikai's case by now. She committed a number of serious political mistakes and yet she has shown little inclination to reform herself," she began in her authoritative voice. "One, she voiced grievances in her ultrarightist husband's behalf; two, she attacked the Campaign to Uproot Hidden Counterrevolutionaries; three, she undermined the great antirightist campaign by concealing Wu Ningkun's rightist utterances and deeds; four, she showed passive resistance to political study by keeping silent at group discussions; five, she has not made a clean break with Wu Ningkun up to this day in spite of all the help we have given her; six, she showed a negative attitude toward the Great Leap Forward and actually refused to take part in launching a satellite; seven, she tried to smuggle cans of food in parcels sent to Wu Ningkun in violation of government regulations and lied to the postal clerk in doing so; eight, when Wu Ningkun was about to be sent to labor reform, she took advantage of her job at the Reading Room to take out all the newspapers that carried government regulations on labor reform. She was hoping to find loopholes in them so as to vindicate her husband. If you have nothing else to add, comrades, our collective appraisal will go into her dossier as it is."

After expressing full agreement with the personnel woman's speech, Zuo announced: "Tomorrow and the day after tomorrow you are excused from work, Li Yikai, so that you will have ample time for packing. Aren't you going to say a few words to show your appreciation of all that we have been doing for you?"

"I thank you all from the bottom of my heart," I choked. "I feel unworthy of the precious time you have wasted on me, when you might have given it to the great campaign of the Great Leap Forward. I beg forgiveness from you all, good-bye."

Two days to get ready for the long journey to exile! There was so much to do and I had to do it all by myself. I had not a minute to lose. In the morning, I rushed from office to office: the personnel office, where I was issued transfer documents by the same woman who had made the summing-up speech; the local police substation, where I had to stand in line in the freezing cold for my turn to have our residence permit canceled and moving permit issued ("Oh, Wu Ningkun's dependents!" the clerk remarked knowingly); the local food grains rationing office, where documents were issued to transfer our rations to Hefei; the school business office, where I applied for two train tickets for myself and my mother-in-law. I walked miles, for a strong north wind made cycling impossible. But there was no one to say good-bye to, and no one came to say good-bye to me.

When I finally returned to my rooms it was supper time. I felt like lying down, but the first thing Mother said was, "Your woman colleague Zuo came to say there will be a meeting for you at seven P.M." "Oh, my God, don't they ever get tired of all this?" I moaned to myself. After eating a quick supper and feeding the baby, I made my way to the office once again. In addition to the usual crowd of a dozen staff members, a few leading cadres had also turned up. Zuo chaired the meeting as usual and called it to order by saying, "This meeting is called because the masses were dissatisfied with Li Yikai's failure to confess to the eight charges against her yesterday. Revolutionary comrades are duty-bound to help her face her mistakes and crimes." Then all those present at the meeting took turns repeating the charges against me. Finally Vice President Yu Wei called on me to admit my guilt and warned me against sinking deeper into the rightist quagmire. My head was so heavy that I closed my eyes and muttered, "I'm sure I was guilty of all the charges against me, for the revolutionary colleagues present would never have said so if they were not true. I thank you all again. I shall never forget your comradely kindness."

I did not get around to packing until the very last day. Now that Ningkun's income had been cut off, I could not afford to leave anything behind. Yet I could not afford to ship the furniture either. In desperation, I called in a junk dealer and watched him carry away the few pieces of good furniture given us by my mother. By midnight, I had finished packing all Ningkun's books into his old trunks and cardboard boxes, and our clothes, the kitchen utensils, and sundry other necessaries into whatever containers I could find. I wore myself out tying up several bedrolls with ropes. The bedding we slept in would be packed in the morning.

By the time I slipped into bed beside my two little ones, I was cold and worn out, and the fire in the coal stove was dying out. I heard the north wind shrieking and feared it would be freezing in the morning. I held the children close to me, one on each side. But before I knew what was happening, the strong wind had turned into a gale. As the building was old and rickety, the doors and windows clattered incessantly. All of a sudden, one window was torn off the hinges and smashed to pieces on the ground outside. Then another window was gone, and another, until we were completely exposed to the elements. Huge snowflakes flew into our room. I piled up all our cotton-padded coats and trousers on top of our quilts and huddled myself underneath, holding the two little ones tightly. I felt as if I were living through the storm scene of *King Lear* or the opening of *Wuthering Heights,* scenes that Ningkun used to read aloud to me. Thank God our storm did not last too long and the two little ones slept through it.

We were to make the fifteen-mile trip to the train station in an old truck provided by the school. When he arrived to pick us up, the glum old driver grumbled, "So early on such a cold day, really now!" I apologized, and he relented a little, saying, "Really, I've never seen such a day before. Been living here nearly sixty years. It's the damned cold wave from Siberia! Sure, it's not your fault. What did your husband want to be a rightist for? I can never understand these dumb intellectuals. Now look at the poor kids!" We loaded the baggage with the help of the driver and his assistant, and then we all climbed onto the open truck and huddled together. It pained me to watch the two grandmothers scramble onto the truck at their great age and with their tiny bound feet. After we had been driving for a few minutes, I suddenly realized that in the chaos of moving I had forgotten to take down from the wall the two paintings by Prince Pu Xinyu in padauk frames, which Mother had given us as a wedding present.

"Oh, Mother, the Pu Xinyu paintings were left hanging on the wall! What shall I do now?"

"Turn back and get them, Yikai."

"But we are already late. We might miss the train if—"

"Your father treasured those paintings. Real gems. If you leave them behind, they will be as good as lost forever. Ask the driver to turn back, I beg you."

I had never seen Mother so insistent in all my life. She made up my mind for me. I twisted my neck and shouted into the driver's cab.

"Old Master, I left something most important in my rooms. I am awfully sorry, but you simply must turn back . . ."

I must have sounded really desperate because the old driver soon made

117

a U-turn, shouting back to me, "I'll oblige you, but you might miss the train!"

A few minutes later, I was back in the truck with the two paintings clasped in my arms. I saw tears in Mother's eyes. The north wind howled all the way to the station and flurries of snow fell on the five of us like confetti, as if to bid us a sad farewell and wish us well on a helpless journey to nowhere. Suddenly it occurred to me that if the cold wave from Siberia is such a scourge here, it must be truly awful in the Chinese Siberia where Ningkun is. I hugged my baby daughter closer to my heart.

At the train station, I had our baggage checked in a hurry and rushed over to the platform where a train was standing, with the baby in my arms and Yiding clinging to my side, only to find it was not my train. I hurried over to another platform with the two grandmothers tottering behind me on their bound feet. By the time I scrambled into a third-class car after Yiding and Ningkun's mother, the train was ready to pull out. I stood at the door dragging up one bag after another, but the train started moving before I could grab the last parcel, which had in it, among other things, diapers for the baby. With the baby in my arms, I waved a hasty good-bye to Mother, who was standing on the platform in tears, the parcel of diapers in her arms. She would take the next train on a solitary return journey to Tianjin.

The train was completely packed, though it was another month until the annual peak around the Lunar New Year holidays. At first I stood in the aisle with Yimao in my arms, but the hectic hassle of the past few days had so worn me out that I slumped to the floor. When I woke in the middle of the night, I found Yiding leaning against me, sound asleep. Having despaired of getting a seat, Grandma stood in the jolting vestibule, grateful that she was at least close to the lavatory, which she had to visit frequently because of her diabetes.

We had to change to a local train in Bengbu, a railroad hub. The waiting room at the station looked even more like a refugee center, with people sitting or sleeping all over the filthy floor. While Grandma and Yiding were seated on our bags, I took the baby in my arms and picked my way toward the ticket line. It took me two hours to reach the ticket window and get our tickets for the slow train to Hefei. By the time we dragged ourselves into a third-class car, we found it was even more crowded than the train we had come in on, with carrying baskets and shoulder poles blocking the aisle. But more people scrambled up after us, pushing us to the middle of the aisle. Grandma was in despair. How was she to get to the lavatory? "Oh my God, what have I done to deserve all this?" she moaned inconsolably. I turned away from her wrinkled tear-stained face. What comfort could I give her? She had to bear the intolerable during the six-hour journey.

3

ANHUI UNIVERSITY, BUILT ON THE SITE OF FORMER GRAVE MOUNDS, WAS A product of the Great Leap Forward. All of the buildings on the suburban campus were brand new. Housing for faculty and staff was designed in strict socialist hierarchical order. The president, the party secretary, and other top officials lived in elegant five or six-room houses in a quiet corner of the campus. The professors and department heads lived in four-room apartments in cream-colored two-story buildings, and the instructors and section chiefs were given three-room apartments in three-story gray brick buildings. The rest were dumped together in the three-story red brick buildings known as "the slums," in units of two or two and a half small rooms with public latrines. I was naturally given one of the smallest units in the slums, with a few pieces of furniture rented from the university.

When I reported to work at the office of the foreign languages department, I asked what courses I would be teaching. The director looked confused by my question.

"What did you say, Comrade Li Yikai? What courses?" he asked.

"The leadership at the party school in Beijing told me I would be teaching English here, because the new department is short of English teachers."

"We are indeed short of teachers, but you can't teach. No, you certainly can't teach. Your husband is an ultrarightist under corrective education. How can his wife teach socialist students in a socialist university? That is as clear as daylight. Comrade Li Yikai, we understand you know how to type. So you are assigned to work under Comrade Wen as an English typist. We are also short of English typists. Typewriting is also revolutionary work, is it not? And we expect you to do your part in the

Great Leap Forward at Anhui University. Please report to her at the Typing Room at the end of the corridor."

I found Comrade Wen at the Typing Room without difficulty. A mother of my own age, she seemed cordial, telling me with a smile about her husband, who was on the department party committee, and their two sons. The elder of the two was just about Yiding's age. A Russian typist herself, she introduced me to the other English typist, a middle-aged man from Shanghai named Chen, and then pointed to a covered standard English typewriter, saying, "This is yours! It has been awaiting your coming! With the Great Leap Forward in full swing, there is so much to do. It has kept Lao Chen busy all the time. Can you start working today?" I was given stencil paper jobs right away. Before leaving Beijing, I had thought I had seen the last of stencil paper. Now after traveling hundreds of miles, I was back at my old job again!

Politics was "in command," as was the case in Beijing and elsewhere throughout the country. Political study took precedence over office work, and study sessions or political meetings took up working hours. Working overtime became a daily routine, and Sundays were often turned into satellite days. With a child to nurse and another to care for, the work load was weighing me down. And Comrade Wen, nicknamed Little Hot Pepper, turned out to be another Zuo the Leftist. She was always finding fault with my work and kept a close watch on my movements, including toilet visits. I was expected to hand in Ningkun's biweekly notes for her inspection. As the leader of the staff political study group, she presided over every session and often made me the butt of her pointed remarks. Periodic sessions of criticism and self-criticism were called to help me with my thought reform. I was to "lay bare my thoughts" and seek the criticism of my revolutionary comrades for my salvation.

As the wife of an ultrarightist undergoing labor reform, I was, needless to say, a "backward element" in dire need of such help. I would always express my gratitude to the party and my colleagues under the leadership of Comrade Wen for their unfailing concern. Then I would confess that my mind was often a total blank because after the day's work and nursing the baby and taking care of Yiding and doing the cooking and washing and other chores, I simply had no strength left to think. Little Hot Pepper would always chide me for hiding my bad thoughts, which she said was a hindrance to thought reform. "How could you not harbor hard feelings against the party with your professional husband denounced as an ultrarightist and committed to labor reform? So long as you have not made a clean break with him but remain on his side, you can never really appreciate what the party has been doing for you, or your husband for that matter. You must begin by laying bare your thoughts, or they will continue to poison your mind, which is very dangerous." She warned me darkly as if I were already on the slippery road to hell. She reiterated the formula "to cure the sickness and save the patient," which sounded all too familiar. But I also remembered a Chinese proverb: "Once bitten by a snake, one is terrified by the sight of a rope for three years." The ostracism I endured was not quite as rigid as that at the party school, but I remained in a social isolation that became part of my way of life.

Daily living also became a struggle for survival, with supplies getting scarce by the fall of 1959, the second year of the Great Leap Forward. Instead of leaping forward, the nation was paralyzed by an unprecedented famine following crop failures, which the party blamed on natural calamities but which the people knew resulted from the party's disastrous farm policies. To make matters worse, when Big Brother pressed for payments in goods not only for the factories built with Soviet "fraternal aid," but for the Soviet weapons and munitions for the Chinese Volunteers in Korea, the government did not hesitate to scour the land for foodstuffs to ship to Moscow. The grain ration per capita was cut from thirty-three to twenty-six pounds a month in the summer of 1959, averaging less than a pound a day. The staples supplied were dried sweet potato strips, sweet potato flour, corn flour, and sorghum flour. Rice and wheat flour were supplied in small quantities on national holidays only. As nutrition was out of the question, the daily concern was how to cook the less than one pound of starches to make it seem more filling. I tried one method publicized in the party papers after another, but was constantly gnawed by hunger all the same. The vegetable oil ration was cut from seven to three and a half ounces a month. Meat and eggs, at first rationed, gradually disappeared from our diet altogether. A black market began to flourish, but the prices were far beyond my means. I began to lose weight, look waxen, and feel weak. My mother-in-law returned to Beijing to live with Ningkun's sister when her diabetes became aggravated due to malnutrition.

* * *

With a full-time job and two underfed small children on my hands, I was forced to hire a nursemaid from a suburban village to care for Yimao and help with the housework. She cost me twenty-two yuan a month, nearly 40 percent of my pay. It was madness, but what else could I do? I felt committed to making the best of an impossible situation, and counted myself lucky that nothing worse had happened. The maid was my own age and also the mother of two small children. She had an honest peasant's face. We got along fine, perhaps because we had much in common. Several months went by smoothly. Then, one morning when I was at work, a phone call came from the college security asking me to go home right away. What now? Flustered, I hurried home. There I found a security man sitting at the small collapsible table in the outer room, the maid standing before him with her head bowed.

"What is the matter?" I asked in alarm.

"You ask her to tell you herself," the security man scoffed.

"Well, Little Gao?" I asked her.

Abruptly she turned around and threw herself on her knees at my feet.

"I am a sinner, Teacher Li," she burst out crying. "I have done you wrong. You have been like a sister to me, and I have done you wrong. I will never, never do it again. Kill me if you catch me at it again. Oh, Teacher Li, forgive me, save me, I beg you. You will forgive a poor peasant . . ."

I was confused and embarrassed. A social outcast myself, I winced at the sight of a distraught sister debasing herself at my feet for whatever aberration she had committed.

"Get up, Xiao Gao, please, and tell me what you have done," I pleaded with her, stretching out an arm to help her to her feet.

She cried even harder and became incoherent when she attempted to speak. The security man took over and told me that a college patrol had caught her passing my food and clothing over the college wall to her sister-in-law, who worked for another family. I had often thought of myself as a pauper, and here this young woman was stealing from me! The security man said since it was apparently her first offense, they would be lenient with her. But there would be no place for her on the college campus. A nice fix for me to be in! If I let her go now, what would I do with Yimao? If I didn't, I would be harboring a thief in my home. Oh God, why did this have to happen to me?

"If she goes now, I will have my daughter on my hands," I said to the security man finally. "I will keep her with me till I find a way out of this, if college security does not object."

"Your risk, Teacher Li," he concurred. "We will hold you responsible, though, if she is caught at it again."

When the security man was gone, I made her wash her face and then sit next to me on the single bed. I couldn't decide what to say to her. Didn't I have trouble enough without her adding to it? Why didn't she tell me if she really needed something? Poor as I was, I would be willing to do whatever I could to meet her needs. Instead she made life even more difficult for me. Now I had to drive home to her what a mortal sin stealing is and how she should turn over a new leaf before she sank deeper and deeper. But then wouldn't I be judging her too harshly? And what right had I to judge her at all? Just because this uneducated peasant woman happened to have taken a few of my things, which would have been worthless under normal circumstances? No, I had to think for her. She had helped me with the baby and the housework and kept me company when I was lonely. It was my turn to help her now that she had run into some difficulty.

"Don't be so emotional, Xiao Gao. You have made a bad mistake, and you can't undo it. Tears won't wash it away. But it's not all that heinous either. The times are hard and people are liable to be tempted. I'm not going to hold it against you, because I have known you to be a nice person. Now you mustn't hold it against yourself. That's what's important, you hear? The college won't let you stay, and I don't think it would be good for you to stay on anyway. You may not want to go home because you will lose twenty-two yuan a month, but you will have your husband and children with you. That's more than I can say for myself. And you will grow stronger from what you learned this time. Stay with me till I decide what to do. And don't carry that on your mind, you hear? We will remain sisters."

She burst out crying again. I patted her softly on the back.

"Stop it, Xiao Gao, or I'll be really mad at you. I must go back to work now. The home is still in your hands. Kiss Yimao for me when she wakes up."

The dilemma weighed heavily on me. It often kept me awake at night. What was I to do? Xiao Gao had to go, but I winced at the idea of starting all over again with another maid. A maid was a luxury I could not afford. I had to save on food in order to pay her wages. At each meal, I always let Yiding have his fill before I would touch a bite. Yimao was fed rice gruel, which took up nearly all of our rice ration. As cow milk was one of the perks for high officials only, I scoured the grocery stores for milk powder for her, though I knew the milk powders for sale were mostly sugar and other nondairy ingredients. My face and ankles showed clear signs of edema, and my menses had stopped. I knew I could not cope any longer.

Around the time of the Lunar New Year, after debating with myself over and over again through countless sleepless nights, I reluctantly decided to part with Yimao and place her in my mother's charge in Tianjin. She had not yet seen her father, and now the nineteen-month-old daughter was to be torn away from her mother!

If life was so hard for us at home, how much harder it must be for Ningkun at the camp in the wilderness!

I dreaded the prospect taking the slow night train to Tianjin with two small children at the worst time of the year. Traveling had once meant pleasure and adventure for me, but now it was like moving through a series of nightmares. The trains were always crowded, but they would be much worse during the Lunar New Year holidays. Before going home for good, the maid accompanied us to the train station. I had warned her against crying, but she cried anyway and bought the children a small packet of hard candy each. After standing in the smoke-filled waiting room for nearly an hour, we were finally jostled by people around us onto the platform. With Yimao in my left arm and Yiding holding my right hand, I climbed into a hard-seat coach that was already full, with the maid pushing me from behind. There were people sitting on the floor in the aisle already. I thought I had better do the same before the space was all taken up. I held Yimao in my arms and made Yiding sit next to me on the floor. The children fell asleep, to my great relief, and I soon dozed off myself. Early in the morning we got off at Bengbu to change trains for Tianjin. The waiting room was a mess, jammed with people and their bags, baskets, shoulder poles, chickens and ducks, vegetables, and whatnot, and stinking with cigarette smoke.

With great difficulty, I managed to find a spot for our bags in the overcrowded room. Turning to Yiding, I said, "You and Yimao sit on the bags. Mama must go and line up for a ticket. You stay where you are and keep an eye on Yimao. You are a big brother now. Don't move, either of you!" Yiding nodded and smiled. It took me an hour to get the ticket. When I came back, I found Yiding sitting on the bags in a daze and Yimao gone. In alarm, I shook Yiding roughly. "Where is sister, Dingding?" He looked frightened. "I don't know. I fell asleep. When I woke up, sis was gone!" I said to him quickly, "Don't be scared, Dingding darling. Stay where you are, don't you move. Be a good boy now. Mama will go and look for sister." But I was scared myself, stories of child kidnapping suddenly surging up from the back of my mind. Picking my way through people sitting or lying on the floor and their baggage, I covered the entire room, from one end to the other, yelling frantically as I went, "Maomao, Maomao, where are you? Mama looking for you! Come to Mama, Maomao! Maomao!" There was no response, no sight of my baby. I was getting panicky. Then it occurred to me that I had not looked in the corners of the large room. I scurried from one corner to another, and when I approached the last corner, I saw my baby huddled up on the filthy concrete floor. She was sobbing and crying "Mama, Mama!" I tripped over several people in my rush to reach her. "Maomao, Maomao, Mama is here! Don't cry, don't cry!" When I had her in my arms, it was I who burst into tears. I hugged her and kissed her with all my might. Only then did I see she was without her cotton-padded overcoat. "Where's your coat, Maomao?" I asked in alarm. "I don't know, I don't know," she cried. "Never mind now, don't cry, darling!" I hugged her more closely. Yiding jumped up to greet us, overjoyed to see his lost sister found. We were the last to get on the train, and of course there were no seats left, but I didn't mind so much with my baby once more safe in my arms.

Mother was greatly surprised to see me and the grandchildren again. When I told her why I was making the trip, she broke down. "Poor Yikai, how could you take so much! Of course, you did right to bring Yimao to

Mother. Where else should you go? What is a mother good for? But you'll miss her, I'm afraid."

She was right. I knew I would miss my baby. But I was thankful that she had such a loving Grandma to go to.

Eight

DEATH BY STARVATION, 1960-61

1

AFTER THREE DAYS AND THREE NIGHTS ON A SLOW TRAIN, WE ARRIVED AT THE small Chadian station on the morning of October 26, 1960. Then we walked six miles of rough road to the prison, with our bedrolls on our backs and our bags in our hands, weary but full of expectations. We hoped that Qinghe State Farm's close proximity to the national capital would bring more humane treatment and better food.

The first thing we saw was a castlelike monstrosity sitting in the middle of desolate fields with barbed wire atop forbidding gray walls. We were taken into the monstrosity by sour-faced officers, through an entrance guarded by several soldiers holding rifles fixed with bayonets. Above them in the turrets were other soldiers holding submachine guns. Once inside, we were ordered to sit on the ground in rows to hear a report from the warden of the Third Branch Farm for rightists and juvenile delinquents under corrective education. He said the purpose of our relocation was to speed up our forced reform. Laying stress on the observance of discipline, he warned against any attempt to escape.

"Any of you who makes an attempted escape will face severe penal punishment, although we don't believe any such attempt can possibly succeed," he warned. "You can only leave the compound when escorted by an officer or with explicit written authorization. The guards will shoot at anyone seeking to flee the compound. You saw the barbed wire on top of the high walls as you came in, didn't you? The wire is electrified. No use pitting your flesh and blood against electrified wire. If you should manage to sneak out, there are mounted guards patrolling the walls twenty-four hours a day. They will shoot any escapee on sight. You're educated men,

I don't expect any such foolishness from you. But I must make things clear to you from the very beginning."

I had no wish to escape, but I certainly found it hard to get used to the idea of being incarcerated in such a heavily guarded prison. Didn't they say over and over again that we were not convicts? Didn't he say we were educated men incapable of escaping? And here we were confined in regular cells inside a formidable prison. I remembered almost with nostalgia the camp at Lake Xingkai, where there were no guards in sight, let alone rifles fixed with bayonets. And in striking contrast to this gray walled prison was the serene lake itself, on the shores of which I had strolled freely on a biweekly or triweekly Sunday. I came to realize, however, that the un-guarded freedom of those days was nothing but an illusion. Guards were dispensed with there only because the swamps around the camp were more deadly than armed soldiers. So long as I was a de facto prisoner, I reasoned, I might as well enjoy all the benefits of a regular prisoner under proletarian dictatorship, lest I be lulled into forgetting the grim reality. The more rigorous the surveillance, the more freely would my spirit soar.

In the morning we would march out of the compound under the watchful eyes of the guards and their bayonets, on our way to the fields for menial labor. The officer on duty gave the number of the men he was taking out to the guard leader, who counted the heads one by one. The same routine was repeated when we were taken back after the day's labor. Political study, or rather denunciation, took up the evening. The officers wore stern expressions all the time, as if to personify the proletarian dictator-ship. None of them remotely resembled Captain Li, who was a poor personification of the system. Now I lived and felt keenly the life of a socialist prisoner.

Before our relocation, I had already had an inkling that all was not well in the socialist state, but I had no idea how far things had gone. On the day of our arrival we had looked forward to the decent meal usually given to new arrivals. But what we got to eat was a clear soup of sliced turnips and sweet potatoes. As there was no trace of oil, there was no need to wash our basins after we ate. Some relished the sweet potatoes, because they were not grown in the cold Northeast. Others thought the kitchen had had no time to prepare a real meal for us, but it would come in due course. The same thing was served in the evening and the next two days, and we were fed twice instead of three times a day. On the fourth day the sweet potatoes disappeared from the soup and turnip leaves were added. We began to feel hungry all the time, but went on laboring in the fields as usual.

One day our job was to harvest acres of celery cabbage and load the produce onto trucks heading for Beijing. When every single head of cabbage had been loaded, the officer on duty ordered us to pick up the loose outer leaves that lay in the fields. "What for?" I asked timidly. "Your food for tomorrow" was the answer. So we put the leaves in wicker baskets and were ready to take them to the kitchen. "Come back here," the officer called. "Why have you not picked up the rest, the dried ones?" Bewildered, I asked again, "What for?" The officer answered in a knowing voice, "Your food for the spring." My heart sank but my hands followed the order.

Food, or rather the lack of it, became an obsession. The inmates talked constantly about the good food they had once eaten, raved about delicious dishes in detail, and swapped recipes. They compared notes on how the gnawing hunger was ravaging their insides and turning them into shameless gluttons for imaginary feasts. Meanwhile, the daily fare went from bad to worse. In the end, real food disappeared altogether and we were fed food substitutes. The regular staple was either gruel or a steamed bun prepared with dried cabbage leaves and a flour made of ground corn roots, which was said to contain 10 percent starch. We had no way of telling how much nutrition there was in the substitutes, but we soon had gruesome bloody excretory problems. One young Russian instructor nearly died of intestinal obstruction following protracted constipation.

For Sunday dinner we were fed dried sweet potato strips, one pound per head. As we lived and ate in squads, our squad leader, with the help of a former specialist in making precision instruments, improvised a steelyard and weighed with great care each portion of this precious food to make sure everyone got his fair share. All eyes were fixed on him and the balance while he carried out the operation, and no one was allowed to eat till the operation was completed. Among the sweet potato strips there were usually some that had gone bad, and it was tough luck if you got them. One day I got a few strips in my portion that were just too much for my stomach. I reluctantly dumped them in the open ditch that the inmates used as a latrine at night. One of the inmates, an ex-Communist, immediately jumped into the ditch and picked them up. Just as he was putting them into his mouth, an officer walked up and shot at him, "Throw them away, you're shameless! And you were a party member!" The man answered, "But I am hungry! Hungry!" He went on munching the strips till he finished. At the evening political study session, I was criticized for wasting good food and he for vilifying the socialist system. The only response he made was, "But I am hungry! Hungry!" Other hungry inmates began to look for new sources of food. One caught a field mouse and cooked it over a fire that he made between two bricks while the officer on duty was not looking. Another caught a snake and shared it with a cook, who turned it into a rich dish in the kitchen.

Lacking in imagination or ingenuity in developing unorthodox food resources, I was the first to come down with a serious case of edema. I became emaciated, my ankles swelled, and my legs got so weak that I often fell while walking to the fields for forced labor. I did not know what I looked like, as there were no mirrors around, but I could tell from the ghastly looks of the other inmates that I must have been quite a sight. Before long I was put on the sick list and given a "humanitarian" food supplement. Each evening I went to the kitchen to receive a bowl of soup made of a piglet that had starved to death on the prison pig farm and a paper bag of wheat bran. I became the envy of the other inmates. My good fortune, however, did not last long, because the supply of sick piglets and wheat bran ran out. More inmates came down with edema, but it was too late for them to share my brief good fortune.

2

ALTHOUGH NEITHER THE PAPERS NOR THE OFFICERS TALKED ABOUT IT, IT WAS common knowledge even at the isolated prison that the land was in the throes of a disastrous famine following the fiasco of the Great Leap Forward. The seriousness of the situation was first acknowledged in a special report by the warden to the inmates. He began by dwelling on the correctness of the Three Red Banners—namely, the party's General Line, the Great Leap Forward, and the People's Commune—and cited figures to substantiate their splendid achievements. Then he blamed the famine on crop failures caused by climatic caprices alone, denying any errors on the part of the party or the government. Finally he announced a new measure in keeping with the party's revolutionary humanitarianism, acting on orders from the capital. In the past food parcels for inmates were strictly forbidden because they were deemed bad for their thought reform. Now, under the new circumstances, family members or relatives would be allowed to hand deliver food parcels to inmates, and inmates themselves might write home for food parcels. A new measure indeed! A government that could no longer feed its prisoners was turning them into a charge of their families while keeping them at forced labor in prison!

The first fruits of revolutionary humanitarianism turned up within a week of the pronouncement, in the form of wheat-flour pancakes hand delivered to a former high school teacher by his wife. All the other inmates followed his every bite with hungry eyes while he munched on the incredible delicacies. I had not written Yikai about the latest manifestation of revolutionary humanitarianism. She was so far away, and I did not want to worry her with my plight. But the sight of my fellow inmate savoring his pancakes made my mouth water. I started thinking perhaps I could ask Yikai's family in nearby Tianjin for help. To ask or not to ask, that's the question I turned over in my mind for another day. Wasn't it bad enough for them socially to have a pariah for a close relation, let alone abetting him in jail with hand-delivered food parcels? Could I afford to get her family into possible guilt by association or to worry my loving mother-in-law with my plight? Then I recalled Yikai's last words on the eve of my arrest: Keep faith with life whatever happens. Now I saw that the question was really whether to be or not to be! In the desperate struggle for survival, I threw away all scruples and appealed to my good relatives for sustenance.

One morning shortly after New Year's Day when I was still too sick to take part in forced labor, I was called into the Visiting Room and found myself face-to-face with Yikai's Fourth Elder Brother. He had been trained as a biologist at the Chinese Catholic University in Beijing and assigned to a research laboratory in the northwestern city of Lanzhou upon graduation in 1952. During the 1955 Campaign to Uproot Hidden Counterrevolutionaries, he was suspected of being a hidden priest and subjected to protracted physical and mental torture until he collapsed with a serious nervous breakdown. The sick man was then sent home, in the winter of 1956, and spent some time with us while receiving treatment at a mental hospital in Beijing. This was our first meeting since then; he was still not well enough to go back to work. Fortunately for me, however, he was well enough to make the trip for a sick brother. The reception officer of the day stood by monitoring our transaction. My visitor opened his little handbag and brought out a dozen boiled eggs, a hunk of boiled mutton, and ten steamed wheat-flour rolls that my mother-in-law had made for me herself. When he brought out some salted turnips, the officer intervened. "No salted stuff. Bad for edema." My brother-in-law at once put them back in his bag, to my great disappointment. He told me all the food was bought on the black market at exorbitant prices, but they would try to get more food to me if revolutionary humanitarianism continued to hold good. Then when the officer was looking the other way, I reached into his bag, grabbed the salted turnips, and put them in my pocket. My brother-in-law, six feet tall but timid, was surprised by my daring.

"What's in your pocket there?" I asked.

"Just two steamed corn buns," he said.

"Hand them to me, quick," I ordered.

"That's my lunch," the honest man pleaded.

"You can eat when you get home. Hand them over now!"

I extorted the two golden corn buns out of his pocket. Poor man, for his good heart and his troubles, he had to walk the six miles of rough road to the station and ride the slow train home on an empty stomach! I felt like the snake in the Greek fable who bit the farmer to death after he had saved it from dying.

I went back to the cell a new member of the "haves" elite surrounded by the envious have-nots. I rationed myself on the precious supply of black-market food, but it was gone by the end of a week. I had no scruples in writing for more, "as if increase of appetite had grown / By what it fed on," as Hamlet put it. On the Lunar New Year's Day in early February, I was surprised to see my aged stepmother come, escorted by Yikai's Second Elder Brother, a high school teacher in Tianjin. They brought me two large traveling bags filled with black-market food, which must have made their six-mile trek to the prison on foot unbearable. I was allowed to spend the night with them in the kindergarten for the children of officers and ex-convicts, outside the prison walls. As I was too weak to carry my own bedroll from the cell to the "hostel," a young officer, newly demobilized and reassigned to prison duty, carried it on his shoulder for me. On the way he remarked civilly, "It wasn't easy for the old lady to make it. You should ask her to spend a couple more days with you. It's the Lunar New Year, after all." I had already been touched by his ungrudging help to a prisoner, and now I was astonished by his simple sentiments. Looking at his rosy peasant cheeks, I realized he was too new to his job to really know what he was doing. Another Captain Li perhaps? I thanked him with all my heart.

We shared the room with a number of other inmates and their visitors. Strangely, everyone chatted lightly as if they were on a regular Lunar New Year's Day visit. I did not notice a single tear shed. Not even a single tear! Perhaps the people were beyond tears and laughter? I was dry-eyed myself, though distraught at the sight of my sixty-six-year-old stepmother, who had walked the long rough road from the station, her bound feet hurting at every step and her diabetes futilely driving her to seek shelter in the treeless country so that she could urinate. This in a nation with an ancient civilization that respects age! She kept her feelings to herself, but gave me all the good news about my sister's family in Beijing, with whom she was staying. My sister had been assigned lighter manual labor because of her pregnancy and her husband recalled from Henan province, where he had been sent for manual labor as a rightist's spouse. Having heard countless stories of people starving to death in prison, Mother was glad to find me still walking. She squeezed herself between two women on the only kang in the room, and Second Brother and I put two square tables together to make a "double bed," in which we whispered to each other throughout the night. He told me about the aftermath of the disastrous Great Leap Forward and the sufferings of the common people. I told him about my forced reform in the wilderness and starvation in prison here. Feeling my body and limbs over and over again, he whispered "Nothing but skin and bones, nothing! We must hurry up and do more for you, before it is too late."

On May 1, my sister came from Beijing, big with child and weary from manual labor on a suburban farm for rightists. In the visitors' room, she found Yikai's First Brother on the same mission from Tianjin, and with him his fifteen-year-old son, Heping, or Peace. I remembered him as a very tough boy. But he broke down at the sight of his ghastly uncle, while my sister tried in vain to suppress her sobs. I put on a bold face and tried to cheer them up: "Come on, you didn't come all this way to cry! You should be happy to see I am still alive, and the food you have brought me here will help bring me back to health." I had to make two trips to carry the food parcels back to my cell, before seeing them turn and start on their trek back.

With plenty of food in my possession, I became the envy of the fellow inmates, especially those who remained have-nots. The families of some of them were in the provinces, and it would take them weeks to make their way to the prison, if they could come at all. Other families, having lost their breadwinners, had a hard time keeping themselves fed. Occasional food thefts were reported. I locked up all my foodstuffs in two big traveling bags and stacked them up behind my pillow. I rationed myself strictly, knowing neither how long I would be imprisoned nor how soon my relatives could come again, though I felt like a miser spending every penny only grudgingly. One day when I came back from laboring in the fields, I was dismayed to find the small padlock on one bag broken and a few food items missing. My first reaction was to report the theft to the officer. It would not be hard to catch the thief among the few have-nots who had been put on the sick list and excused from labor in the fields. On second thought, however, I said to myself, whoever he was, my poor fellow sufferer had as much right to survival as I did, and why couldn't he resort to the only recourse available to him? Furthermore, what mental struggles must he have suffered before stooping to petty theft? Had I been in his worn-out shoes, might I not have done the same thing or worse? After all, he had left most of my things untouched.

One of the have-nots was a young scholar of classical Chinese who slept on my right on the kang. One day he handed me a note written in his elegant calligraphy in the style of the great classical calligrapher Liu Gongquan. "I beg you to lend me one of your pancakes, professor. I solemnly promise to pay you back with double interest when my wife comes from Hunan province to bring me food from home." I hesitated, because I felt I had no right to be generous with the food, which represented the sacrifices my relatives were making to save my life. A second note contained the same message with a proverb added: "He who saves a man's life does a deed greater than building the Buddha a seven-story pagoda." My heart melted at his elegant Liu-style calligraphy. I had always admired and envied people who were expert at the Liu style, which I had imitated in vain in my school days. Such elegant calligraphy reduced to such abject circumstances! What had the nation come to, the nation that tirelessly flaunted its ancient culture! When the others were not looking, I handed Lao Liu a pancake. He gobbled it up in no time.

"You don't know how good it tasted, Lao Wu," he told me in his Hunan accent the next day when he was being removed to the cell set aside for the sick, whose continued presence in the regular cells the officers thought was demoralizing to the other inmates. "I'll repay you with double interest when my wife comes."

"No problem, you take care of yourself, Lao Liu," I said. "If you don't I'll have your IOUs mounted for a souvenir!"

"Not that, please," he pleaded with a weak smile. "If you really like my calligraphy, Lao Wu, I'll write you a scroll under happier circumstances."

"I'll hold you to it," I answered with a weak laugh.

3

WITH THE COMING OF SPRING, THE COUNTRY BEGAN TO LOOK FORWARD TO a better harvest and fewer deaths by starvation. I grew somewhat stronger on the expensive food from my relatives, but my health had been so undermined that I failed to show signs of a quick recovery. My legs remained weak and swollen, and I often fell from dizziness. One day I got permission to go and see a doctor of traditional Chinese medicine at the prison outpatient service. The doctor was a convict himself. After listening to my complaints, he felt my pulse and looked at my tongue.

"It takes more than one cold day for the river to freeze three feet deep." He intoned the proverb with a shake of his head. "I am surprised you are still as well as you are. Even though you've had some good food, as you said, your delicate system can no longer function properly to absorb nutrients. It takes more than one warm day to have the frozen river thaw and melt and flow again. It takes time, and great care. I don't mean to alarm you, anything can happen to anyone under the circumstances. I have seen so much happening, alas! You are a professor, you know what I mean. Take great care."

I was not alarmed, but I certainly found no comfort in what he said.

*   *   *

Then, one day in May, I was called into the room of the officer in charge of our cell and told to take two other inmates with me and go to an outlying plot of the farm to "carry out a task." The task was to dig a pit six feet long, two feet wide, and three feet deep. The officer didn't tell us what the pit was for; it was their habit to keep us in blind obedience.

During the long walk across barren fields, spring was very much in the air, yet there were little signs of life around us. It didn't take the three of us long to do the job. By the time we finished digging, we saw a cart drawn by a scrawny horse moving slowly in our direction. As the cart drew closer, I saw a pair of skinny feet sticking out from under one end of a dirty straw mat. A dead man! When the cart drove up to our pit, the ex-convict driver jumped off and mumbled an order: "Shove him in and cover him up. Be quick about it. No nonsense now!" I removed the mat and I saw to my horror a pair of sunken eyes I recognized. I shuddered, my weak legs began to shake. We gave Lao Liu a quick burial with our spades and shovels. The driver stuck into the newly filled pit a crude wooden marker that bore the number 61301 in black paint. He offered us a lift on his cart, but we all preferred to walk. On the way back, I was tormented by the graveyard scene in *Hamlet*. I wished I had been as cavalier about death as the grave digger was. But then, I told myself in extenuation, he has been at it thirty years, while this was only my first job. In the evening I went to render a report to the officer, as was required.

"The assignment was carried out, officer," I said with a sense of mission accomplished.

"How many pits did you dig?" he demanded.

"One," I replied truthfully, recalling he had not ordered more than one.

"One?" he shot back. "Just one? How many can sleep in one, I ask you? Would you like to share one with another body? You useless bookworm! I should have known better than to give you this soft job. Go back and write a self-criticism."

I didn't mind the homework, but the incident set me thinking. The dead man had been an athlete in college and always considered a sturdy fellow. If he could drop off like that, how did I know I wouldn't be next?

There had been many deaths by starvation in the prison, but death had never come so close to me. I got panicky. I didn't want to go away without seeing Yukai, but I didn't want to upset her either. I debated with myself all night and all day. Should I or shouldn't I ask her to come visit me? I had to: after more than three years of separation, this meeting would mean so much to both of us, now that death was hovering over me. I also wanted so much to see my son again, and my daughter at least once. But would it be really good for her or the children? Wouldn't it be easier for them if they never saw me again? Perhaps I was too selfish. Wouldn't I get her into even deeper political trouble by asking her to come? No, I couldn't do it. Why should I add to her already heavy burden? But, then, wouldn't she blame me if I kept her in the dark till it was too late? Did I have the right to keep her out of my life at this critical juncture? For better or for worse, in sickness and in health! Finally I threw discretion to the winds and sent her an SOS for "possibly a last meeting."

Nine

PRISON VISITS, 1961

Narrated by Li Yikai

1

WHEN NINGKUN WAS TRANSFERRED TO QINGHE STATE FARM, I HAD HOPED IT was a turn for the better, though no explanation was given for the mass relocation. In any case, he was now closer to me, though still hundreds of miles away. Mail was faster. Ningkun wrote twice a month, as was allowed him, short notes telling me he was well and I was not to worry. How could I not worry? I was suffering from edema myself and even little Yiding showed signs of malnutrition. What then could he possibly live on in prison? I knew there was no use worrying, yet my misgivings often kept me awake at night, and the nights were long.

The New Year came, bringing me nothing new except a letter from Fourth Brother, telling me about his visit to Ningkun. "He was as well as could be expected," he wrote. "Not too well, but who is well nowadays? Nothing to worry about. We'll see that more food is sent to him by and by."

In February, I spent another lonely Lunar New Year's Eve with little Yiding. For the great national holiday, we were allowed one pound of wheat flour, half a pound of fat pork, and a small head of celery cabbage. To cheer the poor child a little, I chopped the pork and outer leaves of the cabbage into stuffing for dumplings, traditional food for the occasion. We kept the little heart of the cabbage in a bowl of water to give the drab rooms a little life. It did my heart good to see my boy eat the dumplings with such relish. Then, suddenly, he asked, "Mama, do you think Papa is also eating dumplings tonight?" I had my doubts, but I said, "I hope so. Everybody in Tianjin does, as is the custom." Oh why didn't they release him when they could no longer feed him? I had vaguely hoped to go and visit him when the winter vacation came. But when it was due to begin, I was told to spend "a revolutionary Spring Festival" where I was. A few days later, a letter came from Second Brother, telling me about his accompanying my mother-in-law on a visit to Ningkun. "He had edema, but who didn't? He would surely grow stronger with the coming of spring and the good food that has been sent him. Nothing to worry about!" On May 1, First Brother and Ningkun's sister both went to visit him with more food parcels. With all the good food sent him already, he might be able to cope with his lot. Hopefully I could go and visit him when the summer vacation began. Keep hoping, I told myself over and over.

Then one afternoon in late May, a letter came from Ningkun, even shorter than usual, and terrifying:

> Yikai:
> I'm critically ill. Please come at once for possibly a last meeting.
> Ningkun.

What had happened? I thought he was doing all right, as my brothers reassured me. Had I been living in a fool's paradise? I was panic-stricken. After reading the short message over and over again, I got up from my typewriter and asked the head typist for a few minutes' leave.

"What for? Something has happened?" Little Hot Pepper asked coldly.

"Yes, my husband is critically ill. I must see the party secretary at once and ask for leave to go and see him."

"Well, I don't think it's exactly right to be so concerned about a rightist, and an ultrarightist at that. It's a political mistake to do so. How do you know he is really ill? Don't we all fall ill from time to time?"

"No, this is different. I am sorry, I must go now," I said meekly.

"Suit yourself then, but it's not good for you to loaf around during office hours, Comrade Li Yikai. You should know that."

I swallowed the veiled threat of another session of biting criticism and rushed out. I found the party secretary, a former Army colonel, in his office and showed him the letter in silence.

"How do you know he is as ill as he says?" he demanded in his military voice.

"Party Secretary," I replied as calmly as I could under the circumstances. "My husband has been away for more than three years now. In all his letters before, he always said he was well and asked me not to worry. He would have never worried me unless it was absolutely urgent. I know him too well. Furthermore, as you know, all his letters are censored. The officers would not have let them through if he had said anything that wasn't quite right. Please give me leave to go and see him, perhaps for the last time."

"Don't be sentimental, Li Yikai." He began to raise his voice. "I can't do it. You are a typist. You have plenty of work to do. All the revolutionary comrades in the department are hard at work, and you want to take off to visit your ultrarightist husband? True, you're still his wife, but you're also still a government worker. You must take a firm proletarian stand and draw a clear line of demarcation from your rightist husband. It's a matter of principle. No, no, I can't grant you leave of absence. That's final, Comrade Li Yikai."

He had put me in my place. I was not surprised. I was not angry. Just distressed. When I walked back into the office, I was relieved to find that Hot Pepper had already gone home. With a heavy heart I went home too. Yiding gave me the usual greeting, "Mama, I'm hungry!" It always hurt me to hear him say that, and now it hurt even more. I quickly cooked some sweet potato gruel on our little briquet stove. Yiding gobbled it up with relish. When he saw I wasn't eating, the child asked, "What's the matter with you, Mama? Aren't you hungry? I'm always hungry."

"Eat more then, darling. I am not. Your papa is very ill. And they won't let me go to see him . . ." I could not go on.

"But we must, Mama. Papa must miss us when he is so ill. Why won't they let you? Why can't you go and ask them again? Why don't you, eh, Mama? I want to go and see Big Papa too!"

Then he left the table and disappeared into the bedroom. When he came back, he had in his little hand a large photo of Ningkun holding the child in his arms, taken shortly before he was sent away.

"See," Yiding said, pointing to his father, "Papa is looking at me!"

The child was right. I mustn't give up so easily. When you had lived in fear so long, cowering almost became second nature. But this was a moment of life and death. I must put up a fight.

After putting Yiding to bed, I came out of our bleak little dorm and crossed the campus to the garden house of the party secretary. When I entered his brightly lit sitting room, I found the husband of Little Hot Pepper visiting there with his son, who was the same age as my Yiding. The father was playing with the son, alternately tossing him up in the air and carrying him piggyback. The child and the father were both laughing happily. I remained standing, speechless. The party secretary first lit a cigarette and then turned to me.

"What is it now, Li Yikai?" he began impatiently. "Haven't I told you already, you can *not* go to Qinghe Farm to see your husband. It is politically wrong. Our party practices revolutionary humanitarianism. Even the Japanese prisoners of war and Nationalist captives were given humanitarian treatment. Why should you worry about your husband? He has been fine all these years, hasn't he? He has not died, has he?"

"I hope not."

"There you are. Which goes to show he has received humanitarian treatment. If he is really ill, the farm leadership will surely give him necessary medical care in accordance with the party's policies. What more do you want? You are not a doctor, are you? What's the use of your going, even if he were ill, eh?"

"Party Secretary," I persisted. "I have never asked for a day's leave since I came to work in the department more than two years ago. Now that my husband is dying, I beg you to grant me a leave of absence so I can go and see him, perhaps for the last time. He may deserve what he gets as a rightist, but our children are surely innocent. Yiding, the same age as Little Ming here, hasn't seen his father for more than three years now. And our daughter Yimao was born when he was already in the detention center. All I am asking of you is just a few days' leave, so that we can all see him. I'll come back as soon as I can and make up for lost time. I hope my request is not in contradiction with revolutionary humanitarianism."

"You are certainly a very stubborn woman, Comrade Li Yikai." He sounded disgusted. "What am I to do with you? All right, I grant you a week's leave. You must come back on time. You need to submit a written application for official approval in the morning. You had better go home now."

The laughter of the happy child kept ringing in my ears on my solitary walk home in the darkness. "If only Ningkun would live to play with our children too!" I prayed. When I got home, I found Yiding lying in bed wide awake. I threw myself on him and hugged him again and again. I had to fight back my tears before telling him:

"Yiding darling, we are going to see Papa! Thank you for telling me to go and ask again. I don't know why, but Mama is just plain slow at times. We got seven days!"

My child sprang up from the bed and clasped me by the neck. "Mama, I'm so happy! I'm going to see Big Papa at last! When are we leaving, Mama?"

"Tomorrow, I hope. I must go to the office in the morning to wind up my work and hand in a written application. Then I must go to the train station in town to line up for a ticket. You just go to the kindergarten as usual. I will come to pick you up and ask your teacher for your leave. Now go to sleep at once. You won't be able to sleep much sitting up on the train all night. And Mama must get our things ready for the trip."

2

TWO DAYS LATER, I WALKED INTO OUR FAMILY'S HOME IN TIANJIN WITH Yiding, to the great surprise of my mother and the whole family. I showed them the note from Ningkun, which at once brought tears to Mother's eyes. I regretted my rashness, for too much crying over too many misfortunes in the family had already ruined her eyes. But she quickly wiped away her tears and began to speak in her usual comforting voice.

"How could that be? Your brothers have sent him quite a bit of good food. He ought to be getting better by now. How could this be? It may not be that bad. There may be some mistake. Don't worry, Yikai."

I soon learned from my brothers that Ningkun had been suffering from a very serious case of edema as a natural result of prolonged malnutrition. They did not think it useful or wise to alarm me, although they were quite distressed themselves. Mother wouldn't have allowed it, anyway. They had been hoping the expensive black-market food would gradually bring him back to health. Why then the letter of distress? I could hardly wait to see him. My First Elder Brother warned me, "When we visited him on May Day, Ningkun still looked pretty bad. His sister broke down at the sight of him and even my son Heping cried with her. You'll be going by yourself and I know it will be more than you can take. But you mustn't give away to emotions . . ." He was breaking down himself.

I tried to put his mind at ease. "I promise to rise to the occasion, First Brother," I said. Ever since the premature death of Father a quarter of a century before, First Brother had watched over his seven younger siblings through weal and woe, mostly woe. My sorrows were the latest addition to the burden he carried with such selfless care, never complaining.

Though still sore from sitting up all night on the train, I took the early morning local to Chadian the day after my arrival in Tianjin, leaving Yiding in the care of my mother, who had risen early to make my breakfast. As I was leaving in the half-darkness, she handed me a traveling bag that she had packed with more black-market food for Ningkun. Then she said quietly, "Tell him from Mother to bear it patiently. Good men suffer. Go now, it will be good for you both."

The sun was up when I got off the local train at the small Chadian station. I went into the bleak waiting room to look for the place where I was to get permission to visit the farm. I found a window with a sign in bold letters reading VISITORS TO QINGHE FARM PRISONERS REGISTER HERE. There were already a few women lining up at the window. I stood behind an unkempt, haggard middle-aged woman wearing an old gray man's Mao jacket covered with patches. She had a rusty big shovel in her hand. Why the shovel? A work tool for her man? Why no food bag? After a while, I stammered out a question: "What is that for, the shovel, sister?"

"I don't mind telling you, sister, since you are also going to the same place," she replied naturally. "Yesterday I received a notice from the farm. It says my rightist husband is dead and I can come and bury him. That's what the shovel is for, to bury my dead man. My man is dead, see?"

I noticed a sickly boy in tattered grayish shorts and worn-out black plastic sandals standing close to her. "Is this your son, sister?"

"Oh yes, and the dead man's son too. He is only ten. No food, no clothes, no schooling. When a man is dead, he is dead. Isn't that so, sister? But what will happen to the two of us now?"

"I am sorry," I said helplessly.

"He's dead, he is at peace now. No need to be sorry for him. He no longer needs food. But what will we two, mother and son, do for a living?" After a pause, she asked me, "Is your man a rightist too? You look like an intellectual yourself."

"Yes, I am afraid he is."

"I hope *he* is all right?"

"I hope so," I said weakly, but the shovel made me wince. It had been nearly two weeks since Ningkun wrote. Was I too late? Would I need a shovel too? I shivered at the horrid thought.

After filling out the forms, I left the waiting room with the woman and her son and her shovel. The three of us, two mothers and a son, took to the six-mile-long rough road leading to the prison farm. I learned it was her first visit too. He had written home asking for food. He should have known better. Where was she to find the money to buy food for him? He had been a primary-school teacher earning very low wages, until he was labeled a rightist because he had said the party leader at his school was too bossy. After he had been expelled and sent to prison, she took on odd jobs and earned barely enough to feed the boy and herself. When she answered her husband's last letter asking for food, she had to borrow the eight fen from her neighbor to buy a stamp. She had hoped he would come home one day and get his job back. "Anyway, no more letters to write from now on," she concluded, and there was no irony in her voice.

I looked away from her to keep my emotions down and found the surrounding country singularly desolate, although it was late spring. No trees, no birds, no wildflowers, not even green weeds. What a site for a prison farm! My musings were cut short by the fatherless boy's exclamation, "Look, Mama! What's over there?" In the distance I could make out a monstrous castlelike structure with a high gray wall topped by snakelike barbed wire. It looked more forbidding than the Forbidden City, which had always made me feel depressed. As we approached, I could see armed soldiers in the watchtowers. My heart froze at the sight of the bayonets fixed on the guards' rifles flashing in the morning sun. One of the guards motioned us to the little shed outside the monstrous structure, where a sign read VISITING ROOM. We went in and found several women sitting on unpainted rickety wooden benches. We joined them without a word. After I don't know how long, a man's head poked out of an inner room.

"You people are early," the man said in a loud voice. "What's the hurry? They won't be back from their labor in the fields till lunchtime. You must wait now."

"But I have no need to wait," my fellow traveler shot back at him almost with a touch of triumph, holding up her shovel. "See this? He won't come back to me no more, the hard-hearted man. I can go to him. So can his son here."

"Show me the death warrant." The man in uniform came out of the inner room and stretched out a hand to her. After he read it, he muttered, "Oh yes, you his wife?"

"What do you think I am here for if I am not? Where is he?"

"Well, you're a bit late, see? Bodies don't keep in this weather, see? He was buried last night. I will return his belongings to you by and by. Just wait."

"Why wait?" she asked impatiently. "I want to get out of this place as soon as I can."

"The officer in charge of the dead men's belongings is out to lunch. He won't be back until the visiting hours begin at one, you see? It won't be long now. What's the hurry anyway?"

As he turned back into the inner room, the woman burst out crying and wailing. "Oh, oh, you hard-hearted man, how could you do this to us? Oh, you hard-hearted man, how could you leave us, mother and son, in the world like this? You hard-hearted wretch, oh, oh, oh! . . ." The boy sobbed quietly. All the other women in the room dropped their heads.

I tried to soothe her by patting her lightly on the back. Then I said gently, "There, there, sister. It's a hot day, you must take care of yourself, now that . . ."

"Now that he is gone, and what am I . . ." She started wailing again.

After a while, another man in uniform came out of the inner room carrying a bundle in his hand. He dropped it at the feet of the wailing woman and said matter-of-factly, "Come on now, no use carrying on like this. He was not the only one. We buried five last night. No food, no life, that's all. Go home now and start something new."

"Where is he buried?" she asked. "Can't we go and take a look?"

"What's the use? Take the child home now before you miss the train."

"The train, yes, the train, we haven't even got enough for the fare."

"Now, I don't know what to do about that, sorry." He disappeared into his office. I took out a couple of one-yuan bills and squeezed them into her palm. When she grabbed me by the hand, I said quickly, "Go home now, sister. You've had enough for one day. And your boy is very tired. Go now please, no need to say anything." I pushed gently at her back. She muttered, "Good-bye now. Better luck to you, sister."

As I watched the bereaved mother and son drag their tired feet down the long rough road from which they had only just come, the unused shovel on her shoulder and the dead man's bundle dangling on her back, I prayed for the dead and the living in silence and felt almost reconciled to my own lot. I could still hope anyway. All at once I felt tired, so very tired. I dozed off on my bench for a while. I was roused by footsteps approaching the Visiting Room and I looked up to see a dozen men in rags standing at the door. The officer in the inner room came out and stepped over to the door. He began to address the human figures in rags in a military voice.

"Listen to what I say, you lot. Your families are here to visit with you. They have brought you food. They are not doing this to satisfy your corrupt bourgeois appetites, but to help you reform yourselves thoroughly. We allow this because it's our party's policy to practice revolutionary humanitarianism. You must make greater efforts to turn over a new leaf, to repay the leniency of the party and the government, and also to repay your families for their help. Now I'll call your names. Each of you is allowed fifteen minutes with your family, but mind what you say. One at a time. Wu Ningkun! . . ."

The name gave me a jolt. I had been scanning the faces of the men at the door, but I could not tell which man was Ningkun. They all looked alike in their muddy rags and ghastly pallor. Then I saw Ningkun stepping unsteadily into the room. It was Ningkun all right, but he had changed drastically. How could this be the same man who had been taken away that spring afternoon only three years before? He tried to smile at me, but stopped short. We were led by an officer into a small room along the wall. We stood about five feet apart facing each other, while the officer stood in between and to one side.

"You have fifteen minutes. No foolishness, or you'll be denied future visits," he announced in a voice of authority.

Now I noticed that Ningkun was carrying water in a green enamel rice bowl and that his hand was shaking. It was the same bowl I had sent him, but badly chipped. He stepped forward and stretched out his hand to me. "For you . . ." he muttered and bowed his head. The sight of water made me aware of my thirst. I had not had anything to drink all morning. My man had brought me the water of life! While gulping down the water, I saw his head was covered with an ugly stubble, sparse and sickly, like the withered grass on the grave mounds I had passed on the way. I had a momentary vision of his once well-groomed shining black hair. His ears were thin and waxy, as if they were nothing but two layers of skin pressed together. When he looked up again, I saw his swollen face wore a deathly pallor and his once sparkling eyes were dull and hollow. Tears welled up in my eyes, but I kept them back because I did not want to give the officer the satisfaction of seeing me break down. I had thought I would have so much to say to him. It had been such a long, long time, and now we were wasting our precious minutes.

Ningkun spoke first. "Sorry to have made you come all this way. How are you? And Yiding and Yimao?"

"We're all fine. I have left the two little ones with Mother. We all miss you and hope you get well soon."

"I'm much better now, thanks to the care of the party . . ."

"You are very ill, Ningkun, we must . . ." I began in desperation, but my mind was a tangled skein. "I hear there is a place where we can spend the night together. I must ask for permission from the officer on duty."

Just then a burly officer stalked into the room, dragging behind him a small teenage boy in rags. The big man fell all over the youngster with cuffs and kicks, yelling at the top of his voice, "You thief, you son-of-a-bitch! You dare to steal under my nose? I'll show you, I'll show you, you damned thief!" The boy rolled on the floor, crying and shrieking, "You're killing me, killing me, oh! oh! . . ."

I was scared, wondering if Ningkun had been given the same rough treatment. As if reading my thoughts, our officer turned to me and remarked, "One of the juvenile delinquents under corrective education, a very bad lot. We have to combine punishment with education. Your time is up. Go to the fields now, Wu Ningkun!" Before I knew what was happening, Ningkun was gone. I left the room with the empty chipped enamel bowl in my hand.

I did get permission to spend the night with Ningkun, not by ourselves, but together with other visitors and their men, in a big room in the kindergarten outside the prison walls. The prisoners were not allowed to join their visitors until late in the evening after they had finished their nightly political study—that is, sessions of criticism and self-confession of their bad deeds and thoughts during the day. During the long wait after supper in the dingy little kitchen for visitors, I heard sighs and murmurs from the women around me. I noticed they were all dressed in drab gray Mao jackets. They looked so sad that one might have thought they were all in mourning. No doubt I must have looked the same to them.

When the men finally came, Ningkun was not among them. Where was my man? I bombarded the other inmates with questions, but no one was able to give me an answer. One elderly inmate said ominously, "You can never tell in a place like this." I was alarmed. The men and the women made a hum around me, chattering, sighing, sobbing. How I envied them all! When I could not stand it any longer, I went out of the room to wait for him, hoping against hope. I paced the ground in circles, like an animal trapped in a cage. Around midnight, a guard on patrol passed and asked me what I was doing there by myself. I told him I had permission to visit with my husband but he had not turned up. "Too late now," the man said. "Who knows what has happened to him! Anything could happen to the fellows here nowadays . . . I don't know. You had better go in now. You'll find out in the morning."

In the room, I found the couples huddled up on the kang facing each other, packed like sardines in a tin. They were still chattering, sighing, sobbing. But how I envied them! I slipped into the little space my strange bedfellows had left for the two of us. A naked light bulb glared at me from the ceiling, reminding me of the bayonets flashing in the morning sun. The shabby bed mat made of thin bamboo strips kept pricking through my blouse and trousers, as if to remind me of my plight. When I shut my eyes, my mind was torn by fears. What on earth had happened to him? Had he already . . .? Would I never see him again? I tried to drive the maddening thoughts out of my mind, but my fellow traveler's big shovel haunted me like a specter.

I did not find out what happened to him until morning. According to the officer on duty who had given me permission to spend the night with Ningkun, my husband had been caught smuggling out his supper rations, two rolls of food substitutes, obviously to feed his wife, as he was coming out for the night.

"Violation of rules!" the man declared solemnly. "Caught red-handed!"

"But that doesn't make sense, officer," I reasoned with him gently. "I had my own supper in your kitchen for visitors. I wouldn't dream of touching his rations anyway. I brought him good food myself—"

"That's what he said. But evidence is evidence! So he was locked up in the guardhouse supperless instead."

"Just for carrying his own supper?" I gasped.

"They get locked up for lesser offenses. This is not a school or a dinner party, it's a prison, a reform unit. Severity is the rule. However, we are prepared to be lenient with your husband this time, considering you have come all the way from Hefei to visit him and you have not been able to spend time with him. When he is released from the guardhouse in an hour or two, I give him permission to spend a couple of hours with you. Revolutionary humanitarianism, you know. Just stick around."

Two hours passed before Ningkun walked up to me in front of the Visiting Room.

"Are you all right?" I asked anxiously.

"Don't be alarmed. Anything can happen in this place. I was kidnapped on my way out last night," he said with an amused smile. "I had privacy for a change, all by myself. I was upset only because I couldn't keep my date with you. You must have thought I had simply dropped dead, quite unceremoniously. Oh these petty despots who have us in their power!"

"The officer said you had been caught smuggling food out to feed me!"

"They knew it wasn't true. I just wanted to show you what they feed us here. Food that is not food!"

"Don't be upset now. How are you anyway? How have you been all these years? I couldn't tell from your short letters."

"Sorry I couldn't tell you anything in my letters. They have no right to inspect our mail, since even they say we are not legally convicts. But they read our mail, coming and going. Well, privacy is a Western concept anyway. I have not been able to find a proper Chinese translation for it. Luckily, we can perhaps have a little privacy today. The kindergarten janitor, Lao Wang, is a freed convict. He lives in that little hut over there, all by himself. He lets us use his room for private visits. For a consideration, of course."

We walked over to the little hut not far from the kindergarten. Ningkun knocked on the door and an emaciated old man with a goatee opened the door for us.

"Lao Wang, this is my wife," Ningkun said to him. "We'd like to spend a couple of hours here. Is it convenient for you?"

"No problem, I need to go and clean up the kindergarten anyway. Just make yourselves at home."

"Here, Lao Wang, my wife has brought me these dried persimmons," Ningkun said, taking out of his straw bag a small package and handing it to the old man. "I share them with you. Very sweet."

"I like dried persimmons all right. But I like real food better—cakes, pastry, steamed rolls, you know."

"I know, Lao Wang. Not this time, I'm sorry."

"Next time then. Good-bye."

I tried to be civil by thanking him for the use of the room.

"No use thanking me if you don't bring me some real food next time."

"Lao Wang is an honest fellow," Ningkun said with a laugh when the old man was gone. "The poor man has had a hard life. Five years in prison for something or other. When he was freed, he was not free to go. No family, no friends. Nobody feels sorry for him, he feels sorry for nobody. He expects food in return for the use of his room. Rather straightforward. A product of years of socialist prison life."

"I feel sorry for him. I will bring him some real food next time. But tell me about yourself. Oh, all these years!"

"It's a long story. I'm afraid it will take one thousand and one nights to tell, and we have only a couple of hours. But tell me about yourself and our kids first."

That opened the floodgate to tangled memories of the past three years, memories of the pangs of separation, of sleepless nights and gloomy days, of humiliations and insults, of watching the children grow far away from their father, of one thousand and one trifles of daily struggle for survival. After all these months of solitary living, how I longed to unload everything on the one man who would feel for me with all his heart! But how could I add to the burden of my loved one, who was already weighed down with so much suffering? So I told him I had been all right, working on the typewriter in daytime and spending the evenings and Sundays with Yiding. Yiding was a big boy now, nearly five and a half. He knew a dozen Tang poems by heart and could recite them without a hitch. Ningkun learned for the first time that I had left Yimao in Mother's care since the previous spring. She was very pretty and loved to sing and dance. She would be three in a few days. I said I had promised Yiding I'd bring him to see his papa.

"You don't have to, you know. Maybe he should learn to forget, you know . . ."

To change the subject, I asked him to tell me about himself. "How does this place compare with the other?"

"Well," he sighed. "We had naively hoped that this place, being under direct jurisdiction of the government of the capital city, would practice more humane, or rather a little less inhumane policies, give us a little better food and less harassment. Our life in the swampy wilderness was an unrelieved stretch of hard labor and gnawing hunger, swarms of bloody mosquitoes in summer and mortal cold in winter. But at least there was real food we grew ourselves, though neither good nor adequate. But here we get food substitutes and a guardhouse! One thing I liked about the Great Northern Wilderness was the heavy snow that buried everything, obliterating and oblivious. I wish I could forget!"

"You must have patience, Ningkun," I tried to console him. "Mother says for me to tell you from her you must bear it all with patience. You have done no wrong, she says, but good men suffer as always . . . Maybe they will let you out before too long, since feeding prisoners has become such a burden to the government? You can never tell."

"You can never tell is right. The ironic thing is that they keep telling us we rightists are legally not even convicted. We have not been tried or given a sentence. Thanks to the party's infinite leniency, we are treated as cases of 'contradictions among the people,' not as 'contradictions between ourselves and the enemy.' I can be released when I 'have thoroughly reformed myself through forced labor into a self-supporting laborer,' see? And that could be tomorrow or forever! It will all be a matter of capricious party policies! My life, our lives, are in their hands. Heads, life; tails, death!" After a pause, he added with a weak smile, "Indeed, I must be patient, Yikai . . ."

I didn't know what to say. I could not find a word of comfort for my long-suffering husband.

"I must have given you a fright when you first saw me." He smiled at me with faint amusement. "I knew I looked like a ghost. I don't need a mirror to tell me that. The ghastly looks of my fellow rightists are so many mirrors."

"I'm glad I came and saw for myself how ill you are."

"It's good that you came. I feel better already. You're my seventh visitor. The fellow inmates envy me my food parcels, but they envy me even more the fact that my family and relatives are standing by me in my trial and sorrow. Even as you used to say, 'Man does not live by bread alone.' How true, even when bread does mean life or death! In a moment of despair, I cried out in my heart, What have I done unto you, my people, that you throw me to the wolves? There were live hungry wolves, plenty of them, in the Wilderness. Then I remembered the people had nothing to do with my misfortune. What right have I to blame the people? What use have I been to the people? Then I reproached myself with indulging in self-pity. Haven't my family and relatives all suffered for my sake? Haven't they rushed to my rescue with food and love the moment they heard I was being starved to death?"

"You shouldn't reproach yourself like this. You are being wronged. Your family and relatives will all feel more than rewarded if you just look after yourself and quickly grow stronger."

"Yes, I must, so that all their care and sacrifice shall not be in vain. Has your Fourth Brother told you how I robbed him of the two corn buns that were to be his lunch when he came to bring me life-saving food? He must have been shocked by my shameless behavior. I no longer have the humane feelings you used to give me credit for."

"He was sad to see how desperately starved you were," I said to calm him down.

"What a frail vessel is a man! A few years of malnutrition and a few months of downright starvation reduce him to a wreck. Then it takes so much and so long to bring him back from the brink. Some just don't make it! What is worse, much worse, starvation demoralizes. A starving man is certainly not 'the beauty of the world, the paragon of animals!' For his own survival a starving man is ready to rob another man of his food, the way I robbed your brother. Starvation has always been a formidable weapon in war, but now I have seen and lived it as a terrible weapon in peace."

"You think too much. You are tired. Have you got anything to eat in your straw bag?"

"Oh yes, I nearly forgot. First Brother brought me, among other things, a number of big duck eggs. I have only one left, a huge one. Let's cook it on Lao Wang's little stove."

Ningkun produced the big duck egg and smiled with a childlike triumph.

"See? Also kindling I picked up in the fields."

"How do you like your egg?" I asked. "I haven't cooked anything for you for ever so long now."

"Let's just boil it. I'll make the fire. I learned this when camping in the Wilderness."

When the egg was cooked, I gave it to him to eat.

"No, no, we must share it. You and I haven't had a meal together for ages and ages." So saying, he cut it into two halves with Lao Wang's rusty chopping knife. "Here, one for you, one for me, for good luck!"

That was our first meal together in more than three years. Would it be our last one too? I shivered at the thought.

"Now let me tell you a funny little story, the kind of thing that happens only in a place like this," Ningkun began when we finished our duck egg. "I nearly became a usurer."

"What do you mean? You lent money to other inmates at high interest?"

"Worse! I lent food to a starving man and was promised double interest."

"Did he really repay you with double interest?"

"I wish he had been able to, for his sake, poor man."

"You don't mean he . . . ?"

"I dug his grave and buried him in it. He used to sleep on my right on the kang. Once an athlete in college. That's what scared me into sending you the SOS. I didn't want to go away without seeing you. But I was sorry after the distress message had been sent and I half wished you might not be able to come—"

"You bore it all by yourself too long, Ningkun. You should have sent for me sooner, much sooner," I scolded. My throat was choked. "I must go back and consult my brothers. We must . . ." I did not finish because I had no idea what to do. "You must take care of yourself and not worry about anything. I have only a week's leave. But I will come again if at all possible . . ."

As I walked the lonely rough road to the station, my heart was heavy with Ningkun's tribulations and anguish, with the uncertainties of our future. But two hours of home life in the ex-convict's room had also refreshed my faith in life, and the flame Ningkun had made in the ex-convict's little stove kept flickering for me on my way.

3

WHEN I SAW MY BROTHERS IN THE EVENING, I TOLD THEM I HAD FOUND THAT Ningkun was far from being out of danger. I did not wish to alarm my mother, but we had to find a way to secure his release before it was too late. What was I to do? Perhaps I could bring it up with my work unit when I returned to Hefei, it was first suggested, since everything had to be done through one's work unit. But the idea was soon abandoned, for it was unlikely that my work unit would be so good as to intercede in behalf of my ultrarightist husband, who was in no way related to it. Hefei being far out in the province, the red tape would be too long to get anything started, even if the local authorities could be induced to help, and we were racing against time. The only other option seemed to be taking it up with his and my former work unti in Beijing, although there were foreseeable difficulties. I winced at the prospect of revisiting the places of painful memories and confronting our former bosses, who had sent my husband to prison and packed me off to distant Anhui. But I must leave no stone unturned, however heavy the stone might be.

I took an early morning train to Beijing and got off at the ostentatious new train station, which had been built since I was packed off with my two little children in the dead of winter more than two years before. I felt like an unwelcome stranger in a hostile land. I quickly boarded the rickety bus, which took me to where Ningkun's sister and her family lived. She was astonished to see me. Without thinking, I blurted out, "Ningkun is dangerously ill," and the two of us burst out crying. It was the first time that I had broken down, although I had been on the brink of tears all week long. No time for tears, I reminded myself. Quickly I told her of my visit to Ningkun and of my fears. What must we do to save my husband and her dear brother, before it was too late? Ninghui, too, saw no option other than taking it up with our former work unit. I almost asked her to go with me, for I felt as if I would be groping in the dark by myself. But I quickly realized that I had to brave it alone. It would never do for one rightist to plead for another, even though she was his sister! I anticipated all kinds of evasions and official jargon from our former bosses. But I was determined to "doctor a dead horse as if it were still alive." I also remembered another saying: "How can you catch a tiger cub without venturing into the tiger's lair?"

Early the next morning I set out for the "tiger's lair" by myself. The trip took hours, and I had to change buses in the heart of the imperial city. The buses were packed with unsmiling pale-faced people. Out the bus window, I saw the same faces in the milling crowds. The windows of the butchers' were empty, the windows of the pastry shops displayed only bottles of soda pop. The great metropolis had the air of a city in mourning or in the throes of a mysterious plague. The colorful imposing facades of the new public buildings that had been completed after I left seemed only to set off the pervading gloom.

I got off the bus at the Xiyuan stop. The familiar sights all around brought back memories both happy and sad, but my mind was too preoccupied to dwell on them. I had only hoped I would be spared the pain of meeting anyone I had known on the short walk to campus. But as luck would have it, I ran into one former colleague after another, three English teachers in all, who had been Ningkun's boon companions before he was denounced. They barely nodded to me without saying a word.

On campus, I was stopped by an armed guard and told to fill out a visitor's form in the reception room. The receptionist was surprised to see me back and asked under her breath, "How is Wu Ningkun?" When I told her he was quite ill, she shook her head and didn't say another word. When I walked into the vice president's office, his secretary almost started. I remembered the nasty things she had said against my "evil bourgeois ideas" at the farewell session of criticism for my benefit. Now, when I told her I had come all the way from Hefei to see the school leadership on most urgent business, she said coldly, "I don't know. The vice president is frightfully busy. You no longer have any organizational relationship with us. Really I don't see why . . ." I looked straight into her eyes and said decisively, "Wu Ningkun is dying. I must see the vice president right away."

In a few minutes I was ushered into the vice president's private office. He looked up from a volume of Mao's *Selected Works* and pointed to a chair, the same chair I had sat in when I was called in to be packed off to Anhui.

"How are you, Comrade Li Yikai?" he greeted me in his usual deadpan official tone. "We are always glad to see comrades who have worked with us. You are in Hefei, aren't you? What brings you to Beijing then?"

"Comrade Vice President, my husband Wu Ningkun is frightfully ill at Qinghe Farm. He is dying," I said bluntly. "I come to ask for your help."

"Is he really?" He did not sound at all surprised.

"Yes, indeed. Dying from edema, from starvation."

"Really now. I don't see how we can help. He was expelled from this school when he was labeled an ultrarightist, as you well know. He no longer has any organizational relationship with us. You don't either. You must have faith in the party leadership of the farm, in the party's correct policies. You must go back to your work at once, when all revolutionary comrades are doing their utmost for the Great Leap Forward. If you wish, you could seek the guidance of the party leadership at your university. But loafing around in the nation's capital at the time of the Great Leap Forward simply won't do, especially for a rightist's wife."

Trying to put me in my place again! But I wouldn't accept this, not when so much was at stake.

"I know only too well, Comrade Vice President, that neither Wu Ningkun nor I myself have any organizational relationship with the school. This is why I have never bothered you with our problems ever since we were sent away. Now that he is dying, only the school that condemned him to reform through hard labor can save him, by asking the farm to release him at once."

"I'm sorry to hear he is ill. I know how you must feel. I hope it may not be as serious as you say I am quite certain the farm gives him whatever care is necessary in accordance with the party's correct policies. You must have faith in the party and the party's correct policies. You should go back to your job right away. It is really inappropriate for this school to take any action, since Wu Ningkun is no longer a member of the faculty here."

"Indeed not, but he did work here two years and he was once your best professor, as you had declared at a public meeting, until you sent him away—"

"I must correct you. I said he was a good teacher when we did not know he would degenerate into a rightist. His case was quite serious, but we showed leniency by treating it as contradiction among the people. We did not give him a sentence, we did not send him to prison, we sent him to the farm to give him an opportunity to reform himself through manual labor. If he reformed himself thoroughly, he could eventually return to the ranks of the people. He is an expert in his field, he is still in the prime of his life. He is barely forty, isn't he? He could still serve the people, and make new contributions to atone for his rightist crimes, if only he reformed himself thoroughly. So the pressing matter of the moment is not to get agitated over his health, but to help him reform himself thoroughly."

"I appreciate your solicitude for Wu Ningkun, Comrade Vice President." I was getting desperate. "The most pressing matter of the moment, as I see it, is that he has to stay alive in order to go on reforming himself. I saw him two days ago, and he was very close to death. He has buried a fellow inmate with his own hands. If you refuse to do anything to save him, the lenient treatment you have meted out to him would be no different from a death sentence. Does Wu Ningkun deserve to die?"

"How can you say that?" He raised his voice a little. "We didn't know there would be a famine when we sent him to the state farm to reform himself."

"Of course not." I began to throw discretion to the winds. "But the fact is, he is dying from starvation. He didn't know either that he would be dying in prison when he gave up his career abroad and came home to serve the New China with so much enthusiasm. He didn't know either that he would be condemned as a rightist when you and other leading comrades came to our rooms again and again and urged him to offer candid criticism of the party and the party's policies—"

"But he said the wrong things," he interrupted me. "We expected constructive criticism."

"He was stupid, he did not know what were the right things to say. He has been punished for his stupid mistake, but does he deserve to die a miserable death in prison? Surely our little children are innocent. Yiding is only five, as you may remember. Yimao hasn't seen her father yet. Do they deserve to be orphaned so young?"

"The country is facing another very difficult year, with the famine and the troubles with the Soviet Union. No one has the right to complain. Everyone must give wholehearted support to the party's domestic and foreign policies."

"Of course we must," I agreed. I could see he was stalling. I was already in the tiger's lair; there was no going back now. Perhaps he was only a paper tiger. I went on: "We must also help the party and the government to reduce the burden of feeding so many prisoners by securing the release of someone like my husband who is dying and who has never been convicted anyway. I beg you to act at once before it is too late. Would it be any credit to the school and the government to have a professor die of starvation in prison? And for the school to refuse to save him when it could? All I am asking of you is to give him a chance to live, so that he may serve the people and the party in the future. If you wish, you could send him back to prison when he has been doctored back to health. When I was a child, I used to hear my mother say, 'He who saves a man's life does a deed greater than building the Buddha a seven-story pagoda.' I hope that is not in contradiction with revolutionary humanitarianism. I beg you to take action before it is too late."

"It's too bad what's happening to Wu Ningkun. We certainly don't wish to see him die on the farm. The country needs highly qualified intellectuals. The school lacks competent professors. It was just too bad his saying what he did. I will see what we can do in getting him released for medical treatment, perhaps at home. I make no promises. I will put it on the agenda at the next meeting of the school party committee. You can go back to your job in Anhui now."

"And when will the next party committee meeting be held?" I pursued.

"Oh, in a week or two."

"I told you he is dying, he can't wait that long. I will not leave until you promise to take speedy action. It's in your power to do so, Comrade Vice President. Can I stay in the school guest room overnight to await your decision?"

"No, no, that won't do. I will talk it over with other leading comrades first and then the school will consult the party leadership of the farm. You will hear from us before long, that I can promise you. That's the best I can do for you. You mustn't tarry in Beijing any longer."

I figured that was just about as far as I could push him. He was evasive, but his stiff sternness had perceptibly softened in the course of the encounter. Poor man, he was a hard-boiled party functionary trained in Yan'an, but he was human after all. Perhaps my cause was not lost. I hopped on the city-bound bus with a ray of hope in my heart.

4

ON THE TRAIN FROM BEIJING BACK TO TIANJIN, IT SUDDENLY OCCURRED TO me there were only two days left in my one-week leave. I ought to leave the next day to make the slow train journey back to Hefei. But how could I leave without letting Ningkun see the ray of hope I had found in the tiger's lair? How could I leave without taking Yiding to see his Papa, as I had promised him? The father had been torn away from the son for more than three years now. Who knows when they would meet again, if ever? If I did take him to the farm to see his father, then I would have to overstay my leave and there would be the devil to pay. I could already feel the wrath of the dread party secretary. I could already hear the stinging gibes from Little Hot Pepper. Oh, what was I to do? I tossed all night long and sobbed at the vision of the deathly emaciated visage of my husband, which kept coming back to me. My mind was made up: I must take our five-year-old son to the prison to see his father. I got up early, but Mother was earlier.

"You didn't sleep well, Yikai." I heard soft reproach in her voice.

"No, Mother, but you didn't either," I said softly. "I had to think things out, you see. I am taking little Yiding to the farm to see his father tomorrow."

"Oh," she paused. "I thought you were going back to Hefei today. You will be overstaying your leave now. Are you sure it's all right, Yikai?"

I could see worry in her eyes. Oh, must I keep burdening my poor aged mother with worry after worry?

"It's not all right, Mother," I said bluntly. "But I must do what I must do. If I didn't take Yiding to see him now, the child might never see his father again. I won't mind being punished for overstaying my leave. Don't worry, Mother, please."

"Go then, child. Do what you must," Mother said softly. I could hear tears in her voice, but she was trying hard to control herself.

After a while, she brought out from an inner pocket in her gown a roll of bills and put them in my hand. "Your brothers and sisters give you this. Go and buy some good food for Ningkun. Never mind the prices. We must save his life. I'll get the child dressed when he gets up. Go now."

I quickly left the house with the two empty traveling bags, in which I had taken food to Ningkun last time. I ducked into one side street after another, looking for black-market food vendors in disguise. I felt bad about putting the hard-earned money of my ill-paid siblings into the greedy hands of black marketeers, but I recklessly grabbed what I could find: boiled eggs, cooked meats, steamed bread, pancakes. Food for life, I prayed and hoped against hope.

Yiding was all excitement when he saw me coming in with the heavy bags. The child threw his little arms around my neck and spoke rapidly.

"You really taking me to see Papa now, Mama, eh, Mama? Really, really now?"

"Yes, really, my darling. Are you happy?"

"Very happy, Mama! It's about time, you know. Every one of my little friends in the kindergarten has got a papa. They always ask me, 'Where is your papa, Yiding?' Come on, let's get going."

"We must wait till the morning, little one." I tried to calm him down. "There's only one train that goes to the place daily. And it leaves very early. So you must be a good boy and go to bed early tonight, or you won't be up in time. Also, it's a long walk from the station to the farm. You must get plenty of sleep, so you can have strength to walk."

"But why must we walk?" He looked at me with wondering eyes. "Why can't we take the bus?"

"There are no buses in the countryside, my dear one. Can you walk, my darling?" How could I tell the little one his father was in prison and the government did not bother to provide transport for the families making prison visits!

"Sure, I can walk, Mama! I can walk all the way to see Big Papa!" he bragged cheerfully, as if he were going on a holiday.

I woke up in the dark, but I could hear Mother already moving about in the little kitchen. Yiding was still sound asleep next to me. I turned my flashlight on my watch: four o'clock. The train would leave at five-thirty. I must rouse Yiding now, though I knew the little one needed more sleep. He had gone to bed early, only to stay wide awake for hours. He was only half-awake when I finished dressing him in a clean shirt and a clean pair of shorts Mother had got ready for him.

"Go now, child," Mother said gently when we finished the simple breakfast she had prepared for us. "Be a good boy now, little Yiding, my darling. Papa will be so happy to see you. He loves you so." She paused, smoothing his hair with one hand, and then said to me, "Tell him from Mother again, Yikai, he must bear it patiently, he must get back to health. He has done no wrong. He was just too outspoken. Honest men suffer . . ."

It was beginning to get light when we left the house. I carried one bag in each hand, little Yiding giving me a helping hand on one side. When a rickety bus stopped at the street corner, he eagerly climbed into it and quickly turned back toward me.

"Give me the bags, Mama, quick."

I hesitated at the sight of his outstretched little arms, but the driver was getting impatient. So I handed the child one bag, which he dragged with both hands into the bus. Then I climbed up dragging the other bag. I smiled at him and he smiled back. This operation was repeated when we had to change buses at the next stop.

On the train Yiding quickly fell asleep. When we got off at Chadian an hour later, he dragged himself out of the station. Then he stopped and slumped to the ground. I was alarmed.

"What's the matter now, Yiding dear? Don't you want to go and see Papa?"

"I do, Mama, but I just haven't got the strength to walk."

I suddenly realized the poor child was weak from malnutrition. He, too, had a mild case of edema. Perhaps I was being foolish in taking him on this gruesome trek? I looked around. The other passengers who had gotten off here, all women, were already hurrying toward the distant farm. We two, mother and son, looked so helpless in the desolate country. But there was no going back now. I dropped the bags on the ground and squatted before my child.

"Come on, darling, let's ride piggyback! You haven't had a ride for ever so long now, have you?" I sounded almost cheerful.

"But what about the bags then, Mama?"

"Nothing to worry about, my little man. I can carry you a short distance and then come back for the bags. Back and forth, forth and back! It will be fun."

My child laughed happily as I carried him onward and sang him the nursery rhyme "Little Fat Pig Goes to Town." I stopped and put him down after going forty or fifty feet and then hurried back for the bags. This was repeated several times. The sun was up and I was sweating. My edema-weakened legs were failing. It would take me hours to cover the six miles to the farm in this way. As I took a short rest on the roadside, I looked closely at Yiding by my side. The child was apparently feeling better. My heart hardened.

"Can you walk now, my darling?"

"I will try, Mama, I will try."

"You are a very brave boy. Papa will be so proud of you."

So we moved on slowly, bags and black-market food, toward the prison farm. I don't know how many times we rested by the roadside, but Yiding never wanted to ride piggyback again. By the time we got to the prison, it was nearly noon. But when I handed my visitor's form to the officer on duty, he said, "You are still too early, although you are two hours behind the others. You can't visit with your husband until he comes back from his labor in the fields." I was almost thankful for the respite, for the child and I were both dead tired. We went into the Visiting Room, which was bare except for the same old rickety wooden benches. Our fellow passengers on the train were already in there. Yiding soon fell asleep again, his head in my arms. Half an hour later, Ningkun came in and walked unsteadily up to us. He was the same skin and bones in the same muddy rags I had seen last time, and his complexion was more gray than yellow. He looked at me with a feeble smile, as if he had little strength left even to smile. One officer stood at a little distance from us, monitoring several couples.

"So you are come again," he said gently. "It's such a long way."

"I have brought Yiding to see you." I said the obvious thing.

He stretched out his hand and put it lightly on the sleeping child's head. He said softly, "A big boy now. Three years and more . . ." At this, Yiding woke with a start. At the sight of his father, the child winced and clung close to me. I saw horror in his young eyes.

"Who is this horrible man, Mama? I'm scared, so scared. Take me to see Papa, my Big Papa!"

"But this is your Big Papa, my darling child!" I said desperately. "Now call him, call him Papa!" I held him tight in my arms.

"Pa-pa!" he burst out crying.

Ningkun bowed his head. As I helplessly watched the father and son, a different scene came back to me—how happily the young party functionary had played with his five-year-old son at the party boss's the other night. Then, before we knew it, our fifteen minutes were up. Ningkun rushed from the room with the other prisoners for afternoon labor in the fields. He did not turn back to look at us.

Yiding followed the receding figure of his father with tearful eyes, clinging to me all the while. The poor child looked so worn-out and soon fell asleep again, with tears on his cheeks. Was this the reunion he had so much looked forward to? Or what I had prayed for? No, I mustn't give up so easily. I laid the sleeping child down on the bench and stepped out of the room. I walked up to the room of the officer on duty and knocked on the door.

"Who is it? Come in."

I stepped into the room and saw a middle-aged man in a short-sleeved army shirt and army trousers sitting at the desk.

"What do you want?" he asked peevishly, lighting up a cigarette.

"I am Li Yikai, officer. I have come to visit my husband Wu Ningkun. I need your help . . ."

"I know who you are. A professor's wife, right?" There was sarcasm in his voice. "This is not a university, you know. It is a state farm, a prison, an organ of proletarian dictatorship. You were here a couple of days ago and here you are again. Don't you have anything better to do?"

"I know. But—"

"But you come to visit your husband again. Wu Ningkun is an ultrarightist, and don't you forget you are a government worker, though still married to him. You must draw a clear line of demarcation from him. Your coming to see him so often, it's not good for you, it's not good for him either. He must be made to realize profoundly how heinous his rightist crimes are, how much damage he has done to the party, the people, and the cause of socialism. And to you and your family! Draw a line of demarcation, that's what's most important for you. So leave here and go back to your work unit in Anhui." It all sounded so familiar.

"Thank you for helping me, officer," I said politely. "But as you know only too well, Wu Ningkun is dangerously ill. He may die any day. He buried the person who had slept next to him. I have brought our five-year-old son to see his papa."

"How could you bring a five-year-old brat to a prison farm? It's not good for him."

"Maybe not, certainly not, but I must do what I must do. The child has been separated from his papa for more than three years now. If he is not allowed to spend some time with his father, he may never be able to do it again. As a wife and a mother, I ask you to allow me and my child to spend the night here with Wu Ningkun. I am not asking much . . . My child has no strength left to walk to the train station anyway."

He threw away the cigarette butt and looked up at the ceiling for a while. Then he lowered his eyes at me.

"I suppose it is a long walk to the station for a tired little brat. All right, Li Yikai, in accordance with the party's policies of revolutionary humanitarianism, I give you permission to spend the night here with Wu Ningkun, if you promise not to come back again. Do you promise?"

"I promise, I promise," I said eagerly.

"Wu Ningkun will have permission to come out after supper and political study to spend the night with you and your son in the big room of our kindergarten. He must go back to his cell at five in the morning for the day's labor. Then you must leave."

"Thank you, thank you." I was almost abjectly grateful. After all, it was in his power to grant or to deny my humble request.

"Remember now, you have promised not to come back again." I heard his loud voice at my back as I stepped out of the room.

Yiding looked somewhat refreshed after his nap. I wondered anxiously how he would feel about seeing his father again. I tried to find an opening.

"You didn't have much to say to Papa, my darling. You have always said you missed him so much."

"That wasn't my Papa. Big Papa looks so good in the pictures at home. This man looked so scary. Take me to see my own Papa, please, Mama."

"But he *was* your Papa, Yiding darling. He has been very ill. He had his working clothes on, he was muddy from working in the fields. That's why he didn't look so good just now. Don't you remember how he used to play with you? How he hugged you all the time? You can't judge people by how they look, Yiding dear. Papa is really nice, and he loves you so much. He will be clean and nice when he comes to see us in the evening."

"Is he really coming? Oh how nice! I will speak to him. I won't cry, Mama."

I took Yiding to the dingy little kitchen for visitors to have our supper. A piece of steamed sorghum bread each and a bowl of tasteless boiled celery cabbage between us. We ate standing, for there were no tables or benches. The visitors, all of whom were young or middle-aged women, ate there. Everyone ate slowly and no one said a word. After the meal, we all went into the big room in the kindergarten to await the coming of our men. Yiding stayed behind to play by himself in the children's playground. But we soon learned that the men would not be out until late in the evening. For some reason, they were having a protracted session of criticism and self-confession.

I soon got into conversation with an intellectual-looking young woman sitting next to me on the edge of the kang. It turned out she was a medical doctor visiting her doctor husband who had been denounced as an ultrarightist.

"He had studied at Yenching University and was involved in something called the ABC."

"What, the ABC! My husband Wu Ningkun was involved in that, and some of his best students too."

"I heard my cousins speaking of the professor. I am also a Jiang."

"Oh, Jiang the Elder and Jiang the Younger then! I knew them. I often heard Ningkun speak of them, especially the Younger. He did not know a word of English when he entered the university, but wrote a brilliant essay on Koestler in his last year. How are they? Where are they?" I could hardly wait to hear what had happened to them.

She burst out sobbing. After a while, she muttered, "Dead, both of them. They refused to plead guilty to the charges against them and were given life sentences as incorrigible ringleaders of the ABC. They died in prison. We didn't even know what they died of . . ." She started sobbing again. I patted her on the shoulder, tears welling up in my eyes. My dear sisters in sorrow, I pray for you and yours, the living and the dead.

Then all of a sudden I heard the excited voice of my child, "Here comes Papa, Mama!" I saw him running into the room to my side, Ningkun and other men walking slowly behind him. Ningkun's face was washed clean, and his patched shirt looked clean. He broke into a weak smile at the sight of the child.

"Yiding darling, do you remember Papa now?" Ningkun asked haltingly in a low voice.

"Yes, my Big Papa!" Yiding threw himself into his father's open arms. My eyes blurred. "I mustn't be silly," I told myself. "This is a time for rejoicing. Ningkun still lives. The father and the son are reunited." Ningkun tried to lift the child up as he used to at home. But I saw he was too weak for that now.

"Oh dear, you have grown to be a big boy now. You're no longer Little Dingding, but Big Yiding now. I'm afraid Big Papa can't toss you up in the air any more. Remember how high I used to toss you up?"

"I do, I do, Big Papa! Why don't you come home then? I don't like this place. Mama is busy all the time. She never has the time to play with me. Shame on you!"

"I am so sorry, my darling boy. Papa couldn't have helped it." He laughed a little. I had to fight back my tears. But Ningkun went on jovially, though his voice was strained. "Let's do something to make up for it."

"Tell me a story then. You haven't told me a story for ever so long now."

"Now why don't you recite a Tang poem for Papa first?" I put in. "He has never heard you recite one yet."

"Sure, I'll do that. I know ten and more by heart. What would you like to hear, Papa?"

"I would like to hear any one you recite. I have no idea which Tang poems you know by heart, Big Yiding."

So Yiding rattled off a celebrated four-line Tang poem without a hitch. Ningkun hugged him and kissed him on the cheek.

"Very well done, very well done indeed! You may grow up to be a poet yourself. But tell me what it all means, for I haven't heard any poem recited so long that I have become so slow in understanding it."

"Oh, you're slow all right, Papa! It's an easy one. It's just about a man who left home in his youth. When he comes home again, his hair has already turned gray. The children at home don't know him and ask where the stranger comes from. Isn't that funny?"

"I think it's rather nice. But would you not know me when I come home?"

"Of course I would. Don't be silly, Papa, you won't be away so long. Now it's your turn to tell me a story."

"All right, my boy. Come on, sit in my lap, the way you used to do at home."

When the child was nestled in his lap, Ningkun began as he used to do at home, softly and rhythmically, rocking the child gently at the same time.

"Once upon a time, there lived in a distant land a happy family. The papa was a young pearl-fisher. He was good at diving into the sea to find beautiful pearls. The mama was a lovely young woman. They loved each other very much, and both of them loved their little boy very much."

"What was the boy's name? How old was he?"

"Kino was his name. He was four or five, about your own age. They were poor, but, being together, they were happy. One day, the good pearl-fisher found a very, very large pearl. It was worth lots, lots of money. When the greedy bad people in town saw it, they wanted to rob the honest fisher of his large pearl. So they made some false charges against him and threw the good papa in jail. Then . . ."

I saw the child's head was drooping. Ningkun had lulled him to sleep with the story-telling and gentle rocking, even as he used to do at home.

He kissed the sleeping child on both cheeks before I carried him to the rickety cot that stood incongruously in one corner.

When we stepped back to the kang, I noticed for the first time that all the other couples, ten or eleven in all, were already in bed in their clothes, with their cloth shoes or sandals on. They made a neat row on the kang, sardines packed in salt tears, perhaps. I smiled at Ningkun, and he smiled back at me. We seemed to have lost the power to cry.

"Let's lie down too. You must be dead tired after such a day, Yikai."

"You are the one who is really tired, after laboring in the fields all day," I said softly.

"Okay, we are all tired," said he, pointing to our bedfellows. "Do as the Romans do then. I wonder what the Romans would have done under the circumstances."

I was glad his sense of humor was not dead. We squeezed ourselves into the little space our bedfellows had left for us. I took care that Ningkun slept on my left, for he was deaf in the left ear. When we lay down facing each other, I began whispering into his good ear, which didn't seem to be really good either. Starvation must have weakened his hearing too.

"I hope you didn't mind Yiding crying and not knowing you when he first saw you," I said apologetically.

"How could I mind? It was only natural. I just felt bad about the whole thing. Why should a child ever be brought to such a hole?"

"You don't mean I have done wrong in bringing him to see you?"

"No, no, no! You know what I mean. I'm glad he came and saw his Papa in this sorry plight. He will remember. Who knows whether I will live to see him again!"

"Don't say that, Ningkun," I urged gently. Then I told him about my trip to Beijing and what the vice president of our former school had promised to do for me. "I feel there is hope. Millions of people are dying of starvation in the land, but it's different having a professor starve to death in prison. They may be glad to dump you off on my hands and make your survival or death our own business, just as they are forcing the families to help feed the prisoners. We must always be on the side of life, we must never lose hope. You must be well again, if only for my sake, for Yiding, for Yimao, who hasn't set eyes on you yet."

"I'm sorry, Yikai. I mustn't worry you, your burden is quite heavy enough. It's just sometimes I feel so weak, so low . . . Yes, I must be well again, I must. Even robbing the children of the food that is rightfully theirs . . ."

"You need the food most. It's your medicine. I will take care of the children. Don't you worry."

"I'll feast like a king and leave all the worries and starving kids to the queen, eh?"

"You always tease me, Ningkun." Then, to change the subject, I told him I had taken care of his books. I had carefully wrapped up the manuscripts of his half-finished translations of *Utopia* and *La Chartreuse*. He must grow strong soon and come home to finish them.

"Utopias, by definition, can never be realized, never finished. The poor man paid for his Utopian ideas with his head. I'd rather make a new translation of *Hamlet* if I ever get out of this hole alive. I lived with the play and the Prince's poignant sufferings under the frozen skies of the Great Northern Wilderness. Denmark is a prison! . . ."

Then he talked about his labor in the fields, which he would not mind only if he had the strength to do it, the wardens and officers, some nasty and others rather human, the food substitutes, which were making the prisoners sick, the dead and the dying. He spoke calmly, without rancor, as if he were merely telling stories about others. I told him about the children, leaving out things that might upset him. I kept to myself the death of his two star pupils. We went on and on, never sleeping a wink. When I remembered he had to do hard labor again in the morning, I insisted he get some sleep. Just then, the shriek of a whistle stabbed the silent night. All the men sprang to their feet as one man and rushed out of the room. Ningkun was gone before I knew what was happening. He didn't even so much as glance back at his darling son. I jumped off the kang and went to the door. In the half-darkness I could see the ghastly figure of Ningkun scurrying as fast as he could on his swollen legs. Oh God, how much longer could he endure? When and where would we meet again?

Lost in thought for I don't know how long, I was roused by a frantic cry from my little boy. "Papa, Papa, ah Big Papa! Where are you? Mama, oh, Mama!" I dashed over to the cot and held him in my arms.

"It's all right, Yiding darling, it's all right. Mama is here."

"I want Papa! Where is he?"

"Papa had to go to work. He mustn't be late. You were never late going to school, were you, dear?"

"How mean of Papa! Mean Papa!"

"You know Papa is never mean." I tried to calm him. "He just couldn't help it. He will spend all his time with you when he comes home. How do you like that?"

"But when is he coming home?"

"Very soon, if you are a good boy." I admired my own logic.

His tears and anger were abruptly stopped by a prison guard's rough and rude voice.

"Be quick, all of you! Get out of here! What do you think this place is anyway? Your hotel? The kids will be coming to school now. Time for you people to beat it. Go back, be quick!"

I took Yiding by the hand and started walking the six miles of rough road to the train station. I carried him on my back from time to time. How happy my child sounded when he rode piggyback!

"Mama, Papa was really nice, he took the heavy bags from us. If he didn't, I would have to walk on my own legs again. Oh, Mama, you don't know how tired I was yesterday walking to the farm to see Papa!"

"You were a brave little boy, my darling. You made Papa so happy."

5

JUNE 3 WAS OUR DAUGHTER'S THIRD BIRTHDAY, AND THE POOR CHILD HAD not known her father yet. A visit to an unknown father in prison, dismal as it might seem, was the best gift I could give our daughter. But I had promised the officer at the prison not to go back again. Would he overlook my breach of promise and allow me to see Ningkun once more? Would Yimao be frightened by her father's ghastly appearance, as Yiding was?

I found Yimao playing with my First Elder Brother when I returned from the prison visit with Yiding.

"Where have you been, Mama? I've been looking for you all day! Grandma always stays with me." Yimao pouted.

"I took Yiding to see Papa and we had a nice visit. Would you like to go and spend your birthday with Papa tomorrow?"

"No, I wouldn't. I want to spend my birthday with my Papa right here." She pointed to my brother. As she had been living with Mother in the room next to my brother's, she had fallen into the habit of calling him Papa, as her cousin of the same age did.

"But you have another Papa, Yimao," Mother put in, in her persuasive voice. "You must go and see him. Yiding just did!"

"Oh, yes, Big Papa is so nice," Yiding joined in. "He told me a nice story about a good pearl-fisher."

"I want to hear it too, Mama." So saying, Yimao rushed into my arms.

I was happy to have brought Yimao around so easily. Still, I had to prepare her for the meeting lest she be frightened. And the trek from the station to the prison would even be harder on a three-year-old.

The next morning I started making my way down the long road to the prison, carrying Yimao on my back and a traveling bag of black-market food in my hand. I hadn't gone far before my edema-weakened legs gave way. I put Yimao down on the ground and sat by the roadside to rest. I was at a loss as to what to do. I could not possibly coax Yimao into walking the miles, as I had done with Yiding. Occasionally a peasant walked past us, casting curious looks our way. After quite a while, I saw a horse cart approaching from the direction of the station and recognized the driver as no other than the ex-convict Lao Wang. I scrambled to my feet and hailed him.

"Lao Wang! Nice to see you again. Do you remember me?"

"I surely do. You used my room and promised me some real food."

"I brought it today. This is my daughter. Can you give her a lift to the farm?"

"I think I can. But you can see the cart is loaded and the horse is so underfed. I don't think I can take you too."

"Oh no, I can walk along. Here, Yimao, Grandpa Wang is giving you a ride on his buggy. Isn't that nice?"

"Thank you, Grandpa. I can sing a song for you if you like."

"What a nice little girl!"

As soon as Yimao was seated on the cart, I took a box of crackers out of my bag and handed it to Lao Wang.

"Well, that's nice of you. Put your bag on the cart too."

Lao Wang lost no time in tearing open the box and devouring the crackers with relish. He finished the box when we were still a distance away from the prison. Throwing away the empty package, he smacked his lips and said, "My, that sure tasted good! You're welcome to use my room again. No problem, no problem."

When I found myself face-to-face with the same officer after the long trek from the station, I was prepared for him to jump on me. But there was no going back now.

"What now, Li Yikai?" Surprisingly, he did not sound too angry. "You promised not to come back, and here you are again. A breach of promise, after I have been so lenient with you and your rightist husband. We can report your conduct to your work unit, you know, and what good is it to you, eh? You know very well I'm not going to let you see him again."

"This is our daughter." I pointed to Yimao in my lap. "She was born after her father had been taken away, and she is three today . . ."

"What a place to spend her birthday and see her father for the first time! And such a pretty girl too!"

"I know, I know, but what else could I do?"

"Okay, okay, what can I do with a strong-minded woman like you? I know I am too softhearted, but . . . Okay, you will have another visit with your man when he comes back from the fields. Fifteen minutes, not one minute more, and positively the last, last time. Do you promise?"

"I promise. If he gets well, my mind will be at ease. If he does not, there will be no point in my coming again, right?" I sounded convincing.

"I want it in writing." So saying, he handed me a piece of paper.

I picked up a pen from his desk and wrote on the paper:

My Pledge
I promise not to come and visit my husband Wu Ningkun again.
Li Yikai, June 3, 1961

Ningkun's dull eyes lit up when he saw me again and his daughter for the first time. I had tried to explain to the three-year-old child how her father would look funny in muddy rags because he was ill but still working hard in the fields to produce food for us to eat. All the same, she was frightened by Ningkun's looks, as her brother had been. I held her tight in my arms and reminded her of what I had told her the night before and on the way. She soon looked at her father with a shy smile, calling him "Papa!"

"So this is my little princess!" Ningkun said cheerfully, but I could detect tears in his voice. "So pretty and so nice! Too bad we can't celebrate your birthday in our palace today, Maomao!"

"I don't mind, Papa. Mama says you're coming home soon and we can celebrate my birthday next year in *my* palace."

"But where is *your* palace, my princess?"

"In the woods in my storybook, of course! How silly of you not to know!"

Both Ningkun and I laughed.

"Aren't you going to give me a kiss for my birthday, Papa? Mama did. Grandma did. Everybody did."

Ningkun hesitated.

"My muddy rags will spoil your good looks and your pretty clothes."

"Don't be silly, Papa. Grandma will clean me up. Come on!"

Ningkun held her in his arms and kissed her on both cheeks.

"You're a determined young lady, like your Mama. I am so glad. Someday this little Phoenix will sail the heavens and sing at heaven's gate!"

Our fifteen minutes went by all too quickly. Rationing had become a way of life in the land, so it never occurred to us to protest. When Ningkun turned back to look at us as he rushed out toward the fields, I saw tears running down his pallid cheeks.

Ten

RETURN FROM THE DEAD, 1961-66

1

EARLY ON THE AFTERNOON OF JUNE 29, 1961, AS HUNDREDS OF SWEAT-drenched inmates were gathering wheat under a merciless sun, I was sent for by a personnel officer from the Qinghe Farm headquarters. I felt uneasy: a visit from a personnel man usually meant trouble. The middle-aged man in loose army pants squatting in the shade near the threshing ground began in an almost normal human voice:

"Wu Ningkun, you have been ill, right? How are you feeling now?"

"Somewhat better." I tried to sound appreciative.

"That's good. The farm leadership has decided to let you go home on parole for medical treatment. Revolutionary humanitarianism, you see?" he announced in a more official tone of voice. "So you go back to your room now, settle your accounts, and pack up. At eight in the morning, a horse cart from the farm headquarters will stop at the gate of your branch farm and take you and several others on parole to the train station. A train ticket to Hefei will be handed to you by an officer from the personnel department. We expect good behavior from you while on parole, you understand? Is there anything you wish to say?"

"I am very grateful," I said, nearly choked from mixed emotions called up by the sudden turn of events, which, though not totally unexpected, seemed almost bizarre in its simplicity. "You go home on parole," as simple and as arbitrary as that, even as I had been summarily given an indefinite term without a trial or sentence. A thinking reed at the mercy of the whim of the Socialist political wind! It was more than three years since my arrest on April 17, 1958, and I had been dreaming of my release every day and every night. I could not wait to return to my dear ones again, but I had no idea of what lay ahead of me. The thinking reed could not even think anymore. I was so weary, I did not even have the strength to feel bitter; I just wanted to shake off the shadow of death that had been following me over the past months.

I was the envy of my cellmates when I climbed onto the horse cart the following morning and received my hard-seat train ticket and parole papers from the personnel man. As I had to change trains in Tianjin, I took a pedicab to Yikai's family home on Happiness Lane. The familiar streets and bustling pedestrians seemed almost unreal. Was I really among the living now? At the entrance of the lane, I ran into one of Yikai's nephews, who had been six when I last saw him four years ago. He did not recognize me, just like the children in the poem that Yiding had recited. When the poor boy had recovered from the fright my appearance had undoubtedly given him, he rushed back into the house, yelling at the top of his voice, "Uncle Wu is back! Uncle Wu!" My mother-in-law was astonished into tearful silence and at once went about making me a hot cup of tea, which she knew I always liked. When I explained to her I was on parole on my way home, she broke down again. All Yikai's brothers and sisters shed tears at my sorry sight, but were relieved at my survival and release. I had to restrain my feelings and tried to cheer my mother-in-law up by telling her how all the costly black-market food from her and the family had saved my life, only to make her cry again. Yimao was brought back from Yikai's First Sister's house, where she had been staying. My daughter did not recognize me at first, but threw herself into my arms when she suddenly remembered, saying, "You are Papa. Mama took me to that funny place to see you. Oh Papa! I won't let you go back to that awful place again!" I promised her I wouldn't return there, while Grandma shed tears again.

The next morning, after sending Yikai a short wire advising her of my arrival on the fourth, I boarded the train for Beijing for a brief reunion with my sister Ninghui and my stepmother. It happened to be July 1, the day on which the Chinese Communist party was founded in 1921. At Tiananmen Square, I was struck by the giant portrait of Mao Zedong, which dwarfed the passersby. Memories of the charismatic "Great Leader" waving from the rostrum atop the Gate of Heavenly Peace to a sea of fanatic paraders five years ago mixed with more recent memories of his antirightist campaign, which had undone hundreds of thousands of intellectuals, and his Great

Leap Forward, which was still causing death by starvation all over the nation. The bright red banners on the imposing new public buildings "warmly celebrating the fortieth birthday of the great, glorious, and correct Chinese Communist party!" made a weird contrast with the pallid faces of the people on the buses and the desolate grocery store windows along the streets. I recalled the feelings of venturing into an unknown land that I had experienced upon arriving in the imperial city for the first time nearly nine years before. Now I felt more like a ghost come back from the dead, the parole papers in my pocket marking a line of demarcation from the living multitudes. What would the good people feel if they were shown my ghastly ID? Would they be horrified the way the good citizens of the little French town were by the yellow passport of Hugo's newly liberated Jean Valjean in *Les Misérables*? Or would they give me food and shelter as the bishop did for the "dangerous convict"? Luckily, I had no need to find lodging at an inn, but the good fortune to be received with tears by my sister and stepmother.

We didn't have much to say to each other. What was there to say? It was enough that their worst fears and anxieties had been dissipated. The rest was left unsaid. In the afternoon we went for a stroll in the nearby Happy and Carefree Pavilion Park, only blocks away from the Half-Step Bridge detention center. Far from being happy or carefree, I celebrated my return from the dead with my loved ones in the sun, which shone with the promise of a new life.

In the morning I took an early train to Tianjin, where I boarded a night train for Hefei, which happened to be my mother's birthplace. I felt as if I were going back to the dark womb and starting life all over again. Arriving at high noon, I walked into the waiting room drenched in perspiration, dragging my bags and my legs, and collapsed onto a grimy bench. Minutes passed before Yikai rushed into the room, saying breathlessly, "Sorry I'm late. But I'm so happy you are home at last. Dingding can't wait to see Big Papa again." I had so much looked forward to this moment of reunion, but now I could not find a word to say. After years of separation and anguish, we were together again in a new town. My heart was so full that I felt I would burst into tears if I attempted to give voice to my feelings. I just said softly, "Home at last!" Seeing how hot and exhausted I was, she dashed off for a couple of cheap ice-suckers to cool me. Then she rushed out of the room again to hire a pedicab. Moments later we were seated on a double-seat pedicab under the blinding and scorching sun, on our way to the university campus. Now she told me what a hard time she had had in getting permission to meet me at the station, partly because my wire was unsigned. "To save a few fen for an ice-sucker," I mumbled. "I understand," she concurred. "But they always read things differently. 'How do you know it's your husband?' Little Hot Pepper demanded. 'He is under labor reform, isn't he? How can he all of a sudden come here? Escaping or what? You can't take a couple of hours off on the pretext of an unsigned wire. You outstayed your leave only last month going off to see him. You promised to make up for lost time at the last session of criticism. And here you want to goof off again!' In desperation, I went to a party functionary and promised to make up for the lost time at night if you didn't turn up. Oh, how they put me in my place at every step! But I'm certainly happy I did not venture into the tiger's lair in vain!"

The two little rooms were not much bigger than "a nutshell," but I counted myself "a king of infinite space," now that I was with my wife and my son again. I soon found, however, I had been too hasty in taking my joy of homecoming for granted. In the morning, when Yikai took my parole papers to the university security to apply for my residency permit, she was dismayed to hear from the security boss, an ex-army officer by the name of Shi Baoyu, that the permit was denied because the parole papers were incomplete. We would need a more formal document, as well as my dossier, before the application could be processed. If nothing came before the end of the month, I would have to return to the labor reform farm or be turned over to the local security bureau as an escapee. When Yikai inquired whether an official wire might be sent to the farm for the required documents, Shi Baoyu retorted, "Do you think we have nothing better to do than send wires to secure the stay of a virtual convict?" The foreign languages department leadership was of a like mind. Thrown on our own resources, I drafted a long wire to the Qinghe Farm personnel department, which Yikai sent at our own expense, in the hope of getting the red tape of proletarian dictatorship moving a little faster to beat the arbitrary deadline. Meanwhile, I was tortured by nightmares in which I was bound hand and foot as an escapee, like the ex-convict Chen I'd known at Lake Xingkai, to be transported to a remote new camp, or in which I was in a small French town with Jean Valjean's yellow passport and denied food or lodging. The suspense poisoned our reunion until the very last day of the month, when the security boss let Yikai know the papers had arrived. We did not find out until later that the papers had in fact arrived soon after my return. But the security man deliberately kept us in the dark as part and parcel of the ceaseless war of nerves against class enemies.

With Valjean's bitter experiences lurking in the back of my mind, I was reluctant to show my face on campus, in spite of Yikai's insistence that I see a doctor as soon as possible. A week went by before I ventured out of my hideout to seek medical treatment from the school clinic. People I passed on the way stared at me with abhorrent eyes, glancing back over their shoulders for another look. At the clinic it took the doctor only a minute to diagnose my trouble as a serious case of edema with a swollen liver, for which he prescribed vitamin B_1 pills and one pound each of sugar and soybeans. I thanked the doctor warmly, because I knew this was precisely what I needed and that it would have cost a lot on the black market. When I went to the dispensary with the prescription, however, the woman pharmacist stared at me with a look of nonrecognition and asked to see my medical card. It did not take her long to find out what I was. Instead of filling the prescription, she tore it up and threw the bits into the wastebasket.

To supplement my rations of dried sweet potato strips, corn flour, and sorghum flour, Yikai cycled to black markets around town in her off hours in search of food bargains. While detained on the farm, I was able to subsist on my own forced labor and save up a few yuan a month. Now apparently free, but only free to starve, I became Yikai's "kept man." With three mouths to feed, she had to count every fen of her income, averaging 196 fen a day. After paying for rent, rations, electricity, furniture rent, kindergarten fees, and union dues, she had little left. With the monthly allowance of thirty yuan my sister sent me, we could purchase one bottle of vegetable oil, eggs, some brown sugar, some soybeans, some rice, and a few bits of pork on the black market. Eggs usually cost fifty or sixty fen each. One Sunday morning Yikai came home with four small eggs tied up in a handkerchief. "One yuan for four, quite a bargain," she said, pleased with the purchase. "We can have scrambled eggs for Sunday dinner!" Yiding cheered. But when she broke the eggs into a bowl, a bad smell filled the room. "It stinks! Stinks!" Yiding hollered. She quickly left the room and dumped the smelly mess into a garbage can. "You bad egg! You bad egg!" she muttered, as if scolding an invisible presence. As Yiding ate lunch at home only on Sunday, we opened a precious can of pork stew from the hoard I had brought back from the farm.

When I was strong enough to go out on the old English bicycle we had bought in Tianjin, I would also make an occasional visit to the black market looking for food bargains. My mouth watered at the sight of wheat-flour rolls or cooked meats, but all I could afford was an ice sucker with red beans for ten fen, in the dead of winter. Another time I came upon a peddler with a basket of big red apples, which immediately brought to mind the apple Yiding had lost to the elephant in the Beijing Zoo. "You must buy one for him," I said to myself. "One yuan each, good bargain!" the man hawked. The price made me wince, but I dug out a precious one-yuan bill anyway. Yiding cheered when he saw the apple, "Big red apple! Smells so good!" When he bit into it, I asked eagerly, "Is it sweet?" He mumbled, "It's sweet all right, but it tastes like cotton." Apparently there was no way to make up for his lost apple of gold.

Strength gradually returned to my ravaged body. Trying to be a good "kept" husband, I learned to do housework. The hardest chore was to light the little briquet stove with wastepaper and kindling, poke up a good fire when needed, and cover it up and keep it alive during the night. It usually took me two or three tries to make a fire, and no flames ever shot up when a good fire was needed, however hard I fanned with our tattered palm-leaf fan. My heart would sink when I found the stove stone-cold in the morning, just like finding the life snuffed out of a starving fellow inmate during the night. When this happened, Yiding would go to the kindergarten with a handful of "children's crackers" out of his monthly ration of half a pound, and Yikai would simply do without breakfast.

Hefei is notorious for its steaming summer heat. Our little rooms, intolerable during the day, would be suffocating at night, with clouds of mosquitoes humming and not a breath of wind stirring. We tried to cool ourselves and drive off the bloodsuckers with our rationed big palm-leaf fans. When consistent fanning brought diminishing returns, we took refuge inside the mosquito net. Drenched in sweat and unable to sleep, I would regale Yikai with one thousand and one stories of life and death in the wilderness camp or the prison fortress and wonder what the future had in store for us.

Once Yikai asked me whether, after all that had happened to me during the past ten years, I ever regretted coming back to China. "Not really," I said. "I did have moments of bitter regret when I was tortured by fears of imminent death. But they soon went away when I remembered how many others were already dead or dying from starvation with even less reason. Snowbound in the Great Northern Wilderness, I had time to ruminate on my own life and the Communist rule of the past ten years. Though there were apparent options at the time of my return to China, I could have made no other choice than the one I did. My decision was a natural outcome of my life, my dreams and illusions, my virtues and failings, and the chance of circumstance. Of course it would have been better to have been spared the bitter cup, but it was certainly better to drink the cup than to join the informers and henchmen. In any case, I would never have found you had I not returned!"

"Now you're teasing me again!" she laughed softly.

"No, I'm not. I do feel sorry that I have made you pay heavily for my unfortunate choices, but for myself I have found the experiences of the past few years more uplifting than degrading. I can't tell yet how they have affected me in an all-around way. But I am sure I shall not have suffered in vain. The Communists have also been paying heavily for their gross mistakes, but it is too early to tell whether they have learned much from them. We can only hope for a turn for the better."

To help overcome the famine, university people, like other government workers, were called upon by the party to supplement government rations with food produced with their own hands, as part of the nationwide movement to develop the spirit of "self-reliance and arduous struggle" advocated by Chairman Mao. The media lauded the great example set by the "Wise Leader" himself, who had turned the flower beds in his imperial gardens into vegetable plots. Small plots of uncultivated land about the campus were allotted to faculty and staff members. I planted soybeans on the small plot allotted to Yikai. By the end of the summer, I was strong enough to roam the campus with a spade in hand, looking for bits of unclaimed land in which to plant broad beans or mung beans. My movements and ghastly appearance soon attracted the attention of Yikai's colleagues. One of them, an English instructor named Ming Liang, who had served as an army interpreter in the Korean War and who had later incurred the displeasure of the party leaders with his gibe "The rightists turned out to be right," now remarked in public, "Wu Ningkun's presence on campus is a walking reproach to the party's policy toward intellectuals. He should be given a teaching job rather than allowed to waste his talents planting broad beans." With the all-too-visible failures of the Great Leap Forward, the tongues of some intellectuals were loosened again. I kept mum, contented with my new lease on life. My survival was the envy of some of Yikai's colleagues, who had lost dear ones by starvation in the villages but were not even permitted to wear the black armbands of mourning.

2

DURING THE LUNAR NEW YEAR HOLIDAYS IN 1962, EIGHT MONTHS AFTER MY homecoming, Yimao was brought home by Yikai's Second Brother. Grandma was coming down with edema because she had saved every possible bite for the poor grandchild, who was virtually an orphan. We felt guilty about Grandma's sacrifices, but rejoiced that the family was together for the first time in nearly four years.

With magnificent magnolias enlivening an otherwise drab landscape, spring brought further improvement in my health, as well as in the party's policy toward intellectuals. On Sunday mornings we would spend hours with Yiding and Yimao in Xiaoyaojin, or the Free and Unfettered Ford, the only park in town where a great battle took place in ancient times. It was the kind of outing common to many families at the university, but to us it seemed such a precious gift of life. There was really not much to do in the park. But, free and unfettered for the moment, Yikai and I sauntered back and forth between two lines of blooming white and purple magnolias bathed in sunlight, watching the children playing in the sand pits or flying down the slides. In spite of the obvious difficulties posed by my political status, Yikai and I toyed with the idea of my teaching again. Finally Yikai plucked up her courage and brought the matter up with Colonel Li, the party secretary and chairman of the department. The colonel was not only unexpectedly congenial, but actually called on me in our small rooms a few days later. Our move turned out to be well-timed.

"I should have come to see you sooner, Mr. Wu," began the ex-colonel. "But it would have been to no practical purpose without the recent change in the party's policy toward intellectuals. You have read about what happened at the recent Guangzhou conference, haven't you?"

"Yes, in the papers."

"Good. Intellectuals are now to be considered part of the working class and to be trusted more and treated better. This applies to you too. You were hit hard in 1957; well, that's history. Now it's time to look forward. Do you have any complaints or grievances to air?"

"No, none at all. I am all gratitude," I hastened to reply, wary of another bait.

"That's good. I like your attitude. You see, some intellectuals don't understand that our party's policies have always been going alternately left and right. In 1957, we went left, and now we turn right. It all depends. When Professor Mao of the Russian faculty started attacking the party's leftist policy of yesterday with the right policy of today, I immediately warned him. 'Lao Mao,' I said, 'watch out, you may get caught tomorrow for what you are saying today.' I joined the revolutionary ranks in my early teens, I have been through a lot."

"I am certainly grateful to you for giving me such good advice before I return to work," I responded with a sincere appreciation of his unexpectedly frank and succinct analysis of the party's capricious policies. "I was very naive about politics, and still am."

"That's why you got into so much trouble. You were trained as a student of English literature, and we are very much in need of competent teachers like you. You do your teaching, we mind the politics. With two caps still on your head, an ultrarightist and an element under corrective education, you cannot come back to the faculty, not yet. Perhaps you will be hired as a temporary worker. In any case, your employment will have to be formally approved by the party committee. But I don't foresee any problem, given the party's new policy and your talent and expertise."

The next day the head of the English faculty, Professor Yang, a former law student from a missionary college in the city of Suzhou, called on me, speaking English and engaging me in a discussion of modern English fiction. The professorial visit was meant as a sort of oral examination. A few days later, I was informed of my employment as a temporary contract worker;

the contract was renewable every three months. I was to be paid sixty yuan a month, less than a third of what I was paid before my 1958 expulsion, with none of the benefits available to all faculty and staff. Neither was I eligible for free medical care, which all regular workers and college students were entitled to. But I had learned to live by the sage proverb "He is happy who knows contentment with his lot."

A few days later, Professor Yang called again to give me my assignments for the new academic year beginning in September. I was to teach Advanced English Composition to some twenty seniors, an assignment that I later learned no other teacher would accept, and Extensive Reading to some twenty juniors. Professor Yang also brought two books for me to use as texts for the reading course. One was the *Notes from the Gallows* by the Communist Czech martyr Julius Fuchik, which was widely read in a Chinese translation at the time as a testimony of revolutionary heroism. The other was the short novel *Good-bye, Mr. Chips* by the popular British novelist James Hilton. Both books were new to me, although I had seen a movie based on the novel during my college days in Kunming. And I was glad to refresh my starving mind with new nutrients, though the combination did seem a little incongruous.

Fuchik's *Notes*, which had allegedly been scribbled on scraps of paper smuggled out of the Gestapo headquarters in Prague, tersely recorded the brutal tortures he went through and his courageous endurance in the face of certain death. While often brought to tears by his hellish nightmares, I could not help but feel the irony that the supreme sacrifices made by Fuchik and others only paved the way for the establishment of regimes that rivaled the Nazis in restricting freedom. And the further irony that it was allotted to a survivor of a Communist labor camp to bear witness to the sufferings of a Communist victim of a Nazi torture chamber! Mr. Chips was a hero of a totally different character. In his lifetime devotion to his pupils, I found something infinitely gentle and infinitely noble to guide me in meeting my students, regardless of my ambiguous status. Both Fuchik and Chips made me feel humble in the face of the new challenge.

Using our only chair as a desk, I sat on a little wooden stool and worked out detailed notes for the two texts in the sweltering room, while other teachers took their summer vacations. I submitted the notes to Professor Yang for inspection and clearance before they were typed and mimeographed. When school began in September, I started the Extensive Reading course with Fuchik's revolutionary *Notes.* The course, designed as a sort of rapid-reading supplement to the core course known as Intensive Reading, was never taken seriously by teachers or students. To begin with, under Soviet influence reading as such had been reduced to a study of words and grammatical points. Students of Intensive Reading were expected to learn new words by rote and a battery of terms for the analysis of grammatical structures. Texts disintegrated in the process, and students never really learned how to read. A teacher of Extensive Reading was expected to do even less; students were expected to learn a few new words from the text and to do a bit of retelling. I had called this mechanical approach the best way to produce pedants and slaves, a modern variation on the traditional approach to classical Chinese, which aimed at preparing scholars for the composition of stereotyped essays for the imperial civil service examinations.

Now that I had no say in matters of pedagogical principles, I could at least take my own teaching seriously. With the copious notes prepared as reading aids, there was no need to spend time on vocabulary or grammar in class. Remembering how I had lived *Hamlet,* the poems of Du Fu, and the works of Shen Congwen in the camp, I searched for an intelligent and sensitive approach that would help cultivate a responsive sensibility to humane ideas and feelings and the ultimate growth of a free mind. When I read aloud the *Notes from the Gallows,* I put so much feeling into it that the Communist freedom fighter lived again in the person of a prisoner of Communist camps. The image of Chips as a loving and loved teacher somehow brought my students closer to me, in spite of repeated warnings from their political tutors against "fraternization" with an enemy of the people. I was nicknamed Mr. Chips by my students. Affectionate and admiring notes appeared in some of the papers my students handed in, which, in my ostracized state, brought me to tears. One note from a bright student named Zhang Zuwu thanked me for my "explication and analysis, which have opened up a new world of wonders" to him. Another student by the name of Xu Zhen, always subdued and unsmiling, wrote to say how much he felt for me since his father, a high school teacher, had also been labeled a rightist, and to tell me how my teaching had "lit up" his life under a cloud. I destroyed the notes and warned the writers against such indiscretions, which could easily land us all in political troubles.

Meanwhile, with my students doing volunteer publicity for me, their fellow students from other English classes, as well as junior faculty members from the department and the Hefei Teachers College, came to sit in on my classes. Sometimes the latecomers had to stand in the hallway and follow my lectures from the open windows. This unexpected phenomenon soon alarmed the party functionaries, who issued an order banning all auditors except younger faculty members authorized by the department to learn what they could from my teaching and keep an eye on my ideology. Yikai reminded me of the popular saying, "A big tree catches the wind." I found myself in a dilemma. On the one hand, I had to live up to the expectations of my employers, who had given me the precarious rice bowl on the understanding that I was a competent English teacher. On the other hand, I had to steer away from the shallows of professional jealousy and political hazards. The golden mean of Confucius was perhaps what might have served me best in the situation, but, alas, what use would I be to my good students if I stopped teaching language as a humane discipline? Well, come what may, I could only be guided by the light of my own understanding, even though I was surely treading on thin ice.

In the writing course, I had to struggle with some twenty English compositions a week. There was only one little desk in our rooms. Now that Yiding was in grade school, he had the use of the desk until nine, when he was ready to go to bed. By the time I sat down to the compositions, my eyelids were drooping. To keep myself awake, I started smoking Big Iron Bridge cigarettes, the cheapest brand at nine fen a packet, the only kind I could afford, though my colleagues smoked cigarettes costing five or six times as much. One night, after Yikai and the kids had gone to sleep, a lit cigarette slipped from my unconscious fingers onto the old rug Yikai had put under the desk to keep my feet warm. Awakened by the smoke from the smoldering rug, Yikai jumped out of bed, shook me awake, and stamped out the incipient fire. "Come to bed now," she said decisively. "No more burning midnight cigarettes from now on." In spite of the drudgery, I often found it refreshing to come upon a startling novel idea or an unexpected turn of phrase that opened a window to a young mind.

3

WHEN I WAS HIRED BY THE DEPARTMENT IN THE SUMMER OF 1962, A YOUNG English teacher named Feng Xiangchun, a party member and a former army lieutenant, was assigned to do advanced study with me and supervise my thought reform at the same time. He would write book reports for me and I would hand him a biweekly report on my progress in thought reform. Presumably I was always making some progress, but there was still much to be desired before my rightist label could be removed. An amiable man by nature, Feng would usually say a few words of encouragement upon reading my reports, but if the "bowstring of class struggle" happened to be a bit tight at the moment, he would stop smiling and deliver a short lecture on my easygoing attitude. When he came to my room for tutoring on readings I had assigned him, he was as a rule all respect and admiration. And when he returned from his home in Nanjing or his wife's home in Shanghai after a vacation, he never failed to bring my children chocolate bars or toffees, which they loved. I often wondered how he felt constantly switching roles with me throughout those two years.

Feng's role as my political confessor ended the day my rightist label was removed. On July 4, 1964, as if to mark the third anniversary of my homecoming on parole, a faculty-staff meeting of the foreign languages department was held in a lecture room in the seven-story main building. After recounting my rightist crimes, a personnel officer announced my "decapping" by reading a decision to that effect made by the university party committee. As advised beforehand, I made a short speech, acknowledging my guilt once again and thanking the party for "giving me a new political life." My voice became choked with uncontrollable tears, as if all the dammed-up anguish of seven tortured years had burst open the floodgates. A few colleagues shook my hand to congratulate me on my "return to the ranks of the people." The department leaders assured me I would be put back on the English faculty with a substantial raise in pay.

The same night, before we could take comfort in our new prospects, an urgent wire came from Yikai's family with the terrible message that her mother was critically ill. Rushing off the next day, Yikai arrived in Tianjin on the sixth to find her mother rapidly failing after futile surgery for cancer of the liver. When her dying mother asked after me, Yikai told her about my "decapping," which had been her fervent wish all these years. She also comforted her mother with the white lie that I had been reinstated as a professor with my previous pay. What other comfort could a grieved daughter have given her dying mother, who had given her and me and our children so much of her love and understanding? How could I ever forget the message she had sent me on Yikai's three prison visits, simple words that had lit up my dark world? She died two days later, on July 8, which happened to be the eighth anniversary of our wedding. I remembered we had once celebrated it with her over a simple dinner. She had lived a simple life full of suffering, and from her own suffering she had found the strength to love and to stand by the insulted and the injured. She was certainly worthy of her suffering.

When Yikai returned from Tianjin early in August, she was called in by Professor Yao, vice chairman of the department. He informed her that the department leaders had decided she should start teaching English to nonmajors when the new school year began, now that her husband was no longer a rightist. As to my own reinstatement on the English faculty, it was clear by the end of the year that all of Colonel Li's negotiations with the personnel department had come to nothing. "Once expelled, always expelled," as the personnel chief put it. Before the new year began, Little Hot Pepper's husband, who was on the department party committee, called me in and announced a ten-yuan raise "as a token of the party's recognition of my progress in thought reform and performance in teaching work." The token raise meant more eggs in our diet, but I was brought face-to-face with my "new political life," which meant nothing more than that I was a "decapped rightist." Decapped yes, but rightist nonetheless, a political reality I had to live with for many more years to come.

In the relative lull in class struggle that followed, I was left pretty much alone. For a senior reading course, I took the liberty of including selections from *Gulliver's Travels,* which seemed to relate to life in present-day China by refraction. Once my rightist label was removed, I was assigned to teach a course in listening comprehension, using selected items from the Voice of America, the BBC, the ABC, and the NHK, in addition to Radio Peking, as teaching material. The students loved it, perhaps partly because they were listening to trained native speakers of English for the first time in their life, and perhaps partly because they did not fail to notice the differences in news reporting between Radio Peking and the Western media. As it was a penal crime for citizens to listen to "enemy broadcasts," the university had to apply to the city's Bureau of Public Security for special permission for me to monitor all foreign stations and make necessary recordings for teaching purposes. Of all the populace of the capital city of the province, only one "enemy of the people" could listen in to subversive enemy propaganda with impunity! Meanwhile, I was still excluded from certain political reports, including a presentation by an army officer on "how the Chinese People's Liberation Army won a crushing victory over the Indian invaders on the Tibetan border."

However, the relative lull in those few years soon gave way to renewed emphasis on perpetual class struggle, with the mounting of polemics with Moscow following Mao's open split with our Big Brother. Stormy political campaigns repeated every few years were asserted by the "Great Teacher" to be the only effective means to keep Socialist China from going revisionist the Soviet way. By December 1964, the intelligentsia found itself trapped in the midst of yet another political campaign—the nationwide movement to study the nine polemical articles attacking Soviet revisionists and their allies published in the name of the Central Committee of the Chinese Communist party. We had no way of knowing how the Soviet revisionists fared under the vitriolic fire, but Chinese intellectuals, now charged with carrying the virus of revisionist ideology, once again bore the brunt on the home front. To expose and then purge themselves of pernicious revisionist ideas, all faculty members took turns at making a self-criticism and then accepting "help" from their peers in the form of merciless critiques. I was once again castigated by my colleagues and party functionaries alike as the worst of all, an ex-rightist imbued with revisionist ideas, although I could never figure out how I got hooked up with the Chinese Communists' Big Brothers of yesterday.

Meanwhile, to ensure the rural communes would not "go revisionist," a "four cleanups campaign" was unfolding in the countryside to weed out corruption and political aberrations among commune and village leaders. Younger teachers and upperclassmen were sent for a year at a time to carry out the campaign. The senior faculty, spared from the stint, were sent early in January 1966 to a nearby rural commune to "observe" the ongoing four cleanups campaign, led by Colonel Li, now director of the united front department of the university party committee responsible for the thought reform of senior nonparty intellectuals. Though only a temporary contract worker, I also enjoyed the dubious status of a "united front personage" and went on the tour in the company of a few dozen professors and senior instructors. We stayed at a commune primary school and visited one village after another to hear talks on how village and commune leaders had been "cleaned up" politically, morally, and economically. The Socialist revolution, we were told, was now poised for another leap forward.

As a complement to three weeks in the countryside, Colonel Li took us to Huainan, a major coal-mining town in the north of the province, to "observe the excellent situation on the industrial front" for another week. The city of Huainan was actually made up of five small towns, each centering around a colliery. The streets were black with coal dust and the air foggy with smoke from coal-burning stoves. As guests of Mayor Pan, an old friend of Li's, we were accommodated at the plush Dongshan Government Guest House, complete with carpets and modern bathrooms. There were big lunches at every factory or mine following a conducted tour, and banquets and theatrical performances in the evenings. At the sumptuous banquet hosted by Mayor Pan, Professor Yao, known as a good drinker, downed so many cups of 120-proof liquor that he staggered back to his room afterward and slipped on the bathroom floor. A surgeon had to be summoned to stitch the cuts on his forehead and nose. When our return banquet followed the next evening, to my surprise I was drafted to offer "bottoms up" toasts with the same liquor to the mayor and his ranking colleagues, one by one, in the place of Professor Yao, who had discreetly confined himself to his room.

What impressed me most on the whole tour was our visit to the No. 1 Xie Colliery, the showpiece of the mining town. Arriving in two chartered buses on a fine winter morning, we were met by polite party functionaries who conducted us to the large reception room. On one wall hung a huge portrait of Chairman Mao; the other walls were covered with varieties of awards in the form of red flags or banners, awards for overfulfilling the production quota, for the best pit safety record, for pit sanitation, and so on. We sat in armchairs and sipped tea while the party secretary gave us a warm official welcome. He briefed us on the sad past of the colliery under Japanese occupation and Nationalist exploitation, its salvation by Chairman Mao and the Communist party, its growing annual output, and the miners' happy life. Then several functionaries guided us to the visitors' dressing room, where we changed into protective outfits complete with headlamps. We were taken into the pit by elevator and tram, while our guide explained how things operated underground. I eagerly looked forward to seeing with my own eyes how the miners worked. But the guide had his orders and stopped short of taking us to the coal face. Above ground again, we went back to the dressing room and changed into our own clothes. Then we were taken through the public bath for the miners, which boasted four huge concrete pools filled with water. These heated pools, the guide explained, were used by turns. When one shift of miners turned the water in the first pool black, the second pool would be opened to newcomers. "These pools were built after liberation," the guide added proudly. "Which one are we going to use?" I asked. The guide replied with a laugh, "Oh, no, how could we do that to our distinguished visitors?" He soon conducted us to a separate hall marked DISTINGUISHED VISITORS' BATH. An attendant handed us each a snow-white bath towel, a pair of bathroom slippers, and a small cake of toilet soap. We bathed ourselves in a white-tiled pool with limpid hot water, which did not turn black.

Our next stop was the Class Education Museum in a secluded part of the colliery. We first went through several rooms with pictures on the walls and exhibits in glass cases showing how local capitalists and Japanese aggressors had mercilessly exploited and oppressed the miners. The rooms led to a large hall, which had been used by the Japanese as a sickroom for the miners dying from prolonged hard labor and diseases. The walls were covered with pictures of the dead and the dying. Facing the sickroom was a place with a prominent sign in huge characters: WAN REN KENG, or Pit of Ten Thousand Corpses. The guide explained how the Japanese had thrown the dead and dying miners into an open pit, totaling, over the years of occupation, some ten thousand bodies in all. We were then taken behind a huge wooden screen and suddenly faced with the spectacle of heaps upon heaps of human skeletons, skulls, limbs, and trunks, walled in with glass panels. I could hardly breathe. I had been familiar with stories of Japanese atrocities since I was a schoolboy, but this was my first sight of their unbelievable inhumanities. And these corpses were only an infinitesimal fraction of the millions of victims of Japanese aggression! The sight of the pit made us all somber and speechless. How could any Chinese who had survived forgive and forget? My mind, however, soon wandered to the millions of victims of the recent famine and the preceding political campaigns. Would a museum be built for them too?

Life on the whole was much better for me and my family than in the days when I was close to dying in prison and the family was scattered here and there. By now it was an open secret that millions in the agricultural province of Anhui alone, mostly peasants, had died of starvation; yet I survived. I wondered at my good luck, but my heart was heavy. The political atmosphere relaxed somewhat with the removal of the former provincial party boss, whose despotic rule had wrecked the economy and sent thousands of critics to jail. The university was also freed from the yoke of the same tyrant, who had served concurrently as its party boss and president.

The family was reunited. Following the homecoming of our daughter in the winter of 1962, my stepmother also joined us from Beijing that summer. Another boy was born to us on July 2, 1963, whom I named Yicun or One Village, after a line by Lu You, the celebrated poet of the Song dynasty. In one of his best-known lyrics, the poet jubilantly hailed the sudden appearance of a village flourishing with green willows and bright flowers just when he thought he had come to the dead end of a boat trip on a tortuous river through a mountainous country. Little did we know that on the political horizon of our disaster-ridden homeland, storms were again gathering that would plunge the nation and my family into the abyss of disasters!

Eleven

SWEPT INTO A COW
SHED, 1966–68

1

THE YEAR 1965 WITNESSED THE OMINOUS CLOUDS GATHERING ON THE CUL-
tural scene. On Sundays teachers and students would be issued tickets to a
downtown cinema to see films that were being attacked in the official media
as "poisonous weeds." There was no free show, however, for we were
expected to join in the chorus of condemnation at the next session of
political study. I found nothing wrong with these films, except that they
were artistically much nicer than those formulistic productions extolling the
great party and superhuman Communist heroes. The papers were rife with
critiques of "bourgeois" films and stage plays, as well as traditional Beijing
operas, reminiscent of Hitler's attack on "degenerate art." Before the year
was out, newspapers all over the country front-paged violent attacks on a
new historical play about the unjust dismissal of a righteous mandarin
named Hai Rui by a tyrannical Ming dynasty emperor. The play was
denounced as an oblique attack on the "Great Leader" for his 1959 dismissal
of the outspoken Marshal Peng Dehuai, who had protested the excesses of
the Great Leap Forward and the People's Commune. The playwright, Wu
Han, formerly an eminent professor of Ming history at my wartime university in Kunming and a longtime fellow traveler, was at the time a vice mayor
of Beijing. During the past fifteen years, each major political campaign had
invariably been spearheaded by vanguard action on the cultural front, and
each new campaign had proved more violent and extensive than the previous one. The all-powerful "Great Leader" at the head of an all-powerful
great party supported by an all-powerful army had proved incredibly para-
noid about literary and artistic works, or any form of intellectual expression,
for that matter. What was he up to now?

"The turbulent wind precedes the mountain storm," as a familiar Chinese verse puts it. The spring of 1966 saw an escalation of the critique of the playwright and two other high-ranking scholar-officials who had collaborated on a series of miscellaneous essays. Their writings were denounced as "great poisonous weeds" attacking the "Great Leader." The upshot of the critique was summary dismissal not only of the three culprits, but of the powerful mayor of Beijing himself and his city Party Committee, which was accused of masterminding the conspiracy. On May 16, the Central Committee issued a militant call for the unfolding of a Great Proletarian Cultural Revolution throughout the country to eradicate the "four olds," short for "the old thought, the old culture, the old customs, and the old habits." In the days that followed, the party and army organs were filled with high-pitched editorials and press reports on intense political activities in the nation's capital and other major cities. Obviously, the critique of one historical play was but a pretext for another major political campaign, but nobody knew exactly what it was all about or how it would be carried out.

On the first of June, the 6:30 morning news of the Central People's Broadcasting Station, blasting through loudspeakers, aired a *People's Daily* editorial hysterically calling upon the revolutionary masses to "sweep away all cow demons and snake spirits." It singled out "reactionary academic authorities" as representatives of the bourgeoisie who were dreaming of restoring capitalism in China. The tone was even more hysterical than that of editorials attacking the rightists in 1957. I saw a disturbed look in Yikai's eye, but I was at a loss for what to say. Yiding asked, "What are cow demons and snake spirits, Papa?" While I hesitated, Yikai came out with an answer: "We don't know, Yiding. We have never seen any. We'll find out."

I hurried off to my eight o'clock class. On entering the liberal arts building, the first things I saw were big-character posters plastered on both walls of the hallway. There were attacks on Professor Mao of the Russian faculty, Professor Yang, head of the English faculty, and Professor Yao, vice chairman of the department. I was relieved to see there was none on me. Perhaps as a temporary worker I would hardly rate as a "reactionary academic authority." When I found the classroom deserted, I walked into the department office to ask what to do, only to find some of my students busy writing posters on old newspapers. I ventured to say hello, but nobody seemed to know me anymore. At a loss, I left the room and ran into the department chair, Yang Xingfu, pacing in the corridor. "Are classes suspended for good, Chairman Yang?" I asked anxiously. "No, no, just for the time being. How can we afford to suspend classes for long?" His stutter was stronger than usual. Yang, the son of a revolutionary martyr and a former naval officer, had been brought from a military academy in Nanjing to succeed Colonel Li as party secretary and chairman of the department when Li was promoted to the united front director of the university party committee. His career included a stint of several years at the University of Moscow teaching modern Chinese. Unlike his predecessor, Yang was a man of few words who laid more emphasis on academic values than political verbiage.

Contrary to Yang's expectations, classes were suspended for the next few years, and I never taught at the university again. Instead, there was a hue and cry for heads at the university. Since party directives had named "reactionary bourgeois academic authorities" as targets of the revolution, the party leadership deemed it safe to throw three senior professors and one prolific instructor of Chinese to the wolves. Almost overnight, the campus was transformed into a labyrinth of hastily erected fences lined with reed mattings, which were plastered with abusive big-character posters indicting other teachers, especially senior faculty, in addition to the four chosen arch–cow demons. I wandered through the bizarre maze of poster boards to see whether I might be spared this time, hoping against hope. Soon my eye was caught by a caricature that represented me as a smiling tiger, with the caption "The dead tiger isn't dead." I was mildly alarmed: did that mean they would see me really dead this time? One poster enumerated my heinous ultrarightist crimes. Another exposed my "criminal past" as an interpreter for the American Flying Tigers and the Nationalist Air Force. Still another denounced my teaching work as an infamous plot to corrupt the minds of socialist youths with decadent bourgeois literature and revisionist ideology. I was charged with resisting educational reform by persisting in using original literary works in English rather than English translations of Chinese political articles as teaching material; spreading enemy propaganda in my listening comprehension course; advertising the decadent bourgeois life-style depicted in O. Henry's short story "The Cop and the Anthem," which happened to contain a mallard duck, Chablis, and a demitasse; holding up a bourgeois English schoolteacher as a model to prettify all bourgeois intellectuals; attacking the New China by innuendo with *Gulliver's Travels;* and so on. I had hoped to be spared, but I was wrong again. A rightist, even though "decapped," was by definition a cow demon or snake spirit. I was quickly nicknamed "smiling tiger" by my children at home, who had no idea yet what the fuss would mean to us all.

The night of June 6 was a typical muggy night in Hefei. Under the mosquito net, I was not able to fall asleep until midnight. Then I felt Yikai nudging me repeatedly, saying under her breath, "Listen. The uproar, the slogans!" I began to hear the hubbub of hysterical shouts coming from the center of the campus. "Students having nothing better to do," I said drowsily. "Let's go back to sleep." Then, still half-awake, I heard Yikai whispering more urgently, "Listen, they are shouting your name, coming our way!" Before I knew what to make of it, the rooms shook with fists banging and feet kicking at the door. Grandma, who slept in the outer room with the two older children, got out of bed and opened the door to a band of my own students, who rushed in, shouting, "Down with the ultrarightist Wu Ningkun! Down with U.S. imperialism!" Leading the band was Wang Chongde, who the head of the department had assigned to me for special tutoring on account of his "good" peasant family origin and slow progress in his studies. They pulled me out of bed and ordered me to follow them. On the way out they dragged me past Yiding and Yimao, huddled up in the corner, shivering and sobbing. "Don't be scared," I told them. "These are my students. You know them." I was then half dragged and half pushed to the basketball court. There I was shocked to see dozens of professors and lecturers on their knees while an angry male student made a hysterical harangue on their sins. I was soon on my knees myself, with fists banging on my back and feet kicking at my legs. Finally a shrill man's voice announced over the loudspeaker: "Revolutionary students! Tonight we just scored a great victory over the cow demons and snake spirits at Anhui University! These enemies of the people have been dreaming of restoring their bourgeois paradise! But we have won! Now let us withdraw our forces and prepare to carry on the struggle against the class enemies tomorrow! Long live the Great Leader Chairman Mao!" By the time I dragged myself back to our rooms, it was 2:30 A.M. Sore and dazed, I wondered what such hooliganism had to do with the so-called Cultural Revolution, but my mind failed to cope with what was so preposterous and not amenable to rational understanding. It brought to mind, however, what the storm troopers had done to the Jews in the early days of the Nazi terror—only this crazy wholesale violence of students against their own teachers, in dead of night, was surely more bizarre.

The next morning, all "cow demons and snake spirits," some forty middle-aged or elderly faculty in all, were summoned to a meeting room to hear a party functionary lecture us on the seriousness of our sins and crimes in working for capitalist restoration over the years. What the students did the night before, he asserted, was revolutionary action provoked by "suspicious activities" on the part of the "demons and spirits." Its righteous power had smashed our restoration dreams to smithereens. Therefore we were ordered to go home and reflect, in writing, on how much we had benefited from it and how it had "touched us to our very souls"—in short, to admit it was what we richly deserved and to give thanks to the party and revolutionary masses for going out of their way to "rescue us from the quagmire of capitalism and revisionism."

So I was in for it again, less than two years after I had "returned to the ranks of the people." I had tried to sit very small, I had kept my thoughts to myself, yet I was not spared. Obviously I had been permanently stigmatized, not because of what I did or didn't commit, but because of what the regime wanted to make of me. In 1958, I was the only senior faculty member singled out as a rightist and denounced by my peers with such righteous indignation. I was an exception; even I had wondered if I did not have only myself to blame. Now I suddenly found myself in the company of so many "kindred spirits" who had so recently been given the laurel of "working class intellectuals." I figured that the party, under the personal command of the "Great Leader," was giving Marxist dialectics a new turn of the screw to meet its own political needs, independent of what the intellectuals might have or have not done. So far as the intellectuals were concerned, the Cultural Revolution was a logical development and escalation of the antirightist campaign. Finding no reason to reproach myself, I felt strangely relieved, although I had to start "reforming myself through forced labor" again, a temporary worker among professors and senior instructors.

My wife was again harassed with injunctions to inform on me, "to expose my counterrevolutionary words and deeds." At the same time she was told to guard against my "doing anything foolish to myself." Yikai reassured them: "Thanks for the concern. But Wu Ningkun won't be that stupid. Furthermore, his mother hanged herself when he was a child. He was immunized early." My daughter, Yimao, who had passed her eighth birthday three days before the midnight incursion into our rooms, was accosted by some of my students on her way home and taken into their dormitory. The child, who had barely learned to write, was made to copy a slogan in large characters with a writing brush and put her name under it. The slogan was then prominently displayed on a placard at a crossroad: "Down with Wu Ningkun the Counterrevolutionary!" All three children were constantly jeered at by other children as little rightists and little counterrevolutionaries. Yimao, now a first grader, watched with envy as other schoolchildren organized into a group of Young Pioneers, from which she was excluded, and paraded and shouted slogans on campus. Yicun, hardly three years old when the Cultural Revolution erupted, was all at once shunned by his little friends in the kindergarten. While the others played, he often sat in a corner by himself with his hands on his knees.

2

IN MID–AUGUST, SOON AFTER THE RED GUARDS WERE FIRST FORMED IN BEIJING with the blessings of the "Red Supreme Commander," college students from Beijing wearing Red Guard armbands descended on the campus to pass on their "revolutionary experiences in sweeping away all cow demons and snake spirits as well as the 'four olds.' " Meanwhile, students from all over the country visited Beijing and other cities for "mass revolutionary linkups" and "exchange of revolutionary experiences," which was made easy by the provision of free rides on trains, buses, and ships, as well as free food and lodging. When our students returned from their free tours in September, they sported faded grass-green army uniforms with Red Guard armbands. To intensify the dictatorship against the "cow demons and snake spirits," they brought back copies of big-character posters and handbills from Beijing, now designated the "center of the world revolution," extolling the godly virtues and infallible wisdom of Chairman Mao, now better known as the "Reddest, Reddest Sun in Our Hearts," and denouncing the counterrevolutionary crimes of "reactionary academic authorities" as well as "capitalist-roaders," short for "top persons within the party taking the capitalist road," party and government officials branded as opponents to the "Great Leader." Horror stories of savageries perpetrated by Red Guards against varieties of "cow demons and snake spirits" and cultural treasures in Beijing, Shanghai, Tianjin, and other major cities began to spread by word of mouth and handbills. Under their Red Commander, the Red Guards vowed to "smash the old world to smithereens and build up a bright red new world on its ruins." The reign of Red Terror had begun.

One day in September, during our lunch break, a band of Red Guards broke into our rooms again, shouting "Down with Jiang Zhongjie! Down with landlords!" Jiang Zhongjie was my stepmother, who was classified as a landlord because my father had inherited farm land from his father. She was shaking with fright on the edge of her narrow bed when two college girls wearing Red Guard armbands grabbed her and ordered her to go with them.

"Let me go to the toilet first, please," she pleaded.

"Are you trying to play for time, you landlord hag?" one of the two girls retorted.

Yikai intervened. "Grandma is diabetic. She has to go often, especially when she is nervous."

"Can you guarantee that she will not attempt to escape, Li Yikai?" another Red Guard demanded.

"Yes, I can. You can go and see for yourself that the public toilet has only one door," Yikai explained quietly.

"Okay, get going, Jiang Zhongjie. We'll wait for you outside. Be quick about it." The same Red Guard gave her a push toward the door.

Two hours passed before Mother staggered back on her bound feet, her gray hair straggling over her face. She collapsed onto her bed, and Yiding quickly refilled her tea mug with hot water from a thermos.

"Have some tea first, Granny," Yiding said softly, helping her to the tea. "What happened?" I suddenly sensed how much Yiding had grown during the past few months. He was only ten, but his boyhood had come to a blighted end.

"Well, well, Yiding my darling," she began slowly, in a feeble voice. "You are going to lose your granny." She burst into tears.

"Grandma, try to calm yourself, please. Tell us what happened," Yikai implored, sitting on the bed beside her.

After a while, Mother resumed. "Well, I was first escorted to the basketball court," she began. "I trembled all the way, shaking, scared. I don't know how many other old people were also there, men and women, quite a few. Then we were lined up and made to parade around the campus under escort by Red Guards. They shouted slogans all the way. 'Down with the landlord class! Down with landlords! Down with landlord So-and-So! Drive them out of Anhui University! Long live Great Leader Chairman Mao!' And on and on. Then we were brought back to the basketball court again. A male Red Guard lectured us on crimes committed by the landlord class. Finally he gave the order that we all get out of the university and the city within twenty-four hours. If we failed to comply with the order, there would be dire consequences. Oh, what am I to do? What am I to do now?"

I knew I was helpless, already denounced as a "cow demon" myself. How could a society that was known for its respect to age now stoop so low as to persecute defenseless old women? How could college students, the cream of the nation, be so quickly transformed into inhuman tools of tyranny? Again it was Yikai who took it upon herself to look for a way out.

"Please calm down and rest, Granny, please do," she said gently. "I always say, 'Heaven never seals off all the exits.' I will go and try to reason with the Red Guards."

Nearly an hour passed before she came back.

"I told them Granny is seventy-one years old and very sick with diabetes. She can only stay with us. She has no other place to go to. I don't see how her stay on the campus could do anybody any harm. Their answer was 'Too bad, but that's none of our business. Beijing and Shanghai have taken the lead in driving landlords out of the cities and back to their native places. You have no doubt heard how that's done there. By comparison, we are too lenient as it is. How can we make an exception? This is Red Terror! Obey the order or else!' They are fanatics now. No use hoping for their mercy."

After a brief discussion with Grandma, we decided she could only go back to my hometown, Yangzhou, which she had left fifteen years before to join me in Beijing. At least my cousins there would take her in and look after her. Perhaps she could rejoin us when things quieted down. Early in the morning Yikai again sallied forth and had Grandma's residency permit and rations transferred to Yangzhou, while I helped her pack. In the afternoon, Yikai went to the train station and lined up for a ticket to Yangzhou. After we put the children to bed, a pedicab we had quietly hired came to the door. With tears in her eyes, Grandma had a hard time tearing herself away from Yiding, her favorite grandchild. I went along to see her off, carrying her parcels. For fear of attracting attention, she did not even take a suitcase with her. Watching her board the train for the lonely journey home, I felt much worse than I had eight years ago when I was picked up by an army jeep for my lonely journey to the labor camp. When would I see her again? But she was lucky to have got away alive, for several of Yikai's aged relatives in Tianjin, her paternal step-grandmother and her daughter, and Yikai's own mother's brother and wife, were denounced as evil capitalists by marauding Red Guards, summarily murdered in their own houses, and dumped on trucks carrying bodies to the burning ground. Who could tell me why these defenseless old men and women had to be so brutally butchered by youngsters whom they would have loved as their own grandchildren? Why were these and a million other outrages perpetrated in the name of the Cultural Revolution? Yikai had been inconsolably grieved when her mother had died two years ago, but now she took comfort in the thought that her mother had been spared the ordeal of the revolution. Death seemed to be the only comforter in the land under the reign of Red Terror.

Soon the Red Guards started raiding and ransacking houses of university professors and instructors. On the way to a house targeted for their foray, they would shout the usual slogans to the accompaniment of gongs and cymbals, keeping everybody wondering who would be the next victim. Guards armed with red-tasseled spears would be posted at the entrance of the building in which a home was being searched, in the fashion of the Hunan peasants of the 1920s, whose plundering of landlord homes their "Red Commander" had gloated over in his now-famous report.

One morning an order from the Red Guards of the department of foreign languages and literature was broadcast over the loudspeakers, enjoining the "cow demons and snake spirits" of the department to report to the concrete basketball court at 9:00 A.M. sharp to face denunciation and struggle by revolutionary masses. The list included four senior members of the Russian faculty, five of the English faculty, plus myself. When I showed up a few minutes before nine, the other nine "cow demons" were already lined up on the court, their heads bowed in dismay. At their feet was piled a motley of clothes shoes, art objects, radio sets, and household utensils, apparently plundered from their homes. The "cow demons" were surrounded by a throng of spectators, just as a traditional public execution never failed to attract a large crowd. As soon as I found my place next to the last "demon" in line, the presiding Red Guard started denouncing us all for our counterrevolutionary crimes in carrying out a revisionist line in education. He pointed to the heap of personal articles (which reminded me of American garage sales) as proof of our decadent bourgeois life-style. Then, he announced, as our wages were far too high compared with those of workers and peasants, we were enjoined to volunteer cuts on the spot, one by one. I had thought my pay was already quite low, but I stammered I could live on thirty yuan a month. So forty yuan were withheld from my meager income of seventy yuan. Then we were paraded around the campus, each with a dunce cap on his or her head, under the escort of Red Guards who shouted slogans beginning with "Long live" or "Down with," as the case might be. After the parade, we were taken into a classroom in the liberal arts building, where Xiao Jun, a Russian teacher, former naval officer, and party member, announced the "cow demons and snake spirits" were now organized into a special group for the purpose of political study and labor reform. To my great surprise, I was appointed the group leader. Once again I felt as if the mocking purple was thrust upon me!

We were to meet for the first political study session at 2:00 P.M. the same day. Approaching the building a few minutes ahead of time, I saw from a distance my fellow "cow demons," including a gray-haired woman Russian instructor, squatting on the ground in front of the building, busy pulling up weeds, their dunce caps bouncing up and down. It might have been a scene out of *A Midsummer Night's Dream*. "What are you doing?" I asked Professor Yao, a gray-haired Harvard man. "Better than doing nothing," he answered seriously. "It wouldn't look right sitting or standing around idle." Then all followed me into the room. The first order I gave was for everyone to remove their dunce caps, which each person then stood on their desks. I was a little annoyed by their gratuitous obsequiousness.

"Who asked you to bring and wear the dunce caps?" I asked the group.

"Well, the Red Guards never said we might remove them," answered the Harvard man, who was known for assiduously following party instructions to the letter. "We are criminals all, revisionist as well as capitalist. I think we should show our penitence through humility."

"Lao Wang." I turned to a former Nationalist diplomat who had defected to the Communists in 1950. He was supposed to enjoy a sort of immunity due a defector. I was curious whether he felt betrayed. "You were used to top hats in Paris. How do you feel about trading your top hat of the old days for the dunce cap in front of you?"

"The group leader's question touches me to my very soul," the former diplomat from my hometown replied in all earnestness. A typical minor scholar-official of the old type, Wang always guarded his tongue and watched his step. I often wondered what had given him the guts to defect. "The top hat disguised my hideous reactionary past. The dunce cap is much more fitting, because it shows my true colors. I am grateful to the Red Guards for their revolutionary action, which has helped me to face my own crimes, past and present, helped to touch me to my very soul."

Then Wu Baotai, a hoary old man hired to teach translation from Russian into Chinese upon his retirement as a translator from the military academy in Nanjing, followed in his heavy Jiangxi accent.

"I feel the same way as Lao Wang does. Except that my case is even worse, for I was once a party member. I joined the party in 1922, less than one year from its founding. Unfortunately, I lost contact with the organization shortly afterward. The party was underground and I had no way of re-establishing contact. To eke out a living, I worked for the reactionary Nationalists. But I never betrayed the party or any comrade. So I never saw myself as a renegade or traitor. After all, wasn't I one of the earliest members of the party? Was it my sole responsibility that I lost contact with the party? Did I not cherish an undying love for the party throughout all the years of separation? The liberation had brought the party back to me and I have since given myself back to the great cause of the party. Therefore I have been under the illusion that I am a true revolutionary, although I have not been reaccepted into the party. All of a sudden the Red Guards denounced me as a renegade, a traitor. Their revolutionary action touched me to my very soul. I can no longer deceive myself. I never was a revolutionary. I was a renegade, an out-and-out traitor. I stand condemned as a dog renegade."

This man, who had always enjoyed my respect due a senior colleague, was suddenly metamorphosed into a "dog renegade." My feelings were so mixed that I did not know how to respond. Just then Lao Kong, a professor of Russian, asked for permission to speak his thoughts.

"The revolutionary action of the Red Guards this morning really touched me to my very soul. There were so many 'four olds' in my house. I have lived with them so long and taken them for granted. Once they were brought out into the light of day, I was shocked and ashamed to see how long and how fondly I was attached to these relics of feudalism and capitalism. Even gold rings and other decadent things, which the Red Guards rightfully swept away."

"From the bottom of my trunks, the Red Guards discovered many things I had forgotten for a long time," his wife, the gray-haired Russian instructor, put in. "There was my wedding dress, embroidered in brocade, really too decadent. I would never dream of wearing it again, but I suppose I kept it as a memento of our wedding. A terrible lingering nostalgia for the 'four olds.' "

"The Red Guards did not even search my apartment," added the former diplomat defector. "They came in and very affably asked me to turn over things that I considered 'four olds.' So I handed them my tuxedo, along with a pair of diamond cuff links. Good riddance!"

Lao Mao, a professor of Russian and also a former Nationalist diplomat, was denounced as the number-one "cow demon" of the department because of his checkered past and his big mouth. Usually witty at the expense of his colleagues and party functionaries, he now spoke with an ostensibly heavy heart.

"My name is Mao, as in the verb *maochong,* to pretend to be what I am not. I pretend to be a professor, a poet, a scholar, but I am just a fraud. In reality I am nothing but the dregs of the old society. I served the Nationalist reactionaries, accepted a nominal position from the puppet government under Japanese occupation. I have always led a decadent way of life. Most of the stuff that was heaped on the basketball court in the morning came from my house. All the paintings, calligraphy scrolls, painted fans, and whatnot were out-and-out 'four olds.' Some of them were handed down from my parents as family heirlooms I treasured. Now I can see them as exhibits of my dirty soul, which has long been corrupted with feudal and bourgeois ideas and tastes. The revolutionary action of the Red Guards has touched me to my very soul more than it has done any of you, because my sins and crimes are so heinous that they could never be redeemed even if I were to suffer ten thousand deaths. I have always admired the brilliant poetry of our Great Leader Chairman Mao, by the side of which my own poems are mere trash. But now I must assiduously study his poems for the purpose of my thought reform, my soul reform. I am old and tottering, but I am more than willing to reform myself through hard labor."

I was not taken in by Professor Mao's thought-reform rhetoric, for I knew it only too well from my own experience. I only wished the Red Guards would not be so rash as to throw all those precious artworks of his into the bonfire they had talked about building on the basketball court. The university librarian had managed to stop the Red Guards from setting fire to the library by invoking the name of their Red Commander who, according to him, had honored it with a visit on his inspection tour of the newly founded university in the summer of 1958. In the heart of the city, however, a despairing aged scholar threw himself from the window of his second-story study into a bonfire a band of high school Red Guards had built in front of his house to burn up his lifelong collection of three thousand rare editions of classical Chinese literature. Dashed to his death on the spot, he was summarily condemned as a counterrevolutionary who had thus forever severed himself from the party and the people. Though the Red Terror in the provincial capital was nothing compared to that in the national capital or Tianjin or Shanghai, the toll it took was heavy.

The next day our rooms were searched for counterrevolutionary evidence as well as "four olds." The search squad of four Red Guards came shortly after lunch, led by Xiao (Little) Bao, a younger teacher who was a former student of mine until two years before. Instead of showing his usual shy boyish smile, he addressed me with a deadpan look. "Wu Ningkun, hand me all the letters you have received from home and abroad." I told him it was not our practice to keep old letters, a lesson we had learned from the anti–Hu Feng campaign of 1955. So he ordered me to write down a list of people with whom I had corresponded. I readily complied. The Red Guards spent hours ransacking our drawers, boxes, and chests, which was like a repeat performance of what happened at Nankai University a decade earlier. By supper time, the search squad had left with several suspicious finds. They took my Smith-Corona portable typewriter, on the case of which Dr. T. D. Lee had written my name and address in Chinese in white paint before I sailed from San Francisco fifteen years ago. They took two photo albums, one of which contained a photo of myself, Ann and Bill Burton, and T. D. Lee taken on the deck of the USS *President Cleveland* when they came to see me off. They took the Kodak Brownie box camera that had intrigued the public security inspector in Guangzhou, where I'd landed three weeks later. They took the two electron tubes from an old record player that Yikai had to leave behind with my sister when she moved from Beijing, a hundred-watt light bulb, and a handful of my old ties. Our English bicycle was commandeered by one of my male students, Sun Dengfu, who "needed it to make revolution." I was ordered to surrender a number of my books, including a copy of my class of '48 yearbook from Manchester College, ironically named *Aurora,* along with my degree diplomas from Manchester College and the University of Chicago, and carry them myself to an office newly set up as a depository of "four olds," in compliance with an order from the Red Guards. On my way to surrender my "four olds," I passed by the apartment building in which Lao Wang and his wife lived. Mrs. Wang was wailing and screaming from an open window on the third floor, "I'm not a landlord! I'm Lao Wang's wife! I want our valuables back!" A few spectators looked up and said, "The woman has gone crazy." Finding the "four olds" storeroom already clustered with books, art objects, and articles of clothing, I consoled myself with the thought that my loss was infinitesimal compared with those of others. But I was struck dumb when I heard some time later that Yikai's Third Elder Brother, Shiyu, a world authority on Chinese folk religions, had his lifetime collection of thousands of rare manuscript sutras carried away in three flatbed carts.

In the next few days, following the lead of the foreign languages department, other Red Guards took similar "revolutionary actions" against the "cow demons" in their respective departments. When not subjected to criticism and struggle or self-criticism sessions, we labored on the school farm or did menial jobs, such as carrying night soil out of campus manure pits. Meanwhile, most of the students and younger teachers went off on free tours, first to Beijing, then to other cities and scenic spots that caught their fancy, for "revolutionary linkups." The campus was plastered all over with big-character posters the travelers had copied from Beijing and other major cities. Apart from eulogies that frantically deified Mao Zedong, most of them were attacks on party and government leaders who were, one after another, accused of being his mortal enemies. Liu Shaoqi, the head of state, and Deng Xiaoping, the party general secretary, led the list of the "capital-ist-roaders." The Red Guards, deeply involved in the life-and-death politi-cal struggles within the party leadership, soon split into two or more factions fighting each other all over the country. Big-character-poster bickering paved the way for fistfights, which quickly developed into armed conflicts. By the summer of 1967, the country was virtually in a state of civil war.

The campus and the city alike were in the hands of the two opposing armed factions. Bands of teenagers wearing Red Guard armbands and armed with cudgels or daggers roamed the streets, seeking out members of the enemy faction. Stories of horror abounded. People did not venture into the streets if they could help it. At the university, the sixteen-year-old daughter of Colonel Li, still in junior high, made herself famous by being one of those daredevil Red Guards who prided themselves on their blood lineage. She sported a dagger with éclat, because both of her parents had served in the early Red Army. One day, while roaming the streets with a band of teenagers of her faction, she saw a teenage boy coming toward them.

"Who is that? Friend or enemy?" she asked her companions.

"I have seen him before. Enemy, I believe," one of the boys said.

"Then what are we waiting for? Let's get him," she urged, walking up to the solitary youth.

"Stop! Who are you, kid? Which faction?"

"You have no right to stop me or ask me questions. Let me go by."

"Here's for your impudence, you dog!" Her dagger went straight into the youngster's heart. Her companions were dumbfounded. "Come on!" she said cheerfully. "I'll treat you to ice-suckers to celebrate our heroic deed." Leaving the youngster dying on the street in a pool of blood, she walked up to a man peddling ice-suckers and clenched the bloody dagger between her teeth while she fumbled in her pockets for change. "Ten ice-suckers for Chairman Mao's true Red Guards!" she said proudly. The peddler was so frightened that he dared not take money for the ice-suckers. The dead boy turned out to have belonged to the same faction as the killer.

City residents soon began seeking refuge in smaller towns and villages. At a loss as to what to do, Yikai and I went to the train station to look into the situation for ourselves. We found a milling crowd on the platform watching a train that was not only jampacked with people but had people squatting on top of it. I imagined that those squatters would be thrown off to instant death when the train passed through the first tunnel, which is actually what happened from time to time. The sight brought to mind the refugee train I took in 1937, fleeing the invading Japanese, but even then no one had risked his life squatting on the top of the train. Yikai and I decided there and then we would make the best of it where we were, instead of putting our children's lives in such danger.

With the party leadership paralyzed and the Red Guards either touring the country or busy fighting a factional war, the "cow demons" were pretty much left to their own devices. The campus was deserted and ominously quiet at night. One day Yikai brought home our English bicycle, which she had found abandoned in a deserted boys' dorm, beaten up beyond recognition, like an old intellectual. We stored what drinking water we could in our two vats and hoarded as much foodstuff as our coupons allowed. Fuel became a problem. At the height of the summer, the supply of coal briquets was cut off because, like fellow workers in other industries, briquet-makers had also stopped production, taking up arms to defend their own faction or touring the country to "make revolution." In desperation, a young man living above us and I pulled a flatbed cart to a coal yard five miles away in hopes of getting some briquets for our stoves. The yard was crowded with people and carts, and we soon learned we were to make briquets ourselves. After waiting in line for an hour, we were finally able to pay for our monthly ration of 250 pounds of coal each. Then followed a scramble for an iron coal cart to carry the powdered coal up a gangplank to where it was fed into a coal-briquet machine. It was late in the afternoon when we two, stripped to the waist, pulled the flatbed cart with 500 pounds of precious briquets back to our building. Though drenched in black sweat under the still scorching sun, I felt an ironic satisfaction. "Hard work and self-reliance," I said to my fellow briquet carrier with a weak laugh. "Following Chairman Mao's teaching!" After Yikai and Yiding helped me carry the two heavy crates upstairs to our rooms, I went into the kitchen, crouched under the only faucet over the sink, and turned the water on my body smeared with coal dust and sweat.

How I wished some wise oracle would tell me what was going on in this land! A leadership gone berserk or a nation going through some mysterious crisis?

Late in February 1968, a telegram came from my cousin in Yangzhou telling us my stepmother had died. Since the "cow demons" had been left alone by the warring Red Guards, I was able to obtain a week's leave from the head of the department and return to my hometown to make arrangements for her burial. I had long wanted to revisit my hometown, but who would have thought my first visit in thirty-one years should have taken place under such circumstances! By the time I arrived, Mother had already been laid to rest in an improvised coffin, for my relatives did not know whether I would be allowed to come home and bury a "landlord." My heart was heavy when I was told she had died from diabetes because of lack of adequate medication. Now she had been literally "swept away" as one of the "four olds." Perhaps it was just as well, since death had put an end to her sufferings, especially the ordeal of the Cultural Revolution. I recalled how, when I returned from the States in 1951 and invited her to live with me in Beijing, she had looked forward to a happy life in her old age after a decade of lonely widowhood. Maybe she'd had a little happiness, but mostly it was the ordeal of one political campaign after another until the last blow. Now, seventeen years later, I silently followed the flatbed cart that carried her shabby coffin to the burial ground outside the city. Before the coffin was lowered into the pit, my cousin Ningjia, a party member, reminded me to throw some money into it, as was the old custom. I was a bit perturbed by practicing one of the "four olds" in the midst of the Red Storm. But the grave digger nonchalantly collected the money before he shoveled earth into the pit.

I spent the following day walking the streets and alleys of my hometown, which I had left in 1937 at the age of seventeen in the face of an invading enemy. I relived the fears and dreams that had carried me away, into the mainstream of national resistance, which had then carried me farther away, into the great world of men and ideas. Now dreams had turned into an unending nightmare and fear had woven itself into the texture of everyday life. After thirty-one years, I came back to where I had started, utterly crushed and lost, and heaven seemed to have sealed off all the exits. I felt as if I had been groping in a dark tunnel that was leading nowhere. Death had put lingering illusions to rest, but I had no tears to shed for the dead, for it was the living, in their fear and anguish, who were to be pitied.

3

WHEN THE ARMED CONFLICTS BETWEEN WARRING FACTIONS OF RED GUARDS, now renamed Revolutionary Rebels, took a heavy toll of life and property, the Red Supreme Commander dispatched Mao Zedong Thought Propaganda Teams of army officers and industrial workers to oversee higher and secondary education. By the spring of 1968, the warring factions, under the leadership of army officers and industrial workers, had entered into a "great alliance" to intensify proletarian dictatorship against the common enemies. The Cultural Revolution embarked upon a new stage of "purifying the class ranks"—a nationwide purge of allegedly undesirable elements. In their handling of the "cow demons" at the university, the army officers imposed harsh military discipline, the master workers resorted to corporal punishment, and both despised academic learning.

The ranks of "cow demons" at the university rapidly grew to a labor force of well over a hundred strong. Names were called out over the loudspeakers from time to time. Along with Professor Mao, Professor Kong, and Wu Baotai the "dog renegade," I was among the earliest ones ferreted out. Professor Kong and his wife were denounced as "big reactionaries" in a big-character poster by their daughter, who had been admitted as an English major through her parents' influence. Professor Mao was ordered by his son to stand before a portrait of Chairman Mao at home and confess his sins every evening after his day's hard labor. Before long the denounced included not only "reactionary academic authorities," but "counterrevolutionary revisionists" as well—that is, former party leaders, senior administrators, and department chairs. I was once again made the "small group leader" of the "cow demons" of the foreign languages department, which had soon snowballed to more than a dozen strong, including the former boss Colonel Li and his deputy Lieutenant Guo.

Colonel Li, who had joined the Red Army in his teens and fought both the Japanese and the Nationalists on the battlefield, always looked upon himself as the revolutionary par excellence. With a Japanese bullet still lodged in his body, he never took the Red Guards seriously, but only humored their whims, which he considered nothing more than manifestations of the periodic Left adventurism within the party leadership. The veteran Communist revolutionary, however, underwent an abrupt transformation on May 16, 1968. The day marked the second anniversary of the publication of the 5.16 Circular, which was now regarded as the formal beginning of the Cultural Revolution. The Revolutionary Rebels at the university celebrated the historic occasion by making all the "cow demons" labor from early morning till sunset. Li had taken off a little earlier than the rest after declaring nonchalantly, "I'm quitting, Lao Wu. Got a headache." By the time we returned our spades and picks to the tool room, the loudspeakers suddenly blared a most urgent announcement at a hysterically high pitch.

"Attention: All officers and men of the Chinese People's Liberation Army, all master workers of the Mao Zedong Thought Propaganda Team, all Revolutionary Rebels: The following urgent message has just been received from the Party Center in Beijing: 'The Party Center is convinced Li Dongguang and Yang Xingfu of Anhui University are spies of the Soviet revisionists. The said criminals must be taken into custody by PLA Unit 6408 at once pending further instructions.' Revolutionary comrades, act instantly and drag out the two Soviet revisionist spies!"

Before I knew what was happening, a human wave was rushing around me toward the buildings in which Li and Yang lived. A few minutes later, the accursed "Soviet spies," pushed from behind by revolutionary rebels, were sent running along the main thoroughfare of the campus. The spy-catchers shouted deafening slogans: "Down with Soviet revisionist spies Li Dongguang and Yang Xingfu! Down with the Soviet revisionists!" And so on. The arms of the culprits were twisted crosswise behind their backs and their heads tilted upward, with spy-catchers pulling their hair from behind. Their white T-shirts were in shreds, and they wore neither shoes nor socks. At the main gate of the university, a waiting army jeep took them to the detention house of the Provincial Public Security Bureau. That night, the two veteran Communist revolutionaries were brought back to campus to face a struggle and denunciation rally, which again was held on the basketball court. I watched from a distance. After the inevitable slogans, the first man who went up to denounce the two turned out to be a party functionary, Ma Baohua, one of Li's coterie, which he had brought with him from the military academy in Nanjing in 1958. He started by repeatedly slapping his erstwhile boss on both of his cheeks and then railed at him for having deluded his subordinates all these years. Ma was followed by other Revolutionary Rebels, who resorted to both fists and expletives as weapons of struggle. When the revolutionary masses had given vent to their righteous indignation, the alleged spies were taken back to the detention house in town. For the next few years, except for occasional appearances at struggle sessions on campus, the two veteran Communists languished in a Communist prison, though never tried or convicted. Li's youngest daughter, the one who had killed a teenage boy the year before, was serving her time in the city prison not far from where her father was detained.

Class struggle intensified with the coming of summer. Every "cow demon" was ordered to wear on his or her right arm a white armband made of a four-inch-wide strip of new white cloth with his or her name and stigma painted on it in black ink with a writing brush. Yikai rummaged through her drawers, only to find she had no cloth coupons left, nor any new white cloth. Seeing no other way out, she tore a strip of an old white shirt of mine, sewed up the seams by hand, and then wrote my name and "title" on it in her elegant calligraphy. "I hope this will do," she said with a sigh. "These Red Guards seem to forget that their Red Commander has so often harped on the virtue of thrift." When I presented myself for inspection in the afternoon, the Red Guard on duty tore off my armband and tossed it to the ground.

"Wu Ningkun, what is this? Are you looking for trouble?" he shouted at me. "Didn't you know you must make it with new white cloth? Didn't you know the seams must be done on a sewing machine?"

"We have no cloth coupons left. We never had a sewing machine. Also, Chairman Mao has always taught us to be thrifty."

"None of your impudence, Wu Ningkun!" he roared at me. "You had better come with a new one tomorrow or else!"

When I dragged myself home after the day's labor, wearing no armband, Yikai knew at once what must have happened. She reluctantly went to a neighbor's and borrowed a coupon for half a foot of cloth, spent her hard-saved pennies on a piece of white cloth at the college department store, and had the seams sewed on a neighbor's machine. Leaving home in the morning, sporting the new armband with "Ultrarightist Wu Ningkun" written on it in Yikai's handwriting, I said to her, "Sorry to have put you to all this trouble. But I do wish they had allowed me to keep the old one. A museum piece, you know." The party leaders wore on their arms the stigma of "Counterrevolutionary Revisionist." The vice president, Sun Taolin, who had once been arrested by the Nationalists in his youth before he joined the party, was now a "Dog Renegade," and so was Wu Baotai. Returned students from abroad were labeled "American Spy," "Japanese Spy," or "German Spy," as the case might be.

A young chemistry instructor, Wang Yichuan, labeled a rightist, was appointed captain of the work gang, and hoary Wu Baotai, the "dog renegade," his deputy. Each morning, this work gang of more than one hundred senior faculty, party leaders, and administrators would gather punctually at eight on the basketball court and line up in military formation. A Red Guard on duty would first lecture us on our crimes and then announce the tasks for the day. Then it was Wang's turn to divide the gang into small groups with specific assignments.

For some time, I was assigned to the "heavy duty" group led by Wang himself. The other members were the president, Zhang Xingyan, a big man in his early fifties, the Teachers Union director and a former diplomat, Lin Xing, and the Physical Training director, Jiang Haoquan. Under the scorching sun we would work the pedal-driven waterwheel to raise water from a nearby stream to the college farm's draught-stricken fields. We would take turns lugging the dragonlike waterwheel to the edge of the stream, day in and day out, as if we were primitive tribesmen performing some ancient ritual to exorcise an evil spirit. Inured to labor reform myself, I didn't mind the chore so much. But I was certainly pained to witness the president of the top university of the province reduced to shouldering a primitive waterwheel across the campus when he might have led the faculty in educating the Red Guards in modern science and technology. Worse still, we were sometimes ordered to perform absolutely senseless labor. On a sweltering day in August, we were sent to a remote corner of the campus to dig a piece of uncultivated land, which was as hard as rock. My spade managed to turn over only a few square feet of land after struggling with it all morning. One of my hands was covered with bloody blisters and my mouth felt like a smouldering stove. By the time I finally went home for lunch, I was dying for a piece of watermelon. I cried like a child when I heard Yikai say softly, "Couldn't find any watermelon all morning, so sorry." Dragging myself into the kitchen, I turned on the faucet and guzzled the unwholesome water till Yikai came and turned it off. Suddenly I felt so ashamed of myself. Living, even in the best of times, had never been a picnic with plenty of watermelon. Didn't the Austrian poet Rilke write in one of his poems, "Life is heavier than the heaviness of all things"? Didn't my saintly mother-in-law send me the message of patient endurance when I was starving in jail? If I couldn't even do without a slice of watermelon, how could I steel myself to face whatever was yet to come?

On the school farm, when the director was denounced as a "cow demon," our labor reform came under the supervision of a former peasant-soldier under him, a young man named Zheng. He was of a powerful build, and his brawny arms looked like those of soldiers in propaganda posters picturing the iron fist of proletarian dictatorship. He reveled in his sudden rise to power over a gang of helpless men and women who he knew were his betters, taunting them at will and subjecting them to longer and longer hours of hard labor in the sweltering heat. During a break, he would stage a struggle session against one of the school leaders or a senior faculty right on the site. After his own diatribe, he would order the victim's peers to do their part in the denunciation. One day, the victim was an elderly instructor in Chinese classics. Because of approaching blindness, the frail man could hardly walk straight. Accused of being a Nationalist spy in his student days, Shen had been subjected to frequent sessions of struggle and interrogation, but he had consistently denied the charge in spite of beatings from the Red Guards. Whenever he could find the time, he would hunch over a desk, his nearly blind eyes close to the paper, and write out denials and refutations in his beautiful calligraphy. Then he would have them pasted on a wall or posted to the local law court, firmly believing in his own innocence. Now Zheng vowed to break his stubborn resistance.

"Shen the Blind, you think you can fool people by acting blind?" he began sardonically. "No way, you old dog! It's all in your autobiography. What were you doing in 1937?"

"I was a student refugee. To keep myself alive, I worked for a Nationalist military unit as a telegraph operator for three months," Shen answered in his southern Anhui accent.

"And can you deny that's not military intelligence? Even an uncouth peasant like myself can tell you must have joined the secret service." His inquisitor sneered triumphantly.

"I never joined."

"You never joined? Say it again!"

"I never—"

Before he could finish, the scholar of Chinese classics was thrown to the ground with one push of the former peasant-soldier's brawny arm and then lifted up again by the hair, more dead than alive.

"On your knees and confess, you mad blind dog!"

The old man fell to his knees, looking more like a disfigured eyeless statue beside an old tomb than a mad blind dog.

"I never joined any secret service," he said weakly but distinctly.

Now the frustrated bully stamped with fury, a mad dog himself. He fell all over his helpless victim with blows and kicks.

"You confess now or . . ." he threatened.

When the implied threat failed to have any effect, he roared, "You blind dog, you're asking for it!" Instantly he thrust his terrifying fist at the victim's right eye, the one that still had a little vision left. Blood coursed down the old man's cheek. Instinctively, my own eyes shut, and my throat choked up. I shivered and my eyes literally hurt. I could feel sweat pouring down my back. How I wished he had confessed to escape the brutality! Even though I knew, by instinct and my own experience as a student refugee, that he was innocent. When I opened my eyes again, I saw Shen the Blind staggering away, two Red Guards holding him by the arms.

"You have all seen how stubborn the blind dog was! But he was vanquished by the iron fist of proletarian dictatorship!" the vanquisher roared at us triumphantly. "It's a lesson to you all. The trouble with us is we have been too soft with you cow demons and snake spirits. But don't you forget proletarian dictatorship is no vegetarian! We will never be deterred by a few drops of blood. Confess all your crimes or be smashed to smithereens by the iron fist of proletarian dictatorship! Now go back to labor. Put in an extra hour to make up for the time lost on the blind dog."

4

BY SEPTEMBER, THE ARCH-"COW DEMONS," FORTY IN ALL, MOSTLY MALE, were herded into a student dormitory, now designated a "cow shed," and incarcerated under Red Guard surveillance. Though a nonentity, I found myself in the illustrious company of the party secretary and president, the vice president, the Commissar of Propaganda, and other administrators and senior faculty. We were divided into five small groups, four of men and one of women, and each group was assigned to a room with four or five double-decker bunks. I was one of the five group leaders, who were held responsible for the behavior of the members, presiding over sessions of criticism and self-criticism, and reporting on what the others might do or say. Our first job was to decorate our rooms with quotations of Chairman Mao written out in large characters. The one that hung over our heads like a Damoclean sword was: "Leniency to those who confess their crimes and severity to those who refuse to." Then the five group leaders, including the Commissar of Propaganda and the mathematics chairman, also a veteran party member, put our heads together and racked our brains over the phrasing of a collective confession of our unforgivable sins against the Great Leader. The final version ran something like this:

> Most beloved and revered Great Leader Chairman Mao, the Red Sun in our hearts: We are a group of counterrevolutionaries who have sinned against you, against the invincible Mao Zedong Thought, and against your glorious revolutionary line. Our sins are grievous and innumerable. A thousand deaths could not redeem us from our mortal sins. But this Great Proletarian Cultural Revolution you have launched and directed in person is touching us to our very souls. We solemnly vow that we will examine our sinful past with the microscope of Mao

Zedong Thought and make every effort to turn over a new leaf and return to your glorious revolutionary line as soon as possible. Long live the Great Leader Chairman Mao! Long live the Great Savior of the Chinese People! Long live the invincible Mao Zedong Thought! Long live the glorious revolutionary line of Chairman Mao!

This fruit of collective wisdom was committed to memory by all the sinners, who recited it in unison every morning, standing in two lines and facing a plaster bust of Mao Zedong mounted on a pedestal at one end of the hallway.

All the "cow demons," whether under detention or not, spent most of the daytime in labor reform. All the heavy work, all the dirty work, became our specialization, for everybody else was presumably busy "making revolution." The hours of labor were long, and it was the height of a hot and humid summer. Many fell ill, but no sick leave was granted unless you ran a high temperature. One day, when a team of us were pulling a harrow in the fields, like a team of real cows, the president and party secretary, who often suffered from Ménière's syndrome, collapsed from the stifling heat and overexertion. Wu Baotai, hoary and gaunt, began to show symptoms of edema, but in spite of my prompting he was wary of taking time off for prescribed shots at the clinic. The poor old "dog renegade," he was still exerting himself to make up to the party to which he had once given himself, nearly half a century before.

The "demons and spirits" confined in the cow shed were allowed occasional visits from their families on Saturday evenings when there were no struggle rallies or interrogations scheduled. Yikai visited whenever she could. The head "cow demon," Wang Yichuan, who was required to monitor our conversation, would say apologetically, "Sorry, Li Yikai, regulations." We didn't really mind, because we had nothing to hide. It made us feel better to see each other periodically, exchanging a few words and making sure the other half was all right. Once she even brought Yicun, who had insisted on coming along to see me. "What are you doing here, Papa? Why don't you come home and play with me, eh?" Yikai answered for me, "Didn't I tell you, Cuncun, Papa and Uncle Wang Yichuan and others are studying Chairman Mao's works together here?" One evening in mid-September, my little daughter came with a bowl of dumplings to wish me a happy birthday. In North China, dumplings were a traditional delicacy for birthdays and other happy occasions. The sight of the beautifully shaped dumplings, which bore signs of Yikai's handiwork, brought tears to my eyes. Before I touched any, Wang Yichuan started breaking them open, one by one.

"What did you do that for, Uncle Wang?" Yimao pouted. "Mother took special care to make them look so pretty. It's Papa's birthday!"

"So sorry, Yimao. Orders! To check whether there are messages or other things hidden inside, you know."

"They will taste just as good, Yimao, don't mention it to Mom, please," I said.

"I shall never forget this, never," Yimao said slowly.

My only daughter had met me for the first time on her third birthday, when her mother took her to see me on a prison visit seven years before. Now the little girl made a prison visit on her own to wish her father a happy birthday at the great age of ten! But, when I went back to my room and found Lin Xing, the Teachers Union director, fidgeting, I counted myself very lucky to have had birthday dumplings from my family.

"Have a dumpling, Lao Lin." I wanted him to share my luck.

But he only said, with his brows knit, "Jiang Nan was supposed to visit today, but she hasn't come. What has happened?" Jiang Nan was his wife, a good friend of Yikai's. Their daughter Lan and Yicun were the same age and often played together.

I tried to calm him by saying, "Maybe she's busy with political study or something else. Don't worry. Have a taste of the dumplings. Yikai made them." He took one, but remained worried. I continued, "I have been assigned shopping errands tomorrow to get you guys cigarette rations and toilet things at the college store. I will see what I can find out."

During the lunch break the next day, as I approached the college store, the first thing I saw was a big-character poster flanked by two slogans: "Down with Jiang Nan the Active Counterrevolutionary!" "Smash the Bitch Head of Jiang Nan to smithereens!" I scanned the poster quickly and learned that at a political rally she had been found sitting on a sheet of the *Anhui Daily* with a photo of Chairman Mao on the front page. A struggle session had been held at the scene of the crime. Now she was ordered to publicly acknowledge her guilt and redeem herself. When I told her husband of my finding, he heaved a long sigh. "What would happen to our little girl if her mother should also be thrown in here?" He was relieved when he learned later that his wife was spared the ordeal of the cow shed, but little did he know at the time what a harsher fate was in store for her.

Denunciation meetings and rallies, to which we were dragged en masse or separately, were staged one after another. I was often pulled onto the auditorium stage as Exhibit A, showing how the president and party secretary or the vice president had "scraped together demons and spirits," or how the vice president had carried out a revisionist line in education. Attendance at these rallies was mandatory for Yikai, especially when I was billed. One night, both the president and the vice president were subjected to denunciation and interrogation for three hours, while standing on the stage "jet style"—that is, with their bodies bent forward at right angles and their arms twisted backward in the air. The two elderly men had to be carried back to their beds after the rally and excused from labor the next morning.

The "master workers" from the steel plant in the nearby city of Ma'anshan complained that the Red Guards were too soft with the "demons and spirits." A husky young master worker vaunted, "At the steel plant, we made them sleep in real cow sheds and kneel on bricks in the sun for two hours a day. How else could they be touched to their very souls?" This same "master" often took a postprandial excursion to our cow shed to mete out his own brand of revolutionary justice. Reeking of strong liquor, he slapped Wang Fangxun in the face evening after evening, when he was frustrated in extorting a confession from the obdurate man, who was a professor of economics with a Ph.D. from Columbia.

"Why did you cross out the characters in the quotation from Chairman Mao on the matchbox, Wang Fangxun?" He asked the same question every night.

"I was absentminded, because I was thinking of my poor mother all the time. I didn't know what my hand was doing." Wang gave the same answer.

"You lie, you keep repeating the same lie, you dog!"

The husky inquisitor started slapping the fragile elderly professor in indignation.

"Why did you smear the glorious words of our Great Leader and Great Teacher, Wang Fang-un?"

"I was absentminded—"

The steel-making hands were on the detested culprit again before he had finished.

"You liar, I'll teach you! I'll teach you!" His teaching was imparted in loud slaps. "You did it deliberately! You're a dirty U.S. imperialist running dog. You oppose Chairman Mao. You oppose the glorious Mao Zedong Thought. You are an active counterrevolutionary of the worst kind! We will be lenient with you if you confess. Now!"

"I didn't do it deliberately. I—"

Professor Wang was ordered to submit a written self-confession the next day. Unexpectedly, he was kept in suspense for the next two days, for our regular visitor did not turn up. On the third day, when I was sent to the college store to buy cigarettes and soap and toothpaste for the inmates, who should I run into but this dread petty tyrant! I did not recognize him at first, because his face was patched with bandages and his right arm was carried in a sling.

"What happened, Master Diao?" I blurted out in alarm.

"Oh, an accident bad luck." He sounded almost human.

"Did it hurt?" I asked stupidly. He glared at me and quickly walked away. Back in the cow shed, I handed Professor Wang his cigarettes and soap and, under my breath, related to him my little encounter. He smiled weakly but did not say a word. He had to be careful, even though Shi Baoyu, the informer, was not in the room at the moment.

5

THE SECURITY BULLY TOOK A SPECIAL PROFESSIONAL INTEREST IN AN INSTRUC-tor in Marxism-Leninism and Mao Zedong Thought named Yang Bolian. Yang was in his early thirties but looked much older than his age, his face unshaven and his graying hair straggling around his balding pate. His tattered gray Mao jacket hung loosely on his small build, making him look more like a scarecrow than Don Quixote, which was his colleagues' nickname for him. Badly nearsighted yet without glasses, he would thrust his head forward and narrow his eyes, and walk about this way, with his big toes sticking out of his wornout sneakers. Known on campus as an eccentric bachelor living in a world of his own, he had no friends, ate irregularly, and read avidly. He had stopped teaching even before the Cultural Revolution started, because his views were often at variance with the party propaganda of the day. As he did not read current newspapers, he was out of touch with political developments of the times. Soon he got into an argument with a master worker over Liu Shaoqi and Deng Xiaoping.

"Liu Shaoqi and Deng Xiaoping have always opposed our Great Leader Chairman Mao." Master Worker Wang repeated this latest line at a meeting called to denounce Liu and Deng. "They are top persons in power within the party who are taking the capitalist road. They have been working for the restoration of capitalism in China. They are serving the interests of Soviet revisionists and U.S. imperialists—"

"But this cannot be true," interrupted Yang in his thin voice.

It was audacious to contradict a master worker, it was heretical to defend the arch–capitalist roaders. Familiar with his eccentricities, Yang's colleagues just had a good laugh. But Master Worker Wang was in no humor to put up with such a challenge to his authority.

"What did you say, Yang Bolian?" the master worker demanded with suppressed rage. "You dare to defend the arch–capitalist roaders and oppose our Great Leader Chairman Mao and his close comrade-in-arms Vice Chairman Lin? That makes you an active counterrevolutionary."

"Liu Shaoqi is the president of the People's Republic of China, Deng Xiaoping the general secretary of the Chinese Communist party," Yang went on calmly, totally oblivious of the political reality around him. "They are still in office, are they not? I believe it's a counterrevolutionary offense to slander leaders of the party or the state—"

"You shut up!" bawled Master Worker Wang. "I officially pronounce you an active counterrevolutionary, here and now! Down with Yang Bolian!"

"Down with active counterrevolutionary Yang Bolian!" the crowd responded in unison.

"Take him to the cow shed and put him in solitary confinement. We will deal with him by and by," the master worker shouted to the captain of the college Red Guards sitting behind him on the stage.

Thereupon three Red Guards took the instructor in hand and marched him to the cow shed, showering cuffs and kicks on him all the way. After supper the same evening, we "cow demons in residence" were assembled in the hallway to play our part in the denunciation of Yang by his peers. The criminal was dragged out of the cell for solitary confinement by two Red Guards and ordered to kneel before the bust of Chairman Mao. "Now acknowledge your counterrevolutionary guilt before our Great Leader, Yang Bolian!" ordered Master Worker Wang.

"I don't know what I am guilty of," mumbled Yang.

"You dog! You dog counterrevolutionary!" Master Worker Wang flew into a rage and started slapping Yang in the face. "You liar! You committed the unforgivable sin of defending Liu and Deng in public and now you say you don't know what you're guilty of! I dare you to say it again."

"As a teacher of Marxism-Leninism and Mao Zedong Thought, I can only tell the truth. Otherwise I really would be a liar. I just don't understand how anyone can accuse the head of the People's Republic and—"

The master worker came down on him with cuffs and kicks, screaming "I'll teach you! I'll teach you! You active counterrevolutionary, you stinking ninth category!" Now the security man Shi Baoyu walked up to the master worker and offered the service of his expertise. "Master Worker, please take a rest. I'll teach him a thing or two." He grabbed the little man by his wrists and gave them a resounding twist. The instructor of Marxism-Leninism screamed and slumped to the floor. The security man demanded triumphantly, "Now are you going to confess or not, Yang Bolian? Confess! Confess!" There was no response. Shi kicked at the prostrate body and shouted "Stop pretending to be a dead dog! Get up and get down on your knees!" The body remained still. Shi turned to the master worker, who shouted orders to two Red Guards: "Put him back in solitary confinement and keep a close watch over him." Then he turned to us. "You have all seen how stubborn an active counterrevolutionary can be. You have also seen how it has not done him any good. This is a lesson to you all. Take him as a teacher by negative example and confess all your crimes, the sooner the better!"

The next morning, word got round that Yang Bolian had escaped while visiting the toilet during the night. Squads of master workers and Red Guards were dispatched to the train station and the bus depot to track down the dangerous criminal. In the evening, as soon as we were again assembled in the hallway, Yang Bolian was dragged in by two Red Guards to the front of the hall and ordered to kneel before the bust of Chairman Mao. His hands cuffed and his face badly bruised and swollen, the small man looked even smaller than usual in his tattered Mao jacket, more like a half-dead sacrificial lamb than a dangerous criminal.

"Yang Bolian," Master Worker Wang started shouting. "I pronounced you an active counterrevolutionary yesterday after you committed the unforgivable sin of opposing our Great Leader Chairman Mao, but I was hoping that you would learn a lesson and turn over a new leaf. But what did you do? You thought you were smart, you thought you could slip out of our hands. Now you see, all of you see, there is no escaping the iron fist of proletarian dictatorship! Any attempt to escape from proletarian justice is a counterrevolutionary crime. Now you are twice an active counterrevolutionary. Are you ready to confess today?"

"I attempted to escape," the culprit answered in a weak voice. "I did want to escape, because I could not endure the torture any more. And I don't know what I have done to deserve all this. I never opposed Chairman Mao, I never opposed Chairman Liu—"

Before he could finish, Shi started slapping him in the face. "You stubborn counterrevolutionary dog! You and your Chairman Liu! I'll show you, you dog!"

"I can see all our leniency has been wasted on him," Master Worker Wang sneered. "Show him something else, Shi Baoyu!"

Shi brought forward a large traveling bag and pulled out of it a pile of thick ropes. With the help of the two Red Guards, he tied the rope around the culprit, looped it over a beam, and then hoisted Yang into midair. Even from a distance I could see that he was quite adept at it. Before I knew what was happening, Shi and the two Red Guards started lashing the body with leather army belts, yelling all the while, "Down with active counterrevolutionary Yang Bolian! Down with the escaped criminal Yang Baolian!" All the "cow demons" present also yelled in unison, which made me feel like an accomplice. I could hear Yang's cries and screams first growing louder and louder and then gradually trailing off. The lashing stopped, but the victim was left swinging in midair while the master worker again admonished us to learn a lesson and surrender ourselves to the people. My mind went back to the happy-go-lucky young hooligan tied to a tree after his attempted escape from the labor farm on Lake Xingkai. At least he was not tortured or taunted then, nor were his peers forced to play a part in his ordeal. The Socialist revolution had come a long way in ten years! To forestall further escapes, all our cells were locked from the outside at night, even though there were no toilets in the rooms.

The fate of the instructor in Marxism-Leninism and Mao Zedong Thought was soon sealed when Liu Shaoqi, whom he had naively defended as the president of China and senior vice chairman of the Communist party, was formally condemned as a "renegade, traitor, and scab" in the service of imperialists, modern revisionists, and Nationalist reactionaries at a plenary session of his own party's Central Committee late in October, with only a solitary woman member abstaining. A few days later, while the revolutionary students and teachers of the university were celebrating this great victory of the invincible Mao Zedong Thought by parading on campus and in town, Yang Bolian was formally arraigned as an active counterrevolutionary in the service of Liu Shaoqi. He was not released until Liu Shaoqi was posthumously rehabilitated ten years later.

Twelve

AMONG RED GUARDS
AND MASTER WORKERS,
1968-70

1

LATE IN NOVEMBER 1968, IN THE MIDST OF A NEW CAMPAIGN AT UNIVERSITIES
to carry out "struggle, critique, and reform"—short for "struggle against
bourgeois academic authorities, critique of capitalist and revisionist line in
education, and reform in higher education"—the nation hailed another
"latest supreme directive from Chairman Mao" with the usual parades of
revolutionary masses shouting slogans and beating drums and cymbals. The
new edict called upon the nation's intellectuals to go to the countryside and
receive reeducation from the "poor" and "lower-middle" peasants. In
response to the oracle, the soldier-worker leadership of the university
decided to kill two birds with one stone by sending the entire student body
and faculty and staff, totaling three thousand men and women, old and
young, sick and healthy, to an agricultural people's commune in Hexian
County some hundred miles east of the provincial capital. Days were spent
in sessions devoted to the study of the "great strategic plans of historic
significance." Everyone said the right things, no one ventured into the
transparent political motivation behind it all: it was now imperative to
remove the Red Rebels from their urban bases, where they were beginning
to pose a threat to those in power.

On December 20, one day before the scheduled departure, I was given
leave in the afternoon to go home and get things ready. I found our rooms
in chaos, as if they had just been ransacked again. Yicun ran into my arms,
saying with a broad smile: "Papa, I'm going to live in the kindergarten with
my brother and sister, Mama says. What fun! I wish you could all come."
I only hugged him and didn't know what to say. Yikai was having Yiding's
and Yimao's things packed for their stay at the kindergarten during our

absence. Now she showed me the things she had put into a shopping bag for me, which was like a repeat of what had happened ten years before, on the eve of my arrest that April afternoon. For supper Yikai cooked long noodles. "For good luck," she said with a wry smile. It was the first meal the family had eaten together in quite a few months, and also the last supper before we would be reunited again many months later. Then Yiding took it upon himself to make some steamed rolls for us to take along, in case we got hungry on the way. When he lifted the lid of the big steamer, he was dismayed to see the rolls all dark brown. "Oh God, what happened?" Yikai solved the mystery with a smile: "A little too much baking soda, Yiding dear. Good for digestion. Don't feel bad about it, please. It was good of you to have thought of making them." Then Yiding and Yimao took off first, bedrolls on their backs. "I'll look after Maomao and Cuncun," Yiding said. "Don't you worry, Papa and Mama," Yimao added. "I'll look after Cuncun too." I was at once glad and sad that the children were so composed. When Yiding and Yamao had left, I asked Yikai, "Do you have the plaques ready? You know we must all carry one each on our backpacks. With a quotation from Chairman Mao, written on red paper." Yikai exclaimed, "Ah, I nearly forgot! I did pick up two small boards from the college carpenter shop. They must be somewhere. The red paper I filched from the department office. They always have reams on hand for Chairman Mao's latest directives." Yicun began rummaging through a pile of things heaped on the bed and found the boards and the red paper buried underneath, and then brought us a writing brush and a bottle of black ink from the desk drawer.

"How will I cope without your help, Cuncun darling?" Yikai hugged him. "Now you might as well tell me, which quotation shall we use? Mama's head is swimming."

"I know an easy one the teacher taught us, Mama." So saying, he recited in a standard singsong tone: "People, and the people alone, are the motive force in the making of world history."

"Very good, very true, Cuncun, we'll use that one for Mama. Now can you think up one for Papa?" I prodded him.

"I really don't remember any more, Papa. How about a poem by Du Fu you taught me?"

Yikai laughed. "That won't do, Cuncun. It must be a quotation from Chairman Mao."

"Why is that, Mama?"

"Because that's what everybody is supposed to do, dear. Leave it to Papa. He knows so many of them."

I did know quite a number of them by heart, as was required of everybody, but I was supposed to use one that would relate to my status as a "cow demon." Yikai suggested an oft-quoted one on people making mistakes: "It is hard for any political party or person to avoid mistakes, but we should make as few as possible. Once a mistake is made, we should correct it, and the more quickly and thoroughly the better." She added, "People could read into it an admission of guilt and a readiness to turn over a new leaf. But it's really just a truism that applies to everyone, including the sagacious speaker himself." We both laughed a little and Yikai wrote the quotations on the red paper before pasting them on the boards. Then it was time to take Yicun to the kindergarten. Yikai asked Yicun whether he would like to ride piggyback on her. The kid said in a whisper, "I want to ride piggyback on Papa. We haven't done it in ever so long now." It was so little to ask on the eve of an indefinite separation. "But Papa has to carry your things, Cuncun," Yikai said softly. "Won't you let Mama carry you on my back, eh?" I was afraid the child might start crying, but he gave in without a word, which made me feel even worse. Carrying his bedroll on one end of a shoulder pole and a traveling bag of clothes and odds and ends on the other, I walked side by side with my youngest child on his mother's back. The night was very dark and none of us said a word. Once I called him softly, "Cuncun!" He answered softly, "Yes, Papa!" Then we fell silent again.

When we reached the kindergarten, the night nurse grumbled that we were so late. We quickly unpacked his bedroll and tucked him in on the floor between two other boys of his age. Then we peeked into two other rooms for bigger kids and found Yiding in one and Yimao in another, sleeping on the floor among other children. On the way home, we held hands in the dark but said nothing. Back in our rooms, Yikai said, "It's getting late. You had better go back now. There will be a lot of walking to do the next few days. How I wish we knew where we are heading, but no matter. At least we are not the only ones, and we are on the same road . . ." She put a few chocolate-colored rolls into my bag and handed me the plaque, before I left her alone to the chaos and solitude.

The next morning I got up earlier than my cellmates, because I was slow in tying up my bedding into a backpack that would not come loose on the way. When I had finally done it, with the help of a cellmate, I tied to it the plaque with the quotation from Chairman Mao. After breakfast, we marched to the basketball courts to join the ranks of students, faculty, and staff of our respective departments. The "cows and demons" were placed behind the ranks of revolutionary students, faculty, and staff. We marched four abreast. Yikai was with the women teachers of the department just ahead of me. As the columns marched off the campus, the families, led by the caretaker staff, lined the road to stage a "warm send-off," shouting slogans and beating drums and cymbals. Suddenly I caught sight of our children in their cotton-padded coats, together with others from the kindergarten, also waving their little arms and shouting slogans under the direction of their teachers. "Long live the Great Leader Chairman Mao! Long live the revolutionary road of Chairman Mao! Down with the renegade, traitor, scab Liu Shaoqi!" When we passed by them, Yiding and Yimao cried excitedly, "Good-bye, Mama!" "Good-bye, Papa!" But little Yicun looked lost, his nose running. Yikai quickly walked up to him, wiped his nose, and rejoined the marchers at a run. We were already a distance away when I heard Yicun shouting at the top of his small voice, "Good-bye, Mama! Good-bye, Papa!" Yikai turned back to wave to him. I just went on walking with my eyes fixed on the quotation from Chairman Mao on the backpack of Wu Baotai, the "dog renegade": All reactionaries are paper tigers.

In answer to the infallible oracle, the top university of the province, three thousand strong, pressed forward on a new "long march," one and all carrying backpacks covered with Chairman Mao's quotations on red paper. The whole city had been ordered to turn out and give the marchers a warm send-off, lining the streets on their way and hailing their "unprecedented revolutionary action" in identical slogans. I overheard one elderly woman onlooker exclaim to another, pointing at Wu Baotai and Lao Yao marching ahead of me, "Look at those snow-white heads! They too! Oh my, my!" As we marched on, other onlookers commented on the quotations on our backpacks: "Why, the quotations on the backpacks of those older people are quite different from those on most other backpacks. Ah, these guys must be cow demons and snake spirits. Well, well!" A big cart that would usually be drawn by a horse was instead pulled by the tall president and party secretary of the university, carrying the bedrolls and bags of the Red Guards, who moved back and forth beside the columns to lead the marchers in shouting slogans or singing revolutionary songs. An empty college bus followed the columns slowly as a relief vehicle for individuals who might fall sick on the way or succumb to exhaustion.

The columns zigzagged through the streets like a mammoth legendary Chinese dragon with thousands of pairs of feet. The dragon was said to be on a new historic long march, but no one really knew where it was heading. At midday the hungry and tired marchers came to a halt at the suburban town of Feidong, where lunch had been prepared by college cooks. After lunch, the Red Guards and revolutionary teachers started performing the newfangled collective "loyalty dance" to the accompaniment of the song "Revered and Beloved Chairman Mao, the Red Sun in Our Hearts," for the benefit of the local people. The "cow demons and snake spirits," who had no right to take part in the revolutionary dance, were led to the main street corners of the small town to perform sessions of denunciation and struggle, with the imposing president playing the part of the leading villain. The townspeople seemed to enjoy the "demon show" more than the loyalty dance, for they applauded the emotional self-confession of the president of the top university of the province instead of shouting "Down with So-and-So!"

We covered more miles in the afternoon, reaching the county town of Zuozhen by sunset. After a hot supper, we were assigned sleeping quarters in the classrooms of a local high school. I reluctantly undid my backpack and laid out my bedding on the floor next to that of Guo Renfu, the former deputy party secretary of the department. When I mumbled I would have a hard time redoing it in the morning, Guo said he would help. As a former army lieutenant, he was quite adept at that. In addition, he pricked the blisters on my feet with a clean sewing needle and bandaged them, something he had learned as a foot soldier. Before bedtime, two Red Guards called the department's dozen "cow demons" together for a session of political study.

"What have you learned from the new experiences of the day, Wu Baotai?" one of the two Red Guards asked.

"I truly believe this is a great new adventure," the hoary veteran ex-Communist responded earnestly in his heavy Jiangxi accent. "As I marched, my mind kept going back to the heroes of the Long March. I drew strength from their revolutionary heroism. They had no fear of sacrifice, no fear of fatigue, but surmounted every difficulty to win victory. What are my difficulties compared with theirs? A little fatigue, a few blisters on my soles, nothing at all. This long march will carry the revolution into my very soul—"

His effusion was cut short by the Red Guards, who were called by their comrades-in-arms to join them on a cruise of the small town. "That's good. Have a discussion among yourselves. Don't go out."

The next day went by in much the same way except for a little incident. In the middle of the morning, after we had covered five or six miles, Guo Renfu, who was marching next to me, started moaning.

"Oh, oh, my stomach, my stomach hurts . . ."

"What's the matter, Lao Guo?" I was startled. "Let me ask the liaison Red Guard to send for a doctor. I know the college doctors are on the road too."

"No, no, it's my ulcers," Guo said quickly, his hand pressed against his stomach. "What I need is some food. Some solid food will smother the pain. That's what I do every time it happens, since my army days. Doctors are of no use."

It suddenly occurred to me that I still had Yiding's chocolate-colored rolls in my bag. I fished one out from the bag and handed it to him. "It looks terrible, Lao Guo," I said apologetically. "Yiding put too much baking soda in it. I don't know if you can stomach it."

"Oh, thank you, thank you, Lao Wu, this is just what I need." Guo's pained face broke into a smile. "Baking soda will be good for my stomachache." The roll was pretty hard, but the sick man finished it in no time and went on marching. We spent the night in a classroom in another high school in the county town of Caoxian. The ex-lieutenant dressed my blisters again with even more care.

Before bedtime, two Red Guards called the dozen "cow demons" of the department together for political study.

"How do you feel today, Wu Baotai?" one of them asked the "dog renegade."

"The long march is certainly good for me, for my thought reform. But

I must admit I am so exhausted and my blistered feet hurt a lot. I am getting on in years, after all."

"Do you think you can carry on tomorrow, Wu Baotai?" Now the other Red Guard questioned him.

"I suppose I can try—"

"You don't have to try if you feel you are not really up to it." The first Red Guard cut in. "What do you take us for anyway, Wu Baotai? We are Chairman Mao's Red Guards. We treat you cow demons in conformity with revolutionary humanitarianism. We shall see in the morning."

In the morning, just as we were about to set off on the long march again, Wu Baotai was given permission to board the bus. When he rejoined us at the night stop in the county town of Hanshan, the same Red Guards came up to him.

"How do you feel now, Wu Baotai?" one of them asked.

"I feel much better. I am very grateful to the party and the Red Guards for showing me such leniency. I must redouble my efforts in thought reform."

"That's fine. Will you be able to walk tomorrow?"

"Well, I would like to, but my blistered feet—"

"Do you mean you prefer to ride on the bus again?"

"Well, that is, if you allow me to."

"So after a day on the bus, you decided to enjoy it another day. And all the fine talk about thanking the party and intensifying thought reform! Who are you trying to kid anyway? We have given you an inch, and you reach out for a yard! You are no different from all reactionaries and imperialists. Think it over and hand in a written self-criticism in the morning."

In the morning, just as we were about to start, Wu Baotai handed the Red Guards his homework, which he had managed to do under a dim ceiling light on the auditorium stage of the county high school where we'd slept that night. The seventy-year-old ex-Communist limped the rest of the way the next two days, and the bus, empty except for a couple of women teachers taken ill, followed the columns of marchers like a slow-moving hearse.

We arrived at our destination, the Wujiang Commune, on December 25. We were all given one hour's leave to shop for some necessities, but the "cow demons" were warned against buying eatables. Looking for soap and toothpaste, in a grocery store, I ran into Yikai with her friend Jiang Nan, the wife of Lin Xing. When no one was watching, I smiled at them and said under my breath "Merry Christmas!" Yikai's eyes brightened. I did not see her again until many days later. Different departments were billeted in different villages in the commune, while I was one of the twenty university-class "targets of proletarian dictatorship" detained in the storehouse of an old pawnshop in town, arch-demons all and literally hostages to fortune.

The next day was Chairman Mao's seventy-fifth birthday. The four group leaders, including myself, decided we must also take part in the national celebration to show our loyalty to the "Red Sun," despite being consigned to the disgraceful limbo of the cow shed. The only means available to us was to eat a meal of "longevity noodles" and a meat dish or two. I was again assigned to do the shopping at the market, with money collected from the inmates. In this regard we, the bad people, had an advantage over the revolutionary good people who were billeted in the surrounding villages. I bought ten pounds of pork cooked in soy sauce, averaging half a pound per head, twenty fresh eggs, three pounds of spinach, and fifteen pounds of fresh-made long noodles. Two of the "cow demons" turned out to be good cooks. The pork, cut into thin slices, was served in two enamel washbasins. It was beautifully arranged into the shape of a sunflower with a hard-boiled egg yolk in the center. The sunflower was the symbol of the people's loyalty to the "Red Sun." Two more basins contained an egg-drop soup with shredded pork, which was to go with the noodles. The spinach was expertly stir-fried and looked soothingly green. We ate our fill, and nobody made any reference to the birthday that was the occasion of the longevity noodles. But in the evening, the Red Guard on duty who came to lead us in our political study took us to task for indulging in shameless gluttony on the pretext of celebrating the Chairman's birthday.

The next morning we were taken to the main street and divided into four groups for denunciation and struggle meetings for the benefit of the townspeople. The president, the vice president, Lin Xing, and myself were posted outside the department store at the center of the town. The morning hours were the busiest of the day, so that the street was crowded with peasants peddling their farm produce, tools, kitchen utensils, earthen pots, and whatnot, giving us a sizable audience. A couple of young men standing in front carried on a conversation before the show began.

"Hey, what's going on?

"The Red Guards of Anhui University are putting on a cow demon show."

"What were cow demons doing in the universities?"

"Doing counterrevolution! Doing revisionism!"

"What did they do that for?"

"Come on. You know Liu Shaoqi had them do it."

"Why did Chairman Mao let them do it?"

"Don't be stupid."

"But what did they do anyway?"

"Don't ask me. The Red Guards will show you. Just you watch and listen now."

The presiding Red Guard began by giving a talk on the significance of the Great Proletarian Cultural Revolution, the brilliance of Mao Zedong Thought, and the absolute authority of Chairman Mao's directives. He went on to explain that the thousands of students and teachers of the university had come down to the countryside to carry out the latest supreme directive on "struggle, critique, and reform." So the first step was to struggle against the cow demons. Then he vehemently denounced the four of us one by one, beginning with the president. From time to time he made each of us confess to the crimes indicted against us, including gluttony committed on the pretext of celebrating the Great Leader's birthday. The show ended with the shouting of the usual slogans, with the spectators joining in. Similar shows became the standard repertoire in the following weeks.

2

BEFORE LONG THE ARCH—"COW DEMONS" WERE ORDERED TO JOIN THE OTHER "demons" of their respective departments scattered in dozens of villages. The cow shed of the foreign languages department was in Nanzhuang, the South Village, about a twenty-minute walk from the market town. Professor Mao, Professor Kong, and myself followed the country road to the village and found the cow shed. The tile-roofed house belonged to a woman whose former husband, now deceased, had been a "rich peasant," a bad class status that became her legacy, though she had long since been married to a "poor peasant." While Red Guards and revolutionary teachers lived with good "poor peasant" families, the "cow demons" were housed with the only bad "rich peasant" family, following the principle that birds of a feather flock together. It so happened too that this was the only house with a room large enough to pen in a dozen "cow demons." The head demon, a Russian instructor and activist, denounced because of his past service with the Nationalist military, assigned us sleeping spaces on the dirt floor covered with rice straw. Two Red Guards shared a bamboo cot in the kitchen opposite our doorless room to keep watch over us.

Our day began with a march to the Loyalty Wall, in the center of the village, which had a huge portrait of Chairman Mao painted on it. Standing in a row before the wall, the twelve of us recited a collective confession of guilt and begged the "Great Savior" for his forgiveness and salvation. The three meals became the major business of the day. We bought the same food as the revolutionaries from a kitchen run by a fat cook from the university with two "cow demons" detailed daily as his help. The cook himself ladled food into our bowls from a huge basin. But no one was to line up for food before he or she bowed to the Chairman's portrait on the wall and recited a quotation from the Little Red Book. When one finished eating, he or she went back to the portrait and shouted "Long live Chairman Mao!"

Nanzhuang was a fairly prosperous village of over two dozen families. Thanks to its location, its rice paddies were protected against both drought and flooding. In addition to good crops, it boasted a hill planted with fruitful peach trees and raised hundreds of ducks a year, which were driven down the Yangtze River and sold to poultry buyers in metropolitan Nanjing, thirty miles away. All the families were of "poor peasant" origin, except for one man in his thirties whom everyone jocosely referred to as "landlord" because his father had been executed as a landlord when he was still a child. It was this "landlord," however, whom the village team leader, a party member, put in command of the hundreds of ducks. The team leader, a short, stocky middle-aged man of few words, was liked and respected by the peasants because he assured them of a good income. He showed due respect to the master workers under the banner of the Mao Zedong Thought Propaganda Team and drank hard liquor with them from time to time. Once, after a few drinks, Master Worker Li, who was always mindful of class struggle, asked him how he could trust the "landlord element" with such an important responsibility. "He knows his job," replied the team leader. He was civil to all the people from the university, revolutionary or otherwise. When invited to speak at sessions of denunciation and struggle staged for the benefit of the villagers, he would always criticize the "cow demon" under fire for not valuing the peasants' hard work. "Can you eat the words you scribble on a piece of paper?" he would always ask, and we would all answer truthfully in the negative. But even though his son might have made good money working on the farm like other teenagers, he insisted on keeping the boy in school to learn to "scribble on a piece of paper," because he had once been tricked by people who took advantage of his illiteracy.

It was the slack season of the year. There was really nothing to do in the fields, but at the insistence of the master workers the team leader found odd jobs for us. As luck would have it, in the midst of a heavy snow that kept us housebound several days, I was ordered to take a cart to the grain store in town and bring back sacks of rice and flour for the kitchen, all because I happened to own an old pair of rubbers. As I pulled the heavy cart through the slush of snow, over the broken stone slabs of the street and the dirt road full of bumps and potholes, I heard lines from T. S. Eliot's "Journey of the Magi" singing in my ears, "saying that this was all folly." My role on this long march was not much different from that of the slaves who carried the giant bricks uphill to build the Great Wall in the time of the first tyrant of the Qin dynasty. What were we building? Much time was spent in reading aloud and then discussing writings by Chairman Mao or newspaper articles and editorials. Self-confessions were required from time to time. The villagers were baffled by the university people's presence since none of them seemed to *do* anything, although the master workers and Red Guards kept telling them we were there to carry on the educational revolution and receive reeducation from them at the same time. The slogans "Learn from the poor and lower-middle peasants!" and "Long live the poor and lower-middle peasants!" were roared at every political rally, but a "poor peasant" in his thirties, known as the village wag, remarked to the Red Guards: " 'Long live' indeed! Who would have kept the emperors on the throne dynasty after dynasty, or you young gentlemen making revolution, if the peasants had not lived long?" Some Red Guards accused him of "reactionary thinking" behind his back, but there was nothing they could do about it since they were supposed to learn from the "poor peasants."

Then the villagers started getting ready for the annual celebrations of the Lunar New Year. The village tailor went from house to house making colorful new clothes for children, and the butcher slaughtered a pig for each family. Stone mills busily ground soybeans into milk, which was then treated with coagulants and turned into snow-white bean curds. Children ran around munching crisp candies made of sugar and peanuts or sesame or puffed rice. The drab front doors of houses were enlivened with couplets written on bright red paper. Before the Cultural Revolution, people used to choose auspicious traditional couplets. Now the newspapers recommended new ones composed in the spirit of the times. Our landlady, illiterate and wary of her class status, asked me to select one for her that no one could find fault with. To put her mind at ease, I settled on the surefire slogans "Long live Chairman Mao" and "Long live the Communist party," which Professor Mao wrote in his incomparable calligraphy.

The villagers' bustling preparations for the coming festival, which were occasionally interrupted by political rallies to denounce the "cow demons" as a preemptive security measure for the holiday season, only served to heighten our plight. A few days before the Lunar New Year, Yikai, who was staying in the village of Liuzhuang, a ten-minute walk from Nanzhuang, came to see me on a monthly visit and hand me my monthly allowance, which had been further reduced to fifteen yuan by the master workers. She told me one woman teacher from each department with a child or children left behind would be allowed to return to the university for the holidays. With all three children left in the kindergarten and no relatives nearby, she had thought she was the most eligible for the leave. So she submitted an application and started dreaming of spending the holidays with the kids. But the privilege went to Little Hot Pepper instead, whose two boys were living with her mother in their home. "Politics in command even in a thing like this," she sighed. Then she showed me a letter from Yiding, written in pencil in minuscule characters on a sheet of notebook paper. It took me a little while to make out that he had not been able to go home and see how things were until a week after we had left. To his dismay he found the good cakes that Mama had specially bought for them

235

from the pastry shop at the Yangtze River Hotel downtown had gone bad. He reluctantly dumped them on the garbage heap outside the building. Three days later when he went home again, a greater disaster was awaiting him. He found the floor covered with water, which had overflowed from the sink upstairs when the occupants had forgotten to turn off the tap before they went out for the day. He managed to sweep the water out of the rooms onto the stairway. Then, by himself, he removed the heavy suitcases from under the bed and lifted them onto the bed. At the kindergarten, the cook Uncle Liu asked him to be his assistant and fed him extra food. Finally he said his kid brother was getting along fine, except for one little mishap. Whether the food disagreed with him or he had caught a chill during the night, he'd had an attack of diarrhea and made a mess of his bedding before getting up one morning. The nurse scolded him and sent Yimao to the huge pool to clean up the mess. The wet bedding became so heavy that Yimao lost her footing and got herself soaked in the chilly pool. But everything was all right now, and Mama was not to worry. Yikai had been so alarmed by the last piece of news that she had showed the letter to the master worker when applying for leave to go home for the holidays. "Can you imagine what the guy said to me after reading it?" She was getting agitated. "Li Yikai, look here,' he said, 'your son certainly gave you a detailed account of petty family affairs, but not a word of how he was studying Chairman Mao's works. The important thing for you is not to spend the holidays with them, but to fill their heads with Mao Zedong Thought.' The next day he crossed the river and went home to spend the holidays with his family at the Ma'anshan steel mill.''

When the Lunar New Year celebrations were over, the villagers started making preparations for spring plowing. After working with the villagers in the fields in the mornings, we would spend the afternoons in political sessions, studying party documents or newspaper editorials, or taking turns in making self-confessions in preparation for the eventual decision on our cases. From time to time one of us would be fetched for interrogation by the Red Guards and master workers on questionable points in his personal history and urged to seek leniency by making a clean breast of all his offenses, like "spilling beans out of a bamboo tube." The slogan "Leniency to those who confess their crimes and severity to those who refuse to" was repeated ad nauseam.

One rainy day in April we were taken to the old theater in town for a university rally. The dingy place was jampacked with hundreds of students, faculty, and staff members. A huge banner of red cloth ran overhead from one side of the stage to the other, carrying big black Chinese characters on squares of white paper: ANHUI UNIVERSITY LENIENCY / SEVERITY RALLY. Major Dai Hong, an army political commissar and now director of the university's Revolutionary Committee, opened the meeting by reviewing the "fruits of victory already reaped in the current political campaign." Among other things, he asserted, "more than a hundred cow demons and snake spirits have been ferreted out by the revolutionary masses armed with the invincible Mao Zedong Thought. The leniency / severity rally is being held to push the campaign to a new climax, to demonstrate the wisdom and correctness of the party's policy, and to admonish the criminals to take the road of seeking leniency through confessing all, and not the road to ruin by refusing to confess."

Then the head master worker announced a list of four cases being given lenient or severe treatment. Wang Yichuan, a chemistry instructor and until recently captain of the "cow demon" work gang, was cleared of the "rightist" stigma, which he had been stuck with for ten years through a bureaucratic error. This was hailed as a brilliant example of the invincible Mao Zedong Thought. The second case of leniency had to do with Sun Taolin, the vice president who had confessed to the Nationalist police his connection with the party as a Communist Youth League member in his student days. It was an age-old story, but he was given credit for never seeking to deny it. His lenient treatment consisted of demotion from government service grade 9 to grade 18, with a sharp cut in pay and reassignment to the job of an administrative assistant in the department of mathematics. The first case of severity had to do with Sun Xianglin, the dean of academic affairs, who had been in my group in the campus cow shed. Though confronted with a copy of an old Nationalist newspaper with a list of Communist renegades containing a name identical to his, he staunchly denied the charge that he had ever been a renegade. He was deprived of both his job and his rank and was allowed thirty yuan a month to live on. He had once been a high-ranking official in the Ministry of Justice; I had to wonder how he felt about the way he had fared in the hands of the Red Justice.

The rally came to a climax when the head master worker shouted an order: "Bring out the counterrevolutionary enemy agent!" Two security guys pushed an old man, his bald head bowed, to the center of the stage. "Lift your head, Shen the Blind!" shouted one of the security guys. My heart sank when I saw how much he had aged since I saw him last. His eyes were two sockets of despair. Then I heard the head master worker read out his indictment and verdict. He was charged with (1) working for the Nationalist intelligence service in 1937, and (2) frantically putting up small-character posters to deny his crime during the Cultural Revolution. For his implacable attitude, the counterrevolutionary enemy agent was given the severe punishment of five years of reform through forced labor. "Do you plead guilty?" asked the master worker. Shen shook his head and said, "No, I am not guilty of—" Before he could finish, deafening slogans of "Down with the counterrevolutionary Shen the Blind!" burst out from the audience. "Whether you admit it or not, sign the arrest warrant here," one of the security guys ordered, thrusting a pen into his hand. The blind man screamed, "I will not sign. I can't see anyway." The security guy grabbed his hand, pressed his right thumb into a box of ink paste, and then pressed it on the arrest warrant. He then produced a pair of handcuffs and shackled the wrists of the old scholar of classical Chinese literature. What was taking place before the eyes of the college-educated audience, it occurred to me, undoubtedly brought back to some of them the last scene in Lu Xun's classical story *The True Story of Ah Q,* in which the innocent peasant Ah Q was forced to sign his own death warrant. More slogans were shouted and the convicted man was dragged off the stage. Coming out into the street, I saw Shen the Blind standing alone in the rain on a truck that was to transport him to Hefei, a living or perhaps dying reproach to the forces that had brought him to such straits. Red Guards and teachers passed by chattering and laughing. Undoubtedly glad that the meeting was over, they could now give themselves a treat to some local delicacies at the snack counters.

3

THE LENIENCY / SEVERITY RALLY MARKED A NEW STAGE IN THE CAMPAIGN TO clean up the class ranks. The "cow demons" were reassembled by department at the local high school. We took turns in making a final self-confession and helping each other by exposing loopholes and inconsistencies in the confessions, in preparation for leniency or severity to be meted out to one and all. At the end of a week, most of us returned to our respective departments, or as the jargon had it, "returned to the midst of revolutionary masses," presumably a higher circle in the limbo, pending the eventual conclusion of our cases. A few were detained for further self-examination. The "cow demon" squads were disbanded and the "demons" were assigned living quarters in different peasant households like the others. With the ten other "cow demons" of the department sent to other villages, Professor Mao and I shared the old room with our new guard Chen Yu, a peasant boy majoring in Russian, each of us occupying a narrow bamboo cot. An avid reader of Chinese and foreign literature, our guard relished the opportunity for nocturnal conversations with two professors of literature. Coming from a great scholarly family, Professor Mao had been taught classical Chinese literature at home and Russian literature at the first Chinese academy of Russian. An irrepressible talker, he regaled us with endless literary anecdotes from his own life and recitations of his own poems in classical Chinese style. Chen Yu would laugh aloud irrepressibly from time to time. Fortunately our "rich peasant" landlady and her "poor peasant" husband slept soundly after a day's labor in the fields.

An independent spirit, Chen Yu would come in with stories of how he got into one tiff after another with the master worker Pox Lin, who monitored the thinking and reading of the dozen Russian majors living in the village. "I ran into Pox Lin in the afternoon," he told us one night. "When he saw I had a book in my hand, he asked, 'What are you reading, Chen Yu?' I said, 'The Dream of the Red Chamber.' He said, 'What's that? You should study Chairman Mao's works instead.' I replied, 'It's the great classical novel recommended by Chairman Mao.' He said, 'But I don't think it can be as good as the Chairman's works, no?' I doubt if he reads

Chairman Mao's works himself, with his marginal literacy, ha ha!" Chen Yu also told us that most of the master workers were heavy drinkers who spent the evenings together in the house of a local cadre to get soused on 120 proof "white spirit" distilled from sorghum. The spirit was usually kept in used normal-saline bottles. Once Pox Lin saw a fellow worker coming back from the market with a full bottle. He went up to the man, wrenched the bottle out of his hand and pulled out the rubber stopper. "I've been thirsty like hell for a drink. Don't you dare stop me!" So saying, he turned the bottle upside down, took a quick swill, but immediately spewed it out. "Damn you! What's the awful stuff?" The other worker burst out laughing. "Kerosene for my stove! Serves you right, you greedy old souse!" Chen Yu concluded, "How could they find the time to read anything even if they wanted to?"

Another night Pox Lin descended on us without warning, smelling of white spirit. Professor Mao and I were already in bed. Chen Yu was reading under a dim light. "What are you reading, Chen Yu?" Pox Lin asked. "Guo Moruo's essay commemorating the three-hundredth anniversary of the peasant revolution led by Li Zicheng," Chen Yu answered, not expecting any objection this time. "Why don't you study Chairman Mao's works instead?" asked Pox Lin. "But it is recommended by Chairman Mao and forms an appendix to the Chairman's *Selected Works,* Master Lin!" "Can it be as good as the Chairman's own writings? Yes?" Master Lin retorted triumphantly. When he had left, Chen Yu muttered to himself in a rage, "Oh God, can these guys lead a *cultural* revolution?" The next night, Chen Yu was absorbed in a Chinese translation of *Spartacus,* a novel based on the story of the Thracian gladiator who led the historic slave revolt against the Roman rulers in the first century B.C., when he suddenly heard a neighbor's dog barking. Hastily thrusting the book under his pillow, he opened the *Selected Works of Mao Zedong.* When Pox Lin entered and found him poring over the only book under the sun worth reading, he declared with satisfaction, "I'm glad to see you reading the Chairman's works as I told you to, Xiao Chen. I am glad, I am glad! Nothing can be as good as Chairman Mao's writings, that's what I say. Keep it in mind, Xiao Chen." When he had left, Chen Yu could not wait to share his amusement with us. "Lao Mao, Lao Wu, this is simply fantastic! I was breathless with excitement following Spartacus galloping away from the pursuit of his enemy, when all of a sudden I heard the neighbor's dog barking. My heart galloped as fast as Spartacus's horse! Oh, what an adventure!"

With Chen Yu as our guard, Yikai dropped in from time to time on her way to or from the market town. Chen Yu would excuse himself as soon as Yikai made her appearance. We would chat quietly about the children, left on their own, or speculate a little about our future over a cup of green tea. Yikai always brought some spicy roast peanuts or dried bean curds, which she knew I loved. Yikai would tell me about her life in the house of a "poor peasant" family. Liu the peasant and his wife were very nice, but as a "cow demon's" spouse Yikai was under the surveillance of a Russian major, with whom she shared a narrow bamboo cot. The Red Guard protected herself by sleeping against the wall, leaving Yikai hanging precariously on the outer edge of the cot. To make things worse, rats kept running over the cot at night. "One night, I was rudely awakened by two rats fighting right over my face. I screamed and woke my bedfellow. I hurriedly said I was sorry. She only said it was quite 'unrevolutionary' to be scared of rats. Well, I never was revolutionary anyway. The next morning, while ladling out water from the vat for my morning wash, I was alarmed to see a big rat floating in the water. I did not scream this time, but fetched Liu to see it. He simply grabbed it and dumped it in the urine bucket. 'Nothing unusual,' he remarked. At the next political study session, my bedfellow denounced me as a coward scared of rats and resisting reeducation by peasants." We would compare the current visit with her visits to me in jail or in the college "cow shed," agreeing it was quite an improvement over the past. Sometimes, when Jiang Nan, the Russian instructor, came with her, our conversation invariably centered on what the authorities would do with the "cow demons" in the end. Inured to the party's caprices, Yikai and I had ceased to worry about what was not in our power to seek or prevent. Jiang Nan, however, was anxious, because her husband, Lin Xing, had been classified as a serious case at the leniency / severity rally and escorted back to campus for intensive interrogation in solitary confinement. Yikai and I tried to assuage her worries by assuring her that all would end well, although we had little ground for our assurance.

While the villagers were busy with spring plowing and sowing in the fields, the revolutionary teachers and students stayed indoors and engaged in endless desultory discussions of educational revolution. When excluded from the sessions, Professor Mao and I would take ourselves to the small plot of land where we had been given the task of growing bok choy for the kitchen. Professor Mao could not even walk steadily, so it was always I who carried water or diluted night soil in two buckets on a shoulder pole to the plot. Then both of us would spread the manure or water on the vegetables with a long-handled dipper. There wasn't really much to do, but we loathed going back to the midst of Red Guards and master workers. So I ended up digging a cavern on the side of a ridge, large enough for the two of us to sit in comfortably. Lao Mao was so pleased with our hideout that he named it "Two Cow Demons' Land of Peach Blossoms," after the legendary land of bliss of the classical poet Tao Yuanming. He would alternately doze off in the warm sun and regale me with reminiscences of his glamorous early life, first as a well-connected student of Russian in the old Peking and then as a young diplomat in Moscow. Away from the heat of denunciation, he turned unashamedly nostalgic. Once I teased him by giving him a stereotyped lecture:

"Lao Mao, I'm afraid you are relapsing in your thought reform. All this nostalgia for your reactionary past is proof enough that you hold on to your reactionary class stand. I'm afraid I'll have to turn you in."

"I stand convicted, Lao Wu," he said with affected seriousness. "My son charged me with the same sin at home. He often made me bow before Chairman Mao's portrait and beg the Great Leader for his forgiveness. I went along, the way I used to play games with him when he was little. But when he ordered me to get down on my knees, I thought it was going too far. 'This is feudalistic. I never made you kowtow to me or to our ancestors, did I?' But he retorted triumphantly, 'Feudalistic indeed! It should suit you perfectly, because you are a feudalistic relic yourself. To use a phrase you taught me, this is "to combat poison with poison." Now get down on your knees and beg the Chairman's forgiveness!' "

"But did you get down on your knees?" I pursued.

"On second thought, I did. Since we had been forced to kneel in public on the night of June 6, I said to myself, why shouldn't I do it in the privacy of my home? So down I went. But when my wife called me to dinner, I was too stiff to get up. The boy had to come and help me up. Then the three of us ate our good dinner as usual and the boy even poured me a glass of grape wine. What a farce!"

"You are not only nostalgic for your feudalistic past, Lao Mao: what's more serious, you are cynical."

"Aren't you, Lao Wu? Come on, what else can one be these days?"

I told him I could not afford to be a cynic, because my life experiences were worlds apart from his. So off and on I would tell him stories of the labor camp in the Wilderness or death by starvation. He was touched by the story of the young calligrapher who had not made it, but he turned the tables on me by declaring with mock earnestness:

"I don't believe a word of what you have said, Lao Wu. You know very well the revolutionary humanitarianism advocated by the party and the Great Leader himself. During the war with the Japanese, the POWs were never mistreated. During the war with the Nationalists, the same policies were enforced. It is a matter of revolutionary principle. Then how is it that the offenders under corrective education should have been badly treated and even starved to death? It doesn't stand to reason. It must be a figment of your imagination, or else you have gone out of your mind. I'm afraid I'll just have to turn you in." Then he burst out into a guffaw.

By mid-April, the topic for political study was the "Great Leader's" directive that cadres, that is, all those in public service, should settle down in the countryside and receive reeducation from the "poor and lower-middle" peasants. The university was getting ready to answer the Chairman's call by sending a number of its faculty and staff for the honor and glory of "going down under." The master workers lauded "the wisdom of the Great Leader and the far-reaching significance of his great strategic plan." Everyone declared his or her eagerness to go, but nobody really relished the prospect of being so glorified. It turned out that the honor and glory only went to those who were former "cow demons" recently freed from proletarian dictatorship, spouses of "cow demons" still under it, or those who were thorns in the flesh of the master workers. That Yikai would be among the chosen was a foregone conclusion, even before the list was officially read at a department meeting on May 10. In the evening she came to give me the expected word. Trucks would take them back to the university the next morning, and a few days were allowed for them to get ready to move to their separate villages en masse. I was distressed by the prospect of Yikai suffering all by herself another ordeal of going into exile with the three children. What had happened ten years before was repeating itself with a vengeance. What had she or I or the children done to deserve all this? What was the party or the nation getting out of all this? Was that really the way to build China into a great socialist country? I had no answers and I had no comfort to give my wife. But what upset her most was the news that I would eventually be sent back to a rural village in my hometown of Yangzhou for reform through manual labor under peasant surveillance. I only said, "Let tomorrow take care of itself. I can never forget what you said to me when I was taken away from home eleven years ago: 'Keep faith with life.' Now you just take care of yourself and the kids." I walked her back to her village and said a silent farewell in the darkness.

4

ONCE YIKAI WAS GONE, I BEGAN TO SUFFER THE SUSPENSE OF WAITING FOR MY doom. I was left alone, not even required to repeat my confessions any more. Perhaps just to break the monotony of my days, one hot day in July I came down with a high fever. Dr. Wu from the university clinic stopped by to see me a couple of times and prescribed some pills to bring down the fever. But the fever went up instead of coming down. Finally the doctor decided to send me to the local commune hospital for treatment. Just as I was preparing to go, getting up from my bamboo cot on my weak legs, Yikai suddenly turned up with Yicun. It was the first time I had seen him in six months. I tried hard to hold back my tears. I slumped into the cot again. Yicun came to my side and brought out from his inner shirt pocket a tiny packet. After tearing off layer after layer of wrapping paper, he picked up the hidden treasure with two fingers and put it in my mouth. "The best candy in my box. I saved it for you, Papa. Do you like it?" I could only nod in answer, tears running down my cheeks.

"What happened, Ningkun?" asked Yikai.

"I have been running a high fever. I was just about to leave for the hospital when you walked in. How did you know I was ill, Yikai?"

"I didn't know. Yicun came home from Hefei a few days ago. I thought I would bring him to see you. It's been such a long time. What did the doctor say?"

"Fever caused by unknown viral infection or something else. So to the commune hospital I go."

Seeing I was too weak to walk the distance to town, Yikai pushed me on her bicycle to the hospital, leaving Yicun behind with the landlady. I was admitted and put in a ward with a dozen other patients, although still not entitled to free medical care. Dr. Li the superintendent, who had only recently been released from proletarian dictatorship, examined me and refrained from making a diagnosis. After a few days of drip injection of antibiotics, the fever was brought down and Yikai was able to return to her village with Yicun.

One afternoon in August, Yiding suddenly turned up in my room, drenched in sweat.

"What happened, Yiding?" I was alarmed. "How come you are here by yourself?"

"Sister has been critically ill. Mother was summoned to Hefei by the university. I boarded at the high school in Xiangchuan for a while, but the school would not open on schedule because of the flood. The dining hall was closed, so I went back to our village and lived by myself a few days, eating my meals with Granny Sun next door. She didn't have much to feed me and I was lonely, so I decided to come to you. Do you think they will let me stay?"

"Of course you will stay," Chen Yu put in.

"Okay, that's settled." I felt relieved. "But tell me how you got here."

"I walked."

"Walked? How far? How many hours?"

"Twenty miles, I suppose. I rested now and then. Left early. Ate plenty of watermelon on the way."

Yiding was only thirteen, and he had been on the road six or seven hours on a sweltering day. The landlady was amazed by the boy's stamina and made him a huge bowl of fried rice with eggs. That night, he developed a fever. Chen Yu took him to see the college doctor and came back with APC (aspirin phenacetin caffeine) tablets and herbal drops for heatstroke. When he was well again in a few days, Chen Yu took him for a swim in the Zhuma He, a historic river where the armies of Xiang Yu the Conqueror, of the Age of the Three Kingdoms, watered their horses before their disastrous defeat by Liu Bang, the founding emperor of the Han dynasty.

Yiding's coming added a new dimension not only to my life, but to that of Professor Mao and Chen Yu as well. I had been separated from my firstborn for the greater part of a year. He had grown a little but was still small for his age because of undernourishment. The boy had learned to swim all by himself, and now he found a willing coach in Chen Yu. I was grateful that Chen Yu acted like a big brother to Yiding and never made him feel his father was a "cow demon" under his surveillance. On a long afternoon when there was no political study or manual labor, we would all sprawl out on our bamboo cots (Yiding sharing mine) and Chen Yu would take the lead in reading from a volume of the great modern writer Lu Xun's works, with Yiding taking part. Sometimes we would even stop in the middle of the readings and argue over a passage or clear up a point.

Yiding, reticent by nature but a good storyteller, was full of stories of his months at the kindergarten. "One morning after the regular breakfast time the nurses found all the kids sound asleep in my room," he told us one day. "When they were all up at last, the nurses asked them why they had not got up on time. They said Wu Yiding had kept them up late by telling them stories of the Golden Monkey."

"Did you get into trouble for breaking the rules?" I asked anxiously.

"In a way I did." He smiled. "The teachers made me tell the stories to all the classes from then on!"

"That's wonderful! You did a great thing in cheering up the poor kids left behind by their parents," exclaimed Chen Yu. "I always liked *Journey to the West* myself, but I haven't read it for I don't know how long. Now you cheer us up with the stories, Yiding!"

"Are you sure it's all right, Chen Yu?" I asked.

"No problem. The Golden Monkey is the archetypal revolutionary held up by Chairman Mao. All Red Guards are supposed to model themselves upon him. Go on, Yiding, tell us the stories." So on drowsy summer afternoons the thirteen-year-old boy would tell fairy tales to cheer up three adults adrift on raftlike bamboo cots in the midst of a tempestuous revolution.

One afternoon, just as Yiding was in the midst of the Monkey's exciting bouts with the White-boned Demon in the guise of an alluring woman, Pox Lin barged in.

"What are you doing?" He asked sternly.

"Lao Wu's son here is telling us a Golden Monkey story," replied Chen Yu. "Chairman Mao recommends the classical novel most highly, you know."

"I know, but you are not to indulge in such pastimes with people under your surveillance. You should see to it that they study Chairman Mao's works as much as they can. The same applies to this boy here."

When Chen Yu came back from supper, he looked upset. After a while, he said, "Pox Lin has decided Yiding mustn't tarry any longer. It's not good for your thought reform, neither is it good for the boy, so he said."

In the morning Yiding took the ferryboat to Ma'anshan, where he boarded the train to Hefei to join his mother, who had been nursing his sick sister.

With Yiding gone, our life returned to the monotony of daily meals, occasional sessions of political study, and regular manuring and watering of the vegetables. When the vegetables showed signs of undernourishment, the Red Guard in charge ordered me to spread plenty of chemical fertilizer on them. They did grow faster, but the leaves had turned from green to dark purple by the time Lao Mao and I carried our harvest to the kitchen. After one look at the fruit of our labor, the fat cook asked, "What are you bringing it here for? This is no vegetable, but kindling! Go away!" So Lao Mao and I carried our harvest to the garbage dump instead. I felt like a piece of junk pending disposal myself.

One morning in the fall I was on duty in the kitchen while the revolutionary people of the department were holding a meeting in the nearby public room. All of a sudden I saw a man from East Ying village run toward the public room. A moment later Yue Weizhang, the deputy party secretary of the department, burst out of the room and followed the peasant at a run toward East Ying village. Some emergency, apparently. But what? When the meeting broke up and people came to the kitchen for lunch, I was shocked to overhear that Jiang Nan had been found hanging in her room in the peasant's house where she stayed. In the afternoon I found the kitchen walls and the ground in front of it covered with big-character slogans on yellow paper:

Jiang Nan killed herself to escape punishment!
Forever severing herself from the party and the people!
She died an active counterrevolutionary in vain!
A reed mat she gets! Like a dog be she buried!

Inured to the revolutionary rhetoric of the times, I didn't take the slogans literally. A couple of days later, however, word got around that Jiang Nan's shallow grave, in which her body had actually been wrapped in a cheap reed mat, had been robbed. The body was left exposed after a woolen sweater had been stripped from it. It was then hastily reburied under shovelfuls of earth. Before another day passed, word came around that the grave had been robbed again, this time by a wild dog that tore the body to pieces. The villagers complained angrily, "What had the woman college teacher done that she deserved to be devoured by a wild dog? What have we done to deserve such bad luck?" The master workers called a departmental rally to announce several emergency measures: 1. Jiang Nan, whose suicide is a treacherous betrayal of the party and the people, is formally denounced as an active counterrevolutionary; 2. The incident is to be kept secret and anyone who leaks the information to her husband will be denounced as an active counterrevolutionary; meanwhile her husband, already in solitary confinement on campus, will be forbidden any contact with outsiders; 3. The Red Guards and revolutionary teachers should help the peasants to overcome superstition with Mao Zedong Thought; 4. An investigation will be conducted into the incident and any irresponsible speculation or gossip will be treated as a serious breach of revolutionary discipline.

But the peasants, who were not bound by "revolutionary discipline," spoke freely. It soon became public knowledge that Jiang Nan had been repeatedly raped by one or more master workers, who threatened her with dire consequences against her husband if she talked. Later, finding herself pregnant, she went to see Shen Wenwu, the master worker who ruled the department, and asked for leave to have an abortion done at a hospital. But for that purpose a father had to be named. Instead of helping her out of the dilemma, Shen threatened her with the charge of "corrupting members of the working class" if she talked. Driven into a corner and overcome with shame and despair, she had confided to a close friend that she saw no other way out. Her husband had already been in solitary confinement for some time, but was still allowed to take his meals in the dining hall under escort. From the day of her death on, he was not allowed to leave his room anymore and his meals were brought to him. He was alarmed by the tightening security, assuming it to be a sign of the gravity of his case. He was indeed kept in the dark until the end of the Cultural Revolution, when the master workers returned to their steel mill in Ma'anshan. The investigation into Jiang Nan's death never got anywhere, because no single master worker could be held responsible for the pregnancy, although several were known to have been involved in the rapes. Many years passed before Jiang Nan was exonerated from the mortal crime of betraying the party and the people and a small compensation allotted her daughter.

The death of Jiang Nan dissipated the momentary idyllic illusion under which I had lived during Yiding's unexpected visit. My mind went back to my fellow inmate's death by starvation ten years ago, but this death was far more horrifying. The sad news would soon reach Yikai, and it would be such a blow to her. A shadow seemed to have been cast over the lives of all the people around me. The villagers sighed and shook their heads. They could never understand how such a terrible thing could have taken place at a university. Both Lao Mao and I became subdued. Chen Yu, who used to talk and laugh easily, grew silent and spent more time absorbed in his reading. One night he was engrossed in the heroics of the rebels in the classic novel *All Men Are Brothers* when he heard the neighbor's dog bark. Quickly turning off the light, he ducked under the mosquito net and started snoring. We heard footsteps approaching and the doors creak, then footsteps going away. A few minutes later, Chen Yu came out of the mosquito net and went back to the legendary heroes, swearing under his breath, "Damned nuisance!"

* * *

With Liu Shaoqi and his followers overthrown and discredited, Mao Zedong and his new heir designate, Marshal Lin Biao, moved to consolidate their power. Simultaneous with the disbanding of the unruly Red Guards and the sending of millions of high school graduates down under among peasants, the spearhead of critique at colleges was now directed at the younger teachers. Few were spared. I saw a number of big-character posters attacking my former political confessor Feng Xiangchun for allegedly sitting at my feet. Then it was the students' turn. One freshman English major, a boy from a "poor peasant" family, was taken from village to village for sessions of criticism because he had raised the question, "If the Chinese table tennis players are said to have won world championships because they were armed with Mao Zedong Thought, then how do we account for the victories won by players from Japan and other countries?" He was publicly denounced as an active counterrevolutionary who flagrantly opposed the Invincible Mao Zedong Thought. Only his good class origin saved him from dire consequences.

Several Russian majors in our village were denounced at political sessions, one after another. But Chen Yu got the worst of it because he had repeatedly talked back to Pox Lin. When it was his turn to be denounced, Lao Mao and I were told to attend the session, which was to be held in the village tool room. On an afternoon in late fall, a dozen students and a few teachers came to the meeting place with a little campstool each and found a place among picks and shovels, wicker baskets and shoulder poles. Pox Lin was seated in a bamboo chair. The walls were plastered with the usual slogans, "Down with Chen Yu!" and the like. A huge white cloth streamer hung across the room proclaimed "Death to Chen Yu if he does not surrender!" The Red Guards who had spearheaded the Cultural Revolution were now its targets! What was this revolution coming to? And where was it heading?

The session was presided over by Xiao Pei, Chen Yu's classmate and the class monitor, a favorite of Pox Lin's. "Chen Yu has good class roots because he comes from a 'poor peasant' family in the economically backward north of the province, like myself," he said, starting with the usual class analysis. "Yet because of his arrogance and neglect of thought reform, he has succumbed to the evil influence of bourgeois literature and bourgeois intellectuals, instead of learning modestly from master workers and poor and lower-middle peasants. In fact, he is quickly sinking into the quagmire of reactionary bourgeois ideology. I call upon Chen Yu to lay bare his soul today and make a self-criticism that touches him to his very soul."

Looking subdued, Chen Yu said in his usual brusque way: "Chairman Mao teaches us 'No man is perfect, no gold is pure.' I am certainly no exception. But my twenty-one-year-old life is an open book. I have never tried to hide my defects and foibles. I welcome criticism from my classmates, master workers, and peasants." Then he raised his voice a little, his big eyes flashing with anger. "But surely I am not one of the enemy and should not be treated as such!"

Before he could go on, Xiao Pei put in: "I warn you, Chen Yu, this is no time for you to bluff, or to prettify yourself. You have gone far enough in defying the master workers and opposing Mao Zedong Thought. It's time for you to make a clean breast of your sins and save yourself from perdition."

"I can't believe my ears, Xiao Pei." Chen Yu raised his voice again. "I have heard such charges uttered against cow demons and snake spirits too many times. I have done it myself. And now you say that to me! Are you not confusing your class brother with the enemy?"

"It's you who have done that, Chen Yu," said another class brother of his, nicknamed Little Nun, coming to Xiao Pei's support. "The party has entrusted you with the political task of keeping Mao Xiaolu and Wu Ningkun under surveillance. And what have you done? You have become their friend or, rather, their captive. You never turned in a single report on their reactionary doings or sayings. Instead of giving them manual labor, you went out with them on pleasure strolls. Instead of supervising their thought reform, you wallowed in their bourgeois literary tastes and ideas! Did you not?"

"Down with Chen Yu! Chen Yu must make a clean breast of his crimes!" shouted his class brothers and Pox Lin.

Keenly aware of our role as Exhibit A, Lao Mao and I sat very small and kept very quiet. But there was no escape. Another class brother accused him of circulating a reactionary poem he had allegedly written in collaboration with Lao Mao and myself. All eyes turned to us and Xiao Pei ordered Mao Xiaolu to confess.

"One Sunday Lao Wu and I took a stroll to the Conqueror's Temple under the escort of Chen Yu," Professor Mao said in his loud voice. "Unsteady on my feet, I slipped and fell on all fours before the statue of Xiang Yu the Conqueror. It was Chen Yu who kindly helped me up. To mock myself, I threw off two lines of doggerel: 'Making an exhibition of myself at the Conqueror's Temple / The professor turned out to be a stinking example.' It was Lao Wu who finished it off with two more lines."

"I did," I confessed. " 'Cow demons I don't admit / Back to the cow shed beat it.' Chen Yu took no part in it."

"Perhaps I have been a bit too lenient with Lao Mao and Lao Wu," Chen Yu said. "But I thought I was only following the guidelines set down by the party in giving them humanitarian treatment. And the literary works I read with them were all classics recommended by Chairman Mao—"

"Chen Yu is trying to throw dust into our eyes," another class brother put in. "He not only winked at the reactionary poem by Mao Xiaolu and Wu Ningkun but spread their poisonous sentiments of malcontent by reciting it to us. He shows no penitence for all that, but invokes the name of our Great Leader instead. Chen Yu blasphemes Chairman Mao! Chen Yu deserves ten thousand deaths!"

"Chen Yu befriends not only the cow demons themselves, but their families as well," put in a class sister. "When Wu Ningkun's son stayed with them without permission, Chen Yu took him to the river and gave him swimming lessons. I heard the boy call you 'Big Brother Chen,' didn't he, Chen Yu?"

"Indeed he did, so what?"

"That makes you a brother of the son of a class enemy!" the girl retorted triumphantly.

"How should he have addressed me then?"

"Not at all. You should have had nothing to do with him to begin with!"

The attack on Chen Yu's "fraternization" with class enemies turned out to be only a prelude to the more serious charge of opposing the

Workers Mao Zedong Thought Propaganda Team in the person of Pox Lin.

"Chen Yu frequently talked back to Master Worker Lin when the master earnestly tried to help him with Mao Zedong Thought," Xiao Pei declared. "Not only that, he spread rumors and libel against the master, whom we all respect and admire very much. Master Worker Lin is a representative of the working class sent by Chairman Mao to lead us in making the Cultural Revolution. Chen Yu's opposition to Master Worker Lin is nothing less than an assault on the working class, and opposition to Chairman Mao himself! Down with Chen Yu! Chen Yu must hang his head and admit his guilt!"

"Down with Chen Yu! Hang your head and admit your guilt!" echoed his other classmates.

"When I was a child, my parents always taught me to be an honest boy, to hide nothing from them." Chen Yu seemed to be sidetracking. "Then Chairman Mao taught me to 'say all you know and say it without reserve.' Just because Master Worker Lin represents the working class and is sent by Chairman Mao, I thought I could do no less for him than what I did for my parents, my teachers, or my classmates. If I have inadvertently offended Master Worker Lin in any way out of ignorance or arrogance, I hereby publicly ask for his forgiveness."

"Chen Yu is treacherous! Chen Yu must admit his guilt of opposing the working class and Chairman Mao!" Xiao Pei took the lead in shouting the slogans.

Surprisingly, Pox Lin took the floor and rose to the occasion.

"Fellow students, we are gathered here to help Chen Yu, not to knock him down with one stroke. I'm a member of the workers propaganda team; my task is to help you all forward on the revolutionary road, not to fuss over offenses to my personal dignity. Chen Yu worried me because he wasted time reading about dreams and mansions, Ah Q and Guo Moruo, Lu Xun and Monkeys, and what have you, all ancient and dead. Why not study the writings of Chairman Mao instead? Nothing is as good as the four volumes of the Chairman's works. What I always said to him, I say to you all here and now. Xiao Chen, go back to your room, think it over, and write a self-criticism."

Pox Lin had his triumph, I suppose, and could afford to act the part of a lenient victor. Word got around the next day that Pox Lin had celebrated his triumph over Xiao Chen with half a bottle of white spirit in the company of his fellow workers.

As for Chen Yu, when he returned to the room in the evening, he burst out laughing: "Trying to put me in my place! No way! But you two had better be more careful. I don't believe there is much they can do about me, but they can always give you a bad time. I must read more of Lu Xun's essays. His sharp critiques of his times and contemporaries are equally applicable today. Had he survived into our time, he would also have been labeled an ultrarightist, for sure!" Two days later, Chen Yu was sent to room with one of his class brothers in another house. Lao Mao was also sent to live with another family. With me left behind by myself, the young man of the house, Xiao Jin, moved back to the room and put up his four-poster again.

With half of the "cow demons" of the department liberated and sent to settle down in the countryside, the five who remained were now placed under the surveillance of an English senior named Sun Shaoru. He was trusted by the master workers because he came from a good "poor peasant" family and because he was too shy to talk back. He stayed in another village, where the department leaders were housed, but from time to time he would gather us together from our separate villages for political study or manual labor. He never lectured us, never raised his voice, and blushed easily. He would drop in on me of an evening and take me out for a long walk. He knew my story inside out from my public confessions and autobiographical materials, he said, and he could find nothing wrong with me. So he told me about himself. Orphaned at an early age, both he and his younger brother were brought up by his married sister. A few years later, when the brother-in-law was finally fed up with the continuing care of the orphans, his sister simply got up and returned to their parents' hut in a nearby village, bringing with her the orphaned brothers and a daughter and a son of her own. The commune was known for the luscious pears it produced and marketed all over the country and was therefore named Liangli, or Fine Pears. His sister worked extra hours in the orchards, earning enough not only to keep the four children fed and clothed but to keep the two brothers in school. When Shaoru was admitted to Anhui University after passing the National College Entrance Examination in the summer of 1965, the whole village celebrated with banquets and firecrackers. The sister quietly took the two brothers to their parents' grave mounds nearby, burned incense, and all three kowtowed three times each. Then came the time for Shaoru to take the train for the capital city of the province. The station was five miles away, and Shaoru was short and slight of build. The sister carried his bedroll on her back as a matter of course and walked him all the way to the station.

"You are certainly fortunate in having such a loving sister," I said. "She must be awfully proud of you."

"I know," said Shaoru. "She never went to school, never learned to read or write. She was determined that her brothers go to school. She wanted us to study hard, but never scolded us, never lectured us on what to do or what not to do."

"Is that why you never lectured us, never raised your voice?" I asked.

"I don't know," he said, blushing. "Sister always speaks softly, never hurts anybody. I would have died of shame if I had lectured you or raised my voice or hurt anyone's feelings. My classmates criticize me for having a soft character, but my face burns when I watch them put on airs and bully their teachers. I know we are in the midst of a great revolution and there are many things I don't understand, but that does not give us the right to hurt people for nothing. Anyway, I would have disgraced my sister and my dead parents if I had done some of the things other Red Guards did."

He had not quite finished his freshman year when the Cultural Revolution erupted. Now he would be graduating with a certificate of "having satisfactorily completed a four-year program in English."

"What can I do when I graduate?" He sounded bewildered. "I studied very hard the first year, but I have nearly forgotten everything I learned. I want to serve the people, but what am I going to serve the people with?"

"It's not your fault, Xiao Sun." I tried to comfort him. "I myself lost five years serving in the air force during World War II, but I went back to college when the war was over to make up for lost time. Why don't you start right now, reviewing your old lessons and learning new ones?"

"Do you think you can help me? I'm not bright, but I'm willing to learn . . ."

"There is not much for me to do these days. I have time to kill, pending the conclusion of my case."

Thus we began going over his old lessons. Then we moved on to the standard English reader for sophomores. I warned him against a mechanical approach to the study of English and tried to teach him how to read sensitively and intelligently. One day, when he brought a textbook for first-year French, we began to work on the rudiments of a second foreign language, although my French was quite rusty. Finding him eager and receptive, I also urged him to read classical Chinese literature, especially poetry, with which Chairman Mao was more than familiar. The young man was blessed with a good heart, which unbelievably had gone through three years of Red Terror uncorrupted. An exposure to fine literature, I hoped, might help to enrich his sensibility and add dimensions to his vision of life. What better use could I have made of the forced idleness of a "cow demon"? Of course we had to be very careful, lest he be caught fraternizing with a class enemy, like Chen Yu before him. Luckily, he had few enemies, and we were left in peace.

Another winter came, flurries of snow signaling the beginning of hibernation for the peasants and their water buffalos, for the Red Guards and their "cow demons." Graduates of the classes of '66, '67, and '68 had long since left. Only students of the class of '69 lingered on as the main force of the revolution. But they were only biding their time while maneuvering for a good assignment upon graduation. News and reports of political intrigues that went on in the great capital city and elsewhere echoed only faintly among the faculty and students. There were routine political studies, perfunctory discussions, rumors and gossip, but little passion or interest. Mao buttons and loyalty dances faded out of fashion. One day several Red Guards went into the kitchen for lunch and started the usual ritual of bowing to the portrait of the "Great Leader," reciting a quotation from the Little Red Book, and shouting "Long live Chairman Mao!" Pox Lin abruptly came down on them with the injunction, "What d'you think you're doing? None of that feudalistic rot!" It suddenly dawned on the flabbergasted Red Guards that they were falling behind the capricious political winds again.

When the peach trees on the village hill blossomed with the coming of spring, Xiao Sun often took his small herd of "cow demons" to the orchard, ostensibly for political study. We would sit under the flowering trees and take in the fragrant fresh air. One sunny afternoon, just as we were about to gather there as usual, we were surprised to see a number of villagers cutting down the trees. "What's going on here, Uncle Lou? I can't believe my eyes!" Xiao Sun asked the team leader, flushing with agitation. "Orders, Xiao Sun!" replied the glum man. "Digging up roots of capitalism! Fruit is a capitalist luxury, and the extra income from our peaches will corrupt our souls, so they say. Don't you see?" Xiao Sun was speechless, but I saw tears in his eyes. During our walk after supper, he said to me, "There are so many things about the revolution I just don't understand, I will probably never understand. I grew up among fruit trees. They were my playmates and life-givers. Wantonly cutting down a flowering fruit tree is like killing a laughing youth. I'm afraid I'll never make a good revolutionary . . ." Soon afterward, Xiao Sun was sent back to his commune to be an English teacher at the local high school, while his more revolutionary classmates were given assignments at the university or in city government departments.

Toward the end of April, I was called in by Yue Weizhang, who announced the official conclusion of my case: 1. No new problem has been unearthed, past or present; 2. I will no longer be employed as a temporary worker, effective May 1; 3. I am to join my family in the village of Gaozhuang to "receive reeducation from the poor and lower-middle peasants." He added, "You realize this is a very good political conclusion, although you will no longer have a regular income. Anyway, Li Yikai still has her monthly wages. I hope you appreciate what we are doing for you and express your gratitude to the party at a meeting to be called for the purpose." He sounded as if I had been granted a great favor. I dashed off a note to Yikai, giving her the "good news." At least, I was not sent to a village in my hometown all by myself, as had been threatened. Two days later, on the last day of April, a department meeting was held at which Yue read the "Decision of the Party Committee of Anhui University Regarding the Case of Wu Ningkun." Then I stood in front of the faculty and students and mumbled my thanks to the party, the university and department leadership, and the faculty and students for treating me so magnanimously. Back at the Jin family house, one villager after another dropped in to tell me how outraged they felt at the way I was being treated. "How do they expect you to make a living? Especially when they say they haven't unearthed any new evidence of wrongdoing, past or present!" The village wit said, "Didn't Chairman Mao pronounce just recently, 'A policy of not providing people with the opportunity to earn a living is no proletarian policy?' Well, Lao Wu, as the saying goes, 'As long as the green mountains are there, one need not worry about firewood!' You're barely fifty, take good care of yourself!" In the evening, Chen Yu came to say good-bye. "It doesn't look like either you or Teacher Li will ever teach at a university again. Do take care of your health and help the children grow up healthily. I had a good time with Yiding. Tell him I miss him." He sounded almost wistful. "Come on, Xiao Chen," I said. "I'm not all that pessimistic. If there is no place for someone like me in China, I don't know where the country will end up. Let's just wait and see. My personal lot should not weigh all that much on your mind, if it doesn't on mine! Take care of your big mouth!" We both laughed.

Thirteen

REEDUCATION BY
PEASANTS, 1969-70

Narrated by Li Yikai

1

HOUSE-MOVING AGAIN! WHEN THE GREAT PROLETARIAN CULTURAL REVOLU-
tion erupted in 1966, I would never have thought that it would mean
another exile for the family! My simple mind could never figure out what
we had done to deserve all this, or how in the world it would benefit the
nation. But the very thought of house-moving brought back daunting
memories of the stress of the journey of exile from Beijing ten years ago.
And this time going down under to an unknown village alone with three
kids! As soon as I learned I would be among the first to go, I went to ask
the department's head master worker if my man might be given a few days'
leave to help his wife with the moving.

"Come on, Comrade Li Yikai, you know very well that's out of the
question," Shen Wenwu said, a cigarette smoldering between his lips. "Wu
Ningkun is still a target of proletarian dictatorship, and a university-class one
at that. How can such a person be allowed to roam at large, eh? After all,
it's only house-moving, and the packing and moving will help you prepare
yourself for manual labor in the countryside, don't you agree?"

"But I'm a woman comrade with three kids to care for," I said, hoping
he might see what was so obvious.

"So what? Didn't Chairman Mao teach you that 'women hold up half
the sky'? And 'what men comrades can do women comrades can too!' The
children, oh yes, it will be good tempering for them too, don't you agree?
Don't forget either, Comrade Li Yikai, you live in a big Socialist revolutionary family. Which comrade wouldn't lend you a helping hand when
one is needed? Rest assured."

*   *   *

So I had to go it alone again. "You're holding up more than half the sky, Comrade Li Yikai, rest assured," I told myself blithely when the children ran into my arms after a six-month separation. The first thing I did, with the help of the kids, was to throw open the windows of our musty rooms, clean the moldy furniture, and air the bedding, so that we could all sleep together again in our own home for a few days.

"It's just too bad that Papa couldn't come home to see you and help with the moving," I said helplessly.

"Don't you worry, Mama, I'm the man of the house now!" Yiding said proudly.

"I'm a man too, Mama!" Little Yicun chimed in eagerly.

"But women hold up half the sky, boys!" exclaimed Yimao.

Perhaps it *was* good tempering for the kids!

I had only four days to get ready, and half of the time was to be spent making the rounds from one political session to another, to be told again and again that it was an unprecedented honor and glory to be a *xiafang ganbu,* a cadre going down under, and from one office to another to surrender various permits for city and campus residency in exchange for documents for rural residency. None of my colleagues came to our rooms to share my honor and glory, let alone lend a helping hand. For the first two days it was Yiding who did the packing, with the help of his eleven-year-old sister and six-year-old brother. I suddenly noticed that my thirteen-year-old firstborn was no longer the carefree boy I thought he was, but a "man" grown up under the stress of circumstances. I was amazed to see the care with which he packed his father's books and papers, and his ingenuity in hiding the two paintings by Prince Pu Xinyu among his own drawings, lest they be seized as "four olds."

On May 15, the morning before our scheduled departure, I had to attend a final briefing at the concrete basketball court that had witnessed so many denunciation and struggle meetings over the past three years. The leaders of the Workers' and Soldiers' Mao Zedong Thought Propaganda Team once again praised the first group of faculty and staff going down under and then solemnly declared:

"The cadres going down under are sent by Chairman Mao to go

among the poor and lower-middle peasants and learn from them. You will be most enthusiastically welcomed by commune leaders and the poor and lower-middle peasants as their own. When you arrive at your village tomorrow, the poor and lower-middle peasants will have everything ready for you. A clean house for you to live in, rice and wheat flour for you to eat, a vat of clean water for you to drink, and farm tools for you to work with. Long live the victory of the proletarian revolutionary line of our Great Leader Chairman Mao!"

I felt somewhat reassured. But on the way home from the meeting a woman colleague cautioned me in a whisper, "It all sounded very good. But, if I were you, Li Yikai, I would go by myself first and see how things really are down there before dragging all three kids with me. Haven't you had a glimpse of life in the villages these past months?" I suddenly realized how naive I still was, after all these years. By the time I got back to our rooms, I had decided I would take only Yiding with me, leaving the two younger children behind for the time being. I hated the idea of separation after such a brief reunion, but that seemed to be the lesser evil. After a last supper of a bowl of noodles each, I walked my two little ones back to the kindergarten again. I promised to come for them when I had settled into our new home, but in truth I did not see clearly what lay ahead of me. With the help of Yiding, I spent the last few hours of the day taking apart the beds and tying up the pieces into bundles, packing up quilts and mattresses and pillows into bedrolls with thick ropes, and putting kitchen utensils, chamber pots, lamps, and sundry odds and ends into boxes and crates. By midnight Yiding and I managed to carry everything, including crates of briquets and bundles of firewood, onto a battered truck assigned to us and parked alongside other trucks a short distance from our building. Finally I lay down next to Yiding, on the cotton mattress on the cement floor, hoping to catch a few hours' rest. The worn-out boy soon fell into a deep sleep. I was only half-asleep when I was roused by big raindrops spattering on the windowpanes. "Oh dear! What am I going to do now? Our bedrolls will be drenched and the coal briquets will simply dissolve!" Not knowing what to do next, I got up and went out to see. I found my fellow cadres busily covering up their trucks with tarpaulins.

"Where did you get the tarpaulin, Lao Sun?" I asked my neighbor, a business clerk in the department office.

"It came with the truck," he answered brusquely.

"But there was none in my truck," I said desperately.

"Oh, there's nothing I can do about it," said he. "Perhaps you can go and see Master Worker Wang in charge of the operation. Perhaps he can help."

I dashed across the campus in the rain to Wang's door and roused him out of his sleep. He did not open the door, but answered my plea sleepily, "Go and try your driver, Lao Huang." I was glad to find Huang still up drinking with the other drivers, but he only said, "Your truck happens to be the only one without a tarpaulin, too bad!" Back in my room again, I reluctantly roused Yiding from his deep sleep and had him help me unload the bedrolls and crates of briquets and carry them to the doorway of our building. Yiding went back to sleep right away, but I stayed awake the rest of the night. I was numb, body and mind. The only thing I felt was sorrow for my poor boy sleeping next to me.

We got up early, rolled up the mattress and blanket into a bundle, and ate a couple of cold steamed buns with a cup of hot water from a thermos. When the things were loaded again, it was time to show up at the concrete basketball court once more for a farewell rally. The loudspeakers blasted songs from the *Quotations from Chairman Mao,* and red flags hung around the court whipped in the wind. Yimao and Yicun were already waiting for us. Yiding stayed behind to spend the last minutes with the two little ones while I joined the ranks of the more than a hundred cadres going down under lined up in military formation. Leading master workers walked past us, greeted each with a condescending smile, shook hands, pinned a large red paper flower on each chest, and wished each "victory on Chairman Mao's revolutionary road!" Then, a thunderous applause greeted the arrival of the supreme ruler of the province, General Li Desheng, who commanded a large army and had a seat on the Central Politburo. The dignitary made a brief speech, commending us for being the first in the province to take the road of "integrating with the poor and lower-middle peasants." Then he walked past our lines, shook hands with each of us, and bade us each a hearty "Good-bye!"

Now we were ready to be shipped off. The children ran up to me. I hugged Yimao and Yicun again and again, suppressing my tears. We found our truck in the middle of the convoy. Yiding climbed into the driver's cab first. I clasped Yicun in my arms, no longer able to hold back my tears. The driver was honking impatiently. I put Yicun down and hugged Yimao once more. As soon as I seated myself next to Yiding the driver started off. Through my tears I could see my two little ones waving to me. I was glad Yicun's nose wasn't running, as it had six months before, when Ningkun and I had left on the long march. "Where is this revolutionary road of Chairman Mao's taking me?" I groaned in my soul.

2

IT TOOK US NEARLY FOUR HOURS TO COVER THE SIXTY MILES FROM THE university to the village of Gaozhuang in the Sunbao Commune of Hexian County. The ancient truck jolted badly on the bumpy highway. My whole body ached and I dozed off from time to time. Yiding slept nearly all the way and did not wake up till the truck came to a rude stop outside the village. I could see men and women working in a paddy field at a distance. The driver got out of his cab and waved to them, yelling at the top of his voice, "Come on, get your xiafang ganbu, the down under cadre!"

Within minutes, the men and women started walking briskly toward us on the narrow path leading from the village to the highway, with a few youngsters beating a small drum, a pair of cymbals, and a cracked gong, apparently to give the xiafang ganbu an enthusiastic welcome. Half-naked children ran barefooted beside the adults, laughing and shouting "xiafang ganbu, xiafang xiafang!" While still a dozen feet away, a middle-aged man in front hailed in a hoarse voice, "What's going on? We were only told someone will come down under in our production team soon, but no dates. Welcome, I suppose, but what am I going to do with you, so much baggage and a kid too! I am the team leader. My name is Li Tinghai."

"Just call him Lao Penghai, the Old Crab," a young woman behind him put in. "That's what we all call him. Doesn't he look like a crab running wild?"

"You shut up, you slut!" Lao Penghai turned around and threatened the young woman with a raised fist clutching a folded sheet of paper. "See this? Gong'an liutiao, Six Articles of Public Security! Any of you making trouble or abusing me will fall into the Six Articles as a counterrevolutionary!" Everyone burst out laughing.

"I am Li Yikai from Anhui University," I said, giving him my hand. "I have come down under to receive reeducation from the poor and lower-middle peasants. This is my big boy, Yiding. I have left his sister and younger brother behind and will fetch them later. I will live and do manual labor under your leadership from now on, Team Leader Li."

"My word, three kids to feed! How can the production team afford it? Well, damn it, now that you're already here, I suppose I'll just have to put you up somehow. A woman with so much stuff, rich city folk! Come on, you all, carry her stuff to the public room. That will be your new home until a house can be built for you, Lao Li." So saying, he led me into the village to show me my new home. A stout man with bloodshot eyes, he walked with a swagger that suggested a monstrous, multilegged crab.

The public room was a small mud-brick hut with a thatched roof, out of which a chimney stuck like a minuscule leaning tower. Lao Penghai kicked the door open and I followed him into the dark room, suddenly finding myself besieged by a swarm of flies and mosquitoes. My nostrils were attacked by a mixed stench of urine, cow dung, moldy grains, and rat excreta. Lao Penghai lit a cigarette. I started coughing. After a while, I could see that half of the room was taken up with plows, harrows, a huge threshing tub, urine buckets, rakes, sacks of seeds, and bags of fertilizers. A large straw-burning stove sat in one corner. Lao Penghai said, "You'll just have to get used to living among these things for a while and forget your comfortable city life. I'll get a couple lads to pile up the farm tools on one side and help you clean up the place. You have brought some cigarettes for the boys, I hope?" When I confessed I had not, he looked disappointed. "Any liquor?" He was again disappointed.

Two lads, one nicknamed Darkie and the other Lesser Flood, were given the job of helping me turn the public room into a private home. I soon discovered that nearly everybody in this village had a nickname. Darkie was so called because he was darker than the other youngsters in the village. Lesser Flood was born in the year when the village was invaded by a minor flood, whereas his cousin, the son of Lao Penghai, was called Greater Flood. Both Darkie and Lesser Flood were ruddy and manly teenagers. They did not smoke; they called me Auntie Li and blushed easily. They made friends with Yiding right away and the three of them pushed the farm tools and sacks of seeds to one side of the room and cleaned out heaps of rubbish. There was only room to set up the old double bed the college had sold me at a discount, so the dismantled twin beds we had bought for our wedding were left leaning against the wall in bundles. The trunks, boxes, and suitcases were also piled up against the wall. The little desk stood against another wall, in the company of a long wooden bench and two stools, which I had been allowed to buy at a discount from the college for me and the three children to sit on. No chairs were allowed, for the master workers asked, "Do the poor peasants sit in chairs?" By the time half of the public room was ready for our occupation, Lao Penghai barged in.

"Ah, very nice. See, we take care of you xiafang ganbu," said he. "Is there anything else you need? Just say so, Lao Li. You and I have the same name. We are brother and sister."

"Thank you, Team Leader Li, you have been very helpful. There is one thing I do need. Before we left the university, we were told you would have rice for us to eat, water for us to drink. So I didn't bring any rice or flour. And we haven't eaten since the morning. Is there any rice I can borrow from the team or you?"

"You're joking, Lao Li. New rice is not yet harvested, and the old rice is all gone. I feed my woman and two kids on borrowed rice. Tomorrow you can go to West Town, an hour's walk from us, and buy some from the food grain station with your ration coupons. Today, well, you'll just have to cope. As to water, there's the village pond; drink as much as you like. Darkie, go and fetch Lao Li a pail of water."

As he was getting up to go, his eyes fell on the bundles of twin beds. "What's here? Single beds! Great! You don't need these beds, Lao Li. Lend one to your brother. It's just what my son Greater Flood needs. Lesser Flood, carry this bed here to my home for your cousin to sleep in. I daresay he will like it. If there is anything you need, just let me know. Chairman Mao has absolute authority in China, I have absolute authority in this production team. I am the only party member here, I am the party. You and I will get along, Sister Li, so long as we understand each other."

The sun was already in the western sky, and Yiding and I had had nothing to eat or drink since morning. I was more tired and thirsty than hungry, but I had to find something to feed the famished boy. I recalled I had bought our precious summer ration of one pound of mung beans two days before. While I looked for it among the boxes, Yiding started making a fire in our little briquet stove. The sight of a steaming tea kettle sitting on top of a briquet stove soon attracted not only the neighborhood kids but also their parents, who brought their cheap thermoses in battered wicker cases to be filled. We were the envy of our new neighbors. As their meager annual ration of rice straw from their own crops was hardly enough to cook their meals, boiled water was a luxury! After Yiding and I ate our meal of mung bean soup, we kept the tea kettle going till all the dozen thermoses were filled with boiling water. Then I used some hot water for a bath in the wooden tub I had brought with me, while Yiding went with Darkie and Lesser Flood to bathe themselves in the rear pond of the village.

Once my neighbors had their supper and cold-water bath (men in the rear pond and women in wooden tubs), they sauntered over to the little open space in front of the public room to visit with the newcomer, bringing with them their small bamboo chairs or wooden campstools.

"How come you are by yourself? Where is your man?" was their first question.

I couldn't afford to let them know my man was still in the "cow shed," for that would give me the status of a quasi enemy of the people among my new neighbors. And they were already suspicious that I was perhaps divorced or never married or married to a jailbird.

"Oh yes, I have been married fifteen years. We have two other kids in Hefei. I will go and fetch them when I am settled in. My husband is still taking part in manual labor in Wujiang Commune, along with many others from the university. The leadership will decide when he is to join us here."

"How much do you make a month?"

"I used to make fifty-nine yuan a month. Now that I am in the countryside, I will get two yuan less."

"My word, a woman making so much money a month! We peasants are really poor. We don't see any cash till the end of the year—that is, if we have made enough work points. Half of the families end up owing the production team for their food and fuel when accounts are settled after the fall harvest, after toiling all year round. And you, a woman, getting fifty-seven yuan every single month!"

I had never dreamed anyone would envy me for the little that I made, and now these good peasants made me feel like an accursed exploiter.

"I have three children to feed, you know."

"What about your man then? How much does he make?"

"Well, he used to make more than I did, but there has been some readjustment in wages at the university since the Cultural Revolution . . ."

"Don't tell us if you don't want to. How come you got sent down under?"

"Following Chairman Mao's instructions—"

"Come on, we know all that. Reeducation from the poor and lower-middle peasants, well and good. But smart people in Sunbao are already saying, 'Good people don't get sent down under, among the down under none are good people.' Most people got to stay in towns and universities, right? We just don't know . . ."

All the questions were straightforward and to be expected. A woman with kids was suddenly thrown into their midst out of nowhere, like a pebble cast into the village pond by a naughty boy, disturbing their peace of life. This was certainly a new day in their life, as much as in mine. There was no animosity in their voices, only good-natured curiosity. Their disarming openness almost made me feel welcome.

The next morning I woke early with a hungry stomach and contemplated our new life with a mixture of dismay and amusement. "Is this the world in which I and my family are doomed to spend the rest of our days?" It still seemed inconceivable, but there was no escaping the bizarre reality of Lao Penghai and the home he'd assigned me. Willy-nilly, it was now my lot to hold up half the sky and wrestle with the everyday realities of a new life. In the days that followed, I made several trips to West Town, three miles away, to shop for food for the two of us, as well as for articles needed for country living, including a big water vat, a gourd water ladle, a shoulder pole, a poker for the straw-burning stove, a broomstick, and a pair of water buckets. It was a piece of good luck that I had been able to rescue our English bicycle from the revolutionary baptism of fire, or it would have been even harder for us to get around now. Yiding quickly learned how to carry two buckets of water on the shoulder pole from the front pond to our new vat. And I learned how to cook in a huge iron wok on the straw-burning stove, though my eyes watered from the smoke. We had to save on the briquets, but we managed to fill the neighbors' thermoses from time to time, and we cooked steamed buns for them when they saw how we made them in an aluminum steamer on the briquet stove.

By dropping in on my new neighbors after the day's work, I managed to get acquainted with the eighteen families, which were equally divided in two hamlets about five hundred feet apart. Lao Penghai lived with his family in Rear Gaozhuang in a dingy little hut. His neighbors said he could have built his family a decent new house if he had not squandered so much on liquor and cigarettes. In a solitary tiny hut lived an eighteen-year-old lad nicknamed Xiao Wubao, Little Five Guarantees, because he had been guaranteed food, clothing, and other necessities by the production team since he was orphaned in the great famine of 1960 that had wiped out half of the village. I lived among nine other families in the front hamlet. My next-door neighbor was the elderly widow Granny Sun, who tended one of the team's three water buffaloes. Her son Jisheng, alias Ricefield Eel Basket, was a sturdy fellow married to a gentle young woman whom he occasionally beat, in a fit of temper. They had a sickly three-year-old girl named Little Rabbit and an unnamed baby boy. Sun Kaidao, one of the plowmen and also the water man responsible for monitoring the water level of the paddy fields, was the most senior of the men still doing farm work and was respectfully called Third Elder by everybody. He had two sons, Jigui and Xiao Dan, the Little Egg. Jigui was sixteen, almost of age by rural standards but more childlike than his six-year-old brother. His notoriety had reached my ears even before I set eyes on him. Perhaps the best-looking lad in the whole village, he was the fright of the girls because he often grabbed them from behind by their pigtails. Perhaps also the best-built youth, he earned a fraction of the work points earned by the other boys and girls because he was good for nothing in farm work. He was the disgrace of the family, the butt of the whole village. Everyone, even his own parents and Little Egg, called him Loony Jigui or simply Loony to his face. The only remedy his father had for his aberrations was to give him a sound beating or truss him up with heavy ropes whenever a neighbor complained of a pigtail grabbed, or food stolen from the house, or a vegetable plot divested of half-ripe tomatoes or cucumbers. He was caught redhanded every time because he never tried to hide anything. Next door to Sun Kaidao lived

Darkie and his mother, stepfather, and a teenage stepsister. Lesser Flood's father was one of the two Chen brothers, whose sister was married to Lao Penghai. The other was Chen Anyou, the vice team leader, who was better known as the father of his eight-year-old son Sharp-nozzled Pigling, an adroit little pickpocket and know-it-all. At the entrance of the village lived another Sun family in a big new house with a tiled roof.

Some of my neighbors sold me their hen eggs, which they also used to trade for salt, alkali, matches, thread, and needles at the production brigade store. Taking a cue from Lao Penghai, I kept medium-priced cigarettes in the house, and men began to drop in for a smoke. Lao Penghai himself, of course, made frequent visits and enjoyed his smoke nearly every day. And he lost no time in asking me for a "loan" of a few yuan which he would pay back "in a couple days." I was not greatly surprised, but I still felt upset. Hard up as I was, a few yuan did not really make all that much difference. But this was like blackmail. I did not have the nerve to turn him down, however, because I didn't know what he might do to me with his "absolute authority." No, I couldn't afford to offend him. His bloodshot eyes lit up when he grabbed the few one-yuan bills I laid on the desk for him.

Yiding seemed to enjoy his new friends and surroundings. He swam in the rear pond with other teenagers and played Chinese chess with adults in the dim light of the little oil lamp. He taught the villagers revolutionary songs and told them stories of the Golden Monkey. In line with the village custom, the children quickly gave him a nickname too— Golden Monkey. After his nightly story-telling, he would take me with him on a different adventure: catching fireflies on ridges between the fields. A city-grown boy, Yiding was fascinated by the tiny winged beings that lit up the dark night with their flickering magic lamps. He would put them in a small bottle, bring them into our mosquito net, and then try to catch mosquitoes with the aid of the intermittent light. Every time the little creatures turned on their lights he'd burst into a ringing laugh. What fantasies of joy and wonder did the magic lamps light up for him? It warmed my heart to hear the boy laugh his carefree child's laugh, but it also reminded me of the conspicuous absence of the younger ones and their father.

3

WE WERE ALMOST HAPPY IN OUR NEW HOME IN SPITE OF IT ALL, BUT IT WAS a precarious happiness that I soon learned would easily turn to misery. One morning early in June, I came down with intermittent terrible fever and chills, which panicked me because I had never suffered a fever in my life. Yiding walked the six miles to the market town, Xiangchuan or Fragrant Spring, to send an urgent wire to his father asking him to come home at once, but Ningkun was denied leave by the master worker in charge. It turned out that I had malaria, a common affliction in this area.

When I had just barely recovered from the malaria, after dosages of quinine pills, it began to rain. The rain fell for several days and nights running. Late one night we were awakened by a terrific crash, followed by the explosions of our two thermoses, which usually stood at the foot of the chimney. I stuck my head out of the mosquito net and was dumbfounded to see that the chimney had caved in, smashing the thermoses as it came crashing down. Rain now poured down through the big hole in the roof. Besieged by forces of darkness, I panicked and clasped my boy in my arms. After a few moments I resigned myself to the situation, recalling that, after all, I had come down under to "share weal and woe" with the poor and lower-middle peasants. Luckily, the summer day dawned early and the rain stopped. I hurried over to the team leader's house and reported to him how we had been scared to death by the unexpected calamity.

"What d'you expect with all this rain? That chimney was old and a muddled job to begin with. I'll get a couple men to work on it today, it's no big deal. You will give them a meal, of course. And cigarettes and liquor, of course."

I had to rush to West Town on my bicycle to get two pounds of pork and a live chicken and vegetables, while Yiding started a fire in the briquet stove. I cooked rice in our largest pot, stewed the pork in soy sauce, and stir-fried two vegetable dishes, but I had to beg our neighbor Granny Sun to dress the chicken and cook it for me on her straw-burning stove. It didn't take the two men long to clear away the debris, fix the stove, and build a new chimney with bricks and mud. By noon, just as I was putting the dishes, steamed rice, and a bottle of 120 proof liquor on our little collapsible table, Lao Penghai swaggered in.

"Quick work, these men, Lao Li!" So saying, he sat down at the table, lit himself a cigarette, and poured himself a bowl of liquor. "Come on, you guys, come and have a taste of my sister's cooking! The pork is delicious, better than my woman's cooking, I must say."

"The chimney is not quite straight, Team Leader Li," Yiding remarked.

"That's all right." The team leader dismissed him with a wave of his chopsticks. "You people won't live here long anyway."

The three of them finished the four dishes, the rice, the bottle, and the pack of cigarettes with dispatch. Then the two young men went to work in the field, but Lao Penghai staggered back to his house for a long nap. I was grateful that the job was finished before it rained again.

After a few sunny days, it started raining again, often pouring day and night. The chimney held its own, but the fields were flooded. Some neighboring villages were already under water. One day, in the midst of a downpour, Chen Anyou came into our room.

"Lao Li," he began ominously. "As the vice team leader, it is my responsibility to warn you of the dangers facing us. If this downpour doesn't stop soon, the whole village and your home will be swept away by the flood water. When that happens, we all have our own family to take care of, and who will be able to help you? I want you to be prepared for the worst, to run for your life as best you can. Tonight you and your boy must take part in the patrol to monitor the rising water. When you see any signs of danger, run and report to our water man, Third Elder. We will do what we can to help you and your boy, but I'll have my wife and kids on my hands. I don't mean we will abandon you, but fine words won't help in a situation like this."

I didn't feel abandoned, not quite. As an intruder, what right had I to expect help from the villagers when their own families were in danger? I rather liked the way the man didn't mince words. But what defense had I against surging flood waters, which could easily wash us away? I looked at

Yiding helplessly. My boy said, "If worst comes to worst, Mama, we can use our big wooden tub as a lifeboat and paddle ourselves to safety. I'll sit up and watch the water with you tonight." I hugged him and said, "With a son like you, Yiding, we will certainly pull through." After supper, I put all the cash and food grain coupons I had in a pocket and lay down for a little nap, while Yiding sat on a wooden campstool and looked out into the treacherous night for signs of danger. When I got up again, I took Yiding with me and went out in the rain to check the water level of the fields near us. I could hear the flood water roaring far and near. I held an oilcloth umbrella over our heads while Yiding lit our way with a flashlight. "Mama, the water in the fields is nearly level with the ridge," Yiding said in alarm. "We must let Third Elder know at once." So we made our way through mud and water to his house and roused him. Sun Kaidao came out with a spade under one arm and hurried to the fields to drain off some of the water. Back in our room, I sent Yiding to bed and kept vigil by myself. Before I knew it, I fell into a deep sleep. It was light when I woke up, and joy of joys, the rain had stopped!

The sun was out for several days. The rural bus connecting the county seat of Hexian and the market towns began running again on the highway, which had been under water for many days. It was already July, and I thought I had better get Yiding enrolled in junior high before it was too late. Xiangchuan was the only market town nearby with a junior high school. Aside from a hot spring, which served as the community's public bath, Xiangchuan was also known for its leper colony, one of the few in all China. One fine morning, I took Yiding on my bicycle and started off for the school, with our lunch bag hanging on the handlebars. Halfway to the hot-spring town, I saw Sun Jigui running toward us, frantically hollering, "Save me, Lao Li! Save me, Lao Li!" When he came to a stop before my bicycle, I saw he had only a pair of filthy shorts on, and there was mud in his tousled hair and all over his body and limbs, the very image of the biblical prodigal son. My mother's heart went out to him.

"What are you doing here, Little Jigui? Your dad and mom have been looking for you the past few days. They miss you. Why don't you go home now, Little Jigui?"

"Kaidao no father, he beat me. It hurt, you don't know, Lao Li. Please save me, I'm starved."

"You go back to your father's house. He will kill a chicken for you."

"Not me . . ." So saying, he grabbed my lunch bag and helped himself with his blackened fingers to a pancake I had made the night before. He gobbled it down in a few mouthfuls and started on a second one.

"Jigui, please save the rest for me and my son. We are on our way to Xiangchuan and that's our lunch. You go home now, okay?"

Fishing a big tomato out of the bag, he said, "Lao Li, you take me on your bike too."

"Little Jigui, I can't do that. I already have my boy with me."

While he was munching on the tomato, I hopped on my bicycle and pedaled off vigorously. Jigui ran after me for a distance, but finally gave up.

At Xiangchuan Junior High, I found the registrar and told him, "I am a xiafang ganbu from Anhui University. My son Yiding has finished primary school in Hefei. Can he be admitted to your school when the new semester begins?" The man said there should be no problem and asked Yiding to fill out a registration form. When he saw the address given was Gaozhuang, he turned to me and said, "So you are from Gaozhuang! That's great. That idiot from your village has gone wild at our school, chasing the girls and grabbing food from the students. In turn, the students chase him and cast stones at him. He even barges in when a class is in session, turning the classroom into a madhouse. When he first came, he slept in an empty classroom. Now he sleeps at the hot spring and steals food from restaurants. This can't go on. You must tell your team leader and the loony's parents to take him home." Just then, Jigui ran into the room, yelling, "Save me, Lao Li! Save me, Lao Li!" He was pursued by several boy students throwing stones at him. I went to the door and called to the boys, "Students, please stop baiting this poor boy! I am a xiafang ganbu from his village. He is sick. I will have his parents come and take him home." Then I turned to Jigui. "Why don't you come back to your father's house now, Jigui? No one will throw stones at you there. Your mother will feed you good food. I will make steamed buns for you." He said loudly, "Kaidao he beat me. I like it here." Abruptly he burst out laughing and started singing the national eulogy of the Great Leader, "The east is red / The sun rises / China brings forth a Mao Zedong . . . ," off-key and funny. Before we knew it, he had slipped from the room and vanished out of sight.

When I told his parents the whereabouts of their missing son, his father started cursing, "The damned Loony, a disgrace to the family! I will bring him back and give him the works." I made Third Elder promise not to beat his errant son when he was brought home. "After all, I found him for you. And he is your own son. Please, Kaidao, I won't have it." I was glad Jigui was spared the rod and the ropes when his father brought him home from his self-exile and "showed due respect to my feelings," as he put it.

One day, while I was cooking lunch, the children suddenly burst into my room shouting, "Lao Li, people coming to you!" I looked out and saw Yicun walking along the dirt path into the village clutching a cracker tin with both arms, followed by a young soldier. I had been thinking lately I should go to Hefei very soon and bring the two little ones home. I missed them, and it wasn't safe to leave young children to their own devices. And now this welcome surprise! The young soldier explained he had brought Yicun home on a college truck because the kid had not been feeling well and his sister was worried. It was good to have Yicun with me again, but now Yimao was all by herself. I seemed to find myself in a perpetual dilemma.

Yicun found everything new and intriguing and followed his big brother everywhere. He learned to catch fireflies too, and made his own paper cages for them. Otherwise, he kept to himself, probably because he was used to sitting in a corner by himself in the kindergarten. He would sit on the double bed and play Chinese checkers or Chinese chess on his own. He would laugh happily when he had won a game against himself. Though not mixing with children of his own age at first, he would teach Jigui now and then how to play the games. He would also tell him a story or two of the Golden Monkey. "Jigui is so gentle. I like him," he would say.

I soon took Yicun on my bicycle to Wujiang for a reunion with his father, only to find Ningkun down with an unknown fever. What made things even worse was there was still talk of repatriating him to his hometown for manual labor. As I watched him groaning from high fever in the commune hospital, I was tormented by the lines lamenting the misfortunes of the Tang dynasty poet Fang Gan, "No means to live, going back poor to his native place / Yet difficult to die, lying sick in a strange land."

Then the heavy rain started again, flooding the roads and the fields. Yiding and I took turns keeping a vigil over the rising water. Our supply of food had run very low by the time the rain finally stopped.

4

IN THE MIDDLE OF AUGUST I DECIDED TO TAKE YIDING TO HIS SCHOOL, WHERE he could stay and have his meals, though school didn't start until September. Then I could take Yicun with me to the university and bring Yimao home with us. So one morning I pushed the bicycle toward Fragrant Spring, with Yicun on the seat and Yiding's bedroll and traveling bag on the rack, while Yiding walked on the other side of the bicycle. Halfway to our destination, I suddenly heard a man's voice yelling urgently from behind. "Li Yikai, stop! Li Yikai, stop!" I turned around and saw a man on a bicycle coming toward me. He was a short man in his thirties, and I vaguely recognized him as one of the master workers assigned to the department.

"Li Yikai, this is most urgent! Your daughter has come down with a terrible illness. You must go back to the university at once!"

I could not believe my ears. I was at a loss for words. Yiding held the bicycle to keep it from falling. After a moment, I asked, "What is her illness? Where is she now?"

"We don't know exactly what her trouble is. She came down with a bad fever several days ago and was taken to the teaching hospital of the medical college. Their diagnosis was encephalitis. That's an infectious disease and the hospital has no infectious ward, so she was brought to the army hospital later on. We had no way of getting word to you because of the rain and the flood. Finally I was able to catch the first bus in many days from Hanshan to Hexian. Then I got on a bike and rushed over here to look for you. My name is Dai. I knew you, but never had much to do with you. Now you must hurry and go to your daughter or . . ."

"Or what?" I was full of fear. Was the child still alive or already no more? Was he keeping bad news from me? "Tell me the truth. I need to decide what to do."

"Really, she was admitted to the army hospital, going through examinations. A nurse from the kindergarten was staying with her. I don't know any more. You just hurry up and get going. Don't lose any more time."

I decided to take Yiding to his school as planned before leaving for Hefei. We reached the school before noon. The registrar was surprised to see us.

"You're too early. School won't begin till September, at the earliest. Furthermore, all teachers and staff are fighting the flood and won't be back till it's all over."

I explained my dilemma to him and he readily agreed to have Yiding stay in the boys' dormitory and buy food from the kitchen. The dormitory was one big room with dozens of double-decker bunks. The concrete floor was littered with refuse. I helped Yiding clean up one bunk and parts of the floor and hang up his mosquito net. Then we went to a snack counter in town and lunched quickly on noodles and dumplings. I seemed to be perpetually taking a meal with my children before saying good-bye for I did not know how long. Waving to Yiding, I got on the bicycle, with Yicun sitting in front of me, and sped away. On the way home, I stopped at the commune headquarters to ask for a leave from Guo Renfu, who headed the committee in charge of xiafang ganbu. Then I thought it might be a good idea to stop at the commune hospital and pick up some pills for heatstroke and diarrhea, just in case Yicun or I should need any on the way. Even before I entered the hospital, I could hear the voices of a man and a woman crying and wailing piteously, "Oh my poor daughter, oh oh oh! . . . " It was the lament of death! It wrung my heart. When I asked Dr. Lu what happened, he shook his head and said, "Just too bad. They lost several days before bringing the child to us. Too late when she finally came. Acute pneumonia, just too bad. Came too late. I know the family. A very nice girl." His words threw my mind into a flurry. Had too much time already been lost for Yimao too? Fear tightened around my heart. On my way to the dispensary, I passed by a room and saw the mother crying and wailing, holding the dead girl in her arms. The father was also weeping beside the dead child. I stood fixed to the spot and tears started from my eyes. Sad as it was, this poor girl at least died in her mother's arms. My daughter would have fared even worse, with not a single dear one by her. Hot tears streamed down my cheeks. Dr. Lu came up to me and whispered in my ear, "Teacher

Li, compose yourself. You have so much on your hands . . ." Hurriedly I left the hospital and made my way to the Xinjian Production Brigade headquarters to ask for leave from the party secretary, Song Xianjin. But I was haunted all the way by the picture of the dead girl in her mother's arms and the piteous lament of death. Finally back at Gaozhuang, the first thing I did was to ask for leave again, this time from Lao Penghai, who was now my immediate superior.

"What am I going to do with my home, Team Leader?"

"Your home? Well, it's our public room. I'll just have the lads take turns keeping watch here at night, as they used to do before you came. What have you got to worry about? Don't you trust the poor and lower-middle peasants? Aren't you here to receive reeducation from us?"

There was nothing else I could do, anyway. After supper, I started putting things away before packing for tomorrow. At midnight, just as I was getting ready to join Yicun under the mosquito net, someone started banging urgently on the door. Another midnight raid by Red Guards? My heart sank. Then I heard the pleading voice of Sun Kaidao's wife. "Lao Li, open the door, quick. You must save us. Loony threatened to kill Little Egg with a kitchen knife. I must leave Little Egg with you for the night." The moment I opened the door, she rushed in and pushed Little Egg into the bed. Then she vanished into the dark night as quickly as she had come. I could hear a hubbub of voices from the direction of her house, but I was too tired and anxious about Yimao to care, and I had a long, arduous day ahead of me.

A few moments after I'd lain down between my son and Little Egg, she rushed in again and pleaded breathlessly, "Lao Li, come quick! Kaidao, Penghai, Anyou beating Loony to death. Only you can save him. You are a cadre. You come from Chairman Mao. Come quick, quick, I beg you." Me, a "cow demon's" wife down under for reeducation, going to the rescue of a "poor peasant" boy from his own father and a Communist team leader? I winced, but she had already pulled the mosquito-net curtain open and started dragging me out. Hurrying after her, I tripped in the dark and nearly fell into the cow dung heaped outside Granny Sun's house. Even before I got to Kaidao's house, I could hear him cursing hoarsely, "You no good Loony! You bring shame on me and my ancestors, and now you want to kill your own brother, who is my only hope. I'll show you, I'll show you!" Then I heard Jigui screaming, "I'm dying, I'm dying! You landlord! You killing poor peasant! You bad egg!"

A dense crowd of neighbors had gathered, just like the crowds of spectators who'd watched public executions since time immemorial. Among them were Jigui's first cousins, Jiwen and Jisheng. I had to push my way through to where Jigui was being tortured by his own father, with the help of the team leaders. Now I could see Jigui in the dim light spilling out of the house's open doors. He was half-naked and tightly bound with thick ropes to the solitary tree in front of his home. He was bleeding. His father, the team leader, and the vice leader, all stripped to the waist, each wielded a big wooden club.

I quickly went up to the boy's father and said, "Kaidao, you promised me not to beat Jigui again. What are you doing now? Look at him, he is bleeding to death. Is he not your own son? Is he not your firstborn?"

"I wish he were not, I wish he had never been born. Yes, I did promise you, Lao Li. But he done many bad things since. I tied him up again to keep him out of mischief. He broke himself free and grabbed a kitchen knife and went at Little Egg. He is good for nothing. He must die. I'll end his life here tonight."

"Good riddance!" Lao Penghai spoke with authority. "He deserves to die. Third Elder will be better off, the production team will be better off."

"No, Jigui is sick," I said as calmly as I could. "Let's all calm down. What the boy needs is to see a doctor, not to be beaten to death. You must stop torturing the poor boy at once. A life for a life—no one can get away with murder."

"What business is it of yours anyway, Lao Li?" Lao Penghai shot back at me, his breath reeking of liquor. "You're only a woman, a xiafang. You are here to receive reeducation from the poor and lower-middle peasants. I am the boss here. You have no business meddling in the internal affairs of my production team. You mind your own business. Didn't you ask for leave to go to your sick daughter in Hefei? Go, go. Leave Loony to his father and us."

"Perhaps you are right, Team Leader." I tried to be calm. "I know what I am here for. And I can't wait to go to my daughter. But I can't sit idle and turn a blind eye when a helpless innocent boy, the son of a poor peasant, is being beaten to death by his own father and leaders of the production team. If you don't stop it right now, I'll go and rouse the brigade party secretary, Song Xianjin."

Now Jigui's mother staggered up to her husband and fell to her knees. "Please be merciful, Third Elder. Please spare me my firstborn. It's my fault to have given you a loony son. It's not his fault. Kill me first before you beat him to death . . ." She burst out crying and wailing. Granny Sun also came forward and begged him to spare her nephew once more.

Somewhat calmer now, Kaidao said, "I'll let you off this time, Loony, just this once more. If you dare—"

"Untie him now, Kaidao," I said. "Jigui is in very bad shape. You must feed him, too."

Jigui started groaning and moaning, "Kaidao not my father. Chairman Mao my father. Lao Li my mother. Down with Kaidao! Down with Penghai!"

The onlookers laughed uproariously, but Lao Penghai stamped with fury. "That makes you an active counterrevolutionary, you Loony! You son-of-a-bitch! You dare to down me, me the team leader, the Communist party member! I have the Six Articles of Public Security in my hand! I'll see you dead yet! You, Third Elder, don't come to me again with your Loony troubles. I tried to do you a favor, but you chickened out. Don't expect me to help again, I say." As he turned to go, he added, "And don't you forget the thank-you meal for Anyou and me either."

Unbound now but too weak to stand, the battered boy crawled toward his father's house on all fours, like a dog beaten half to death. I walked back to my room and collapsed onto the bed, between Yicun and Little Egg. I clasped both children tightly to my sides, for I felt I would go loony myself if my burdened mind dwelt a moment longer on what I had just been through. I prayed for the release of both the "poor peasant's" son and my "cow demon's" daughter from the clutches of death.

5

BEFORE DAWN, I CARRIED LITTLE EGG TO HIS HOME AND TOOK TO THE ROAD with a sleepy Yicun on my back. I had to start early for West Town to catch the bus bound for the county town of Hexian, then transfer to the long-distance bus to Hanshan, where I could board the train for Hefei. I carried a traveling bag in each hand and trudged along in the dark. It was like repeating the nightmarish trek to the Qinghe Prison with Yiding on my back eight years before. Yicun had turned six a month ago, just the same age as Yiding was then. Was there no end to the nightmare? From time to time, I had to rest on the roadside. After Yicun awoke, he started walking on his own. About halfway to West Town, we came to a place where a section of the road had been washed away by the flood. A long, narrow plank had been thrown across the gap, through which a torrent was rushing. I could not negotiate it myself, let alone carrying Yicun and the bags. I sat down on the road, not knowing what to do next. I must go on, but how? How long would it take before the road was repaired? After some time, I saw another xiafang ganbu from the university coming my way. I got up quickly and went up to him. "Lao Zhang, you must help me get over the gap. My daughter is critically ill in Hefei. I have no time to lose in getting to her. You must help me." He took a look at Yicun and my bags and shook his head. "Sorry, Li Yikai, I can't help you with all that. I am in a hurry to catch the bus to Hexian to meet my own daughter." So saying, he walked the plank, which shook under his weight, and went on his way. Pretty soon a middle-aged peasant approached. I went up to him. "Big brother, can you help me and this little one cross to the other side? I am in a hurry to catch the bus. My daughter is critically ill in Hefei. I must go to her." He answered warmly, "You must be a xiafang ganbu. Oh, it's just too bad. Sure, I'll certainly help you cross over. You have never come across this sort of thing before, have you? I'll carry your little boy over first. Then back for your bags. Then you." When Yicun and the bags were on the other side, he came back again and gave me one hand to hold on to and led me to the other side. "I don't know how to thank you," I said, heaving a sigh of relief. "I live in Gaozhuang. Drop in when you come by our village." He said he was from nearby Wangzhuang, in the same brigade. Yicun said, "This uncle is so nice. Uncle Zhang wasn't nice, he didn't want to help us." I said, "That's not nice of you, Yicun. Uncle Zhang was in a hurry." The man said with a smile, "I ran into Lao Zhang on the way. Then I had to stop at another village. I know him. He has been made deputy party secretary of the brigade. I don't suppose he could be bothered."

We spent the rest of the day on the road. After walking the three miles to West Town, we were unable to fight our way onto the packed bus going to Hexian. Hexian was another six miles off, and it was a hot day. But I had no choice, my mind haunted by Yimao dying or already dead. Yicun bravely took to the road with me in his little black plastic sandals. We rested on the roadside from time to time, cooling ourselves in the shade. After we had covered a couple of miles I stopped a peasant pulling an empty flatbed cart going the same way. After hearing my story, he told me to put Yicun and the bags on the cart. I walked alongside. We made it to the bus station in Hexian in the afternoon, but all the tickets to Hanshan were sold out. In desperation, I pleaded with a ticket agent until he sold me a standee ticket. By the time the bus got to Hanshan, it was already dark. We finally boarded the local train to Hefei around nine. Yicun fell asleep right away. It was past eleven when the train pulled in. With a sleepy Yicun on my back and a bag in each hand, I was the last to get out of the station. Buses had long since stopped running, and there was not a single pedicab in sight.

Sitting on the curb, I was again at a loss as to what to do. There were no hotels nearby, and I couldn't have afforded to stay at one anyway. Just as Yicun was falling back to sleep in my arms, a pedicab came toward us. I hailed the driver.

"Please, comrade," I started, knowing no pedicab driver would want to go all the way to the other side of the city at this late hour. "Please take me and my little boy to Anhui University. It's an emergency."

"Oh, no, not me." The man shook his head. "Too far and too late!"

"Please, I beg you. My daughter is critically ill, all by herself. That's why I took the late train from Hanshan. If I spend the night here on the curb, this little boy of mine will surely fall ill too. Please, I'm racing against time. Chairman Mao teaches us, 'All those in the revolutionary ranks must care for each other and help each other.' I need your help."

"That's all very fine, but how much d'you pay?"

"Two times, three times as much as you think it's worth for your trouble."

After I was seated with Yicun in my arms and the bags at my feet, the surly driver, stripped to his waist, pedaled swiftly through the streets, deserted but for the people sleeping on bamboo cots on the sidewalk. It was after midnight when we passed through a shortcut to the university, an area I used to avoid even in daytime because it housed the mortuary of the teaching hospital and the dissection lab of the medical college. Death was in the air; I could hardly breathe, and I held tight to Yicun. When we finally arrived at the university, the iron gate was closed and bolted, and I had to shout at the top of my voice to rouse the gatekeeper. He let us in, and the driver reluctantly took me to the kindergarten, where I thanked him with a large bill.

The nurse on night duty was too sleepy to talk. She sent Yicun back to his place on the floor and said I could spend the night with him. I caught sight of one of Yimao's red cloth shoes and the doll she liked so much on her mattress on the floor. From the lone shoe and the abandoned doll, I could tell she must have been carried away in a flurry. Maybe she didn't need them anymore. Was I too late? I could no longer hold my tears. I was dead tired, but I didn't sleep a wink. I only wished morning would come quickly.

Yicun was still sound asleep when I made my way to the army hospital, a mile away. The nurse at the reception desk looked at me in amazement. "What are you here so early for? We don't open until eight." After listening to my explanation, she looked for Yimao's name among the patients registered but found none. I was sent on a search for my daughter, from one ward to another. Finally, it was suggested that since she had been suspected of encephalitis, perhaps I should look in the isolation ward. But her name was not in the register there either. The head nurse allowed me to go from room to room to see for myself. As I approached the last room, I saw a nurse from the college kindergarten standing outside.

"Why are you so slow in coming, Li Yikai?" she asked sullenly. "Your daughter has been in a terrible fever for many days now. They haven't found out what's the matter with her yet. The kindergarten assigned me to look after her till you came. And I had to pretend to be her mother, or the hospital wouldn't have her. Now you go in and see for yourself."

Tears swelled up in my eyes when I saw that Yimao was no longer the pretty girl she used to be, but skin and bones, her emaciated face flushed with fever. I struggled hard with my feelings and said softly, "Maomao, Mama is here. How are you feeling?" She smiled a wan smile. "Mama, I have been counting the days till you came. I think it's been nine or ten days now. I am so happy you are here. What about my brothers?" It was a relief to see she was not delirious, but composed as usual. A strong-minded girl, my little daughter. "Cuncun has come with me; he's back at the kindergarten. Yiding is in junior high school. Don't worry," I said. Then she asked, "Do you think Papa can come to see me?" I said I would try to bring him. Again she asked, "Did you get the sesame cakes and walnut cookies I sent Cuncun by Uncle Wang Zhuxing, Mama?" She was so clearheaded! "Yes, yes, some time now. I wasn't able to write and let you know, because the postal service was cut off by the flood."

Now an army doctor came in for morning inspection. "Who are you? What are you doing here?" he demanded. Before I could give an explanation, Yimao said, "This is my mother, Dr. Wang. She just arrived from Hexian, where she has gone down under." Dr. Wang looked puzzled, "Another mother? What about the other woman comrade?" I took over and cleared up the confusion. Then the doctor gave me an account of her case, how she had been transferred here from the teaching hospital of Anhui Medical College as a case of encephalitis, and how later tests done here were negative. How they had worked on several hypotheses and tried a number of tests and examinations. Malaria was eliminated when quinine didn't work, as was a viral infection when antibiotics didn't work either. Then flu and pneumonia were also eliminated. Typhoid fever was the current theory. She seemed to respond better to the latest drip injections. He was not pessimistic, but refused to give a prognosis.

When Yimao went to sleep, I rushed back to the kindergarten and made arrangements for Yicun to stay there. I also took the time to call on leaders of the Mao Zedong Thought Propaganda Team and ask for permission for Ningkun to join me at the hospital. My request was flatly denied. I went back to Yimao with a large slice of watermelon, which she said she craved. But she pushed it away after one bite, which worried me a great deal. By strange coincidence, however, Yimao's temperature began to drop the day I arrived. The next day she began to take some liquid food for the first time since she had come down with the unknown fever. To my great relief, her temperature was back to normal within a week. She was able to eat solid food again. With the feverish flush gone, her small face was gaunt and pallid. To speed up her convalescence, I knew I had to get her some good food, which I couldn't do at the hospital. But she was still too weak and unstable to live in the village.

I got permission to stay in a room in the college hostel until Yimao was strong enough to go home with me. When she was being discharged, the entry for final diagnosis was left blank. When I asked Dr. Wang for an explanation, he said it was really difficult to be positive. Given their limited means of diagnosis, I thought that was understandable. It would be even more difficult, I thought, to give a definitive diagnosis of the fevers of the Cultural Revolution. But I suggested he had to put something down. After a brief hesitation, he wrote: typhoid fever strongly suspected.

I brought Yimao to the hostel on a borrowed flatbed cart. She still looked so sick that one passerby asked me whether I was taking her to the hospital. At the hostel, we found a good neighbor in Wu Baotai and his wife, who occupied the room facing mine. Finally cleared of the charge of being a "dog renegade" but dismissed as a "temporary worker" like Ning-kun, he was awaiting repatriation to his hometown, Jiujiang in Jiangxi province. They offered us the use of their briquet stove, kitchen utensils, and even food. For the first time in many years, I felt the warmth of comradeship. No doubt common experiences in the cow shed had brought him closer to Ningkun. Our next-door neighbor was the elderly lecturer of classical Chinese literature, Shen the Blind, who had been given a five-year sentence at a public trial in Wujiang a few months before. It had turned out the trial and the sentence was just part of a war of nevers to break him. But the obdurate man really had nothing to confess, and those in power refused to admit they had been wrong. So he was also awaiting repatriation to his hometown of Huaining County in southern Anhui. As his wife was long since dead and they had no children, a niece of his had to come all the way from the southwestern province of Guizhou to escort the blind uncle back to his hometown in disgrace and destitution. Since the public toilet was at the end of the hall, the blind old man had to pass our room to get to it. More than once he groped into our open door. On another occasion, his cane upset the pot of milk I was heating for Yimao on our neighbor's briquet stove. When he learned who I was, he said Ningkun had been kind to him and he wished him better luck. "Things will get better for you too, Teacher Shen," I tried to comfort him. "Me? My life is not worth living anymore," he said bitterly. "I'm going back to my roots to die. There will be no more torture and anguish for me." I turned away from his empty eye sockets of despair under his straggling gray hair. I thought, he must know the lines "No means to live, going back poor to his native place / Yet difficult to die, lying sick in a strange land." I learned much later he had died of internal injuries shortly after he was repatriated.

6

SHORTLY AFTER I SET UP HOUSEKEEPING IN THE HOSTEL, YIDING UNEXPECT-edly arrived in the middle of the night. I was amazed to hear how he had walked all the way to Wujiang to join his father and how he had enjoyed his stay. Yiding remarked dryly, "Though Yimao's illness was a terrible thing, it brought us all together for the first time since May sixteenth. This is called 'turning a bad thing into a good thing,' Mama, even as Chairman Mao teaches us." When the color began to return to Yimao's cheeks, I decided it was time for me to end one exile and return to another with all three children. Also, school had started, and both Yiding and Yimao were already late. When the next college truck went to our commune, the Wu family, mother and three kids, were among the passengers. It was autumn. We huddled together on the truck bed, facing the three crates of briquet I had managed to buy with ration coupons given me by Mrs. Wu Baotai and a woman colleague of mine. Since we sat against the wind, we were smeared black with coal dust by the time we got home, verily a family of demons and spirits.

Back in our public-room home, I was alarmed to find our bicycle missing. It was our only means of transportation. "This is serious," I said aloud. Just then, Lao Penghai barged in. I handed him a pack of cigarettes I had bought in Hefei.

"Beng Yue, good brand, thirty-five fen a pack!" So saying, he lit one with a match and put the pack into his pocket. "It tastes so much better than Big Iron Bridge, nine fen a pack. So this is your daughter, pretty girl. We took good care of your things, Lao Li. You have everything now?"

"My bike is gone. I left it right here, standing against the wall."

"Oh, the bike, sure, the bike. Lao Feng borrowed it. He saw you riding it in town and hankered for a ride on your foreign model. So he came to me and said he wanted to borrow it for a day. It was standing there idle anyway."

"But I had it locked."

"Indeed you did. Well, we broke the lock, that was a cinch," he giggled. "Lao Feng is the poor peasant representative on the commune's committee in charge of you xiafang ganbu. You don't want to offend him, do you, Lao Li?"

"But where is my bike now?"

"That you will have to go and ask him."

The next morning, I went to Sunbao to look for my bicycle. Lao Feng, very fat and very heavy, was busy selling fish.

"You're back, Lao Li! Nice to have you back. Say, I used your bike when you were not using it. I didn't think you would mind."

"But I need it now. Where is it?"

"Right there against the wall. Sure good bike, Lao Li."

I stepped behind him. The bicycle was battered beyond recognition. Furious, I turned around and asked him, "Lao Feng, what did you do to my bike?"

"It broke down when I took my wife with me, going uphill near Xiaobao. You were lucky we didn't get hurt, or it would be your responsibility, you know, because it's your bike. I don't think there is much wrong with it. You can leave it here and I'll find someone to fix it by and by. Damned foreign make, the guys round here don't know what to do with it. You can wait or, if you like, you can take it home and have it fixed. Perhaps you'll need it."

I swallowed my rage and pushed my crippled bicycle home. It was the second time it had done its bit for the Great Cultural Revolution.

After three years of suspension, classes were in session again at high schools and colleges, in response to a supreme directive from the "Great Teacher" to resume classes while making revolution. At the same time, senior and even junior high graduates went down under among the poor and lower-middle peasants, and college graduates were assigned to rural communes or factories. Education and learning were in disrepute, and intellectuals became the "stinking ninth category," joining the odious company of landlords, counterrevolutionaries, and other enemies of the people. Enterprising parents put their children in uniform or found openings for them on athletic or acrobatic teams. All that was beyond my ability or understanding. I was determined that the children stay in school, chaotic as the schools were at the time. After a few weeks at Xiangchuan Junior High, Yiding was switched to the newly established Sunbao Commune Junior High, only a mile from home. Now he could help me with housework, especially carrying water from the village pond, while I could teach him English. Yimao went to the commune primary school in Sunbao. Yicun entered the one-room lower primary school of Xinjian Brigade. There was a straw-burning stove behind the teacher's desk in a corner of the school-room, where the teacher cooked his lunch during breaks in his instruction, filling the room with smoke. The teacher, a middle-aged Muslim itinerant peddler, taught his pupils so little that Yicun did not have much to unlearn later on. Eventually the teacher quit because the brigade paid him so little, and he went back to his old job of peddling from village to village. By then, Yicun was ready to join his sister at the commune primary school in Sunbao.

There was only room for the double bed in our makeshift home, so all four of us slept together. "The more numerous the people the greater the heat," Yiding remarked, citing a quotation from Chairman Mao with a straight face. Yicun simply said, "The more the merrier!" The child turned out to be prophetic. One snowy afternoon we had an unexpected visitor, another woman xiafang ganbu from a neighboring village. Chen Ruixuan was a lab technician from the Provincial Institute for Prevention and Cure of Schistosomiasis, based in the city of Wuhu. She came down under alone, for her husband, a pharmacist at Hexian County Hospital, was still under proletarian dictatorship, an ex-rightist like Ningkun. Lonely and unhappy, she closeted herself in a small room in a peasant's house. We met at political study sessions regularly. Aside from the similarities in our situation, we were delighted to discover we were both from Tianjin and literally spoke the same language. And my children loved her, because Aunt Chen was frank, outspoken, and guileless.

Yicun was excited to see Aunt Chen suddenly appear out of the snow flurries. "Aunt Chen, you can't go back to your village in this snow. You must stay with us."

"I may very well stay, Little Cuncun."

"The more the merrier!" Yicun shouted with a laugh.

"What made you come out in this weather, Ruixuan?" I asked anxiously, sensing there was something wrong.

"I am literally homeless, Yikai. You know how I lived. The landlady came this morning and told me she wanted the room back. Her son is getting married during the Lunar New Year holidays. So I went to see the team leader and asked him to find another place for me. He said the only place he could offer me was the team's cow shed. He could fix it up for me. When my allotment of lumber arrives, he will build a new shed for the cows."

"That's preposterous!" Yiding almost shouted.

"But that's reality, children. Furthermore, he said I couldn't even move into the old cow shed unless I agreed to his arrangements. I said he could keep his old cow shed and walked out. I went to see the brigade party secretary, but he was busy getting ready for the festivities and said he would look into it after the holidays. I will insist on having a small hut built for me with my allotment of lumber. But meanwhile I am homeless."

"We only have room for this double bed, but it's pretty big, and it's wintertime. I am sure we can manage, Ruixuan. The children will love it."

The kids chanted aloud in unison, "Welcome, Aunt Chen!"

Ruixuan was visibly affected. "Aunt Chen will make dumplings for you. Would you like that?"

Ruixuan was good at making dumplings. So they were made on the first night of her stay. At bedtime, we put our heads together and tried to figure out the best plan for the five of us to sleep in one bed. After much discussion, it was finally decided that Ruixuan and I would sleep on either side, with the two little ones in between, and Yiding lying crosswise at our feet. This arrangement held good until the holidays were over and Ruixuan went to share a house with another woman xiafang ganbu.

Spring came early in our part of the province along the Yangtze. It was time to build houses for the xiafang ganbu with the lumber allotted to them for the purpose, 0.30 cubic meters per capita. Lao Penghai himself went to the county lumberyard with two young men to supervise the shipping of the 1.20 cubic meters of lumber for the four of us. Brought by flatbed cart, the dozen logs were then stacked into a neat pile under his eaves.

"I'm going to build a big house for you, Lao Li, with all this good lumber. You just leave it to me," he said reassuringly. As I didn't know how to go about it myself, anyway, I was thankful that he was taking it into his hands. He decided I was to get a four-bay house of sun-dried mud-bricks with a thatched roof on a wooden framework. I said it sounded fine. On a sunny day the village threshing ground was covered with mud-bricks made of local dirt. The main building job was to have a framework made. The new house was to be built on the ground next to the public room. Instead of working near the site, however, the carpenter, his apprentice, and the other helpers did all their work in front of Lao Penghai's house. When all the beams, rafters, and pillars were processed and ready, they were shipped from the rear hamlet to the front hamlet to be assembled on the site. All the men turned out to build the thatched roof and the mud-brick walls. All the expenses were paid out of my government funds, which were in Penghai's control. I had to show my appreciation with a carton of good cigarettes and two bottles of 120 proof liquor.

The finished hut had one room on either end, partitioned off with a bamboo and mud wall, leaving a broad space in the middle with a straw-burning stove in one corner. There were no doors. "What d'you want doors for? Wasting good lumber," Lao Penghai said when I asked him. There were no windows either. To humor me, he told a bricklayer to leave a hole in the front wall of my room and that would be my window. The front door of the house could not be closed properly. "So what? No one closes the door anyway," Lao Penghai said, dismissing my objection with a wave of his hand. "Lao Li, you really ought to be grateful to the Communist party and Chairman Mao for this wonderful new house. You are better off than a landlord in the old society. You get it all free, no rent to pay, free water, and free electricity when we fix up your lights for you. And you get paid fifty-seven yuan a month, fifty-seven!" I said of course I was very grateful, not only to the party and Chairman Mao, but to the poor and lower-middle peasants under his leadership. All in all, house-moving this time, out of the rat hole into a clean new hut, was almost a happy event. Yicun slept with me in one room, Yimao in the other room, and Yiding in the open space in between. Yiding observed there was a technical reason behind the design of the door that could not be tightly closed: to protect him against gas poisoning by the briquet stove that kept him company. "I'm sure Papa will support my theory," he added. "Like father, like son!" Yimao said. "How I wish he would come home now to enjoy the new house with us! He wasn't even able to come and see me in Hefei when I was so close to dying."

Our joy of moving into the new home was soon spoiled by a band of midnight visitors, who roused us rudely long after we had gone to bed. At first I had thought it was another nightmare, but I was soon face-to-face with half a dozen real men and women armed with blinding flashlights. "We are part of a nationwide political campaign to ferret out counterrevolutionaries in hiding. This is a unified action beginning at two A.M. throughout the country," a young man declared solemnly. "Are you Li Yikai?"

"Yes, I am, a xiafang ganbu from Anhui University."

"How many people in your family?"

"Five. But only four here, me and my three kids. My husband is still in Wujiang."

"Why isn't he with you?"

"The university hasn't sent him."

"Are you sure there are no bad people hidden here in your house?"

"I am certain."

While I was being interrogated, the rest of the band searched the house with their bright flashlights.

Then one of the women reported to my interrogator, "Found one little boy in that room, one big boy in this central room, and a girl in the other room."

"Did you look under the beds?" asked the man.

"Yes we did."

"Li Yikai, can you vouch that there are no counterrevolutionaries hidden in your house?" The man turned to me again.

"Yes, I can."

The visitors filed out of the house. I knew the children were all awake, holding their breath. I quickly went over to Yimao first, then to Yiding, and finally to Yicun, saying to each, "Go back to sleep now. The day will soon be dawning." How I wished my children could sleep in peace at night!

In the morning, after taking Yicun to the brigade school, I went into the brigade office in the hope of finding an explanation for what had happened the night before. I ran into Zhang Weiwu, a Russian lecturer and fellow xiafang ganbu. The first thing he said was, "Did anyone come to your house last night, Li Yikai?" I told him what had happened. He explained that the action had been mapped out two days before, right here in this office. Two families were selected as prime targets: one was the landlord Li Shanzhu, the other me. Village militiamen dug into the dirt floor of Li Shanzhu's house, three feet deep, presumably looking for hidden title deeds for land or for gold and jewelry. Nothing was found, of course. It dawned on me that politically I was on a par with the only living landlord in the brigade. Only they did not have to bother with digging my new dirt floor.

How I wished I knew when the nightmare would end!

Fourteen

A COW DEMON AT LARGE, 1970-73

1

AFTER TWO YEARS IN THE COW SHED, I WAS FINALLY GIVEN A BUS TICKET TO move on to another village to join my family, but more importantly, to "receive reeducation from the poor and lower-middle peasants." All of a sudden, I was given an ironic sort of freedom. Freed from proletarian dictatorship, I was also freed from my job as a temporary worker. Speaking up for the freedom of speech, I was rewarded with the freedom of starvation. I was literally a nobody. While walking me from the bus stop to our village home on the afternoon of May 1, 1970, Yikai asked me what was my status now; I could only laugh and quip, "A cow demon at large, my wife's fourth dependent!"

The family was happily reunited for the first time in two years. I had felt guilty about my family's circumstances, but I was more than happy to find all three children tolerably healthy and contented. Yiding was as dark as the other teenage boys in the village, Yimao was thin but had color in her cheeks, and Yicun laughed constantly. But where would we go from here? The family of five now depended on Yikai's meager wages, which had been further reduced to fifty-seven yuan a month because life in the countryside was presumably cheaper than in the city. I felt bad about being dumped on her hands again, but Yikai was gratified that I had been spared a lonely exile after all. She was not quite forty, but her hair was beginning to turn gray, and she complained of a backache. She accepted her lot cheerfully, saying it was all in the design of things and citing the age-old axiom "though falling short of the best, yet being better than the worst."

The villagers, officially known as "glorious members of the people's commune," eyed me as an anomaly. A returned student from America, once a university professor in the national capital, now dependent on a woman for his daily bowls of rice! Either I was untouchable, like those in the nearby leper colony, they felt, or someone in power was out of his mind, like Loony of the village. Lao Penghai was disappointed to hear that I was devoid of any income. "Well, I can't help you moneywise, but I can help you politically," he said significantly. As I was not a glorious member of the people's commune, I could not even work in the fields with the villagers and take a share of their annual income. A freed cow demon, but not free to graze in any pasture!

It so happened that the villagers had been unhappy with the chaotic records of their daily labor for some time. Each able-bodied villager, man or woman, earned ten work points for a full day's work. But, being illiterate, most of them could never tell just how many points had been jotted down for them at the end of the day's labor by one of the teenagers with one or two years of schooling, as dictated by the whims of their team leader. The villagers saw in me a dependable and disinterested "work-point recorder," and Lao Penghai conceded to their wish, partly as a favor to me. I was now a temporary worker hired by the production team. My new job earned me one work point per day, worth three to four fen, depending on the cash value of the year's work point. The team's work-point record in hand, I would find my way to wherever the villagers happened to be working toward the end of the day's labor. Lao Penghai would dictate to me the number of points to be awarded each of the villagers. Often a row would break out when he penalized a younger villager for poor work or for talking back to him. He would always give himself ten points, whatever he had or hadn't done for the day. It was not uncommon for him to assign the villagers their tasks in the morning and then disappear. At the end of the working day, he would return to the village and stop by our house, his face flushed and his eyes bloodshot from too much hard liquor.

"Lao Wu, let's go and get the work points down!" he would shout.

"Where have you been, Team Leader Li?" I would ask him on the way.

"Oh drinking and eating all day in the restaurant in Sunbao with other cadres. Have to do business with them and get on good terms, you know," was his invariable answer.

When I found a spot on a ridge or a path to seat myself and do my job, I would ask him, "How many points for you, Team Leader Li?"

"Ten points, of course!"

"What about your type of work?"

"Diplomacy, of course!"

I was filled with admiration. The man certainly lived up to his name of Old Crab. Though illiterate and crude, he was a consummate political leader who impudently subverted words to serve his self-interest. He was absolutely dauntless, because he wielded absolute power as the one and only party member. Sometimes, when one of the younger villagers rashly questioned the propriety of his getting full work points for doing nothing or wining and dining at the team's expense, he would crush the impudent greenhorn with his classic argument: "The party gave me everything. I was a poor peasant before liberation. Now I am a party member. I'll have you know it's the party, the Communist party, that gives me the right to eat and drink to my heart's content. Okay, you green-eyed rascal? Now you had better behave yourself, before you fall into the Six Articles of Public Security!"

I was given other odd jobs, which earned me a few more work points. At the height of the national campaign to learn from the model production brigade of Dazhai in Shanxi province, I was sent up onto the tile roof of the Sun family's new house to paint on it five giant Chinese characters in white: IN AGRICULTURE LEARN FROM DAZHAI. During another political campaign, the brigade party secretary, Song Xianjin, ordered me to spend a whole day in his home village applying my calligraphy to the mud-brick walls of the better houses. In addition to learning from Dazhai, the peasants were exhorted to REARRANGE THE MOUNTAINS AND RIVERS, BUILD THE COMMU-NIST PARADISE ON EARTH, and so on. The villagers did not seem impressed by the heroic slogans, probably because most of them were not literate enough to know the characters. For my trouble I was given a free lunch of rice and boiled cabbage at a peasant home. During lunch, my gray-haired host thanked me for making their houses look nice with my calligraphy and pointed to his grandson's report card prominently displayed on the wall. "Look, my grandson done well at the school. He's only ten, but knows more characters than the party secretary," said the grandfather proudly. I was amused to find that his grades for three of the five subjects were F, written in red ink; but of course red always meant "double happiness" to the old man.

I was also told to join the villagers for political study in the evenings. My job was to read aloud editorials, important dispatches, and political articles, and explain what I read. Everyone came, because attendance earned each of them two work points. After a hard day's work in the fields, it was time for them to relax. The younger men would indulge in horseplay, while the younger women would breastfeed their babies or work on soles for cloth shoes. None of them seemed to care what I was reading. One day, Darkie said, "Please read some more, Uncle Wu." (All the younger villagers addressed me as Uncle Wu, while the adults simply called me "Lao Wu.") Surprised, I asked, "What would you like to have me read, Darkie?" He said, "I don't care what you read. They're not written for us peasants anyway. I just love to hear the way you read, and the tone of your voice." I was flattered, but also disconcerted. Was I unconsciously subverting party propaganda with my voice? Would I be denounced as a counterrevolutionary at the next campaign? Still I was pleased to see that the peasants had better sense than the party gave them credit for.

2

AS THE FAMILY ENTERED THE ORBIT OF LIFE DOWN UNDER, A DIVISION OF labor came about naturally. Yikai, now the sole "ricewinner" of the family, was kept busy with political study sessions and political meetings at every level—for the team, the brigade, the commune, the district, and the county. The meetings often overlapped, and identical documents were distributed and studied at all levels. "Much ado about nothing, a plague spread throughout the land," observed Yikai. My sister and her family, Yikai's brothers in Tianjin, my cousins in my hometown, and other relatives in different parts of the country were also going through the same rigmarole.

As an ex-rightist and ex-temporary worker with no other status, I was luckily exempted from all the xiafang ganbu ado. I was now a genuine househusband, holding up the half of the sky that had traditionally been the housewife's concern. I became the family cook. The central room, in which Yiding slept on a single bed, was also the kitchen. I did my cooking on the briquet stove, which stood near the front wall, across the open space from

Yiding's bed. Near the stove was the water vat. Tucked away in one back corner was a makeshift cupboard, which Yiding had made with firewood. It stood on three legs because he had run out of material for the fourth leg. Yiding also shared his bedroom with a rooster and a dozen young hens, who spent the night in a coop he had built for them in another corner, facing the door, a few feet away from his own bed.

In addition to providing us with eggs for food, the young hens held an important place in the family as the children's pets. Each was given a distinctive name: Big Yellow, Little Black, Pearly, Snow White, and so on. When the eggs were laid, one of the children would write the date in pencil on each of them. Our neighbors taught us how to hatch chickens, twenty at a time, and it was such a joy for the children to watch little chicks break out of their shells one by one, after weeks of eager expectation.

It was not long, however, before our innocent joys were spoiled. During the night, eggs began to disappear from the basket. Annoyed and puzzled, Yikai and I decided to keep vigil one night. By and by, we were amazed to see a fat yellow weasel appear out of nowhere. It approached the basket noiselessly at a run, pushed the lid off with its forelegs, and grabbed an egg between its teeth. Then it disappeared. A few minutes later, it came back and repeated the agile operations. I threw a shoe at it as it ran off with the second egg. In the morning I told Third Elder what had happened to our eggs and asked him for advice on what to do with the "damned weasel." He was shocked by what I called the animal thief. "Lao Wu, don't say that! It's a fairy, a grand fairy. You mustn't use that foul language. Blasphemy will bring bad fortune on you and your family. The grand fairy likes your eggs, you should feel honored." I didn't have the heart to contradict the honest fellow, but I certainly didn't relish the honor. We locked our eggs up in a wooden box. Two days later, Sharp-nozzled Pigling dropped in. "You lost your eggs, Uncle Wu?" said he knowingly. "Maybe I can help you find them, if you give me two of your steamed buns." I suspected he was trying to hoodwink me, but two steamed buns was no big deal. So I followed him to Third Elder's backyard and found a huge hole under a big tree. I removed a heap of leaves and rice straw from the hole. Lo, there were our eggs, with their penciled dates, neatly piled up in the cache! Third Elder was scandalized when he heard I had violated the sanctity of the grand fairy's abode.

Every evening when our chickens trooped home, one by one, the children would stand by and count them by name until the last one was in. One evening, however, they found three chickens missing. Thinking perhaps they had strayed into our neighbors' coops, the children searched their coops for the missing birds. Not a single one was found. I said, "Yellow weasels are notorious chicken thieves too. It's that damned weasel, I bet." Third Elder warned me again, "Lao Wu, what did I tell you last time about your eggs? You didn't listen to me. And now you are blaspheming again. Oh, I fear for you, Lao Wu!' Just then, Lao Penghai happened to go by. I reported our loss to him, hoping to enlist his help. He said, "Impossible. You just have so many of them that you lose count. Or you must have offended the grand fairy." The children went to bed unhappy over the loss of their friends. The next day, Sharp-nozzled Pigling dropped in again. "Uncle Wu, too bad about your chickens. I wouldn't look for them if I were you." I knew at once he was in the know. "Well, what happened to them? In that hole again?" He squinted and shook his head, "Oh no, not that. If you really want to know . . ." "Okay," I said, "two steamed buns." He lowered his voice and said rapidly, "This time it's my uncle, Lao Penghai. Yesterday afternoon he came with Jiwen to our house. He said to my dad and Jiwen, 'Lao Li and Lao Wu raising too many chickens, breeding capitalism, we must do something about it.' When the three of them went over to the public room, I tagged along. I saw you were reading in your room when I passed your house. They left the door of the public room open, and your chickens wandered in to pick food grains off the floor. Then they slammed the door shut and caught three of your chickens. My uncle went home with your chickens in a sack and all the cadres of the team shared a chicken dinner at his house." "Who else was there?" I asked. "Just me," he said. "I had a drumstick, real tender. But they wouldn't let me taste the liquor." Yikai was outraged that evening when I told her the story. But mindful of Penghai's absolute authority, we thought we had better keep quiet about it.

As part of our reeducation, we were given two small plots of land to grow our own vegetables. On one plot we grew cucumbers, tomatoes, chives, string beans, and radishes for spring, summer, and fall consumption. The other plot was planted with turnips and ivory bok choy, which we hoped to gather for winter storage. To provide fertilizer for the vegetables, we built an open-air latrine next to our house, which consisted of half a vat buried in the ground, surrounded by a low mud wall with an opening. A passerby could look the other way when he saw it was occupied. Once or twice, however, while squatting by the broken vat, I saw Third Elder walking directly toward the latrine. I bowed my head in embarrassment, only to hear him give me the usual local greeting, "Have you eaten, Lao Wu?" After that, I would always serve as a door when Yikai or Yimao had to use the "toilet."

Yiding was the heavyweight in the family's division of labor. When he came home in the late afternoon, he would carry two buckets of water on a bamboo shoulder pole from the front pond to fill our water vat, or he'd fill one of our neighbor's urine buckets with night soil from our family latrine, diluted with water from the rear pond, and bring it to the two vegetable plots. We lost some of our tomatoes and cucumbers to Jigui, but we still had enough vegetables to eat. Yiding's turnips and ivory bok choy were the pride of the family and the envy of the villagers. We looked forward to the harvest. When the day came, the whole family turned out with a spade, a large wicker basket, and a shoulder pole. But when we approached the plot, we were flabbergasted to see our precious kitchen garden lying in shambles. The outer leaves of the ivory bok choy were left standing, so that the bok choy looked intact from a distance though the heads were gone. And the green leaves of the turnips were strewn all over the place, like broken limbs on a battlefield. The children were in tears. Yikai soon found Lao Penghai and told him about the theft of our vegetables. He said it was impossible. Every family grew its own vegetables. Why should anyone steal ours? Then he added, "If anyone did it, it must have been someone from the team on the other side of the highway. Your plot is too close to the road. And your turnips and ivory bok choy were certainly better than any I have seen." His nephew Sharp-nozzled Pigling knew better, for he made no secret of how much he loved "Lao Wu's luscious turnips," which he had tasted at his uncle's table.

We were upset by the petty thefts, mainly because they killed the joy in our children's life. We collected enough eggs from the remaining hens and bought vegetables from our neighbors. We even felt mollified when Lao Penghai unexpectedly returned our single bed to replace Yiding's makeshift mud-brick bed. When we thanked him, he said, "No problem.

Lao Li is my sister. And this is your bed." Once he was gone, Sharp-nozzled Pigling dropped in and remarked, "So you have your bed back, Aunt Li. Do you know why?" "It's our bed. Your uncle borrowed it from us," Yikai said. The boy, who was much wiser than his age, said with a grin, "I know, I know. But it's really because my cousin Greater Flood had a new bed made for him. With your wood, Aunt Li." We were incredulous. Sharp-nozzled Pigling went on: "Come with me. I'll show you something in the public room." We followed him into Yikai's former home and came upon a new plow, a new harrow, and a new dipper-shaped wooden container. "What's that for?" I asked. Our young guide answered, "That's what the families steam sweet rice in, come the Lunar New Year. All these were also made with Aunt Li's wood." Dismayed, Yikai turned to me. "This is impossible. The wood is government property, given me for the explicit purpose of building our house. I'll be held accountable." Sharp-nozzled Pigling added, "One whole log was left over. It's lying under my uncle's bed. He said it's just what he needed to make furniture for Greater Flood when he gets married."

We gave Sharp-nozzled Pigling some candies on top of the usual two steamed buns, because we really appreciated what he had done for our reeducation. Yikai decided she must report the occurrences to the brigade leadership and see what they might do about it. The deputy party secretary of the brigade was ostensibly outraged. "This is Nationalist behavior, unworthy of a member of the Communist party. We will look into it and do something about it." Some time later, word came to us through the local grapevine that the brigade leadership had reprimanded Lao Penghai at a meeting. But he defended himself by saying he was weeding capitalism from the team by ridding us of our surplus chickens and vegetables and logs. We never heard from the brigade leadership again.

Lao Penghai was undeterred in his avowed commitment to weeding capitalism from the team. Shortly after he had been chided at the brigade meeting, he held a "mass criticism" meeting on the edge of a field during a break. Yikai and I happened to be passing by. We heard him raise his voice, denouncing manifestations of capitalism in the team: "There are people in this team who don't work in the fields but raise too many chickens that steal grains from the public room. People who don't labor but get work points for scribbling here and there. Parasites! Exploiters! Capitalists! Class struggle!" He had his revenge, and we took it with a grain of salt.

But Lao Penghai did not stop there. Another day, he barged into our central room, sat down at the collapsible table, and lit himself one of our cigarettes. "Lao Wu," he said, "scribble a *daibantiao* for me." The daibantiao was a sort of purchase affidavit written on a piece of paper by the purchasing party. It was acceptable in lieu of a receipt or invoice in the financial system of the people's commune, especially at the team level. I had often done it at his bidding and thought nothing of it. "In West Town the other day I bought two large wicker baskets, five yuan each, and two coarse sieves, two yuan each. That's all. Put my name on it for me." I always wrote his name for him, because he did not know how to write his own name. He went away with the paper and I forgot about it. Then I learned through the local grapevine that a counterrevolutionary slogan had been found on the wall of a public latrine in Sunbao. Anxious to crack the case, the commune security asked the teams to obtain handwriting samples from possible suspects. The diabantiao I scribbled for him was submitted. To Lao Penghai's disappointment, the security personnel found no resemblance between my scribbling and the handwriting on the wall. Undeterred, he reported to the commune security that villagers had overheard me stealthily listening in to enemy broadcasts on our short-wave radio set. He was closer to truth this time, because we actually often tuned in to the Voice of America "English 900" program for Yiding's benefit. After Nixon's visit to China in 1972, English was once again a favorite subject in colleges and schools, but good teachers were scarce, especially at the commune level. We thought it would do Yiding good to listen to English conversation taught by native speakers. Though doing nothing criminal, we kept the volume low, but the mud-brick walls had ears. When the security cadre went to check with Guo Renfu, my former boss at the university told him, "I'll have you know Lao Wu was the only man in the whole province authorized by the Provincial Public Security Bureau to listen in to all foreign stations."

To learn from the poor and the lower-middle peasants, I also raised a pig myself. It was a male hybrid white piglet, of the "small and round" variety. Our Small-and-Round also shared the room with Yiding. I made a comfortable rice-straw place for him next to the front wall and fed him boiled sweet potatoes. I was tickled to see how he peeled the potatoes before gobbling them down. Lao Penghai claimed I was raising a capitalist pig, because he fed his own pigs sweet potato peels. Small-and-Round was also pretty wild, often breaking away from the tether and rushing into the fields. It took both Darkie and Lesser Flood to bring him back. One day when I was feeding him with freshly boiled sweet potatoes, he actually bit the hand that fed him. That was too much for me; and he was growing too slowly anyway. Lao Penghai was all for getting rid of this capitalist pig. He set a date and did the killing himself for a fee. I had never witnessed the slaughtering of a pig before. The frantic rushing about of the animal, the desperate squealing, the shining knives, the fatal thrust, the spurting blood, the death throes, the half-naked Lao Penghai cursing, "You capitalist pig! You capitalist!" and the merriment of the onlooking villagers provided another lesson in my reeducation. After losing its hair in a boiling water bath, the capitalist was sliced into different cuts. Then the slaughterer went to the pond to wash the blood off his face, hands, arms, and chest. After a dinner of plenty of fresh pork and a bottle of liquor, he went home tipsy, carrying the pork liver and a huge hunk of meat. We never raised a pig again.

With free time on my hands, I could now do a little reading. Yikai had kept my books packed in cardboard boxes, even when some of our colleagues had sold theirs to the salvage station as wastepaper, for books and bookworms had been thoroughly discredited. When the boxes were opened, we found that many of the books had been damaged by the flood that had invaded the village the year before, and others had been gnawed by rats. Among them I found the copy of the *Selected Poems of Du Fu* that had kept me company in one prison after another. Also half-chewed was the manuscript of my translation of Stendhal's *La Chartreuse de Parme*, which I had started in 1957 but had never been able to finish. I felt sad and Yikai was dismayed. Then it occurred to me, "The poor rats! They must have been hungrier than I was in the winter of 1960!" We spread the books out on the ground in front of our home to air them in the sun. Some of the curious young men passing by picked up Helen Gardner's *Art Through the Ages*, a textbook from my Manchester College days. They giggled and nudged each other when they saw the nudes from the Sistine Chapel. The next day I was called to the commune by Guo Renfu to answer Lao Penghai's charge that "Wu Ningkun corrupts the young peasants with lurid pornographic pictures." When I explained what had happened, Lao Guo laughed and called my informer "a nosy crab."

3

WE REALLY HAD NO REASON TO COMPLAIN WHEN WE SAW HOW THE POOR and lower-middle peasants, supposedly comasters of the country along with the working class, were faring under proletarian dictatorship, in the despotic and greedy hands of the local cadres.

Lao Penghai throve on every new political slogan. In the name of the campaign to "dig up roots of capitalism in the countryside," he went around with an axe to chop down the one or two trees in front of the villagers' houses, for he was too lazy to plant a tree himself and at the same time he envied the others for their shady trees. Gaozhuang had always been known for its scarcity of trees; now it was completely denuded. Then he carried his campaign into the peasants' chicken coops. Each family was theoretically allowed only four hens, but no family observed the quota. Eggs and chickens were their only source of small cash. One night, he went from house to house, a storm lantern in hand, to look into the coops and check the number of chickens. He began by insisting on the families having their surplus hens killed, but settled for each family surrendering to the team one hen, to be sold on the market. The hens were caught and sold, but the money did not end up in the community fund. The families also raised pigs and had one slaughtered from time to time. Lao Penghai never missed the slaughtering of a pig. He was always the guest of honor at the fresh pork dinner that followed and always went home afterward with a big hunk of good lean meat plus either the tenderloin or the liver. He was also the guest of honor at every dinner for every special occasion at every house. When agricultural mechanization was the order of the day, Lao Penghai spent a whole day shopping in the county town with Sun Jiwen, the buyer and cashier, and came back in the evening with a walking tractor, sodden with hard liquor. He gave himself and Sun Jiwen fifteen work points each for the day's labor, plus expenses. Since no one really knew how to operate the novelty, it quickly broke down after a lot of fumbling. The team leader had to spend another day taking it back for repairs. This process was repeated many times until the walking tractor was abandoned outside the public room. The cost to the villagers of agricultural mechanization ran to several hundred yuan, including considerable per diem expenses for the traveling team leader.

It was my job to take notes at the team's business meetings. At the year's end, the team bookkeeper would make public a detailed account of each family: how many work points it earned, how much it owed the team for the food grain, the rice straw, and other fuel it received, and whatever cash it was able to borrow from the cashier to meet emergencies. The families in the black would receive whatever cash was due them, ranging between a few and a hundred yuan. For the families in the red, a full meeting of the village was usually called to look into their accounts and discuss their applications for relief from the community fund. At the first meeting I attended, Lao Penghai was at the top of the list of five families in the red. He owed the team a hundred yuan, because the team's cashier readily lent him whatever he asked for. The question under discussion was whether or how much of that debt might be canceled. Most of the villagers said nothing, but several young men spoke up against any cancelation. Then Captain Tang, representing the brigade party committee, summed up the discussion. He first praised Penghai for all the good things he had done for the team during the year, then deplored his difficulties in raising two children (knowing well that his son Greater Flood was making ten work points a day), and finally suggested that, out of class feelings for a fellow poor peasant and party member and a model team leader, the "tail be cut off" for him, meaning the debt be canceled. "Does anyone have a different opinion?" asked the powerful brigade cadre. Silence. "Then it's unanimously passed. Meeting dismissed." Lao Penghai turned to me: "Lao Wu, keep on record that all the members of the production team unanimously agreed at a full meeting to have the tail cut off for Team Leader Li Tinghai, in the presence of Captain Tang."

On the way home, I asked Darkie why the problems of the other four families in the red had not been looked into. Third Elder, for example, was really hard up, because Loony earned few work points and Little Egg was only six. "If you don't mind my saying so, Uncle Wu, you may know books, even foreign books, but you don't know how to read this book of life in the production team," Darkie said, holding my arm to help me negotiate the rugged path in the dark. "Everybody knew what the meeting was all about, except you. Well, we grew up here. You do need reeducation, Uncle Wu!"

Another meeting was held after *shuang qiang* or "double rush," which was the most arduous time of the year for the villagers. All the men and women worked round the clock at the height of summer, rush-harvesting early rice and rush-planting late rice almost simultaneously. The government collected from the peasants an annual agricultural tax paid in grain in three installments—that is, when the early, the middle-season, and the late rice were successively harvested. But the local authorities, prompted by the higher authorities, suddenly called on the communes to have their total annual tax paid in full as soon as the early rice was harvested. Captain Tang descended on Gaozhuang to tell the villagers to answer the call.

"I was pleased to learn Gaozhuang reaped a good harvest of early rice this year," he began smoothly. "You have worked hard, and shuang qiang is really backbreaking. Don't I know? I toiled for landlords before liberation. Now, thanks to the party, thanks to Chairman Mao, we are liberated. How do we express our gratitude to the party and Chairman Mao? How do we show our support for the Great Cultural Revolution? By harvesting better rice, more rice, and paying your tax in grain, you will all say. Fine and good. But is that enough? I say we must do better than that. All advanced brigades will pay their annual tax in grain in full with the harvest of early rice. The brigade party committee has adopted a resolution to make Xinjian Brigade an advanced brigade. Do you want an advanced brigade? Or a backward brigade?"

"We want an advanced brigade, most certainly," responded Lao Penghai without a moment's hesitation.

"You have a good, advanced team leader. What do you all say? Come on, speak up, we are democratic. I welcome everyone to speak up."

"Captain Tang, I will open my heart to you," said Third Elder. "You know me. I am an old poor peasant. I love Chairman Mao. But the fact is we have nothing left in our rice crocks. We have worked ourselves to death these past days, and thank God the early rice is harvested. Can't we possibly borrow a little from the team to tide us over for a few days, say ten or twenty catties per person? And that would not make a great difference in the total—"

"Kaidao, I am shocked to hear this from you," said Captain Tang, turning very stern. "You are an old poor peasant, as you say, and you are senior. What a bad influence on the whole team! The brigade calls on all of you to give all your early rice harvest for the tax paid in grain, and you want to keep some of it for your own stomach. We want to be advanced, and you want to hold us back. That's what our class enemies want, you're talking their language. I say you had better make a self-criticism."

"I'm only an illiterate poor peasant, I'm ready to make a self-criticism anytime," said Third Elder. "But our stomachs are as empty as our rice crocks. Not just in my own home, but in most homes. We have been living on borrowed rice, so as to be able to do shuang qiang. I hate landlords, you know that. But we all know, the landlords used to feed us the best food in the time of shuang qiang. The better to exploit us, I know, but—"

Lao Penghai cut him short. "Are you going loony, like your son, Kaidao?" You don't know what you are saying. If you don't mend your ways, you will fall into the Six Articles of Public Security, poor peasant or no poor peasant. Captain Tang, let's get on with our business. On behalf of all the poor and lower-middle peasants of Gaozhuang Production Team, I pledge to the brigade party committee that we guarantee to pay our tax in grain in full with all the early rice harvested. If our harvest is not enough, I will go and borrow more early rice from other teams to make up the difference."

"That is very well said, Tinghai," said Captain Tang warmly. "I'll make sure that you are nominated an advanced team leader of the brigade."

"Meeting dismissed," concluded Lao Penghai. "Beginning tomorrow morning, we will deliver our rice to the grain collecting station. Lao Wu, put down in the records that all the poor and lower-middle peasants of the production team unanimously . . . oh damn it, you know what to write."

In addition to the agricultural tax paid in grain, the peasants provided labor and brought their own tools and food when the highway needed repair or a river needed dredging or a flood had to be fought. Troublemakers, usually younger peasants who disobeyed the team leader or spoke out against a brigade decision, would be punished with doing unpaid labor for the brigade. When the peasants heard over the loudspeaker, "So-and-So report to the brigade in the morning for a day's labor. Bring tools and food," they would take the lesson to heart and remember their place in the socialist countryside. Good boys would be selected annually to join the ranks of recruits for the armed forces, with the prospect of being given a paid job in the commune headquarters or the county seat if they came back alive. Xiao Wubao, the orphan of the village, was awarded that good fortune and sent to the Vietnam front because he never disobeyed orders and always worked hard. He had another advantage over the other young men of his age: there would be no one to worry about his safety on the battlefield or mourn his death if he got killed.

I used to think only intellectuals were vulnerable to the capricious changes of the political weather. But reeducation taught me otherwise. One day in the spring of 1971, the team leader of Wangzhuang was paraded from village to village for criticism and struggle because he had remarked that Lin Biao, who had emerged in the Cultural Revolution as the "Great Leader's closest comrade-in-arms and successor designate," had a "villainous smile." Counterrevolutionary slander! He was stripped of his job and did days of unpaid labor. When he was brought to our team to be denounced, Yikai immediately recognized Lao Wang as the kind man who had come to her rescue when she was stopped by flood water on her way to West Town two years before. A few months later, Lin Biao reportedly died in an air crash as he was fleeing in a Trident passenger plane after an abortive plot on the "Great Leader's" life. Thus the nation was plunged into another political campaign, to criticize Lin Biao the arch-villain.

One afternoon Lao Wang walked into our central room all smiles. "Lao Wu, I come to ask a favor of you," said he. "Now that everybody says Lin Biao did have a villainous smile, the brigade party secretary wants me to hand in an application for party membership. He says I have shown a 'high degree of political consciousness.' I am an open-eyed blindman, an illiterate peasant. I come to ask you to write an application for party membership for me."

"No problem," said I. "But you must tell me something about your-self and why you want to join the party."

"It really doesn't matter, Lao Wu. Okay, say I am a poor peasant, my folks were poor peasants for generations. I love the party. I love Chairman Mao. I hate the smiling villain Lin Biao. That'll do the trick. I don't really know what they want me to join the party for." A few minutes later he left with his application for membership in the great, glorious, and correct Chinese Communist party on a sheet of paper torn from Yiding's notebook.

Darkie's young life was affected in another way. A date had been set for his wedding while Lin Biao's "three loyals" campaign was in full swing. The most loyal heir designate called upon the nation to be "loyal to Chairman Mao, loyal to Mao Zedong Thought, loyal to Chairman Mao's revolutionary line." The triad of the Chinese character *zhong*, meaning loyal, became a dominant decorative motif throughout the land. When Darkie's bridal bed was finished, the carpenter mounted a carefully carved character zhong into each of the three interlocking wooden rings as the centerpiece of the front band of the four-poster. Before the wedding took place, however, the "three loyals" had become as discredited as the dead advocate himself. The carpenter was called back to knock out the infamous characters, leaving three blank rings as blind witnesses of an age of double-dealers.

Even the confines of the leper colony were no defense against the storms of the Great Cultural Revolution. At the height of the "three loyals" campaign, Dr. Lu was called in to the colony for consultation. He found the patients afflicted with the age-old curse were divided into two hostile factions, each faction claiming to be more loyal to the Great Leader. "One faction tried to shout down the other as 'counterrevolutionary lepers,' " Dr. Lu told me. "Both factions waved the same Little Red Book held between equally truncated fingers. I have never seen anything more lamentable." "The place sounds like a perfect epitome of China," I remarked.

The "three loyals" also had a small impact on my family. The two older children had had their names changed before I came down under because the name Wu was odious and embarrassing. Following the fashion of the times, Yiding called himself Li Nong, Li the Peasant, and Yimao called herself Li Zhong, Li the Loyal. When the Lin Biao conspiracy was made public to the students at the junior high, Yimao came home one day and told me, "I must change my name again, Papa." When I asked her if she had thought of a new name, she confided to me, "I have thought it over. The character zhong is made up of two parts. The upper part alone is also pronounced zhong, the lower part is *xin,* the heart. I'll simply drop the heart and use the upper part by itself. What do you say?" I was amused. "Great!" I said. "Now you are Li Zhong the Heartless!" My daughter did not like my little joke and walked away pouting, but she did not change her name again. When our life down under came to an end, she went back to the name I had given her from my cell at the Beijing Detention Center.

4

ANOTHER SCOURGE OF COUNTRY LIFE WAS ILLNESS. SINCE THEY COULD AF-ford neither the time nor the expense, the villagers never went to see a doctor at the commune hospital until an illness grew serious. For an attack of malaria, the sick one would swallow a few quinine tablets and lie down in bed under a heavy cotton-padded quilt to sweat it out. The minute the fever and chills were over, he or she would be back toiling in the fields. When our neighbors discovered Yikai's first-aid kit with patent medicine for common ailments, they would come to her for sulfaguanidine tablets for dysentery or diarrhea, aspirin compound for a headache or a common cold, or Chloromycetin eyedrops for eye infections.

Darkie's ugly bald spot, surrounded by rich black hair, always reminded me that he had contracted favus of the scalp in childhood. Lesser Flood's mother, a garrulous but kindhearted elderly woman, moved about on her filaria-afflicted legs, which the peasants called "rubber legs." When first afflicted many years ago, she knew no better than to apply the folk cure of having little boys piss on her affected legs. By the time it was diagnosed, several years later, a cure was no longer necessary. Though she loved to banter with me, I never had the heart to ask her whether she still suffered. Judging by the way she talked and laughed, you would never believe she had lost ten of her eleven children, by three husbands. Lesser Flood, by her present husband, was the only survivor. It was touching to see her doting on the shy robust young man, but when she needed to have him home from a distance, she would cry at the top of her voice, "Lesser Flood, you cannon-fodder, you who will never live to the age of sixteen, you come home right now, quick . . ." I would tease her, "Lesser Flood's Mom, he is already seventeen. You didn't mean it. It wouldn't work. Who would carry water to our vat if he did not live to sixteen? Who would be there to save me from drowning when I go bathing in the rear pond? Who would play us that tear-jerking tune on his bamboo flute night after night?" She would laugh uproariously and chide me for "making fun of a helpless old poor peasant" and in the same breath offer Lesser Flood to me as an adoptive son.

Granny Sun was a different type. She was busy all day long, tending the cow, cooking for the family, and looking after the two little grandchildren. Her gray hair straggling over her mournful waxen face plowed with wrinkles, she moved about barefooted, rain or shine, summer or winter. As she really had little time to spend with the grandchildren, Little Rabbit, now four years old served as her baby brother's sitter. Yimao used to go over and play with Little Rabbit. One day, when Yimao came home from school for lunch and heard that Little Rabbit was in bed with a fever, she went into their dark central room to see her A minute later, she dashed out and cried in a frightened voice, "Come quick, Granny Sun, Granny Sun! I pushed Little Rabbit, she didn't move!" The grandmother rushed inside and came out a few moments later, holding the dead child in her arms. "My poor, poor Little Rabbit," she cried and wailed till the child's parents ran home across the fields. Jisheng, the father, made a little coffin with thin boards, and the child was buried the same day. They never bothered to find out what the little girl had died of.

We also had our share of illness. Yikai was the first to come down with malaria, and she was also the only member of the family entitled to free medical care. The three children took turns in running high fevers. It was my job to carry Yimao or Yicun on my back to the commune hospital a mile away. When Yiding was too sick to walk, one of the young men would carry him. Though often unable to find out what was wrong with them, the barefoot doctors did everything within their power to bring down their temperature and send them back to school. Once when Yiding was too weak to walk to the latrine, Dr. Lu carried him there on his back.

I suffered periodic attacks of malaria in summer, which threatened to reduce me to a physical wreck once more. One rainy day during my second summer in the village, a high fever developed and I grew delirious. Yikai hurried to the commune hospital and brought back Dr. Lu in the pouring rain. During her absence, our hut had become flooded with rainwater, which came in through the door that could never be closed properly and the roof that had started leaking in the rainy season the year before. I was laid up in my daughter's narrow bed in the only dry corner of the hut. The drenched doctor at once set to work on me and soon improvised an apparatus from which to administer drip injection. The next moment he appeared to help my wife bail out the muddy water with washbasins. An hour after the rain stopped and the muddy water was gone, a couple of cadres from the commune poked their heads in the doorway and hollered, "Lao Li, we are touring the production teams to see what help the xiafang ganbu might need in the rainstorm. Is there anything . . .?" "Thank you for your concern," Yikai said. "You might have helped if you came two hours earlier. But thank you anyway."

But of course we had Dr. Lu. The first time I went to the commune hospital, not long after I came down under, he received me with a politeness to which I had long been a stranger and prescribed some pills for my liver complaint. When he asked for my medical card number, I said I had none. "You mean you don't remember it, Teacher Wu?" I said, "No, I have none. I am not a xiafang ganbu. I am Li Yikai's dependent." He looked incredulous and mumbled to himself, "How is this possible?" He quickly learned about my situation and went out of his way to be nice to us ever after. When we accepted some service or help from him, he would act as if it were we who had done him a favor.

At the age of thirty, Dr. Lu was already a father of four. His peasant wife lived in a nearby village with their three boys and one girl. Born in a peasant family and with two years of schooling, he had learned herbal medicine from a neighbor and picked up rudiments and techniques of Western medicine from his colleagues and medical books and journals. He had to do the job of a general practitioner in both Western and traditional Chinese medicine. It was by no means unusual that he would do two surgeries in the morning and then walk miles in his straw sandals to an outlying village to deliver a child in the afternoon. A lifesaver in the eyes of many peasants, he never forgot his own limitations as a doctor, and constantly strove for self-improvement. On evenings when he did not have an emergency call, against the warnings of his boss, he would drop in on us, bringing with him a basic English reader. He would spend hours under a dim lamp trying, with our help, to fathom the mysteries of the foreign tongue. It was his dream that one day he would be able to read medical papers written in English. It was also his dream that his children would receive more and better education than he did. To make up for his deficiencies in a general education, he read avidly any Chinese classics and modern literary works he could lay his hands on and frequently discussed his readings with us. It was his belief that a doctor needed not only good medical skills, but a good doctor's heart. And reading good literature "helps to nurture a love of man and a love of life." For me, Dr. Lu was greater than the great imperial physicians in the Forbidden City. In him I saw something no tyranny could ever hope to corrupt or subdue. I was almost grateful to the forces that had granted me the opportunity to receive reeducation from this peasant doctor, as well as the good peasants themselves. He brought me back to health, he taught me to reaffirm my faith in life.

Dr. Lu was a friend in need when we had few friends. Our only regular correspondents were my sister and Yikai's family in Tianjin. My sister and her family were sent down under in Gaixian, Liaoning province, after her husband, a senior engineer at the Anshan Steel and Iron Complex, had survived weeks of interrogation and torture by steel-making master workers. All Yikai's three elder brothers in Tianjin were sent down under to the outlying suburban communes after undergoing various atrocities. It was a time when friends and relatives seldom wrote each other, for fear their letters might be seized as counterrevolutionary utterances in the next political campaign. A "cow demon" was naturally incommunicado. Thus I was greatly surprised when, toward the end of 1973, a letter came from Shen Congwen in Beijing, whom I had lost touch with when I became an "untouchable" in 1958. The six sheets of traditional eight-column letter paper were covered with small, closely written Chinese characters in his inimitable *zhangcao,* a cursive hand formerly used in memorials to the throne. A month later, there came another letter on eight sheets of the same paper, in which he urged me not to "give myself up as hopeless" just because I was suffering the double misfortune of poverty and sickness. Moreover, he spoke of his own lifetime experiences, which gave me much food for thought: "I have reached seventy-two this year, yet in doing my work, I am still full of childlike innocence." Still that transparent, candlelit voice! I read the letters word by word, sentence by sentence, to my wife and three children, who were sharing my tribulations. Even the ten-year-old Yicun was touched to tears, and a few years later started reading Shen's books one by one.

5

YEAR IN AND YEAR OUT, LIFE DOWN UNDER SEEMED TO BE ANOTHER GRATUI-tous indefinite term, a repetition of what I had been through before. Aside from the intolerable suspense, daily life was becoming more and more difficult. With incidental expenses and frequent small loans to Penghai, we found it very hard to live on Yikai's fifty-seven yuan a month. We had little money to spend on clothes, so Yikai turned patching holes with colorful bits and ends of materials into an art. Yicun, the youngest, often ran around the village in summertime stark naked. Except for the children's textbooks, we never bought a single book. Lao Penghai was more of a threat to our peace of mind than a drain on our scanty resources. I did not understand until late in the day what he had meant when he'd said upon my arrival, "I can't help you moneywise, but I can help you politically." What with one thing happening after another, it finally dawned on me that he had made it very plain that if I didn't help him moneywise, he could certainly make me pay politically. We overlooked his petty thefts and bad debts, but we could do no more than that, and it was certainly not comfortable to cope with his unscrupulous blackmail.

After the fall of Lin Biao, the political struggle in the national capital reached a new turning point. By 1973, Deng Xiaoping was recalled from exile in Jiangxi province to bring the country out of chaos. Rehabilitation of intellectuals was once again on the agenda. As I did not even have an ID card, I could not travel freely and could not present my case to government offices. So I posted one appeal after another to the university, the provincial authorities in Hefei, and the central authorities in Beijing, seeking rehabilitation and employment. Yikai was on the road again, venturing into one "tiger's lair" after another, repeating her performance of 1961, which had succeeded in bringing me home from Qinghe Farm on the brink of death.

At Anhui University, she was rebuffed by Shen Wenwu, the master worker who ruled the foreign languages department. "If we couldn't even keep one Wu Ningkun out of the department, the Cultural Revolution at Anhui University should be considered a total failure. Furthermore, what do you want to get him a job for? You still have your fifty-seven yuan a month, and that's a lot of money for living in the countryside. What more do you want? Reeducation is what both of you need." She moved on to Beijing and found our old school was no longer in operation. She visited the Ministry of Education and the State Council, only to be told that my case fell under the jurisdiction of the provincial authorities of Anhui.

Back in Hefei again, she tracked down President Zhang Xingyan, now reinstated as the director of the university's Revolutionary Committee (nominal chief administrator under the control of the master workers and army officers of the Propaganda Team) but staying in the hospital at the time. I had written him months before and sent through him an appeal to Yang Xiaochun, a veteran party member who was labeled a rightist in 1957, denounced again in the early years of the Cultural Revolution, but now reinstated as deputy director for culture and education at the Provincial Revolutionary Committee, a new name for the provincial government. President Zhang was delighted to see Yikai and congratulated her on the settlement of my case.

Baffled, Yikai asked, "What are you talking about, President Zhang?"

Rising from his sickbed, Zhang said excitedly, "I saw with my own eyes Director Yang Xiaochun writing down his instructions on Lao Wu's report to him. Lao Wu should be reinstated at Anhui University or given a job at another university as soon as possible. He should also receive a minimum of one hundred yuan a month. I thought it's all settled. I know there is resistance against rehabilitation of intellectuals from the ultraleft, but I didn't know they were so brazen as to ignore Director Yang's instructions. I am outraged. Go and see Director Yang himself or the head of the education bureau and the personnel department of the university."

Yikai went to the Provincial Revolutionary Committee, hoping to call on Director Yang, but the gatekeeper adamantly kept her out, despite hours of arguing and pleading, because she did not have the special pass required for admittance. She moved on to the education bureau and luckily got admitted to the deputy bureau chief in charge, who said Director Yang's instructions had been passed on to Anhui University weeks before. So back to the university again. One personnel man said he had never heard of such a thing, another said he had heard of it but didn't know what happened to it, still another said the man in charge of the case was out of town and no one knew when he would be back. It was the cat-and-mouse stratagem all over again. Apparently the ultraleftists were playing for time, waiting for the next change of the political weather to overturn Yang's decision. Yikai was told to come back two months later. When she did, she was told, yes, the document was found, but it would have to be discussed at the next meeting of the university party committee in December. The upshot of it all was that Major Dai Hong, the army officer who headed the university party committee, had openly defied Yang's instructions because my reinstatement would amount to "an admission of the failure of the Great Cultural Revolution at the university." Through the intercession of Director Yang, I was to be reassigned as a regular teacher to the English faculty of Anhui Teachers University in the port town of Wuhu. Yet, Anhui University being the keeper of my dossier, my transfer papers had to be issued by its personnel department, which took the liberty of setting my wages at seventy yuan a month, as had been the case before the Cultural Revolution, in defiance of Director Yang's explicit instructions.

After many months and three arduous trips to the "tiger's lair" in Hefei, Yikai came home tired and sick, but with the news of our reassignment to Teachers University in Wuhu. The papers for our transfer, however, did not arrive till January 1974, when the radicals reluctantly gave up their obstruction and stalling tactics. For fear of any unpredictable change in the political weather, I lost no time in reporting to duty at my new work unit in Wuhu. Though the roads were treacherous due to a heavy snow, I managed to scramble into a crowded boxcar after crossing the Yangtze on a steam ferry. A urine bucket stood in the middle of the car, bringing back to me the stench of my cell at the Half-Step Bridge detention center in Beijing.

The new party secretary and director of the Revolutionary Committee at the university received me with unaffected warmth. I found him in his office in the middle of an informal meeting. On seeing me enter, he dismissed the meeting and talked with me for an hour. Once deputy to Yang Xiaochun, who had headed the Propaganda Department of the Provincial Party Committee, Wei was denounced as a "right opportunist" in 1959 in the wake of Yang's fall as a rightist. He was reinstated two years later, but denounced again as a "counterrevolutionary revisionist" in the early years of the Cultural Revolution. Now reinstated once more, Wei was all enthusiasm in his new job under Yang's jurisdiction and anxious to revitalize the largest university in the province with a new respect for learning and the learned. He said he had been looking forward to my coming as a shot in the arm for the English faculty.

After making the rounds of the various offices concerned, I went home the next day with 140 yuan in my pocket, which one of the department leaders, against the opposition of another leader, insisted on lending me from the department's funds as advance payment for two months' wages, so that "Teacher Wu can celebrate a happy Spring Festival with his family." Having been deprived of an income for four years, this was an astronomical sum for me. It was the first time in eight years the family was able to enjoy a good Lunar New Year dinner together! Yikai's spirits were not even dampened by the news that once again she would not be given a teaching job as she wanted, because the department chairman, a party functionary, said, "a typist is just what we need, and typing is also revolutionary work."

Unfortunately we had to split up again when the festival was over. The overcrowded university had no housing for the family, but I was scheduled to start teaching when classes began in February. With the special permission of Secretary Wei, I was put up at the nearby Jiujiang Hotel, sharing a small single room with Yiding and Yimao, who went to the high school attached to the university. Yikai and Yicun had to stay behind in Gaozhuang till a place for the family of five could be made available by the housing officer, who had put my name at the bottom of the waiting list.

6

THE CHILDREN WERE HAPPY ABOUT RETURNING TO THE CITY, BUT THE YEARS of their life down under left poignant memories in their mind, as can be seen from my daughter's reminiscences.

SHOES
by Wu Yimao

After six years in the States, I've got used to most things. Still I don't wear high heels, I only wear walking shoes or sneakers. For these feet of mine are not very long, but awfully broad and thick. I could never find high heels to fit them.

"These pig's trotters of yours," Mom used to say, "grew out of walking barefooted all those years."

Now the fact is, I was barely ten when Dad and Mom lost their teaching jobs at the university during the "cleanup" and the family was packed off to the countryside.

Early one morning, I took after the kids of the village and went off with a basket on my back to collect with a long-handled hook the dogs' and pigs' droppings, to be used as fertilizer. Every ten pounds of manure turned in to the production team was worth one work point or a few fen in cash.

"Ha-ha, look at this city girl, collecting manure with shoes on!" Doggie laughed at me.

"She doesn't yet know shoes are hard to make," Sister Ying next door defended me.

From that day on, I stopped wearing shoes. Besides, Mom could no longer afford shoes for her three kids on her small wages and Dad had no income at all.

My feet were toughened by and by. On a hot summer day when I walked on the gravel road, my feet felt neither burning nor pain. On rainy days when I walked on muddy crooked paths, I could stick my toes deep in the mud to keep from falling. When it snowed, I either stayed home all day, or went out dragging my feet in Mom's old rubbers with a big wad of old cotton stuffed in.

Then came the Spring Festival or the Lunar New Year. All the village kids put on new clothes and new shoes.

"I want new clothes, new shoes too, Mom," I pouted, refusing to go on New Year visits to the neighbors with her in my old threadbare cotton-padded jacket.

"Yimao dear, the village people are superstitious, that's why they have to put on new things for the New Year. We don't go in for that sort of thing. It will soon be spring. What do you want shoes for anyway?" So Mom coaxed me into going with her.

When spring itself came, I already knew how to tend cows. And Sister Ying, now fourteen already had her marriage arranged for her and she was learning how to embroider and how to make shoes. Her parents were poor, and her elder brother could not find a girl to marry him. So her father arranged a "marriage exchange" for them—Sister Ying's elder brother was to marry the younger sister of her man.

Dad wouldn't let me learn how to make shoes. It would be better for me, he said, to spend the time reading. So when the cows grazed, Sister Ying and I would sit together on the grass, one reading, the other patching up soles for cloth shoes.

"How could you understand all that?" Sister Ying asked me. There was envy in her voice.

"If you went to school, you would be able to read too." In the one-room school of the production brigade, I was the only girl pupil.

"The folks won't let me. What could I do?" She rubbed the needle on her scalp and then forced it into the thick sole.

One day, Sister Ying said abruptly, "You tell me the stories from your books, and I make you a pair of shoes."

"Really? Really, Sister Ying? I'll tell you stories, I'll sing songs too!" I was on the Mao Zedong Thought Propaganda Team. Every time we went to the riverside to salute the peasants dredging the river, I would take the lead in shouting slogans and then would solo an aria from a model Beijing opera.

All of the *Journey to the West* was told, all the eight model Beijing operas were sung, and my new shoes were also done. Thick, solid white cloth soles, dark blue uppers, and even tiny flowers embroidered on the tip of the shoes. I went mad with joy.

Sister Ying said shoes were only to be worn when you went visiting relatives during the New Year holidays or on other festivals. As it was neither the New Year nor any other festival, I would wash my muddy feet before going to bed and then walk around on the bed once in my new shoes every night. The new shoes would have been spoiled if I had walked about in them on the dirt floor of the hut.

"When are we going to visit our relatives, Mom?" I kept asking.

"Next year, Yimao, next year Mom will take you to Tianjin to see your uncles and aunties and cousins."

"Why don't we go this year?" I wouldn't be put off.

"Tianjin is hundreds of miles away."

"I can go on foot."

"Go, go, go. Go away, stop annoying me." Mom got rid of me.

By the time the shoes became too small for me, we hadn't yet visited our relatives even once. And Sister Ying had married, so there was no one to make shoes for me anymore.

In the years after she got married, Sister Ying gave birth to two girls in a row. When she was lying in for the third time, it happened to be the Lunar New Year again. I heard she had given birth to twin girls, and I hurried to visit her on the third day of the festival.

"Let me see your twin babies, Sister Ying, quick!" I started jabbering the moment I entered her room.

The room was very dark. She was lying in bed. I went closer and saw she was weeping.

"She is confined. Let her rest." Her mother-in-law came in.

"I'm going, Sister Ying." I left a handful of candies posted by my relatives from Tianjin by her pillow and followed her mother-in-law out.

"Why is Sister Ying crying?" I asked the moment we were out in the central room.

"Alas, cruel is her fate!" The mother-in-law's eyes reddened. "She already had two little things which had to be given away, and now two more to be fed. For luck, we didn't do it on New Year's Day, but waited till the second and then my son threw the two 'debt-collectors' into the river."

I don't remember how I left the house. The two poor little girls, at least, flowed away with the river, fresh and clean. Other girls of the same fate were usually held upside down by the father and drowned in a urine bucket the minute they were born.

Not long after that, my family left the countryside when Dad and Mom were rehabilitated, and I never saw Sister Ying again.

Dad and Mom returned to the university, and I went to high school in the neighborhood.

On the first day of school, I was in high spirits and combed out my long pigtails till they were smooth and shiny. Immediately as I reached the classroom door, the head teacher of the class stopped me.

"Good morning, teacher!" I said respectfully, all smiles. There were so many girls in the room and I could hardly wait to join them.

"Where are your shoes?" the teacher asked, without answering my greeting.

"I, I . . ." I stuttered, not knowing what to say. It was not New Year's Day or any other festival, neither was I visiting relatives—why shoes?

"Go home, put on your shoes before you come back to class."

When I finished telling Mom in sobs the reason why the teacher had sent me home, Mom broke into laughter.

"Oh dear, in the hassle of moving, plus living in the country so many years, I'd forgotten all about that. Stop crying, dear, I will take you out and buy a new pair of shoes for you."

On my term report card, in addition to uniform comments such as "able to hold high the Great Red Banner of Mao Zedong Thought," the head teacher wrote these words: "A simple country girl who has learned to wear shoes."

Fifteen

A PRECARIOUS REPRIEVE,
1974-78

1

SEVEN AND A HALF YEARS HAD ELAPSED SINCE I HAD TAUGHT MY LAST LESSON in May 1966. As a result of the educational revolution, the period of schooling was shortened from four to two years. Students were no longer enrolled through a unified national examination, but were selected from among workers, peasants, and soldiers (including high school graduates who had gone down under for two or more years) on the basis of their class origin and political behavior in the Cultural Revolution. The newcomers were known as "worker-peasant-soldier students," as distinguished from "bourgeois college students" of the past. I was assigned by the department's gray-haired vice chairman for teaching, Zhang Jiaotan, to teach a course in intensive reading for the second-year English majors. Half of the class of twenty students were city youths who had taught themselves some English while down under by listening in to "English by radio" programs. The other half came from factories, rural communes, and the army and were mostly interested in getting a college diploma. Zhang told me to select my teaching materials from English translations of Chairman Mao's writings, party documents, party periodicals, or party-approved current fiction. There was not much I could do with the materials as texts, after all the new words and allusions were translated and explained and all the grammatical difficulties cleared away. I would often read the text aloud once or twice to fill up the time. Some of the better students, who enjoyed my reading, would often drop in just to chat, against the warnings of their political instructor. I was amused to think there must be something subversive in my voice, recalling how the young villagers in Gaozhuang liked to hear me read newspaper articles that they did not quite understand.

The only other member of the English faculty who had studied abroad was C. K. Zhang. Trained as a sociologist at an American university, C.K. was a professor of sociology at Shanghai University in 1949 when the Communists took over the city. By 1952, his university, being a missionary institution, ceased to exist and sociology was denounced as a bourgeois pseudoscience. C.K. was reassigned to the university in Wuhu, not as a professor, but as an untitled English teacher earning 66.50 yuan a month. Following the cycles of political campaigns, he had been in and out of prison camps three times for the same unverified charges of conspiracy against the Communist takeover of Shanghai University. A devout Baptist, C.K. never complained, never showed self-pity. His motto was "Life begins at sixty." Once out of prison, he would go on rendering service to his country and giving help to students and colleagues with the same childlike enthusiasm. He taught spoken English, and the students loved him, not only because he spoke perfect American English, but because he cared for them. Typing was not his job, but he was often, too often, found in the typists' room, his fingers flying over the keyboard of an aged standard English typewriter with incredible speed, rhythm, and precision (he also played the piano), to help clear away a backlog or rush out the English translation of an important party document or a *People's Daily* editorial within hours of its publication. His service was never recognized, neither did he ever get a raise, and he never expected anything. He was a living legend in the college community, a walking reproach to those who unscrupulously exploited his talents and his love of the motherland after wrecking his life and academic career. At my very first appearance in the department, he briskly walked up to me and welcomed me with open arms, as if he had found a long-lost brother. Ten years my senior, he always called me his "kid brother." C.K. shared a dilapidated two-room hovel atop Ocher Hill with his wife, a piano professor also trained in America. When we were both free, he would take me home with him, climbing the hill with difficulty. We would chat over a cup of tea and sweets or a meal he cooked himself. He never alluded to the misfortunes that had befallen him. It was touching to hear him eagerly exploring ways and means to improve the students' proficiency of the English language. His first name, Chun Kiang, means Spring River, and he did flow like a spring river through the lives of many during a severe long winter.

The other Zhang was a totally different character. He had graduated from Wuhan University in the 1930s as an English major, though he did not seem to have profited much from the well-known English scholars with whom he had studied. Assiduously watching his steps and guarding his tongue, he was accepted into the party and always towed the party line of the moment, shifting with every change in the political wind. As a party member, he held the vice chairmanship for teaching without doing any teaching himself. He issued me a piece of chalk before I started teaching every morning, as he did all other teachers. He always came to his desk a few minutes before the first bell rang in the morning, and never left before five in the evening. His punctilious observance of the office hours alone earned him the honorary title of "model party member" year after year. Holding the rank of an associate professor, he was the highest-paid man in the department. A resentful worker in the department office remarked one day, "I wonder how much the handling of each piece of chalk by Lao Zhang is costing the country. It's the only thing the professor does for his nearly two hundred yuan a month." That wasn't really quite fair, because the professor had other important political functions to perform. During a recurring political campaign against bourgeois ideology, Spring River was singled out for criticism by a worker-peasant-soldier student for teaching the subjunctive mood and illustrating it with the clause "If I were a king." He was charged with the double offense of "calling a stag a horse" and "harboring a counterrevolutionary dream." The professor and party member threw his weight, as a self-styled grammarian, on the side of the accuser.

2

THE SITUATION OF THE FAMILY LIVING IN TWO SEPARATE PLACES BECAME increasingly untenable with each passing day. The two children and I ate our meals at the college dining hall, but the meal tickets alone cost us more than my monthly income of seventy yuan; and life for Yikai and Yicun still down under was simply intolerable. Lao Penghai had ordered Third Elder to plow up our vegetable plot the day after I left for Wuhu and declared Yikai persona non grata because he could not wait to tear down our hut and make better use of the wood. I kept imploring the housing office for a shelter for my family. In mid-April, I received notice that my housing assignment had been made. I could not wait to see my new home and bring the family together under the same roof. What I saw was a room in a temporary building that was similar to our hut in the village. The room had been the home of a tailoring shop until it moved into a better place. It was seventeen square meters in size and had a dirt floor. I could not figure out how to accommodate my family of five in that room and reported the same to the department leader who had given me an advance when I first reported to duty. She was miffed and sent me back to the housing office to seek a more reasonable deal. Surprised that I didn't know my place, the unsmiling housing officer put my name back at the bottom of the waiting list. By and by, both the political and the finance offices served notice that I would have to pay my snowballing hotel bill if I did not move very soon into the college housing assigned to me. Some of my colleagues were worried, because I could never afford the luxury, and also because the radicals could turn it into a political issue. When Yiding and Yimao went back to the village to spend the summer recess with their mother and Yicun, a Russian instructor from Shanghai named Gu Yongnian invited me to stay with him while his wife and their two children returned to their Shanghai home for the summer. To extricate me from my dilemma, he gave me his bed and slept on a mat on the floor himself. But the hotel bill was not paid until months later when the finance officer was personally reprimanded by Secretary Wei for "violating the party's policy toward intellectuals."

In August I was assigned an "apartment" near campus in a former American Protestant church that the university had taken over and converted into faculty-staff housing. It stood on a terrace at the foot of Phoenix Hill, overlooking a driveway that led into the Iron Hill Hotel, a plush government guest house. With God evicted under proletarian dictatorship, his house was partitioned into six cubicles, each of which was further partitioned into two rooms, so that six homeless families could be housed. The burden of house-moving fell on the shoulders of Yikai and Yiding again. By happy coincidence, Yikai's Third Elder Brother, Shiyu, was visiting with her at the time. An eminent scholar of Chinese history, Shiyu was shocked to find the village so similar to the Neolithic Hillside Village found near the city of Xi'an, and marveled at how we could have survived all those years. But we had grown so attached to the villagers that it was in fact quite hard to tear ourselves away when we waved good-bye to them from the college truck, the family huddled on top of our shabby baggage along with the few remaining hens in a large box. Just as the truck started moving, Jigui the village loony suddenly appeared from nowhere, half-naked and filthy, as usual. He ran after the truck. "Take me with you, Lao Li! I'm your son!" he cried desperately. "Take me with you, Lao Wu!" He was already a distance from us when Yikai and I both shouted at the top of our voices, "Good-bye, Little Jigui, Good-bye! You go home now!" Yikai muttered, half to herself and half to the family, "What will happen to the poor boy now?"

Our new home was smaller than the village hut, but it had a cement floor. We cooked on the same briquet stove, outdoors in good weather, and indoors when it rained or snowed heavily. Instead of a public pond, the seven families shared a water pump that froze in winter. Instead of an open-air private latrine, there was a public privy at the top of the hill, and neither the privy itself nor the rugged path leading to it were lighted at night. Any member of the family who had to make an adventure to the place of necessary evil after dark would be cautioned by the others against "a false step leading to everlasting grief!" Privacy in the apartments was out of the question, for the partitions only went halfway up, leaving a common air space above the six families. Words spoken in normal volume at one end of the church building could be heard distinctly at the other end. (Perhaps the architect was mindful of acoustics, I thought.) When Yiding began to take violin lessons from Professor Lei Yuan of the mathematics department, his practice at home so disturbed our next-door neighbor, another English teacher, named Shen Shiliang, that his wife, an elementary school teacher, often cursed between her teeth "the rotten rightist!" When my gray-haired colleague personally enjoined my eighteen-year-old son not to practice at home anymore whether he was in or not, Yiding first moved outdoors and then gave up altogether, but the staccato cursing went on until they moved into a better place.

The Wu-Li family enjoyed the additional concern of Yikai's fellow typist, Qin Youze, who occupied the vestibule and the belfry of the former church with his wife and their small child. In the relatively relaxed political atmosphere of the time, a couple of former rightists in town as well as a few of my less discreet students dropped in on us occasionally. Once, after seeing a visitor off, Yikai and I walked past Qin with his child in his arms. He asked us, "Who was that man?" I said, "A high school teacher." "Which high school?" he went on. "Number Ten," I said. Finally, he asked point-blank, "What's his name?" I said, "Zhu Huarong." "Oh, that rightist," Qin said knowingly. "He stayed with you quite a while, didn't he?" Zhu used to be a law teacher at the People's University in Beijing before he was labeled a rightist in 1957 and turned into an English teacher here after years of labor reform. It dawned on us why the department leadership was so well posted on our private comings and goings. But we thought it quite understandable, for Qin was trying his best to get accepted into the Chinese Communist party.

The reunion of the family was short-lived. In the spring of 1975, Yiding had to go down under again for reeducation upon graduation from senior high. He was sent to a production team in the county of Dangtu, where he began to work as a full-fledged peasant. Less than a year later, it was Yimao's turn to go down under, to a production team in the county of Jingxian in the mountainous region of south Anhui. Restless with misgivings, Yikai boarded the chartered bus with Yimao in hopes of seeing with her own eyes what the place was like, but was pushed off the bus by the man in charge. Undaunted, the next morning the determined mother slipped in through the back door of a postal van bound for the commune. After being jolted for hours, huddled among the postbags in the closed van, she arrived at the commune half-dead with acute pyelonephritis. She received emergency treatment at the commune hospital, then hitched a ride on a passing tractor to get to Yimao's production team, five miles away, and found Yimao still recovering from car sickness, which had caused her to throw up all the way on the jampacked bus the day before. When Yimao started working in the fields the next day, the sick mother started the five-mile trek to the commune to catch a bus back to work in Wuhu. Mother and daughter alike had shared another lesson in reeducation.

At first we had thought Yiding and Yimao might be spared, since they had just returned from the countryside after more than four years with us "receiving reeducation from the poor and lower-middle peasants." Yet here they were, going down under again on their own. There was nothing we could do about it, nor did we know what the future had in store for them. We could only take comfort in the thought that millions of young people of their age were in the same boat. Now that they were both gone, the two little rooms suddenly looked half-deserted. I started rereading *The Decline and Fall of the Roman Empire* and Yicun was often absorbed in the story of the Golden Monkey or the *Romance of the Three Kingdoms*. Whenever she could find the time and privacy, Yikai would return to her favorite reading, the *Imitation of Christ*.

As a result of the ongoing educational revolution, "open-door schooling" became part of college education. The teachers and students spent several months of the school year off campus, to "integrate themselves with workers, peasants, and soldiers." During the first semester I was sent with my students to the Guanghua ("to glorify China") Glassworks in town to "learn from the workers." My first job was to translate a short history of the factory into English for later use as part of the teaching material. Then I spent several hours a day watching a rotating machine that turned out glass liners of thermos flasks, trying to spot and trash the defective ones. Luckily, I reaped a good harvest of rejects, or I might have been criticized for "failing to accomplish the task."

The next summer I spent several weeks in an army camp outside the county seat of Fanchang, where dumps of military materiel were stored in warehouses scattered in a mountainous area. Except for military drills, from which I was excused in consideration of my age, I joined the students in "learning from the army." We visited a warehouse under the care of a "model warehouseman," who knew exactly where everything was and could put his hand on a particular item in the dark in seconds, in response to the "Great Supreme Commander's" call to "be prepared against war." We sat in on meetings at which the regimental commander read documents of the latest military trials to the rank and file, as part of the education in military discipline and criminal code. It was certainly hair-raising to hear cases like the one in which the regimental commander and the political commissar in a military corps for city youths sent down under in outlying Xinjiang Autonomous Region had been given death sentences for raping one by one, between the two of them, all the teenage girls under their care. Scandals of sexual harassment of city girls sent down under for reeducation were no longer news, but the exploits of the two military criminals certainly taught us a new and unforgettable lesson in reeducation.

I also had occasion to spend several weeks at a commune high school with a graduating class for student teaching. On a stint at a commune senior high in the county of Jingxian, we were first greeted by the commune's deputy party secretary for culture and education, who turned out to be a political science graduate from the university. A tall, outgoing young man, Secretary Qiu was delighted to see us and promised to come down and pay his respects to a veteran teacher from his alma mater. The school was housed in a dilapidated Buddhist temple surrounded by terraced fields planted with tea trees. A horizontal board inscribed with four Chinese characters in faded gold—DA XIONG BAO DIAN, the Grand Sacred Temple—looked down upon a desolate hall, from which the statues of Buddhas and arhats had been swept away as the "four olds," like the Christian God from his church, which had been converted into our refuge in Wuhu.

Secretary Qiu, as good as his word, soon descended on a Saturday. The middle-aged principal and party secretary of the only senior high school in the commune showed his appreciation for my being the occasion of a friendly visit from his supervisor by inviting me to the dinner he gave in honor of his young superior. When Qiu heard I was abstaining from drinking because of a weak liver, he laughed and downed a cup of 120 proof liquor. "My doctor told me the same thing, when I got over my hepatitis recently," he declared. "I do exactly the opposite! Defy the doctors, Teacher Wu!" We all laughed. The other guests included the vice principal, the party secretary of the local production brigade, and his deputy. When dinner was finished and the bottles were empty, the hospitable principal asked the guest of honor whether he would like to climb the mountains or go fishing the next day. The young party secretary said, "To tell you the truth, I have been hankering for a game of mah-jongg, but where can one find a damned set of the 'four olds' these days?" The secretary knew only too well that mah-jongg had been condemned as an evil pastime of the decadent landlords and capitalists and the tiles confiscated or burned as evil gambling devices even before the Red Guards started sweeping away the "four olds." The brigade secretary, however, had a pleasant surprise for his superior: "What a happy coincidence! In the campaign to sweep away the 'four olds,' I confiscated two sets from landlord families. They are still sitting in a corner upstairs at the brigade headquarters. Surely we can pick out enough pieces for one complete set." Secretary Qiu was delighted.

The next morning, after a breakfast of seven poached eggs in a bowl of chicken soup from one of the teachers ("There is no arguing with these people. They would be unhappy if I didn't eat them all," the helpless man complained gently), Qiu invited me to walk over to the brigade headquarters with him. It was housed in a former residence of a landlord, a large two-story wooden structure with huge pillars and a high ceiling, not uncommon in this part of the country. The brigade party secretary took us upstairs, which was largely unoccupied. I followed the two party secretaries to the corner where the mah-jongg tiles were dumped. The three of us squatted around the heap and started matching the pieces together. It did not take us long to make up a complete set of 144 pieces. By the time we marched back to the principal's house with our spoils, Secretary Qiu could no longer wait to start playing. The table was set and the four of us, three party secretaries and a "cow demon," sat down to play game after game until lunch was served. As I had not played the game for at least a quarter of a century, my skills were rather rusty, and I did not win a single game. Luckily, we were not playing for money. Once wining and dining was over, we went back to the table again and played till dinner was served by another family. Elated with his success in mah-jongg, the young party secretary continued to defy his doctor by challenging the two other secretaries to one toast of *gan bei*, "bottoms up," after another. He had wanted to continue the game after dinner, but reluctantly gave up the idea when he found he could hardly walk straight. At the end of the day I had the feeling that the Cultural Revolution had nearly run its course. "Things will develop in the opposite direction when they become extreme," even as the "Great Teacher" was fond of repeating.

3

ON THE WHOLE, OUR MOVE TO WUHU MARKED A TURN FOR THE BETTER IN our life. True, Yiding and Yimao had been torn away from us for an indefinite period of time. Yikai had to leave the family on the eve of our first Lunar New Year in our new home and rush to the deathbed of her dear First Elder Sister in Tianjin. Political discrimination against me was still a fact of life, but I was no longer subjected to meetings of criticism or struggle. The university even built a kitchen with running water and a sink at the rear end of our church home. We were contented with so little, yet our easy contentment was soon threatened again by a new change in the political weather.

When the popular Premier Zhou Enlai died in January 1976, the radicals led by Mao's wife, who rejoiced in the removal of a thorn in their flesh, enforced tight restrictions on memorial activities for the departed national leader. Three months later, on April 5, a traditional remembrance day, what began as spontaneous mourning for the departed premier at Tiananmen Square turned into a mammoth demonstration against the radicals entrenched in the Forbidden City. The crackdown on the demonstration precipitated the third fall from power of Deng Xiaoping, who had been handpicked by Zhou to succeed him. In the wake of Deng's dismissal, Mao's wife and her gang mounted a new offensive against the veteran Communist leaders who had been reinstated during Deng's return to power. The nation was plunged into a new campaign to criticize Deng and the "right deviationist trend to reverse correct verdicts." In the provincial capital, Yang Xiaochun and his followers bore the brunt of the attack. At Anhui University, President Zhang Xingyan and five reinstated department party secretaries were accused of staging a capitalist-revisionist comeback. By the time the new school year began in September, a new work team of model coal miners, officially honored as "ten red banners," had been dispatched by the army leaders in control of the provincial power to lead the new campaign at the Teachers University. As luck would have it, the campaign had to be suspended shortly after its ominous opening salvos, when the nation went into mourning over the death of Mao Zedong.

One September afternoon, I again indulged in my favorite pastime of reading pages from the *Decline and Fall* in our little cubicle, which was made possible by the tedious but otherwise undemanding teaching work. The parallels between ancient Rome and modern China were often very startling. That afternoon I was absorbed in Gibbon's inimitable portrayal of Empress Theodora, who had married the emperor after seducing him and then reigned with terror for twenty-two years. As I came to the end of the chapter, where the historian deplored the irony that "her husband, who, in the room of a theatrical prostitute, might have selected the purest and most

noble virgin of the East," I exclaimed to myself, "What a historical prece-
dent for the Red Empress reigning in the Forbidden City!" Just then, an
announcement from the Central Broadcasting Station came over the loudspeaker outside, saying there would be a release of important news at four
P.M. The announcement was repeated in a subdued voice every few minutes, with funeral music in the background. "This is most unusual," I said
to myself. "Oh, oh, the old man has kicked off! That must be it." At four
sharp, the death of Mao made world news. It was September 9, 1976.

A week of national mourning was proclaimed. The papers were filled
with encomiums for the dead, and everyone sported a black armband. All
recreational activities were banned. A former landlord in town who was
accused of celebrating the event at home with a good dinner and wine was
summarily given a three-year sentence. A clerk in our department had to
make a public self-criticism when he was caught playing a game of Chinese
chess with his son at home. Like everybody else I wore a black armband and
attended sundry memorial activities. Like everybody else too, I wondered
"What now?"

As if racing against time, Mao's widow and her gang renewed the
assault on Deng and the other reinstated veteran leaders as soon as the
national mourning was over. Following closely upon the heels of the
memorial rally, the "model coal miners" of the special work team called
another rally of the student body, the faculty, and the staff of both the
university and the attached high school, numbering some three thousand,
to "criticize and repudiate the right deviationist trend to overturn correct
verdicts." I was fed up with meetings and campaigns, all the more so
because I felt I had absolutely nothing to do with it this time. Yet I had to
sit through the asininities of one more campaign and one more rally. So I
sat as far back as possible, a few feet away from the last row, chatting with
a colleague to while away the time. The speaker, Xu Yan, was a young
woman, a worker-peasant-soldier student recently graduated from Anhui
University. Radical and politically active, she was catapulted into the position of deputy secretary of the Anhui University party committee. She was
sent on a tour of the universities and colleges in the province to give
impetus to the campaign by exposing the right deviationist crimes of Zhang
Xingyan and his cohorts, the five reinstated department party secretaries. I
caught what she was saying off and on. "I wish it were over," I said to my

colleague. "I can hardly wait to go back to my Gibbon." Instead of answering me, he pricked up his ears and said, "Listen, she just mentioned your name." My name? No mistake. I could hear her saying what happened at her university was by no means an isolated incident. An incontrovertible evidence was the case of Wu Ningkun, "a reactionary professor driven out of Anhui University" but reinstated at the Teachers University through the collusion of Yang Xiaochun and Wei Xinyi. "Oh, oh, here we go again!" I said to myself. Then I heard her asking Secretary Wei seated next to her, "How farther right could you go, Wei Xinyi?" Wei responded by saying, "Comrade Song Peizhang, secretary of the Provincial Party Committee, recently remarked at a meeting in Hefei, 'You have always been a rightist.' The 'you' referred to me. I have undoubtedly made many mistakes in my work at the university. I welcome criticism from the students and the faculty and staff." I thought his response was remarkably decorous, worthy of a seasoned veteran inured to false accusations.

On my way home after the rally, I heard people asking from time to time, "Who is Wu Ningkun?" Occasionally, I was pointed out by someone who recognized me, "There, there goes Wu Ningkun!" When I got home, Yikai had already arrived. She asked me with an amused smile, "How do you feel about it, reactionary professor?" I was glad it did not hit her too hard. I said, "Just like a bad penny!" She said, "A bad penny may be a collector's item, you know." We both laughed. There was nothing we could do about it anyway, so why not laugh? We had been sitting very small, but it made no difference. Perhaps political campaigns were bad pennies that kept turning up, even as the dead man had prophesied.

I had no idea how the new campaign would be conducted, or what would happen to me and my family now. Back to the cow shed or another labor camp? No use worrying. I went to work in the morning as usual and first sounded out the party member in charge of my teaching group, a very affable young man of the class of '69, about whether I was to go on teaching. "Of course, Teacher Wu, why not?" he said with a disarming smile. I found the students attentive as usual At the political study session in the afternoon, most of my students made the stereotyped speech that they were ready to take an active part in the current campaign and raise their political consciousness through class struggle, without any reference to me or leaders of the university under fire. There were a few big-character posters plastered on the wall in the hall, but only the one put up by Professor Zhang Jiaotan contained a reference to me and C.K. He accused Secretary Wei of promoting bourgeois restoration by commending the two "reactionary teachers" for taking an active part in "open-door schooling." One colleague who was reading the poster next to me remarked, "Lao Zhang fishing for political benefits again!" Some colleagues began to shun me. In the typists' room, Qin Youze stopped talking to Yikai. When I passed him standing outside his door, he would just glare at me, reeking of "class hatred."

Yikai and I felt somewhat relieved that at least Yiding and Yimao were spared the anguish of sharing their father's new round of persecution. Yicun was in junior high at the No. 1 High School. He usually cut across campus on his way to school. Now, with big-character posters mounted around the university administration building, he would sometimes stop and scan them on his way home. One day, he came home with an impish grin on his face. "Papa, are you a black cat or a white cat?" I was baffled. "What do you mean, Yicun?" He went on, "One poster put up by the finance officer, Wu the Blind, says Deng Xiaoping is notorious for declaring 'Black cat or white cat, a mouse-catcher is a good cat,' and Wei Xinyi was following this capitalist line of Deng's when he invited you to teach here and forced the finance office to pay your hotel bill. Well, what are you, black or white?" We both laughed. I was glad to see the boy wasn't overworried. Just as the campaign was building to a climax, Yimao suddenly came home from her village for a visit. Of course we were overjoyed to see her, but we also told her it was not exactly good timing. "Oh, nonsense! I knew all about it already. Xu Yan has been touring the colleges in the south, denouncing Papa in all her talks. Congratulations, Papa, you're now the number-one reactionary professor in the whole province of Anhui, more famous than anybody I know!" Her best high school friend, Wang Weiyu, the daughter of a physical education teacher at the university, soon came to see her. Weiyu was an athletic tomboy, very open and childlike. "I've missed you so much all these months, Yimao," she said. "But my father says I mustn't be friends with you anymore because your father is under criticism." Yimao said, "I don't care. It's up to you, Weiyu." I put in, "Little Weiyu, your father may be right. Why don't you go home then?" Weiyu shot back at me in her loud voice, "I will not, Uncle Wu! Unless you throw me out." We all laughed.

The mood of the university and the country was perceptibly different from that of the earlier years of the Cultural Revolution. Most people were simply fed up with the endless political upheavals and the increasing hardships of life. In spite of the sound and fury of the "model coal miners," very few students or faculty members responded with any enthusiasm for the current campaign. Many middle-aged party members were cynical and openly critical of the new assault on veteran cadres. The talk of the town was about the slogans that appeared on a college wall, supporting Deng Xiaoping and denouncing Mao's widow as a "demon." A sense of imminent change was in the air and an attitude of wait-and-see was on every face. Then, less than a month after Mao's death, his widow and her radical cohorts, now known as the Gang of Four, were arrested and thrown from power, bringing the ten-year-long Great Proletarian Cultural Revolution to an end. The new leadership openly denounced it as "an unprecedented great catastrophe," the gravest mistake in the political career of Mao Zedong, who remained nevertheless a great Marxist, as well as in the annals of the Communist party of China, which remained nevertheless "great, glorious, and correct."

The "model coal mine workers" refused to clear out in the face of a growing opposition from the university community. When the students openly suggested a send-off party for them, the workers called a rally and threatened to spend the winter on campus. "We have brought our heavy cotton-padded coats. We will see the campaign carried out to a successful conclusion," declared their leader. Before winter came, however, they quietly packed up and went back to the mines, without a farewell party.

4

MY FIRST FRINGE BENEFIT FROM THE DOWNFALL OF THE GANG OF FOUR CAME in the form of unexpected medical care. One morning in November, in the middle of a class I was teaching, a vice chairwoman of the department sent for me. I was taken by complete surprise when she said, "Teacher Wu, we just had a call from the Municipal Schistosomiasis Institute saying you must report to the district hospital at once for treatment of the disease. The result of your tests two years ago was positive. But when the Gang of Four said 'Forget about the little worm, grasp the big problems of class struggle,' prevention and cure of the disease was interrupted. Now, as an elderly intellectual, you are given priority to receive immediate treatment. Go home now with your wife and get ready for the hospital." I hardly knew what to think. Large areas of the province were known to be infested with the worm, but I had shown no symptoms of the disease, which killed millions a year. To make sure there was no mix-up, I first went to the institute for verification. I was shown two positives out of my three tests on record. I inquired about getting new tests, but the lab technician on duty curtly said it was uncalled-for and insinuated that I was not showing proper appreciation of the party's concern for intellectuals. So I reported to the district hospital and was assigned to a large ward with a dozen other inmates admitted for the same reason. The treatment, which consisted mainly of drip injection of antimony, a toxic and dangerous substance, took a little more than a month. Groups of patients were treated at three different district hospitals in town at the same time. We overheard reports of fatalities at the two other hospitals. Luckily we all survived, though death was often very near. A couch outside our ward was often used as a temporary station before the body was removed to the mortuary, so that we were occasionally startled from our sleep in the dead of night by laments for the dead. At the time of discharge, the physician on duty warned us, "You are carrying plenty of toxic stuff in your blood. In the next month or so, be sure not to trip or fall, because bleeding will cause instant death." With the stern warning ringing in my ears, I moved about with great care, and never ventured out of our cubicle onto the snow- and ice-covered ground.

A few days after my return, Yikai came home at noon in the midst of a heavy snow. She found that the briquet stove had gone out and the two thermos bottles were empty. With a thermos bottle in each hand, she went out into the snow again to fetch water from the campus boiler. She was gone longer than usual, which I assumed was because of the weather. But when she did come back, I was shocked to see that her face and coat were smeared with mud and that she was cradling her left arm with her right hand. The girl student who saw her home was carrying the two thermoses, empty and corkless. It turned out that Yikai had slipped on the icy road on her way back with the filled thermoses. Now her arm was in terrible pain and someone had to escort her to a hospital. By sheer coincidence, a young friend of ours arrived from out of town at this very moment. Out into the snow Yikai ventured again, with the godsend of a young man as her escort. At the No. 2 Hospital she had to scramble from one department to another with a broken arm, in excruciating pain, until the comminuted fracture of the elbow was at last fixed. The snowstorm was still raging when she finally returned late in the afternoon with her left arm in plaster splints. With both parents disabled, Yicun, now thirteen, took up the duties of the man of the house until his big brother and sister came home for the Lunar New Year holidays. Unable to continue working as a typist, Yikai started teaching English again in February. Two years later I underwent a thorough physical examination at the No. 86 Army Hospital in the nearby county seat of Dangtu. When the examining physician heard I had received treatment for schistosomiasis, he examined me with a proctoscope and found no evidence that I had ever had the dread disease.

"Luckily you escaped death by antimony!" concluded the army doctor.

"But I saw the positive results recorded in my case history, two out of three," I said.

"I know, I know," said the doctor with an understanding smile. "But what if the lab technicians neglected to clean the used tubes or failed to clean them thoroughly, as they often did?"

"Survival is surely an endless adventure in this land, doctor," I sighed.

"The battlefield is not the only place where one may be killed by friendly fire," returned the doctor.

The new leadership's call to "set to right things which have been thrown into disorder" took effect slowly, against the last-ditch resistance of the radicals. The system of enrolling college students through a national unified examination was reactivated in the summer of 1977, and millions of high school graduates took part in the first such examinations since 1965. Both Yiding and Yimao studied for the examination in five subjects in secret, because the production teams did not wish to lose educated youths. When they returned to their respective villages from the examination at the county seat, both had to make a self-criticism for being "bourgeois college fiends." Yimao was accepted as an English major at Teachers University. Yiding made excellent scores in all subjects, and his scores in English were among the highest. Yet none of the best English departments of the country would take him, because his father was an ultrarightist. Even Anhui University would not have him, because "it would have meant the reincarnation of Wu Ningkun." With tears in his eyes, the ruddy young man took the train to the city of Fuyang in northern Anhui, a region popularly known as "Anhui's Siberia," and enrolled in the Teachers College, which had been newly upgraded from a junior college to accommodate the sudden influx of college students.

As the country began to open up to the outside world, my contact with relatives and friends abroad was also renewed by and by. When the first letter came from my elder sister in Hong Kong, our children were incredulous and excited, because we had kept them in the dark about our overseas relations since the government had abhorred any contact with the outside world. In addition to a new aunt, they soon discovered a new uncle in my elder brother living in New Jersey. In September 1977, a niece of mine, Wang Yu, and her husband, Hsia Peijan, who was a translator at the United Nations, arrived in Beijing from New York for a home visit. I had thought they would naturally visit us in Wuhu. But they telephoned to say that their program person had told them Wuhu was not an "open" city. "You were told a lie," I said. "Dr. C. N. Yang, the Nobel physicist, a contemporary of mine at the University of Chicago, was here recently. He stayed at the Iron Hill Hotel just a few hundred feet away from where I live. I often had the pleasure of watching his motorcade pass by."

Thus my niece was able to meet her uncle after all, for the first time, in her mid-thirties, years after her mother, my sister, had passed away. When the university learned of her projected visit, the housing office got busy moving me out of the church building so that my overseas relatives would not get the wrong impression of how senior intellectuals were treated in Communist China. The party hacks, who still looked upon ex-rightists as the "stinking ninth category" at its worst, reluctantly gave me a two-room apartment in a college residential building. I was not to move in till the evening when my relatives' arrival the next day was confirmed and the former occupants began to move out. Actually, we were not able to move in till the next day, because we had to clear out the rubbish and clean the floor and the windows first. The walls looked terrible, with plaster peeling off here and there, and the kitchen walls were smeared black with soot. In the morning, to cope with the political task of emergency cosmetics, the housing office sent over a young temporary worker with a broom and a pail of limewash to give the walls a quick going over. Yiding, home from his village by coincidence, moved over our large pieces of furniture on a flatbed cart, leaving behind the sundry junk for another day. Master Worker Xia of the department came and handed me thirty yuan, which Secretary Wei had approved as a raise in my monthly pay, to make up for what the radicals at Anhui University had struck off at the time of my reassignment. The young master worker, an obliging newly demobilized soldier, also went to the Iron Hill Hotel to buy, for the entertainment of my guests, two cartons of the deluxe Da Zhonghua ("Great China") cigarettes and two bottles of brand liquor, neither of which were available in the market. As it turned out, my relatives neither smoked nor drank, and the goodies went to the people who had helped with the reception.

My niece, her husband, and their four-year-old boy arrived by train from Shanghai in midafternoon, but we could not have them come from the new Wuhu Hotel to our new home for dinner until the electrician had put in new wires to replace the ones that the former occupant had ripped out. It was a sweltering late-September evening. We had to borrow C.K.'s electric fan to prevent our guests from fainting from the heat. A local relative of mine prepared a dinner of a dozen dishes, which gave a semblance of affluence. Our relatives from America found our rooms clean and comfortable, not knowing we had moved in just a few hours before, with most of our junk left behind in the church. I was dressed in a new white Dacron sports shirt. It was the fashion of the times, and the first one I had bought, just for the occasion. Being the only decent-looking shirt I had, it had to be washed before I went to bed so that I could wear it in the morning. But it was drenched in sweat before lunch and had to be washed again before I could wear it, not quite dry, to the banquet the vice president of the university threw in honor of my relatives from America, who had been among my political liabilities for many years. Though they knew of the political campaigns that had plagued the nation over the decades, my relatives were enthusiastic about the new developments in socialist China and thought their old Uncle Wu was overcritical of the status quo. I found them equally enthusiastic when I saw them again in Shanghai two years later. After all, I said to myself, "seeking truth from facts" about China from an outsider's perspective would be a formidable process, but these young people, with an untainted love for their motherland, would learn, in their own good time.

Sixteen

REHABILITATION
TWENTY-TWO YEARS
AFTER, 1979-80

1

WITH DENG XIAOPING AND HUNDREDS OF THOUSANDS OF OTHER CADRES AT different levels of the party, the government, and the army leadership reinstated, the rehabilitation of the half a million rightists of 1957 loomed large on the party's political agenda, which called for national unity and stability. Deng, who had directed the antirightist campaign, now endorsed "correcting the verdict" passed on most of the former rightists, yet still maintained that the campaign itself was correct and necessary because there were genuine rightists seeking to overthrow the Communist rule. To catch half a dozen "genuine rightists," the great, glorious, and correct party had not scrupled to net half a million innocent intellectuals and their families for a devastating ordeal of twenty-two years. To show that the former rightists were not altogether blameless in getting condemned as such, the ruling party now refused to compensate the victims for their financial losses due to punitive cuts in their wages.

The rehabilitation of rightists was decreed in a Central Committee document in October 1978, and cases were to be reviewed by the work units where the rightists had been labeled as such in 1957–58. Within the first few months following the issuance of Document No. 55, Teachers University alone handled more than 240 cases, an amazing figure for a small provincial college! One former teacher, a man in his late forties, returned for rehabilitation from the village to which he had been banished. As he exited the administration building after receiving his rehabilitation papers, the man dashed his head against the wall. When people rushed over to take the bleeding man to the college clinic, he said, "They ruined my life for nothing, and now expect me to be grateful to them for their pretended benevolence? No way! My blood is on their hands, on their hypocritical facade! I don't want these damned papers, but I have to clear my family of guilt by association, or the curse would be on them for ever and ever."

Though not ready to shed my blood in protest, the fellow rightist's defiant outcry certainly threw a new light on the rehabilitation I was so much looking forward to. My call did not come until early May, when I returned to Beijing for the "correction of my verdict." Ever since Deng's return to power, I had rejoiced in his call for "emancipation of the mind" from old taboos and manacles, which once again promised freedom of expression for the intelligentsia. Once back in the capital city, however, my spirits were dampened by his recent avowal of continued adherence to Marxism-Leninism—Mao Zedong Thought, the leadership of the Chinese Communist party, socialism, and the proletarian dictatorship, which came to be known as the "four cardinal principles" underlying the rule of China.

I presented myself at the former party school, now known as the Institute of International Relations, on a new campus on the other side of the road from the complex of buildings that housed the headquarters of the CID, the Central Investigation Department. I found myself sitting face-to-face with the director of rehabilitation, who turned out to be no other than the very party hack who had played an active role in the antirightist campaign at the school. Even more insolent than I remembered him, Geng told me mine was a marginal case. My offenses were grave, but in consideration of my progress in thought reform over the years, the party had decided to be lenient with me and have my verdict corrected. Begrudging charity, eh? I had been warned by my friends at the university not to expect too much, because resistance on the part of the radicals still ran strong. "Never mind what they say in the conclusion, sign it so long as it gives you rehabilitation." So I glanced over the paper and signed it, as I had signed the so-called conclusion of my case handed to me by the same man in 1958. Then I was called into the president's office. Wang Jun, a vice minister and concurrently president and party secretary of the Institute, was all affability. "We are sorry for all that you've been through these years," he said airily, as if all my trials and tribulations had thus been compensated for by his one word of official apology. I was invited to return and teach graduate students of English at the Institute. Yikai and Yicun could come with me, but Yiding and Yimao would have to wait till they graduated from college two and a half years later.

While in Beijing, I read in the papers that Dr. T. D. Lee was in town again on a lecture tour in his motherland. Recalling how he had seen me off before my homebound ocean liner set sail in 1951 and how a Christmas card from the Nobel Prize winner in 1974 had raised eyebrows in Wuhu, I thought it might be interesting to see him now when our paths crossed again, twenty-eight years later. Through a "back door," I found his phone number at Beijing Hotel, which was the state guest house at the time and called him. I was flattered that he still remembered me. He suggested a meeting over the weekend, but I was leaving town the same afternoon. He was busy preparing his lectures, so we settled for a fifteen-minute chat in his hotel suite. Six years my junior, T.D. had been the youngest in our group of Chinese graduate students at the University of Chicago in the late 1940s; we used to call him Kid Brother.

Now in his early fifties, the Nobel Prize winner still looked young, with a baby face and smooth skin, though visibly balding. We faced each other in two big armchairs across a tea table. As I briefly answered his questions (I did not want to outstay my welcome) about what I was in Beijing for and what I and some of our mutual friends had been through over the years, he showed no signs of strong interest or emotion. Dignified and self-assured, he looked the eminent scientist and scholar par excellence. I quickly sensed we were living in two different worlds, across an unbridgeable gap. Staying behind in America, he was able to reap successes and honors and live a happy life in security and affluence. Returning to China, I struggled through trials and tribulations and barely made it to this day of rehabilitation. Secure in the "imperialist fortress of America," he was hailed as a patriot in Communist China, feted by every top leader of the party and the government, and whisked about in a chauffeur-driven Red Flag limousine as an honored guest of the state. Recalled to serve the motherland, I was denounced as an enemy of the people and had survived labor camps, starvation, and proletarian dictatorship. Even while we were chatting, my ribs ached from the jabs they had received from robust young men of the generation of Red Terror, who had ruthlessly elbowed their way onto the bus to the hotel. An amusing thought flashed through my mind: what would have happened if I had been the one to see him off back to China on that July afternoon in San Francisco? Would I perhaps be sitting in his armchair and he in mine? Oh, no, I decided right there and then, I would never have exchanged my bitter cup of lifetime reeducation for the salutatory toasts from the masters of proletarian dictatorship. No, I would not sit in his armchair and, God forbid he should ever have been in my accursed shoes. When I was ready to say good-bye, his wife went into their bedroom and came out with a paperback edition of James Thurber's *Fables for Our Time* and handed it to her husband, who inscribed it to me. T.D.'s interest in literature and fables at that was something new to me, and I was glad for it. Once when we had chatted deep into the night at the International House in Chicago, before he took his Ph.D. and went to work in San Francisco, I recalled, I had been dismayed to hear him call the Chinese classic *Dream of Red Mansions* "unscientific," because the hero of the novel was born with a "precious jade" in his mouth. I might have taken after Hamlet and said to him, "There are more things in heaven and earth, Horatio, / Than are dreamt of in your philosophy." Now if someday he were to read my life story, hopefully he might not say, "This can't be true. Ningkun must have made it all up as a fable of patriotism for our time."

I had to visit the Institute a second time, six months later, before orders could be issued for my recall to Beijing. While at the school, I was notified that a deputy minister of the CID, Xiong Xianghui, wanted to invite me to an Old Vic performance of *Hamlet*. How I would love to watch my favorite Shakespearean tragedy, an integral part of my life in the labor camps, performed by a prestigious London company! But in no mood to accept a small favor as part of my rehabilitation, I sent my apologies by the messenger. A few hours later, another deputy minister, Chen Zhongjin, who had replaced Wang Jun as president and party secretary of the Institute, sent for me and made it clear I simply must accept the invitation. I was politely cornered, and my recall was yet to be formalized. So to Elsinore I went, riding to the Capital Theater downtown with the deputy minister in a CID Red Flag limousine, nearly twenty-two years after I had been delivered to the detention center at Half-Step Bridge in a CID jeep, later to be shipped off to the prison farm in the Great Northern Wilderness with a copy of *Hamlet* in my old laundry bag, an ultrarightist condemned by the same CID.

2

HOUSE-MOVING AGAIN! THE TIMES HAD CHANGED, AND MANY HANDS helped this time. We were only sorry that Yiding and Yimao, who had been exiled with us all these years, had to be left behind. Leaving Wuhu on the last day of February, the three of us were seen off at the train station by a number of colleagues, including heads of the department, as well as Yiding and Yimao. Before parting, Yimao asked for a book as a memento. I could think of nothing more fitting than the copy of the *Selected Poems of Du Fu* from which I had found a name for her, now dog-eared and rat-gnawed. Darkie came to Wuhu for the leave-taking, bringing with him his elder brother's son, now in his early teens. He insisted on accompanying us all the way to Nanjing, where we had to spend two nights to get tickets on the express train to Beijing. It was their first visit to the historic metropolis, so I took them to as many famous sites and scenic spots as we could manage in one day. I also took the opportunity to call on a former teacher who had taught me Chinese history in junior high and classical Chinese in senior high, bringing with me Yikai and Yicun. Yang Dazhi was now a well-known professor of classical Chinese at the local Teachers University. It was our first reunion since I'd said good-bye to him in 1939 upon my graduation from the wartime National Second High School in Sichuan province. In his late seventies, Professor Yang did not have a single gray hair and could still read without glasses. His wife, about the same age and in equally good health, cooked a meal for us. When he heard a brief sketch of what had happened to me over the years, my septuagenarian teacher of generations of teachers cried like a child. Upon my arrival in Beijing, I found a ci-poem by the Song dynasty poet Chen Yuyi in the mail, written in my teacher's inimitable xiaozhuan (an ancient style of calligraphy adopted in the Qin dynasty) on a sheet of xuan paper (a high-quality paper made in the city of Xuancheng, Anhui province), which read as follows:

> *I remember in former times on the Wu Bridge drinking*
> *With companions mostly young and outstanding*
> *Silently the moon gliding down the long brook*

In the tenuous shadows of apricot blossoms
The bamboo flute till daybreak playing

The twenty-some years were like a dream
Though still alive I feel like starting
Leisurely going up the little pavilion to see the sky clearing
I hear so many things of the past and the present
In the fishermen's songs at the third watch rising

In a note accompanying the precious gift, my teacher wrote, "Your twenty-some years were an endless nightmare, Ningkun. It's an outrage, an absolute outrage, even if you had not been my favorite student. I am so happy that you have survived it all and will now do what you have to do." I had the piece of my teacher's calligraphy mounted and the scroll has since then hung on the wall in my little study at home, as a reminder of the nightmarish "twenty-some years," and "so many things of the past and the present."

This was Yicun's first visit to Beijing. I made a point of taking him through Tiananmen Square when we first arrived on March 2. The boy showed interest neither in the huge portrait of Chairman Mao looking down on us over the Gate of Heavenly Peace at one end nor the new mausoleum with his corpse at the other. "I bet it will be great fun flying kites on the huge square on a sunny spring day," was his only comment.

We were assigned a two-room apartment on the top floor of a four-story gray brick building on campus. The compound used to be the home of Li Lianying, chief eunuch under the Empress Dowager Cixi, who ruled China some fifty years, till Henry Puyi became the last emperor. The short driveway led to a straight-faced four-story red brick classroom building, from the roof of which, I was told on the day of our arrival, a girl student, gone berserk under denunciation and interrogation, had jumped to her death during the Cultural Revolution. Behind this main building were two rows of identical three-story gray brick buildings, which looked more like barracks for the military than dormitories for students and families of the faculty and staff. A couple of one-story brick buildings in classical style, left over from the chief eunuch's days, broke the monotony of a drab campus with no trees, no flowers, no grass. The ghost of castration seemed to be lurking on the campus, still enveloped in an air of secrecy, though it was no longer part of the physical body of the CID.

Some former colleagues dropped in to greet us. Xu Zhiwen, a professor of French and one of my former drinking companions, barged in and burst out in his Cantonese Mandarin, "Lao Wu, I come to apologize to you for the awful things I said against you at the criticism and struggle meetings." I was surprised that he of all people should have had anything on his conscience.

"Lao Xu, you don't rate," I said, clasping his hand in mine. "I never remembered anything you said, I never associated you with my denunciation. Everybody had to speak up, and you were no exception. I don't hold anything against any individual, least of all you. Perhaps we were all actors in a tragedy of the times. Everyone had to play his part. In any case, I survived."

Always loud-voiced, the gray-haired and gray-mustached septuagenarian now fairly shouted at me, "I don't care whether you held it against me or not. I held it against myself. It was base of me to have joined the chorus and said untruthful things against you. I did worse things by my own brother Xu Zhongjie. He was also labeled a rightist in Tianjin and I severed relations with him until his verdict was recently corrected. How low can a man stoop to save his own skin!"

"Please don't feel too bad about it, Lao Xu." I was really touched to see him take it to heart. "After all, it was not your fault. Where is your brother now?" It turned out his brother was living in the same building as we did. With a degree in English from an American university in the 1920s, he had taught English at a local university before he was expelled as a rightist. Moving from the university housing to a dank basement room, he went on working on English translations of classical Chinese poetry until the Institute invited him to teach graduate students of English following his political rehabilitation.

A younger English instructor, Liao Kechang, who had been assigned to the English faculty at Nankai upon graduation from Beijing University in 1954 and subsequently reassigned to the Institute in 1956, also came to make an apology for his part in my denunciation.

"I was your jinx at Nankai University. I was in charge of your case during the antirightist campaign. Did you know that, Professor Wu?" He sounded as if his offenses had been really heinous.

"Kechang, I never numbered you among my persecutors," I reassured him. "You were a recent college graduate. Like many other young people, you were pursuing 'progress' and did whatever the party ordered you to do. You didn't know any better. That's about all there is to it."

"Not quite," he went on in a heavy voice. "There is something in what you said. But I went out of my way to be nasty and mean, because I had ulterior motives. I was trying hard to win the party's favor and personal gains."

"You are too harsh on yourself, Kechang. But it didn't really make any difference one way or another, did it?" I said.

"Perhaps not. But it weighs heavy on my conscience. I beg your forgiveness with all my heart."

I reassured him again that I had never held any grudge against him and that we should be good colleagues from then on.

Another former colleague who did not show any sense of personal guilt asked me airily, "Was it really very bad, Lao Wu?"

"Well, I survived," I answered vaguely.

"You sure did. Damn it, you still look so young."

"Defiantly young!" I laughed a little. "Some of the people here had expected to see me nursing a diseased heart or walking on a crutch. They were disappointed. Thanks to Chairman Mao, I have been tempered in the great storms of class struggle. It has been only a matter of twenty years, and I'll give them twenty more years to break me."

"Listen to him! You haven't changed a bit. You haven't learned your lesson. I fear for you, Lao Wu."

"Just a minute," I retorted. "Who is to learn a lesson? Me or the party who was in the wrong?"

A few days later, the president of the Institute also dropped in. A 1930s graduate of Beijing University, he had later spent two years studying economics at Columbia University. I found him affable and easy to talk to. And there were things on my mind that I needed to get across to him.

"We have been settling in pretty well and meeting some of our former colleagues," I said in answer to his solicitous question about our well-being in the new environment. "Some of the comrades came to apologize for what they did in 1957 and 1958, which I thought was uncalled-for. But one comrade thought I had not learned my lesson . . ."

"Who said that?"

"Never mind who. I haven't learned to give names yet. But who was to learn a lesson anyway, me or the party?"

"It was the party that committed the ultraleftist mistake in 1957. It is the party that has been learning lessons from the serious mistakes it made over the years. There is no question of learning a lesson from the past for intellectuals like you, but the necessity of emancipating the mind and looking forward," said he.

"But I have my misgivings," I said. "My rehabilitation itself seems ambiguous or partial at best. My conclusion did not read like the correction of a wrong verdict, but the handout of a lenient treatment."

"What do you mean, Professor Wu?"

"Well, when I came for my rehabilitation last year, Geng gave me to understand that mine was a marginal case. It was only in consideration of my 'good behavior' over the years that I was granted rehabilitation."

"What nonsense! This won't do. We must have your case reexamined and you vindicated."

When the summer recess drew near, the vice president for administration called on me.

"Comrade Wu Ningkun," he addressed me rather formally. "A group of high-ranking cadres of the CID will soon be going to Beidaihe, the summer resort, for a two-week vacation. The Institute is given the quota of one person. Only one. We have decided Comrade Wu Ningkun deserves it most."

Beidaihe was a sort of summer capital for the top party, government, and army leaders and vacationland for other privileged groups. Only recently rehabilitated, a carefree vacation on its sunny beaches had never been within the reach of my fancy. What temptation! Another small compensation for my twenty-two years of ordeal.

"Comrade President Zhang," I addressed him formally in return. "It is very kind of the Institute leadership to award this rare honor to me. But

I don't see how I can deserve it. I have been back only a few months and haven't done much. Many other comrades have been working hard here all these years. Thank you, I cannot accept the honor."

He did not take my "no" for an answer. "Comrade Wu Ningkun," he said. "You have been working hard all the same, though not at the Institute. Please think it over and get ready to leave in a couple of days."

The next day, the vice president for political affairs descended on me. "Comrade Lao Wu," she began, taking a more personal line. "How come you don't want to go vacationing in Beidaihe? This simply won't do. After all these years, you need a good rest. Come on, be ready to go in the morning."

"Comrade President Ni," I said. "I had plenty of rest in the Great Northern Wilderness, a real vacationland. Lakes, rivers, woods, plenty of fish, and a cool summer. I beg you to give this honor to one of the many more deserving and willing comrades . . ."

But the reexamination dragged on in the face of resistance from the diehard radicals. The personnel chief took my case over from Geng. One day he asked me, "Professor Wu, one thorny point is that you signed the conclusion of your case, didn't you?"

"Indeed I did. What would you expect? I signed the conclusion in 1958, which condemned me as an ultrarightist, didn't I? During the Cultural Revolution, how many veteran party members signed conclusions condemning them as renegades or counterrevolutionary revisionists? Are those conclusions still binding?"

"You've got something there. I'll work on it."

3

EVER SINCE MY CONDEMNATION AS A RIGHTIST, MY WRITINGS HAD BEEN banned. My Chinese translation of *The Scalpel, the Sword,* a story of the Canadian surgeon Dr. Norman Bethune, first published in Shanghai in 1954, was twice reprinted in Hong Kong in the 1970s by a government publishing house without the translator's name. Now the same publishing house came to me for a revised edition in commemoration of the fortieth anniversary of the death of the legendary surgeon, to be republished in Beijing in 1979, this time with the translator's name. My old translations of American short stories reappeared in various collections. I also began to do literary translations to oblige editor friends. The one request that had me savoring strongly the irony of fate came in the summer of 1980 from *World Literature,* the national magazine devoted to the introduction of foreign literary works: I finished a translation of *The Great Gatsby* in less than two hot summer months for the October issue. This was the same novel that had been held up by a student activist at my very first criticism meeting in 1952 as Exhibit A of my crime in bringing home "U.S. imperialist crap to poison the minds of the socialist youths of the New China"!

In October, I heard that the first convention of the All-China Foreign Literature Association, sponsored by the Institute of Foreign Literature under the Academy of Social Sciences, would be held in Chengdu, Sichuan province, in December. Isolated from academia for so many years, I thought I should be able to benefit from the national gathering of specialists in my field, if I could attend the conference. So I went to see what the president could do about it. He picked up his telephone and called Professor Feng Zhi, director of the Institute of Foreign Literature, and asked him why I had not been invited to the conference. "We didn't know Ningkun was still alive," answered the honest professor of German literature. The president laughed and said, "Lao Wu is a professor of English at my Institute, just now sitting right here in my office!" A special invitation arrived a few days later.

Some two hundred people from all parts of China turned up for the occasion. I was delighted to see many old friends, including a few rehabilitated rightists, at the conference, which was held in the Golden Ox Guest House, formerly Chairman Mao's "travel palace." The building in which the late "Great Leader" used to stay was still kept as a sort of shrine, with one of his former attendants as the guide. In another building was his vast swimming pool, now drained and lying in desuetude. When I said it was a pity that it could not be put to use for swimmers in this populous metropolis, the guide looked at me in consternation, as if I had just uttered a sacrilege. I soon discovered that the ghost of the departed was not only still haunting his former palace but also hovering over the conference. In spite of repetitions of the catchphrase "emancipation of the mind," most of the speakers were discreet and noncommittal about controversial issues such as "popular Western fiction" and "modernist literature."

At one of the few plenary sessions, a research fellow in Russian literature from the host institute gave a lecture with the provocative title of "Literature or Revolution?" It was adapted from the title of an essay written by V. I. Lenin years before the success of the October Revolution, a virulent attack on modernist literature as a threat to the revolution. The speaker also appealed to the authority of Andrei Zhdanov, the Stalinist dictator of ideology and culture, in advocating the suppression of the spread of Western modernist literature since the end of the Cultural Revolution. I was outraged, but I told myself I had better observe the decorum befitting a special guest and keep my big mouth shut.

On the last day of the conference, the participants were organized into three groups to engage in discussions in separate areas. I opted for the literary theory group, with dozens of people crowded into one room. The meeting was presided over by Professor Feng Zhi himself. The discussion was not particularly stimulating until a middle-aged man, introduced as the director of the department of theory of art and literature at the Ministry of Culture, took the floor. He began rather jovially by telling an anecdote about his teenage son saying to him, "Daddy, forget your Marxism-Leninism. It's passé. Nobody is interested in that anymore. People need something new." We all laughed. He changed his tone of voice and went on to say that his son was misled by a wrong trend of the day, which he accounted for as a reaction to the Cultural Revolution. But it was time to reverse the trend. He concluded authoritatively, "We must persevere in the Marxist-Leninist stand, viewpoint, and method in our theory of art and literature."

It was customary to dismiss a meeting after a cadre in authority had made his summing-up remarks. The director's speech was obviously intended to be just that. It was time for us to disperse and enjoy the farewell banquet. Should I let him go at that or not? Was it my business to confront this man in authority, when there were many others around me better qualified? It was a split-second decision. I raised my hand and asked tentatively, "May I say a few words now, Professor Feng?" Taken by surprise, the chairman reluctantly invited me to speak.

I also began jovially by referring back to the anecdote the director had told about his son. "Comrade Director, I'm glad you didn't give your boy a good beating, because I have a feeling he was right." There was laughter. I went on to say I had no objection against Marxist stand, viewpoint, and method, nor could I say I was for it, simply because I didn't know exactly what it was in spite of years of political study. And I was not sure how many people knew exactly what it was. It seemed to have been changing constantly over the years with every shift in the political wind. Furthermore, with so many sovereign Communist parties in the world today, there were an equal number of "true Marxist-Leninists." I put a question to him: "Which party's Marxism is the true 'true Marxism-Leninism,' Comrade Director?" As he made no answer, I continued. "After years of confusion, after the ten-year-long catastrophe inflicted on the nation by a gang of self-styled Marxist-Leninists, how can one persevere in Marxism–Leninism before he studies it in all humility and honesty and finds out exactly what it is?"

Then I turned to the question of modernist literature. "The same applies to the issue of modernist literature," I said. "How many people in China, or even in this room, are familiar with modernist literature? How can anyone put a ban on it before the people have a chance to read it and make up their own minds about it? Read before you criticize, not the other way round. The days of self-appointed censors are gone forever, I hope. Our speaker at the plenary session yesterday cited the authority of Lenin in opposing modernist literature against the revolution. Lenin's article was written before the October Revolution. The spread of modernist literature might have alarmed him as a detriment to the cause of the Bolshevik revolution, but the opposition between modernist literature and the revolution in post–Cultural Revolution China can only be a figment of political imagination. As to Zhdanov, I am glad he has long been dead. If the choice is imposed on me, however, I would certainly opt for a free literature, not an enslaving revolution!"

There was quite a stir in the audience. As I walked out of the room, several people shook my hand and said, "Good for you!" At the door, I was stopped by Professor Zhang Yuechao of Nanjing University, a fellow rehabilitated rightist. "Lao Wu, thank you, thank you," he said. "You said what I wanted to say, but I didn't know how to say it, thank you for saying it." There were tears in his eyes.

On my return to Beijing in mid-December, I went to see Professor Bian Zhilin, who had not been seen at the conference and was said to be unwell. The first thing he said to me was, "You put your foot in your mouth again in Chengdu. Shuifu told me Ningkun's mind was certainly emancipated. I knew at once you did it again."

"Aren't we supposed to emancipate our mind in answer to the call of the Central Committee and Comrade Deng Xiaoping?" I asked honestly. Though a party member, Professor Bian was an honest and sincere friend.

"Are you still so naive after all that you have been through? If I were you, I would cherish my rehabilitation and concentrate on academic work and literary translation."

I was thankful to him for his wise advice, given out of his solicitude for a long-suffering friend. But I also realized that emancipation of the mind still had a long and hazardous way to go in post–Cultural Revolution China.

I also called on the president of the Institute, when I learned he was to leave shortly for an international conference in Italy, since the reexamination of my case was still dragging on.

"The resolution of my case has been pending since you gave orders in April. It certainly didn't take them that long to give me the wrong verdict in 1957. Do you think I will have to wait till another year begins, Comrade President?" I tried to sound casual.

"What? I thought it had long been resolved." He sounded outraged. "This will never do. There is always resistance from the left when we try to carry out the party's correct policies toward intellectuals. I'll see to it that they have your case resolved this year, not next year. The wrong verdict thoroughly, not partially, corrected. It is important, not only to you, but to the diehard leftist comrades who need to learn a lesson from this."

A few days before New Year's Eve, I was called in to a short meeting with the vice president for political affairs, nicknamed Madame Marxist-Leninist, to hear a sullen Geng read a new one-sentence conclusion that declared the 1958 verdict against me null and void. It had been more than two years since the Central Committee Document No. 55, decreeing the correction of verdict against the rightists, was issued on October 15, 1978. Condemned as an ultrarightist in 1958, "decapped" rightist in 1964, and now rehabilitation after twenty-two years! Hamlet's lament of "the law's delay" finally came home to me.

Epilogue

AMONG THE DEAD AND THE LIVING

AS I LOOK BACK AND RUMINATE ON THE THIRTY YEARS OF MY LIFE IN Communist China, the dead and the living who have peopled the changing landscapes come to live together in my mind.

At the Institute, Vice President Yu Wei, who had played a leading part in my denunciation and imprisonment, had died of coronary heart disease several months before our return. We were told he had become a wiser man through his own sufferings during the Cultural Revolution. My wife and I called on his widow to offer our belated but heartfelt condolences. We told her I might have died long before her husband did, had he not yielded to Yikai's plea for my release from the labor reform farm twenty years before. Bereaved and grief-stricken, she was a far cry from the part of the personnel cadre she had played twenty-two years before at the sessions of criticism for Yikai's benefit. The former invisible woman president, Mao the Frightful, who had personally ordered my denunciation and imprisonment, was living by herself in semiretirement at the CID's luxurious downtown hostel for ranking officials. I was amused to learn she was serving on the Legal Committee of the National People's Congress, as I had been told on my return by Lao Liu, former secretary of the faculty party branch, that the severity with which she had disposed of me in 1958 was illegal even by the rules in effect at the time. Professor Huang Hongxu, who had committed the indiscretion of shaking hands with me following my formal denunciation as an ultrarightist, was now reinstated as chairman of the foreign languages department and vice president for academic affairs at the Teachers University of Hebei province. His friend, Cao Dun, who had been transferred to the Institute on Huang's recommendation and then bit the hand that fed him following Huang's welcome dinner for him, was now a full professor and head of the English department, and a member of the Institute Party Committee. He greeted me with a lighthearted laugh and, "Long time no see, Lao Wu!" as if nothing had ever happened, as if we had parted half an hour before after a pleasant cup of tea. His booming laughter had gained volume, partly due to his growing self-esteem, partly due to the rotundity of his waist, which bore witness to years of good living and an untroubled conscience. In the Typing Room, Zuo the Leftist was thriving as head of the Teaching Material Section, and actually suggested that Yikai come back to work for her. But Pan, the chic French typist, had killed herself when her suave husband, a French teacher and ex-Communist, was denounced as a renegade and adulterer during the Cultural Revolution. The husband who had survived her and the denunciation was living in Shanghai, happily married to his third wife after his second wife had also died, leaving him a good house.

Bao Qing, the talented English instructor, had escaped the rightist label because her second husband, Dao Sheng, also a talented English instructor at Beijing Foreign Languages Institute, had taken all the blame upon himself. However, unable to bear the growing political pressure on her as the spouse of an ultrarightist, she divorced him a few years later to marry an instructor of Japanese, a party member, as her "political umbrella." Angry and grief-stricken, Dao Sheng was finally driven to suicide while doing forced labor in Jiangxi province. Yikai and I silently mourned his tragic death. We could hardly look Bao Qing in the eye when we remembered how the two families had spent many happy hours together during the brief "Beijing Spring," each with its first child, not knowing what the future had in store. Now her Communist protector, who wielded the invincible weapon of Mao Zedong Thought, had taken control of her ideology as a matter of course. When the charge proved intractable, the returned student from Japan, now a full professor of Japanese, often resorted to cuffs and kicks. Though nationally known as a glamorous teacher of English by radio and swamped with fan mail, Bao Qing lived in constant dread of physical assault from the Red Sun umbrella at home. The breakup of her third marriage was only a matter of time. Later, after they were separated, she would often get down on her knees before the dead man's portrait and ask for his forgiveness. Yikai said with a sigh, "Tolstoy is undoubtedly right when he opens his great novel *Anna Karenina* with the famous axiom, 'Happy families are all alike; every unhappy family is unhappy in its own way.' Yet in a country where politics meddles with family life, many unhappy families are victims the same way. It's a pity that the happy family of Bao Qing, Dao Sheng, and their two bright sons should have come to this, but who can lay the blame on the victims? Again happy families are happy for different reasons. There are those that came out of every political campaign with flying colors, and there are those who bore the brunt of every attack. I am happy that we survived our unhappy ordeal the way we did!"

Among the former English faculty at Yenching University, two were "swept away" in the first assault on "reactionary academic authorities" at Beijing University in June 1966. Professor Yu Da'ying, the ailing and childless Oxonian in her fifties, took her own life when she could no longer endure the insults and abuses of her own students, who accused her of attempting to corrupt their class consciousness with her motherly solicitude. Her husband, Professor Zeng Zhaolun, once deputy minister of higher education, followed her to the grave before long. Professor Wu Xinghua, the talented poet and multilingual scholar, died of bacillary dysentery after drinking polluted water given him by a student slave driver who was keeping surveillance over the work gang of professors laboring in the hot sun. (The water was from the same college lake around which he and I used to stroll on moonlight nights during my first months at the university; it was a delight to hear Xinghua reciting Chinese or English poems from his faultless memory.) An autopsy was performed in search of evidence of suicide, which, if confirmed, would have made him a posthumous "active counterrevolutionary," an enemy of the people of the worst kind. He was only forty-five, younger than Du Fu by thirteen years when the "poet saint" died, also of bacillary dysentery. His bereaved wife and two little daughters were driven out of their college house as soon as his mangled body had been cremated. Hu Jiatai, the Buddhist scholar, did not survive hard labor very long. Dr. Lucy Chao was the only English professor who had survived, but her husband, Chen Mengjia, the archaeologist of international fame, succeeded in his second attempt at suicide when Lucy failed to come to his rescue because of her own schizophrenic relapse. He was not quite sixty.

Among the younger faculty, Yang Yuemin, who had forsworn Christianity and embraced communism in 1949, also took his own life at the Institute of Literature when he could no longer endure the endless tortures inflicted on his paralytic body as punishment for his following a "revisionist line" in literary theory. My former assistant, Huang Jizhong, was recalled to Beijing University as an associate professor of English after surviving years of imprisonment at Qinghe State Farm and subsequent forced labor in his home village in Jiangxi province. Separated from his wife, who had also been labeled a rightist and exiled to the outlying Ningxia province, he had lived in his village with his aged mother whom he had once publicly denounced in absentia. Back at Beijing University, he telephoned one day to say he had a confession to make to me. I was baffled. The university was only two bus stops away from where I lived. When he arrived on his bicycle, I was shocked to hear that he had been assigned to spy on me while working as my assistant. He was relieved of his special duties a few months later, because he had failed to provide incriminating evidence.

Among the former leaders of Yenching, Zhang Dongsun, professor and head of philosophy, died in prison as a suspected American spy. President C. W. Lu, who after his dismissal had been reassigned to the Linguistics Institute under the Academy of Sciences as a senior research fellow, had in his seventies been sent down under to a May 7 cadre school in Henan province, and eventually went out of his mind and died of heart failure while roaming the wild country like King Lear. Jian Bozan, the Marxist professor of Chinese history who had taken over the leadership of Yenching after the ouster of President Lu and confronted me with my autobiography in 1952, later became the chairman of the history department at Beijing University. In the early days of the Cultural Revolution, Jian was unexpectedly denounced as a "reactionary academic authority" who brazenly opposed Chairman Mao's philosophy of history. One day, after months of denunciation and hard labor, he was told his case had been cleared up and he was to appear at a meeting the next morning to hear the official conclusion. Before dawn, the Marxist professor of history and his wife, both in their early seventies, dressed themselves in their best suits and lay down side by side in their double bed after swallowing a fatal dosage of sleeping tablets. Dr. T. C. Chao, Lucy's father and dean of the Divinity College, was the only one who died peacefully in Beijing, at the age of ninety in 1979.

In the city, I found my way to 5 Lamb's Tail Alley, where Shen Congwen and his wife lived. The master worked and slept in a small room with a western exposure in a *siheyuan* (a compound with houses around a courtyard), which was mostly taken up by a bed against one wall, along which were stacked old books. I heard that his wife had to find shelter elsewhere at night. Compared with the setup at East Tangzi Alley in the fifties, things had apparently gone from bad to worse. As I watched the wan faces of the aging couple, I hardly knew what to say. Yet, like Yan Hui, a disciple of Confucius, they felt happy as ever "though living in a mean alley on very poor food." The voice of Shen Congwen was still young, so transparent and candlelit, as if it were "a stream of limpid water," "as if all the rivers I had seen in different places in my life were one by one flowing over my heart. And on the river were lying at anchor small gray boats, and floating around jade-green cabbage leaves." The master never talked about his difficulties, never aired grievances, but always wore a Buddha-like smile, as if to say he took personal sufferings for granted, he took faith in life for granted, so that he never talked about them. But he broke down when we mourned the death of our two mutual friends. In 1973 Ba Jin's wife, Xiao San, my college friend, had died of liver cancer after years of forced labor in Shanghai when her husband, the doyen of Chinese letters, was locked up in a cow shed. Now free to write again, Ba Jin regretted the falsehoods that had crept into his writings when he had indiscriminately followed the dictates of the party. He vowed that he would never write another lie. The other friend was Cha Liangtseng, a major modern poet and my roommate at the University of Chicago, who had died suddenly in Tianjin of myocardial infarction, following twenty years of persecution and shortly after the downfall of the Gang of Four. His posthumous rehabilitation dragged on until Dr. T. D. Lee learned from me at our brief meeting in 1979 about the death of his patriotic old friend and asked to see his widow, Professor Zhou Yuliang, who was still teaching at Nankai University. Shen's rehabilitation also took several years, and he was not assigned a decent apartment until

1986, when he could no longer move about without a walker. Two years later he died of a sudden heart attack; his passing away was not noted by the Chinese media until several days after a long obituary had appeared in the *New York Times*. Declining the offer of an official memorial meeting, his family invited a small number of relatives and friends to a private funeral. It was the first such funeral I had ever attended in Beijing, for I had felt that belated official rituals for victims of persecution smacked of crocodile tears.

Widowed and childless, Lucy Chao also lived by herself in two tiny rooms with a western exposure in a siheyuan that used to be her father's home, while her younger brother and his wife occupied the large sunny rooms. Dispossessed of her own home with her elegant Ming dynasty furniture and other objets d'art, she worked, slept, and received her visitors from home and abroad in the inner room with a single bed and two soft chairs; the outer room was cluttered with books, including first editions of novels by Henry James and autographed copies of works by T. S. Eliot. An avid reader, she could no longer read as much as she liked to because of a failing eyesight. In her late sixties she embarked on the formidable venture of translating into Chinese *The Leaves of Grass* in its entirety. While her brother and sister-in-law entertained their friends with hours of mah-jongg in the spacious central room decorated with elegant scrolls of Du Fu's poems in their father's calligraphy, she would bend over her little desk and recreate Whitman's lines in Chinese characters in her meticulous hand. Her only recreation was music. An accomplished pianist, she would occasionally play a piece on the upright piano made in China (her Steinway was "swept away" with the other "four olds") in the central room or listen to recorded classical Western music in her own cell. Like Shen Congwen, she never touched upon her personal troubles, never even alluded to the loss of her husband. I knew she was still on medication for schizophrenia. One day, when I noticed her lips twitching from time to time, I suggested she might cut down on her medicine, which had side effects. Her face changed color and she shot at me, "You want me to have a relapse?" I regretted my rashness, but I suddenly realized what nightmares she must have been living with all by herself all these years. Not even a Jamesian tragic heroine could have carried her suffering with such courage and dignity.

* * *

In Tianjin, Yikai's family home was destroyed in the great earthquake of 1976, but the family miraculously escaped without injury. For several years, they lived in simple and crude sheds until the home was rebuilt with government help. Meanwhile, two of her elder brothers and another elder sister passed away after years of physical and mental sufferings. Her Third Brother, Shiyu, resumed his historical studies in his tiny shed, freezing in winter and stifling hot in summer. In the hope of retrieving his collection of hundreds of manuscript sutras of Chinese folk religions, he spent weeks going from one government department to another, only to be told in the end that "most likely they were salvaged as wastepaper." A Canadian colleague who had written to inquire whether he might now realize his long-cherished dream of reading at least one of those rare manuscripts was heartbroken to learn what had happened to them all. It was like suddenly losing a dear friend, he said, who one had kept hoping to see again one day.

On a summer lecture tour in Anhui province a few years after my return to Beijing, I was happily reunited with some of my fellow "cow demons," including the reinstated president and vice president of Anhui University and the president of Teachers University. All three were enthusiastic about the reform and "open door" policies. Mao Xiaolu, now a full professor of Russian in his seventies, came to see me escorted by Chen Yu, now a party functionary in the mathematics department. The three of us laughed over the days we had spent together in the village of Nanzhuang. When I confessed I no longer remembered the doggerel lines of verse Mao and I had extemporized, I was amazed to hear Chen rattle them off without a hitch. We mourned again the suicide of the Russian instructor Jiang Nan and lamented the fate of her ailing husband, Lin Xing, who had sought justice in vain. I promised to return again next year, but Mao passed away the following spring. One former colleague told me that both Shen Wenwu, the master steel worker, and Shi Baoyu, the professional security bully, had died, one of cancer of the liver and the other of heart disease. My informant said both "iron fists of proletarian dictatorship" had slumped to the floor when the nature of their ailments was made known to them. "Even as the popular axiom goes," he moralized, " 'Good will be rewarded with good, and evil with evil.' " I found it hard to agree. "How can you then account for good rewarded with evil, and evil with good? Rather it was a pity that such people never seemed to remember that man is mortal, in the midst of so many deaths around them. Perhaps they also believed 'evil will be rewarded with evil' when they hounded their victims with such relentless brutality. Never questioning their own righteousness, the poor wretches undoubtedly had lived under the delusion of reaping their rewards in the Communist heaven on earth and thriving happily forever after. And they were only such small fry!"

Colonel Li, the veteran Communist, was released after five years in a Communist prison when the telegraphic message denouncing him and his successor as Soviet spies turned out to have been a hoax perpetrated by his political enemies. Disgusted with the university, he went back to his native Heilongjiang province and was eventually appointed party secretary of the prestigious Harbin Institute of Technology. No longer a dread boss but a man who had grown more humane through his own ordeal, he would drop in on us for a longish visit nearly every time he came to Beijing on official business.

The one who really made news at the university was my former student Wang Chongde, who had led his classmates on that memorable midnight raid on my rooms on June 6, 1966. His good class origin and radical activism earned him the trust of the party and the Mao Zedong Thought Propaganda Team leaders. Upon graduation he was assigned with the highest political recommendations to the top-secret intelligence department of the Headquarters of the General Staff. Later, while serving as an assistant to the military attaché at the Chinese embassy in an African country, he secretly sent the host government a request for political asylum. Dependent on Chinese economic aid for its survival, the host government understandably turned the secret communication over to the Chinese embassy. Recalled home under escort on a Swissair flight, the defector actually managed to smuggle a message to the captain, under the eyes of his four fellow officers, pleading to the Swiss government for political asylum. When the plane landed in Geneva, Swiss security officers came aboard and took charge of the asylum-seeker, who had hidden in a lavatory. As the Swiss government found no use for his "expertise" and no other government would accept him, the former Red Guard leader became a refugee roaming the streets of Geneva year after year.

*   *   *

My mind constantly goes back to the Great Northern Wilderness. I wonder what might have happened to the good Captain Li. Had he been punished for his weakness, or simply given a different job since he was obviously a misfit in the prison system? Most likely, however, he was back in his home village living with his wife and children and perhaps grandchildren and the other villagers, loving and loved. I should not be surprised if I ran into him one sunny day in this small world. I would instinctively embrace him and call him "my brother." Captain Ge had the sterner stuff of which a good security officer was made. Yet he never abused the power in his hands, never insulted or manhandled the inmates. He was a model servant of the law, which was a rarity among the Red Guards and master workers who took the law into their own bloody hands. Dr. Benjamin Lee also returned to Beijing in the sixties and practiced for a while at a semiprivate street clinic staffed by medical personnel who could not find employment at public hospitals. During the Cultural Revolution, he was fired again and roamed the countryside as a vagabond. Back at the street clinic at the end of the Cultural Revolution, he was again sent to corrective education through hard labor in suburban Beijing on some absurd charge. Released once again, he eventually found his way to America to pursue his study of "concentration-camp fevers," for which he had accumulated plenty of data and experience the hard way.

My mind also goes back to Qinghe State Farm. Lao Wang, the ex-convict who allowed us to use his little room as our prison rendezvous, is most likely gone. Would his successor let visitors use the room for the same purpose, since Qinghe remains a major prison farm? Lao Liu, the young athletic calligrapher I had buried with my own hands—is his shallow grave hidden under thick weeds now? Or did his wife eventually come and take his remains home?

Last but not the least, my mind goes back to the village of Gaozhuang, kept alive by occasional letters from our good doctor. When the commune was abolished and the peasants started working individual plots on their own, Dr. Lu wrote, "Lao Penghai is living in a new house, which the villagers say was built with the wood he stole from you. But he is still unhappy, because he can no longer live off the peasants of his village. He is constantly heard abusing the new system and dreaming of 'the good old days when the party gave him the right to eat and drink to his heart's content.' Freed from his tyranny, the villagers work happily for their own good, though their life is still not free from want."

Both Darkie and Lesser Flood were happily married and beginning to have their second child despite the "one child" policy, but Jigui's fate was a different story. "The Loony unexpectedly rose to fame and wealth," Dr. Lu wrote. "One day, while dashing across the highway, he was run over by a truck and taken to the county hospital for treatment. Driven back in the same truck three days later, we saw he had lost his left leg and now hopped about on crutches. His mother was heartbroken and wailed like a madwoman. His father took it rather philosophically, saying it was a case of 'evil rewarded with evil.' When the truck driver offered him compensation of three hundred yuan, he went dizzy with joy and decided it was 'good rewarded with good,' because he had spared Jigui's life a few years back. Three hundred yuan! An incredible astronomical sum! Compensation for a water buffalo killed is twelve hundred yuan, for an able-bodied adult killed one thousand yuan. The good-for-nothing Loony traded his evil leg for three hundred yuan! How could the father not rejoice! Now permanently disabled, Loony will not be able to go places and make trouble. He can stay home and feed the water buffalo. The money was just what the father needed to pay the bride-price for Little Egg's future wife." Yikai was outraged but helpless. A few months later, Dr. Lu sent a follow-up on Jigui. "Jigui often hops to the hospital on his one leg and two crutches to have me treat infections on the surgery site. He seems to be a more sensible boy than before. I asked him, 'Jigui, you made three hundred yuan. Don't you want to buy an artificial leg with the money?' His answer was, 'What do I want an artificial leg for, Dr. Lu? Stop making fun of me. It would be good money wasted. Bride-price for Little Egg is serious business.' He has made me ponder whether the accident, the amputation, and the suffering have given him a sort of shock therapy that drove the mad demon out of him. I will need to follow him up more closely." Another update: "After his hospital visit, Jigui will often hop to the market and sit next to the young coal miner who had lost one of his legs in an accident in the local pit with no safety precautions. Jigui was delighted when his fellow sufferer once treated him to a cup of tea and a packet of roast peanuts, like a child who had never been given a toy before. The two occasionally play a game of Chinese chess. Jigui went mad with joy when he actually beat the coal miner once. 'I had good teachers in Yicun and Li Nong,' he said proudly."

I could easily imagine Jigui and the coal miner sitting next to each other, crutches by their side, a somber personification of the "alliance between the working class and the peasantry," which presumably provides the power base of the New China.

What about ourselves? Yikai provided an unexpected epilogue to rehabilitation. She started teaching a course in English as a foreign language when the new school year began in September 1980. Then, a few days before the Lunar New Year in February, she had to be carried out of the class she was teaching, suffering splitting headaches and vomiting. One doctor said it was Ménière's disease, another said it was a nervous disorder. After visiting several hospitals, she was finally diagnosed with acute late glaucoma at the former Peiping Union Medical College teaching hospital, renamed the Anti-Imperialist Hospital during the Cultural Revolution and now called the Capital Hospital. When she asked Dr. Hu what were the causes of her affliction, the elderly eye specialist asked her about the kind of life she had led. After listening to her story, the good doctor said, "What do you expect then? All the stresses of the years would take their toll on your system one way or another. If you didn't have a strong character, which pulled you through an endless ordeal, the stresses might have ruined your nerves or your heart. Our mental hospitals are packed with victims of the Cultural Revolution and the other political campaigns. You're lucky to have come to me before it's too late. I will do my best to save your eyes, but I'm afraid you will have to give up teaching from now on, so soon after you have started again." Within the next few years, both of her eyes had to be operated on and she was pronounced partially blind and awarded a mobility cane! It is our three-year-old grandson Erik's favorite toy.

I once summed up my thirty years of a "cow demon's" life in a simple formula: I came, I suffered, I survived. But there was surely more to it. The protracted suffering was by no means mere passive endurance, but a life-sustaining gift. Suffering runs like an unbroken thread through the drama of life and history. It is perhaps precisely because suffering occupies a supreme place in one's life that a great drama like *Hamlet* or a great poem by Du Fu ennobles us with the tragic grandeur of life. Each suffers and learns in his own way, but no one suffers in vain. Perhaps we have grown a little wiser, like Jigui the Loony; perhaps we have grown humbler in the face of so much poverty and suffering among the peasants; perhaps we have drawn strength from their unspoken faith in life and evergreen hope for the future. Perhaps, even as a cow that grazes on grass requites its sustenance with life-sustaining milk, a "cow demon" that grazes on weeds of bitterness can likewise requite his sustenance.

I have come a long way. China has come a long way. "As I look homeward again with a new nostalgia," I wrote in 1986 while winding up a visit at Cambridge University, "it is my fervent wish that the Half-Step Bridge in Beijing become one day a historical curiosity, to adorn the new heaven and new earth of a *newer* China, much like the replica of the Bridge of Sighs in Cambridge!" With infinite patience and goodwill, how we all wished that the party would benefit from the lessons it professed to have learned from its mistakes and sail, on the crest of the nation's euphoria over the ending of the catastrophic Cultural Revolution, toward a *newer* China! The economic reform and "opening to the world" brought the nation an ample supply of consumer goods, imports as well as domestic products. But freedom of expression remained a commodity under tight control. Writers were assured of creative freedom time and again, only to witness the recurring political persecution of those whose works had been condemned as "poisonous weeds." Shortly after my return from Cambridge in the fall of 1986, the attack on intellectual freedom reached a climax in the suppression of the first student pro-democracy demonstrations, the expulsion of outspoken dissidents from the party, and the dismissal of the party's general secretary. A year later, when "The River Elegy," a TV series, lamented the fate of the nation and its intellectuals under the yoke of the age-old feudalistic system, the self-styled defenders of party orthodoxy and national heritage hysterically denounced it as a counterrevolutionary work. An imminent confrontation between the diehards and the advocates of freedom and democracy was inevitable. The explosion at Tiananmen Square during the spring of 1989 was as inevitable as the crackdown that followed. The use of wanton brutal force, which outraged the nation and the world, was not the mistaken choice in a moment of passion, but followed the inexorable logic of the escalation of violent political campaigns over the four decades of proletarian dictatorship, as mirrored in our single tear. Hundreds fell in the bloodbath, but millions of demonstrators throughout the land gave voice to a new awakening of the nation. The tanks and machine-guns might have carried the day, but China can never, never be the same again. Hundreds of those who demonstrated for freedom and democracy at Tiananmen Square were thrown into the same detention center at Half-Step Bridge where I had been incarcerated thirty-one years before. A *newer* China is yet to appear, but appear it will, in the not-too-distant future, with a new heaven and a new earth!